THE TREATIES OF CANADA

WITH

THE INDIANS OF MANITOBA

AND

THE NORTH-WEST TERRITORIES,

INCLUDING

THE NEGOTIATIONS ON WHICH THEY WERE BASED, AND
OTHER INFORMATION RELATING THERETO.

BY

THE HON. ALEXANDER MORRIS, P.C.,

LATE LIEUTENANT-GOVERNOR OF MANITOBA, THE NORTH-WEST TERRITORIES,
AND KEE-WA-TIN.

PROSPERO

CANADIAN COLLECTION

TORONTO
2000

The Treaties of Canada
with the Indians of Manitoba and the North-West Territories,
Including the Negotiations on which They were Based,
and Other Information Related Thereto

This edition first published by
Prospero Books in 2000
from the 1880 Belfords, Clarke & Co. edition

Prospero Canadian Collection edition © Prospero Books, 2000

Canadian Cataloguing in Publication Data

Morris, Alexander, 1826-1889
The treaties of Canada with the Indians
of Manitoba and the North-West Territories...

(Prospero Canadian Collection)
Facsim. reprint.
Originally published: Toronto: Belfords, Clarke, 1880.
ISBN 1-55267-141-0

1. Indians of North America - Northwest, Canadian - Treaties.
2. Indians of North America - Manitoba - Treaties.
3. Indians of North America - Canada - Government relations - 1860-1951.*
I. Title. II. Series.
E92.M87 2000   323.1'1970712   C00-931938-7

Prospero Books
90 Ronson Drive, Toronto, Ontario, Canada
M9W 1C1

Printed on acid free paper

Printed in Canada by Webcom Ltd.

TO HIS EXCELLENCY

𝕿𝖍𝖊 𝕽𝖎𝖌𝖍𝖙 𝕳𝖔𝖓𝖔𝖗𝖆𝖇𝖑𝖊 𝖙𝖍𝖊 𝕰𝖆𝖗𝖑 𝖔𝖋 𝕯𝖚𝖋𝖋𝖊𝖗𝖎𝖓,

Her Britannic Majesty's Ambassador at St. Petersburg, K.P.P.O.,
K.C.B., G.C.M.G., &c., &c., &c.

My Lord,—

Encouraged by the earnest interest, your Lordship ever evinced, in the work of obtaining the alliance and promoting the welfare of the Indian tribes in the North-West of Canada, and in opening up the Territories for settlement, by obtaining the relinquishment of the natural title of the Indians to the lands of the Fertile Belt on fair and just terms, I have the honor, by your kind permission, to dedicate this collection of the treaties made with them, to your Excellency, in the belief that its publication will be timely, and that the information now supplied in a compact form, may prove of service to the Dominion of Canada.

I have the honor to be

Your Lordship's obedient servant,

ALEXANDER MORRIS,

Late Lieut.-Gov. of Manitoba, the North-West Territories, and Kee-wa-tin.

TORONTO, *March, 1880.*

PREFACE.

THE question of the relations of the Dominion of Canada to the Indians of the North-West, is one of great practical importance. The work, of obtaining their good will, by entering into treaties of alliance with them, has now been completed in all the region from Lake Superior to the foot of the Rocky Mountains. As an aid to the other and equally important duty—that of carrying out, in their integrity, the obligations of these treaties, and devising means whereby the Indian population of the Fertile Belt can be rescued from the hard fate which otherwise awaits them, owing to the speedy destruction of the buffalo, hitherto the principal food supply of the Plain Indians, and that they may be induced to become, by the adoption of agricultural and pastoral pursuits, a self-supporting community—I have prepared this collection of the treaties made with them, and of information, relating to the negotiations, on which these treaties were based, in the hope that I may thereby contribute to the completion of a work, in which I had considerable part, that, of, by treaties, securing the good will of the Indian tribes, and by the helpful hand of the Dominion, opening up to them, a future of promise, based upon the foundations of instruction and the many other advantages of civilized life.

M.

CONTENTS.

THE

TREATIES WITH THE INDIANS

OF

MANITOBA, THE NORTH-WEST TERRITORIES,

AND KEE-WA-TIN,

IN THE

DOMINION OF CANADA.

INTRODUCTION.

ONE of the gravest of the questions presented for solution by the Dominion of Canada, when the enormous region of country formerly known as the North-West Territories and Rupert's Land, was entrusted by the Empire of Great Britain and Ireland to her rule, was the securing the alliance of the Indian tribes, and maintaining friendly relations with them. The predecessors of Canada—the Company of Adventurers of England trading into Hudson's Bay, popularly known as the Hudson's Bay Company—had, for long years, been eminently successful in securing the good-will of the Indians—but on their sway, coming to an end, the Indian mind was disturbed. The events, that transpired in the Red River region, in the years 1869-1870, during the period when a provisional government was attempted to be established, had perplexed the Indians. They, moreover, had witnessed a sudden irruption into the country of whites from without. In the West, American

2

traders poured into the land, and, freighted with fire-water, purchased their peltries and their horses, and impoverished the
tribes. In the East, white men took possession of the soil and
made for themselves homes, and as time went on steamboats
were placed on the inland waters—surveyors passed through
the territories—and the "speaking wires," as the Indian calls
the telegraph, were erected. What wonder that the Indian mind
was disturbed, and what wonder was it that a Plain chief, as he
looked upon the strange wires stretching through his land, ex-
claimed to his people, "We have done wrong to allow that wire
to be placed there, before the Government obtained our leave
to do so. There is a white chief at Red River, and that wire
speaks to him, and if we do anything wrong he will stretch out a
long arm and take hold of us before we can get away." The
government of Canada had, anticipating the probabilities of
such a state of affairs, wisely resolved, that contemporaneously
with the formal establishment of their rule, there should be
formed alliances with the Indians. In 1870 the Parliament
of Canada created the requisite machinery for the Government
of the Province of Manitoba and of the North-West Territories
respectively, giving to the former a Lieutenant-Governor and
Legislature, and to the latter, a Lieutenant-Governor and
Council, Executive and Legislative—the Lieutenant-Governor
of Manitoba being *ex officio* Lieutenant-Governor of the North-
West Territories. Subsequently the North-West Territories
were erected into a distinct government, with a Lieutenant-
Governor and Executive, and Legislative Council. The District
of Kee-wa-tin, "the land of the north wind," was also established, comprising the eastern and northern portions of the Territories, and placed under the control of the Lieutenant-Governor
of Manitoba, and an Executive and Legislative Council. Since
1870, no less than seven treaties have been concluded, with the
Indian tribes, so that there now remain no Indian nations in the
North-West, inside of the fertile belt, who have not been dealt
with.

It is the design of the present work to tell the story of these treaties, to preserve, as far as practicable, a record of the negotiations on which they were based, and to present to the many in the Dominion and elsewhere, who take a deep interest in these sons of the forest and the plain, a view of their habits of thought and speech, as thereby presented, and to suggest the possibility, nay, the certainty, of a hopeful future for them.

Prior to proceeding to deal, with the treaties of the Dominion of Canada, it will render this book more complete to present the reader, with information as to three treaties which preceded those of the Dominion, viz., the treaty made by the Earl of Selkirk in the year 1817, those popularly known as the Robinson Treaties, made by the late Hon. William B. Robinson, of the City of Toronto, with the Indians of the shores and islands of Lakes Superior and Huron in the year 1850, and that made by the Hon. William Macdougall, for the surrender of the Indian title, to the great Manitoulin Island, both acting for and on behalf of the Government of the late Province of Canada.

Ere however entering upon an explanation of these two first-mentioned treaties, I submit a few brief observations:

The Indians inhabiting the region covered by the treaties in question, extending in Canadian territory from Lake Superior to the foot of the Rocky Mountains, are composed of distinct tribes having different languages.

The Ojibbewas, Chippawas, or Saulteaux as they now call themselves, are found in numbers in the District of Kee-wa-tin and the Province of Manitoba. In the North-West Territories they are not numerous except within the limits of Treaty number Four. These Indians migrated from the older Provinces of Quebec and Ontario many years ago.

The Crees, inhabit the North-West Territories and are divided into Plain, Wood and Swampy Crees, according to the region of the country they dwell in. The Swampy Crees reside in Manitoba and Kee-wa-tin.

The Black Feet nation are to be found towards the slope of

the Rocky Mountains, in the region comprised within the limits of the Treaty number Seven.

A few Chippawayans, or Northerners, dwell within the North-West Territories.

The once powerful nation of the Assiniboines, or Stonies—a kindred tribe to the Sioux—are greatly reduced in numbers, and are now only to be met with in the North-West Territories.

The Sioux in the Dominion are refugees from the United States, the first body having come over some fourteen years ago. A large influx of similar refugees, have recently fled to the Dominion from, the same country, as the issue of the recent war between the United States and the Sioux.

CHAPTER I.

THE SELKIRK TREATY.

IN the year 1811, the Earl of Selkirk purchased* from the Governor and Company of Adventurers trading into Hudson's Bay, in consideration of ten shillings and certain agreements and understandings contained in the Indenture, a large tract of territory within Rupert's Land described in the Indenture as follows:

" All that tract of land or territory being within and forming part of the aforesaid lands and territories of the said Governor and Company, bounded by an imaginary line running as follows, that is to say, beginning on the western shore of the Lake Winnipic, otherwise Winnipeg, at a point in fifty-two degrees and thirty north latitude and thence running due west to the Lake Winnipegoos, otherwise called Little Winnipeg, then in a southerly direction through the said Lake so as to strike its western shore in latitude fifty-two degrees, then due west to the place where the parallel of fifty-two degrees north latitude intersects the western branch of Red River, otherwise called Asseniboine River, then due south from that point of intersection to the height of land which separates the waters running into Hudson's Bay from those of the Missouri and Mississippi, then in an easterly direction along the said height of land to the source of the River Winnipic, or Winnipeg (meaning by such last named river the principal branch of the waters which unite in Lake Sagenagos), thence along the main stream of these waters and the middle of the several lakes through which they flow to the mouth of the Winnipic River and thence in a northerly

* *Vide* Appendix for copy of the agreement in question.

direction through the middle of Lake Winnipic to the place of beginning." The deed is accompanied by a map intended to show the tract of country, and there is an endorsement on the map that as the surveys were not sufficient to ascertain with precision whether, latitude 52° does intersect the river called Red or Assiniboine River, it was agreed, that in case the waters of of Red River, shall on more accurate survey be found, not to extend so far north as latitude 52°, then the west boundary of the tract of land intended to be within the grant, should be a line drawn due north and south, through the post upon the Red River, marked on the plan as "Carlton House."

The Company reserved the right to call upon the Earl to set off one-tenth, however, of the tract for the use of the servants of the Company—and the Earl covenanted, within ten years, to settle within the tract one thousand families, each of them consisting of one married couple at the least, on pain of revocation of the grant, if on receipt of notice to that effect from the Company he did not, within three years after the receipt of the notice, complete the settlement of the one thousand families.

In pursuance of his obligations, Lord Selkirk, in the autumn of the year 1811, sent out a number of families from the County of Sutherland, in Scotland, who spent the winter at Fort Churchill on the western shore of Hudson's Bay. On the arrival of spring, they travelled thence to the confluence of the Assiniboine and Red Rivers, and thus was commenced the interesting settlement of the Red River, which is now included in the Province of Manitoba. It is not my purpose to notice here the eventful history of the Selkirk colonists, and I will only note the fact that in 1836, the Company bought back the whole tract, from the heirs of Lord Selkirk, for the sum of £84,000, the rights of colonists who had purchased land between 1811 and 1836, being respected.

In the year 1817 the Earl of Selkirk, visited his wide domain, and entered into negotiations with the Indian tribes, for the extinction of their title, to a tract of land described as follows:

* "All that tract of land adjacent to Red River and Assiniboine River, beginning at the mouth óf Red River and extending along the same as far as Great Forks at the mouth of Red Lake River and along Assiniboine. River as far as the Musk Rat River, otherwise called Rivière des Champignons, and extending to the distance of six miles from Fort Douglas on every side, and likewise from Fort Doer, and also from the Great Forks and in other posts extending in breadth to the distance of two English statute miles back from the banks of the river."

The Indians then inhabiting the region were described as being of the Chippawa or Saulteaux and Killistine or Cree nations. They were made to comprehend, the depth of the land they were surrendering, by being told, that it was the greatest distance, at which a horse on the level prairie could be seen, or daylight seen under his belly between his legs. The consideration for the surrender, was, the payment of one hundred pounds of good merchantable tobacco, to each nation annually.

The treaty was signed by Lord Selkirk and by five Indian chiefs, who affixed thereto drawings of the animals after which they were named, by way of signature, a *fac simile* of which will be found elsewhere The surrender was to the Sovereign. Lord, King George the Third. The treaty was accompanied by a map which shows that the tract surrendered extended to Grand Forks in what is now United States territory. A copy of the treaty will be found in the Appendix and will prove of interest.

---

* A large portion of the ceded territory is now comprehended in the Territory of Dakota, United States.

CHAPTER II.

THE ROBINSON TREATIES.

IN consequence of the discovery of minerals, on the shores of Lakes Huron and Superior, the Government of the late Province of Canada, deemed it desirable, to extinguish the Indian title, and in order to that end, in the year 1850, entrusted the duty to the late Honorable William B. Robinson, who discharged his duties with great tact and judgment, succeeding in making two treaties, which were the forerunners of the future treaties, and shaped their course. The main features of the Robinson Treaties—viz., annuities, reserves for the Indians, and liberty to fish and hunt on the unconceded domain of the Crown—having been followed in these treaties. A special feature of the Robinson Treaties, was the adjustment of a claim made by the Indians to be paid, the amount received, by the Government, for the sale of mining locations. This was arranged, by Mr. Robinson, agreeing to pay them, the sum of £4,000 and an annuity of about £1,000, thus avoiding any dispute that might arise as to the amounts actually received by the Government. The number of Indians included in the treaties were stated by Mr. Robinson to be: on Lake Superior, 1240, including 84 half-breeds; and on Lake Huron 1422, including 200 half-breeds.* The relations of the Indians and half-breeds, have long been cordial; and in the negotiations as to these initial treaties, as in the subsequent ones, the claims of the half-breeds, to recognition, was urged by the Indians.

---

* The census return of the Department of the Interior for the year 1878 gives the numbers of these Indians as follows:

Chippawas of Lake Superior 1,947
Chippawas of Lake Huron 1,458

I cannot do better, in giving information with regard to these treaties, than simply to reproduce the Report of Mr. Robinson to the Honorable Colonel Bruce, Superintendent-General of Indian Affairs, in which he describes the course of his negotiations and communicates their results. A copy of the treaties will be found in the Appendix. The Report is as follows:

TORONTO, *24th September, 1850.*

SIR:—I have the honor herewith to transmit the Treaty which on the part of the Government I was commissioned to negotiate with the tribes of Indians inhabiting the northern shore of Lakes Huron and Superior ; and I trust that the terms on which I succeeded in obtaining the surrender of all the lands in question, with the exception of some small reservations made by the Indians, may be considered satisfactory. They were such as I thought it advisable to offer, in order that the matter might be finally settled, without having any just grounds of complaint on the part of the Indians.

The Indians had been advised by certain interested parties to insist on such extravagant terms as I felt it quite impossible to grant; and from the fact that the American Government had paid very liberally for the land surrendered by their Indians on the south side of Lake Superior, and that our own in other parts of the country were in receipt of annuities much larger than I offered, I had some difficulty in obtaining the assent of a few of the chiefs to my proposition.

I explained to the chiefs in council the difference between the lands ceded heretofore in this Province, and those then under consideration, they were of good quality and sold readily at prices which enabled the Government to be more liberal, they were also occupied by the whites in such a manner as to preclude the possibility of the Indian hunting over or having access to them : whereas the lands now ceded are notoriously barren and sterile, and will in all probability never be settled except in a few localities by mining companies, whose establishments among the Indians, instead of being prejudicial, would prove of great benefit as they would afford a market for any things they may have to sell, and bring provisions and stores of all kinds among them at reasonable prices.

Neither did the British Government contemplate the removal of the Indians from their present haunts to some (to them) unknown region in the far West, as had been the case with their brethren on the American side.

I told them that the two chiefs who were ln Toronto last winter (Shinguacouse and Nebennigoebing) only asked the amount which the Government had received for mining locations, after deducting the expenses attending their sale. That amount was about eight thousand pounds which the Government would pay them without any annuity or certainty of further benefit ; or one-half of it down, and an annuity of about one thousand pounds.

There were twenty-one chiefs present, about the same number of principal men, and a large number of other Indians belonging to the different bands, and they all preferred the latter proposition, though two of them (Shinguacouse and Nebennigoebing) insisted on receiving an annuity equal to ten dollars per head.

The chiefs from Lake Superior desired to treat separately for their territory and said at once in council that they accepted my offer. I told them that I would have the treaty ready on the following morning, and I immediately proceeded to prepare it; and, as agreed upon, they signed it cheerfully at the time appointed.

I then told the chiefs from Lake Huron (who were all present when the others signed) that I should have a similar treaty ready for their signature, the next morning, when those who signed it would receive their money; and that as a large majority of them had agreed to my terms I should abide by them.

I accordingly prepared the treaty and proceeded on the morning of the ninth instant to the council-room to have it formally executed in the presence of proper witnesses—all the chiefs and others were present. I told them I was then ready to receive their signatures; the two chiefs, Shinguacouse and Nebennigoebing, repeated their demand of ten dollars a head by way of annuity, and also insisted that I should insert in the treaty a condition securing to some sixty half-breeds a free grant of one hundred acres of land each. I told them they already had my answer as to a larger annuity, and that I had no power to give them free grants of land. The other chiefs came forward to sign the treaty and seeing this the two who had resisted up to this time also came to the table and signed first, the rest immediately following.

I trust his Excellency will approve of my having concluded the treaty on the basis of a small annuity and the immediate and final settlement of the matter, rather than paying the Indians the full amount of all moneys on hand, and a promise of accounting to them for future sales. The latter course would have entailed much trouble on the Government, besides giving an opportunity to evil disposed persons to make the Indians suspicious of any accounts that might be furnished.

Believing that His Excellency and the Government were desirous of leaving the Indians no just cause of complaint on their surrendering the extensive territory embraced in the treaty; and knowing there were individuals who most assiduously endeavored to create dissatisfaction among them, I inserted a clause securing to them certain prospective advantages should the lands in question prove sufficiently productive at any future period to enable the Government without loss to increase the annuity.* This was so reason-

---

* The annuities under these treaties have recently been increased, the following item having been inserted in the Supplies Act of Canada, viz., "Annual grant to bring up annuities payable under the Robinson Treaty to the Chippawas of Lakes Huron and Superior, from 96 cents to $4 per head, $14,000."

able and just that I had no difficulty in making them comprehend it, and it in a great measure silenced the clamor raised by their evil advisers.

In allowing the Indians to retain reservations of land for their own use I was governed by the fact that they in most cases asked for such tracts as they had heretofore been in the habit of using for purposes of residence and cultivation, and by securing these to them and the right of hunting and fishing over the ceded territory, they cannot say that the Government takes from their usual means of subsistence and therefore have no claims for support, which they no doubt would have preferred, had this not been done. The reservation at Garden River is the largest and perhaps of most value, but as it is occupied by the most numerous band of Indians, and from its locality (nine miles from the Sault) is likely to attract others to it, I think it was right to grant what they expressed a desire to retain. There are two mining locations at this place, which should not be finally disposed of unless by the full consent of Shinguacouse and his band; they are in the heart of the village and shew no indications of mineral wealth, they are numbered 14 and 15 on the small map appended to Messrs. Anderson and Vidal's report. I pledged my word on the part of the Government that the sale of these locations should not be completed, and as the locatees have not, I believe, complied with the conditions of the Crown Lands Department there can be no difficulty in cancelling the transaction.

The chiefs are desirous that their several reservations should be marked by proper posts or monuments, and I have told them the Government would probably send some one next spring for that purpose. As I know many of the localities I shall be able to give the necessary information when required.

When at Sault Ste. Marie last May, I took measures for ascertaining as nearly as possible the number of Indians inhabiting the north shore of the two lakes; and was fortunate enough to get a very correct census, particularly of Lake Superior. I found this information very useful at the council, as it enabled me successfully to contradict the assertion (made by those who were inciting the chiefs to resist my offers) that there were on Lake Superior alone, eight thousand Indians. The number on that lake, including eighty-four half-breeds, is only twelve hundred and forty—and on Lake Huron, about fourteen hundred and twenty-two, including probably two-hundred half-breeds; and when I paid the Indians they acknowledged they knew of no other families than those on my list.

The number paid, as appears on the pay list, does not show the whole strength of the different bands, as I was obliged at their own request to omit some members of the very large families. I have annexed to this Report the names of the chiefs, their localities, and number of souls in each band as recognized by me in apportioning the money, thinking it will be useful when paying the annuity hereafter.

This information may I believe be fully relied on for Lake Superior, but the census for Lake Huron is not so perfect; and I would suggest that Captain

Ironside should be furnished with copies of that document and also of the pay-lists, in order that he may correct, in time, any errors that are found to exist.

As the half-breeds at Sault Ste. Marie and other places may seek to be recognized by the Government in future payments, it may be well that I should state here the answer that I gave to their demands on the present occasion. I told them I came to treat with the chiefs who were present, that the money would be paid to them—and their receipt was sufficient for me—that when in their possession they might give as much or as little to that class of claimants as they pleased. To this no one, not even their advisers, could object, and I heard no more on the subject. At the earnest request of the chiefs themselves I undertook the distribution of the money among their respective bands, and all parties expressed themselves perfectly satisfied with my division of their funds.

On my arrival at Penetanguishene I found the chiefs Yellowhead and Snake, from Lake Simcoe, and Aissance, from Beausoleil's Island, waiting to see me, to prefer their claim to a small tract of land between Penetanguishene and the vicinity of the River Severn. I was aware of their intending to make such a claim and took the precaution of asking the chiefs assembled in council at the Sault whether it was well founded, they emphatically declared that those chiefs had no claim on Lake Huron, that they had long since ceded their lands and were in the receipt of a large annuity, this I believe to be the case, and Captain Anderson, whom I met there, is of the same opinion; but I promised to inquire into it and give them an answer, and I will therefore thank you to cause the necessary information from your office to be furnished to me on the subject. Should it appear that these chiefs have any claim I think I could get their surrender of it for a small amount, and there remain sufficient funds at my disposal for the purpose.

The Canadians resident on the lands just surrendered at Sault Ste. Marie are very anxious to obtain titles to the land on which they have long resided and made improvements; they applied to me after the treaty and I advised them to memorialize the Government the usual way, setting forth the manner in which they were put in possession by the military authorities of the time, and that I had little doubt that the Government would do them justice. I think the survey of the tract should be made so as to interfere as little as possible with their respective clearings and that those who can show a fair claim to the favorable consideration of the Government should be liberally dealt with.

It will be seen on referring to the treaty that I have kept] within the amount at my disposal. Of the £4,160 agreed by me to be paid to the Indians of both lakes, there remains £75 unexpended. I could not from the information I possessed tell exactly the number of families I should have to pay, and thought it prudent to reserve a small sum to make good any omissions, there may still be a few who will prefer claims, though I know of none at present. If not, the amount can be paid next year with the annuity to such families as are most deserving; or it may be properly applied in extinguishing the claim made by the Lake Simcoe Indians, should it appear on inquiry to be just.

The whole amount given to me in August was £5,033 6s. 8d., of this sum their remains £800, which I have placed in the Bank of Upper Canada to the credit of the Receiver-General, and I have prepared a detailed account of the whole, which, with the proper vouchers, I shall deliver to the Accountant of the Crown Lands Department.

I have much pleasure in acknowledging the valuable assistance afforded me by all the officers of the Honorable the Hudson's Bay Company resident on the lakes; and the prompt manner in which their Governor, Sir George Simpson, kindly placed their services at my disposal.

The report made last year by Messrs. Anderson and Vidal I found of much use to me, and the long services and experience of the former gentleman in Indian affairs enabled him to give me many valuable suggestions.

Captain Cooper and his officers by attending at the council, and otherwise, gave me most cheerfully all the aid in their power; and Captain Ironside, of your Department, with his assistant, Assickinach, were of essential service to me.

I found it absolutely necessary to have the aid of some one in taking the census of the Lake Huron Indians at the time they were receiving their presents at Manitoulin; and as Captain Ironside was fully occupied in attending to his own duty, I requested Mr. Keating, who had long known the Indians on that lake, to give me his assistance. This he cheerfully and very efficiently did, and afterwards was with me in distributing and paying out the money.

I have, in course of my negotiations with the Indians on the present occasion, collected some information which may be useful to your Department and will at an early day send it to you.

I will thank you to lay the two treaties accompanying this Report before His Excellency, and trust they may meet with his approval.

I have, &c.,

(Signed)   W. B. ROBINSON.

The Hon. Col. Bruce,
Superintendent-General, Indian Affairs.

CHAPTER III.

THE MANITOULIN ISLAND TREATY.

SOME years after the completion of the Robinson Treaties, the then Government of the old Province of Canada deemed it desirable to effect a treaty with the Indians dwelling upon the Great Manitoulin Island in Lake Huron, as a complement to the former treaties, and with the object of rendering available for settlement the large tract of good land upon the Island. The duty was entrusted to the Honorable William McDougall, then Superintendent-General of Indian Affairs, who, in the month of October, 1862, proceeded to the Island, accompanied by the late William Spragge, Esq., Deputy Superintendent of Indian Affairs, and Mr. F. Assicknack, of the Indian Office, Toronto, as interpreter. Mr. McDougall encountered considerable difficulties, but by firmness and decision eventually succeeded in obtaining a surrender from the Indians of the Island, excluding however from the surrender that portion of it easterly of Heywood Island and the Manitoulin Gulf.

The terms of the treaty, which will be found in the Appendix, were adapted to the peculiar circumstances of the Indians and were well and wisely framed. The result has been to render available for settlement a large tract of land on the Island, much of which is now occupied by a prosperous and thriving population. I conclude this brief notice of an important treaty by submitting, to the attention of the reader, the report of the Hon. W. McDougall, to His Excellency the Governor-General in Council, of the results of his mission.

The undersigned has the honor to state for the information of His Excellency the Governor-General in Council, that, under the authority of the Order in Council of the twelfth day of September, 1862, he proceeded early in the month of October last to visit the Great Manitoulin Island, accompanied by William Spragge, Esq., Deputy Superintendent of Indian Affairs, and Mr. F. Assicknack of the Indian Office, Toronto, as interpreter.

The resident agent, Captain Ironside, under instructions from the Department, had caused the Indians residing on the Island to be notified of the intended visit of the undersigned, and of its object, and had summoned them to attend at Manitowaning on the fourth ultimo.

The Chiefs and principal men, with the exception of one or two detained by illness, and nearly all the males above the age of eighteen years, were present at the council.

The undersigned stated the object of his visit, explained the wishes of the Government in regard to the settlement of the Island, and proposed the terms in respect to the Indians specified in the Order in Council authorizing the negotiation. The Indians had selected one of their Chiefs to reply to the overtures of the Government, and without taking time to consider these overtures he proceeded to announce the determination of the Indians to reject them unconditionally.

The undersigned made some further explanations, and directed an ajournment of the council for an hour, during which time the Indians were requested to consider the propositions he had made with care and deliberation.

On re-assembling there was an evident disposition among the bands living westwardly of the place of meeting to listen favorably to the propositions of the Government, but the majority were still unwilling to treat, and by intimidation and threats of violence prevented any open expression of opinion except by the old war Chief, Assicknack, who declared his full assent to the wishes of the Government.

Ascertaining that the Chief's opposition came from Indians living eastwardly of Heywood Sound, the undersigned determined to modify the propositions of the Government, so as to meet in some degree the objections from that quarter.

He accordingly adjourned the council until the following Monday, the first day of meeting being Saturday, informing the Indians that those who were disposed to continue the negotiations would remain while those who had resolved to reject every proposition of the Government might go home. He also informed them that no threats or intimidation would be allowed, and that any one who should attempt violence would be surely punished. Nearly all the Indians remained or returned on Monday, and being apprised of the nature of the proposition the undersigned intended to submit, namely, to exclude that part of the island eastwardly of the Manitoulin Gulf and Heywood Sound from the proposed agreement, they came to the adjourned meeting in a more friendly mood and expressed their willingness to surrender for sale and settlement all that part of the island westwardly of the Gulf and Sound.

The undersigned submits herewith the deed or instrument which embodies the agreement made and concluded between the respective parties. It was executed by the undersigned and the Deputy-Superintendent of Indian Affairs on behalf of the Government, and by nineteen of the Chiefs and principal men on behalf of the Indians.

In consequence of the modification of the terms of agreement authorized by the Order in Council as above-mentioned and the addition of other terms deemed necessary to prevent future difficulty, and which will be found in the instrument, the undersigned caused a provision to be inserted that it was not to take effect until approved by the Governor-General in Council.

The undersigned therefore now begs to submit the same for such approval.

(Signed)   WM. McDOUGALL,
Superintendent-General of Indian Affairs.

CHAPTER IV.

THE STONE FORT AND MANITOBA POST TREATIES NUMBERS ONE AND TWO.

IN the year 1871, the late Honorable Joseph Howe, then Secretary of State of Canada, recommended the appointment, by the Privy Council of Canada, of Mr. Wemyss McKenzie Simpson, as Indian Commissioner, in consequence of " the necessity of arranging with the bands of Indians inhabiting the tract of country between Thunder Bay and the Stone Fort, for the cession, subject to certain reserves such as they should select, of the lands occupied by them." Mr. Simpson accepted the appointment, and in company with Messrs. S. J. Dawson and Robert Pether visited the Ojjibewas or Chippawa Indians, between Thunder Bay and the north-west angle of the Lake of the Woods, and took the initiatory steps for securing a treaty with them thereafter. On his arrival at Fort Garry, he put himself, as directed by his instructions, in communication with his Honor, the Hon. A. G. Archibald, then Lieutenant-Governor of Manitoba and the North-West Territories. A conference took place between His Honor, Messrs. Simpson, Dawson and Pether, and the Hon. James McKay, a member, at that time, of the Executive Council of Manitoba, and himself a half-breed intimately acquainted with the Indian tribes, and possessed of much influence over them. The Indians in Manitoba, in the fall of 1870, had applied to the Lieutenant-Governor to enter into a treaty with them, and had been informed that in the ensuing year negotiations would be opened with them. They were full of uneasiness, owing to the influx of population, denied the validity of the Selkirk Treaty, and had

3

in some instances obstructed settlers and surveyors. In view of the anxiety and uneasiness prevailing, those gentlemen were of opinion " that it was desirable to secure the extinction of the Indian title not only to the lands within Manitoba, but also to so much of the timber grounds east and north of the Province as were required for immediate entry and use, and also of a large tract of cultivable ground west of the Portage, where there were very few Indian inhabitants." It was therefore resolved to open negotiations at the Lower Fort Garry, or Stone Fort, with the Indians of the Province, and certain adjacent timber districts, and with the Indians of the other districts at Manitoba Post, a Hudson's Bay fort, at the north end of Lake Manitoba, the territory being occupied principally by one nation, the Chippawas, of whom the Saulteaux of the lakes are a branch, although there are also a number of Swampy Crees resident within it.

Mr. Simpson accordingly issued proclamations, inviting the Indians to meet him on the 25th of July and 17th of August, 1871, at these points respectively, to negotiate an Indian treaty. The Lieutenant-Governor also issued a proclamation forbidding the sale or gift of intoxicating liquors during the negotiation of the treaty, and applied to Major Irvine to detail a few of the troops under his command to preserve order, which request was acceded to.

The Lieutenant-Governor and Mr Simpson arrived at the Stone Fort on the 24th of July, 1871, but as the Indians had not all arrived the meeting was postponed till the 27th, when a thousand Indians were found to have assembled, and a considerable number of half-breeds and other inhabitants of the country were present, awaiting with anxiety to learn the policy of the Government.

Lieutenant-Governor Archibald, after the Indians were assembled opened the proceedings by delivering the following address :

" On the 13th September last, on my first arrival in the

country, I met a number of you at the mission, I told you I could not then negotiate a Treaty with the Indians, but that I was charged by your Great Mother, the Queen, to tell you that she had been very glad to see that you had acted during the troubles like good and true children of your Great Mother. I told you also that as soon as possible you would all be called together to consider the terms of a treaty to be entered into between you and your Great Mother.

"I advised you to disperse to your homes, and gave you some ammunition to enable you to gain a livelihood during the winter by hunting.

"I promised that in the spring you would be sent for, and that either I, or some person directly appointed to represent your Great Mother, should be here to meet you, and notice would be given you when to convene at this place to talk over what was right to be done.

"Early in the spring, Mr. Simpson, who sits beside me, was made Commissioner. He left his home at once for this Province, by Rainy Lake and the Lake of the Woods.

"The Indians of the lake districts meet, as you know, on Rainy River yearly, about the 20th June, to fish for sturgeon, and they could not be called together sooner.

"Mr. Simpson met them there at that time, and talked over their affairs with them, and made certain arrangements with them. He then hurried on to see you, and reached this Province a week ago last Sunday. He then sent messengers at once to all the Indians within certain bounds, asking them to meet him here on the 25th day of July. Some of you were unable to come so soon, and he has therefore, at the instance of those who were here, waited till to-day to open the talk. I believe that now you are all arrived, and ready to proceed to business.

"It will be the duty of the Commissioner to talk to you on the particular details of the treaty, and I will give place to him presently, but there are one or two things of a general kind which I would like, before I close, to bring to your notice, for you to think about among yourselves.

"First. Your Great Mother, the Queen, wishes to do justice to all her children alike. She will deal fairly with those of the setting sun, just as she would with those of the rising sun. She wishes order and peace to reign through all her country, and while her arm is strong to punish the wicked man, her hand is also open to reward the good man everywhere in her Dominions.

"Your Great Mother wishes the good of all races under her sway. She wishes her red children to be happy and contented. She wishes them to live in comfort. She would like them to adopt the habits of the whites, to till land and raise food, and store it up against a time of want. She thinks this would be the best thing for her red children to do, that it would make them safer from famine and distress, and make their homes more comfortable.

"But the Queen, though she may think it good for you to adopt civilized habits, has no idea of compelling you to do so. This she leaves to your choice, and you need not live like the white man unless you can be persuaded to do so of your own free will. Many of you, however, are already doing this.

"I drove yesterday through the village below this Fort. There I saw many well-built houses, and many well-tilled fields with wheat and barley and potatoes growing, and giving promise of plenty for the winter to come. The people who till these fields and live in these houses are men of your own race, and they shew that you can live and prosper and provide like the white man.

"What I saw in my drive is enough to prove that even if there was not a buffalo or a fur-bearing animal in the country, you could live and be surrounded with comfort by what you can raise from the soil.

"Your Great Mother, therefore, will lay aside for you 'lots' of land to be used by you and your children forever. She will not allow the white man to intrude upon these lots. She will make rules to keep them for you, so that as long as the sun shall shine, there shall be no Indian who has not a place that he can call his home, where he can go and pitch his camp, or if he chooses, build his house and till his land.

" These reserves will be large enough, but you must not expect them to be larger than will be enough to give a farm to each family, where farms shall be required. They will enable you to earn a living should the chase fail, and should you choose to get your living by tilling, you must not expect to have included in your reserve more of hay grounds than will be reasonably sufficient for your purposes in case you adopt the habits of farmers. The old settlers and the settlers that are coming in, must be dealt with on the principles of fairness and justice as well as yourselves. Your Great Mother knows no difference between any of her people. Another thing I want you to think over is this: in laying aside these reserves, and in everything else that the Queen shall do for you, you must understand that she can do for you no more than she has done for her red children in the East. If she were to do more for you that would be unjust for them. She will not do less for you because you are all her children alike, and she must treat you all alike.

" When you have made your treaty you will still be free to hunt over much of the land included in the treaty. Much of it is rocky and unfit for cultivation, much of it that is wooded is beyond the places where the white man will require to go, at all events for some time to come. Till these lands are needed for use you will be free to hunt over them, and make all the use of them which you have made in the past. But when lands are needed to be tilled or occupied, you must not go on them any more. There will still be plenty of land that is neither tilled nor occupied where you can go and roam and hunt as you have always done, and, if you wish to farm, you will go to your own reserve where you will find a place ready for you to live on and cultivate.

" There is another thing I have to say to you. Your Great

Mother cannot come here herself to talk with you, but she has sent a messenger who has her confidence.

" Mr. Simpson will tell you truly all her wishes. As the Queen has made her choice of a chief to represent her, you must, on your part, point out to us the chiefs you wish to represent you, as the persons you have faith in.

" Mr. Simpson cannot talk to all your braves and people, but when he talks to chiefs who have your confidence he is talking to you all, and when he hears the voice of one of your chiefs whom you name he will hear the voice of you all.   It is for you to say who shall talk for you, and also who shall be your chief men.   Let them be good Indians, who know your wishes and whom you have faith in.

" You will look to the Commissioner to fulfil everything he agrees to do, and the Queen will look to the chiefs you name to us, to see that you keep your parts of the agreement.

" It is our wish to deal with you fairly and frankly.

" If you have any questions to ask, ask them, if you have anything you wish the Queen to know, speak out plainly.

" Now chiefs and braves and people, I introduce to you Mr. Simpson, who will say anything he thinks fit in addition to what I have said.

" When you hear his voice you are listening to your Great Mother the Queen, whom God bless and preserve long to reign over us."

Mr. Simpson also addressed them, and thereafter, in compliance with a request of the Lieutenant-Governor, the Indians retired to select their chiefs and principal spokesmen.

On the next day the conference was resumed, the chiefs and spokesmen being presented.   The Indians, on being asked to express their views, " stated that there was a cloud before them which made things dark, and they did not wish to commence the proceedings till the cloud was dispersed."   On inquiry it was ascertained that they referred to the imprisonment of four Swampy Cree Indians, who had been convicted under a local law, of breach of contract, as boatmen, with the Hudson's Bay Company, and on default of payment of a fine, had been sent to prison. The Lieutenant-Governor, as a matter of favor, ordered the release of these prisoners, and the sky became clear. Next day the Indians met again and declared that they would never again raise their voice against the enforcement of the law, but much difficulty was experienced in getting them to understand the views of the Government—they wishing to have two-thirds of the Province as a reserve. Eventually on the 3rd of August, 1871, a treaty was concluded, its principal features being the relinquishment to Her Majesty of the Indian title; the reserving of tracts of land for the Indians, sufficient to furnish 160 acres of land to each family of five; providing for the maintenance of schools, and prohibition of the sale of intoxicating liquors on the reserves ; a present of three dollars per head to the Indians and the payment to them of an annuity of three dollars per head.* (See copy of treaty which will be found in the Appendix.) On the 21st of August Mr. Commissioner Simpson, accompanied by the Lieutenant-Governor, the Hon. James McKay, and Mr. Molyneux St. John (lately Sheriff of the North-West Territories), met the Indians at Manitoba Post, and found them disposed to accept the terms of the treaty made at the Stone Fort, with which they had already become familiar, so that little time was lost in effecting a treaty with them as they had no special terms to prefer. By these two treaties, there was acquired by the Crown, the extinguishment of the Indian title in Manitoba, and in a tract of country fully equal in resources beyond it.

Having submitted these preliminary remarks, I conclude my notice of these treaties by quoting, as matter alike of historical record and practical interest, the despatches of Lieutenant-

---

* In consequence of misunderstandings having arisen, owing to the Indians alleging that certain promises had been made to them which were not specified in these treaties, a revision of them became necessary, and was effected in 1875, as will be seen reported hereafter.

Governor Archibald and the excellent and instructive report, addressed to the Secretary of State by Mr. Simpson, embracing as it does a full and graphic narrative of the proceedings which took place at the negotiation of these treaties, and of the difficulties which were encountered by the Commissioner, and the mode in which they were overcome.

GOVERNMENT HOUSE,

SILVER HEIGHTS, *July 22nd, 1871.*

SIR,—I have the honor to enclose you copy of a proclamation I have caused to be issued, with a view to prevent the danger arising from intoxicating drinks being given to the Indians, on the occasion of the meeting to negotiate a treaty.

I look upon the proceedings, we are now initiating, as important in their bearing upon our relations to the Indians of the whole continent. In fact, the terms we now agree upon will probably shape the arrangements we shall have to make with all the Indians between the Red River and the Rocky Mountains. It will therefore be well to neglect nothing that is within our power to enable us to start fairly with the negotiations.

With that view, I have, amongst other things, asked Major Irvine to detail a few of his troops to be present at the opening of the treaty. Military display has always a great effect on savages, and the presence, even of a few troops, will have a good tendency.

I fear we shall have to incur a considerable expenditure for presents of food, etc., during the negotiations; but any cost for that purpose I shall deem a matter of minor consequence. The real burden to be considered is that which has to be borne in each recurring year.

I doubt if it will be found practicable to make arrangements upon so favorable a basis as that prescribed by His Excellency the Governor-General, as the maximum to be allowed, in case of a treaty with the Lake Indians.

Nor indeed would it be right, if we look to what we receive, to measure the benefits we derive from coming into possession of the magnificent territory we are appropriating here, by what would be fair to allow for the rocks and swamps and muskegs of the lake country east of this Province.

But to this subject I shall probably take occasion to call your attention at an early day.

I have, etc.,

ADAMS G. ARCHIBALD.

THE HONORABLE
THE SECRETARY OF STATE FOR THE PROVINCES,

Ottawa.

LOWER FORT GARRY, *July 29th, 1871.*

SIR,—I have the honor to inform you that on Monday last I came to this Fort with the Commissioner to meet the Indians called here, with a view to negotiate a treaty, intending to open the business on Tuesday morning.

It appeared, however, on inquiry, that some bands of Indians had not arrived on Tuesday morning, and we were therefore obliged to postpone the opening of the meeting till Thursday. On that day the Indians from all the sections of the country to which the invitation extended were found present to the number of about one thousand. A considerable body of half-breeds and other inhabitants of the country were also present, awaiting with some anxiety to learn what should be announced as the policy of the Government.

I enclose you a memorandum of the observations with which I opened the meeting. On reading them you will observe one or two points which may require some explanation.

At the time of the treaty with the Earl of Selkirk, certain Indians signed as Chiefs and representatives of their people. Some of the Indians now deny that these men ever were Chiefs or had authority to sign the treaty.

With a view therefore to avoid a recurrence of any such question, we asked the Indians, as a first step, to agree among themselves in selecting their Chiefs, and then to present them to us and have their names and authority recorded.

Furthermore, the Indians seem to have false ideas of the meaning of a reserve. They have been led to suppose that large tracts of ground were to be set aside for them as hunting grounds, including timber lands, of which they might sell the wood as if they were proprietors of the soil.

I wished to correct this idea at the outset.

Mr. Simpson followed me with some observations in the same strain, after which the Indians retired to select their Chiefs and spokesmen.

On Friday morning the Chiefs and spokesmen were duly presented, and after their names were recorded, the Indians were invited to express their views.

After some delay they stated that there was a cloud before them which made things dark, and they did not wish to commence the proceedings till the cloud was dispersed.

On inquiring into their meaning, I found that they were referring to some four of their number who were prisoners in gaol. It seems that some Swampy Indians had entered into a contract with the Hudson's Bay Company as boatmen, and had deserted, and had been brought up before magistrates under a local law of last session, and fined, and in default of payment sent to prison for forty days.

Of this term some considerable part had expired. A few of the offenders had paid their fines, but there were still four Indians remaining in prison.

On learning the facts I told the Indians that I could not listen to them if they made a demand for the release of the Indians as a matter of right; that every subject of the Queen, whether Indian, half-breed or white, was equal in the eye of the law; that every offender against the law must be punished, whatever race he belonged to; but I said that on the opening of negotiations with them the Queen would like to see all her Indians taking part in them, and if the whole body present were to ask as a matter of grace and favor, under the circumstances, that their brethren should be released, Her Majesty would be willing to consent to their discharge; she would grant as a favor what she must refuse if asked for on any other ground. They replied by saying that they begged it as a matter of favor only. Thereupon I acceded to their request, and directed the discharge of the four Indians. This was received with great satisfaction. I explained again, that there might be no misunderstanding about it, that henceforth every offender against the law must be punished. They all expressed their acquiescence in what I said. The discharge of the prisoners had an excellent effect.

Next morning the Indians, through one of their spokesmen, declared in presence of the whole body assembled, that from this time they would never raise their voice against the law being enforced. After the order of the release, the Chiefs and spokesmen addressed us, questions were asked and answered, and some progress made in the negotiations. Eventually the meeting adjourned till this morning at ten o'clock.

A general acquiescence in the views laid down by Mr. Simpson and myself was expressed; but it was quite clear, by the proceedings of to-day, that our views were imperfectly apprehended. When we met this morning, the Indians were invited to state their wishes as to the reserves, they were to say how much they thought would be sufficient, and whether they wished them all in one or in several places.

In defining the limits of their reserves, so far as we could see, they wished to have about two-thirds of the Province. We heard them out, and then told them it was quite clear that they had entirely misunderstood the meaning and intention of reserves. We explained the object of these in something like the language of the memorandum enclosed, and then told them it was of no use for them to entertain any such ideas, which were entirely out of the question. We told them that whether they wished it or not, immigrants would come in and fill up the country; that every year from this one twice as many in number as their whole people there assembled would pour into the Province, and in a little while would spread all over it, and that now was the time for them to come to an arrangement that would secure homes and annuities for themselves and their children.

We told them that what we proposed to allow them was an extent of one hundred and sixty acres for each family of five, or in that proportion ; that they might have their land where they chose, not interfering with existing occupants; that we should allow an annuity of twelve dollars for every family of five, or in that proportion per head. We requested them to think over these propositions till Monday morning.

If they thought it better to have no treaty at all, they might do without one, but they must make up their minds; if there was to be a treaty, it must be on a basis like that offered.

That under some such arrangements, the Indians in the east were living happy and contented, enjoying themselves, drawing their annuities, and satisfied with their position.

The observations seemed to command the acquiescence of the majority, and on Monday morning we hope to meet them in a better frame for the discussion and settlement of the treaty.

I have, etc.,

ADAMS G. ARCHIBALD.

THE HONORABLE
  THE SECRETARY OF STATE FOR THE PROVINCES.

LOWER FORT GARRY, MANITOBA, *July 30th, 1871.*

SIR,—I have the honor to inform you, for the information of His Excellency the Governor-General, that I arrived in this Province on the 16th instant, and, after consultation with the Lieutenant-Governor of Manitoba, determined upon summoning the Indians of this part of the country to a conference for the purpose of negotiating a treaty at Lower Fort Garry, on Tuesday, the 25th instant, leaving for a future date the negotiation with the Indians westward of and outside of the Province of Manitoba.

Proclamations were issued, and every means taken to insure the attendance of the Indians, and on Monday, the 24th instant, I proceeded to Lower Fort Garry, where I met His Excellency the Lieutenant-Governor.

On Tuesday, finding that only a small portion of the Indians had arrived, we held a preliminary conference with Henry Prince—the Chief of the Swampies and Chippewas residing on what is known as the Indian Reserve, between Lower Fort Garry and Lake Winnipeg—at which we arranged a meeting for the next day at twelve o'clock, for the purpose of ascertaining the names of the Chiefs and head men of the several tribes. At this preliminary conference, Henry Prince said that he could not then enter upon any negotiations, as he was not empowered to speak or act for those bands of Indians not then present.

In the meantime it was found necessary to feed the Indians assembled here, and accordingly provisions were purchased and rations served out.

On Wednesday, the 26th, His Excellency the Lieutenant-Governor and myself met those Indians who had arrived, in council, and addressed them with the view of explaining the purport of my commission, and the matters which were to form the subject of a treaty.

It having been reported that the Indians who had not then arrived were on their road here, we agreed that another meeting should take place on the following day, at which the Chiefs and head men were to be presented to us.

On Thursday, pursuant to appointment, we again met the Indians, when the Chiefs and head men of the several bands present were named and presented. I then explained to them the nature of Indian reserves, and desired them to determine, in council among themselves, the locality in which they desired their reserves to be laid out.

On Friday, the 28th, we again met the Indians, but they were not then prepared to state their demands, and another meeting was appointed for Saturday.

On Saturday, the 29th, we again met them, all having by this time arrived. When the subject of reserves came up, it was found that the Indians had misunderstood the object of these reservations, for their demands in this respect were utterly out of the question. After a prolonged discussion with them, I consulted with the Lieutenant-Governor, and determined to let them at once understand the terms that I was prepared to offer, and I pointed out that the terms offered were those which would receive Her Majesty's consent. On further explanation of the subject, the Indians appeared to be satisfied, and willing to acquiesce in our arrangements as hereinafter mentioned; and having given them diagrams showing the size of the lots they would individually become possessed of, and having informed them of the amount of their annuity, it was finally settled that they should meet on Monday, the 31st, and acquaint me with their decision.

The reserves will comprise sufficient land to give each family of five persons one hundred and sixty acres, or in like proportion, together with an annual payment in perpetuity of twelve dollars for each family of five persons, or in like proportion.

As far as I can judge, I am inclined to think that the Indians will accept these terms.

I am happy to be able to say that the precautions taken to prevent the introduction of liquor amongst the Indians have been wholly successful, and that perfect order and contentment have prevailed up to the present time.

I have, etc.

WEMYSS M. SIMPSON,
Indian Commissioner.

THE HONORABLE
THE SECRETARY OF STATE FOR THE PROVINCES,
Ottawa.

OTTAWA, *November 3rd, 1871.*

To THE HONORABLE

THE SECRETARY OF STATE FOR THE PROVINCES,

Ottawa.

SIR,—I have the honor to submit to you, for the information of His Excellency the Governor-General, a report of my negotiations with the Indians of the Province of Manitoba, and with certain of the Indians of the North-West Territory, entered upon by me, in accordance with your instructions, dated 3rd May, 1871.

Having, in association with S. J. Dawson, Esq., and Robert Pether, Esq., effected a preliminary arrangement with the Indians of Rainy Lake, the particulars of which I have already had the honor of reporting to you in my Report, dated July 11th, 1871, I proceeded by the Lake of the Woods and Dawson Road to Fort Garry, at which place I arrived on the 16th July.

Bearing in mind your desire that I should confer with the Lieutenant-Governor of Manitoba, I called upon Mr. Archibald, and learned from him that the Indians were anxiously awaiting my arrival, and were much excited on the subject of their lands being occupied without attention being first given to their claims for compensation. Amongst the settlers, also, an uneasy feeling existed, arising partly from the often-repeated demands of the Indians for a treaty with themselves, and partly from the fact that certain settlers in the neighborhood of Portage la Prairie and other parts of the Province, had been warned by the Indians not to cut wood or otherwise take possession of the lands upon which they were squatting. The Indians, it appeared, consented to their remaining on their holdings until sufficient time had been allowed for my arrival, and the conclusion of a treaty; but they were unwilling to allow the settlers the free use of the country for themselves or their cattle. Mr. Archibald, and those residents in the Province of Manitoba with whom I conversed on the subject, appeared to think that no time should be lost in meeting the Indians, as some assurances had already been given them that a treaty would be made with them during the summer of 1871; and I therefore, at once, issued notices calling certain of the Indians together, naming two places at which I would meet them. The first meeting, to which were asked the Indians of the Province and certain others on the eastern side, was to be held on the 25th of July, at the Stone Fort, a Hudson's Bay Company's Post, situated on the Red River, about twenty miles northward of Fort Garry—a locality chosen as being the most central for those invited. The second meeting was appointed to be held on August 17th, at Manitoba Post, a Hudson's Bay Company's Post, at the north-west extremity of Lake Manitoba, as it was deemed that such of the bands of Indians residing without the limits of the Province of Manitoba, as I purposed to deal with at [present, would meet there more readily than elsewhere.

On Monday, the 24th of July, I met the Lieutenant-Governor of Manitoba at the Stone Fort; but negotiations were unavoidably delayed, owing to the fact that only one band of Indians had arrived, and that until all were on the spot those present declined to discuss the subject of a treaty, except in an informal manner. Amongst these, as amongst other Indians with whom I have come in contact, there exists great jealousy of one another, in all matters relating to their communications with the officials of Her Majesty ; and in order to facilitate the object in view, it was most desirable that suspicion and jealousy of all kinds should be allayed. The fact of the Commissioner having arrived was sufficient evidence of the good intentions of Her Majesty's Government, and it seemed better to await the arrival of all whom I had summoned, than to press matters to an issue while any were absent. This, however, entailed the necessity of feeding those who were already there, and others as they arrived.

It is customary in dealing with Indians to do so, and in this case it was absolutely necessary, for, obviously, it would have been impossible to invite those people from a distance, and then leave them to starve at our doors, or, in search of food, to plunder the neighborhood into which they had been introduced. At that season of the year the Indians were not engaged in fishing or hunting, and consequently large numbers of men, women and children attended at the place of meeting, for all of whom food was provided. The price of provisions, even at the lowest price for which they could be obtained, was high, pork being fifty dollars a barrel, and flour twenty shillings sterling per hundred, and such cattle as I was able to purchase £16 per head; so that the expense of keeping the Indians during the negotiation of treaty and payment of the gratuity, which lasted eleven days, forms no small share of the total expenditure. In addition to this expense, it was thought necessary by the Lieutenant-Governor that Major Irvine, commanding the troops at Fort Garry, should be requested to furnish a guard at the Stone Fort during the negotiations, and that there should be at hand, also, a force of constabulary, for the purpose of preventing the introduction of liquor amongst the Indian encampments. Other expenses of a somewhat similar nature were incurred, which would be totally unnecessary upon any future occasion of payment being made to the Indians of Manitoba. I may here refer to the apparently prolonged duration of the first negotiation, and explain, in reference thereto, the causes, or some of them, that entailed the loss of time and attendant expense. For some time a doubt has existed whether the Chief, nominally at the head of the Indians of the Indian settlement, possessed the good will and confidence of that band ; and I thought it advisable to require that the several bands of Indians should select such Chiefs as they thought proper, and present these men as their authorized Chiefs, before anything was said as to the terms of a treaty. The Indians having acquiesced in this proposal, forthwith proceeded to such election; but the proceeding apparently involved discussion and consideration amongst themselves, and two days elapsed before the men chosen were presented for recognition, and the business of the meeting commenced.

When the peculiar circumstances surrounding the position of the Indians of the Province were pointed out, the future of the country predicted, and the views and intentions of the Government explained by the Lieutenant-Governor and myself, the Indians professed a desire for time to think over what had been said before making any reply; and when their answer came it proved to contain demands of such an exorbitant nature, that much time was spent in reducing their terms to a basis upon which an arrangement could be made.

Every band had its spokesman, in addition to its Chief, and each seemed to vie with another in the dimensions of their requirements. I may mention, as an illustration, that in the matter of reserves, the quantity of land demanded for each band amounted to about three townships per Indian, and included the greater part of the settled portions of the Province. It was not until the 3rd of August, or nine days after the first meeting, that the basis of arrangement was arrived at, upon which is founded the treaty of that date. Then, and by means of mutual concessions, the following terms were agreed upon. For the cession of the country described in the treaty referred to, and comprising the Province of Manitoba, and certain country in the north-east thereof, every Indian was to receive a sum of three dollars a year in perpetuity, and a reserve was to be set apart for each band, of sufficient size to allow one hundred and sixty acres to each family of five persons, or in like proportion as the family might be greater or less than five. As each Indian settled down upon his share of the reserve, and commenced the cultivation of his land, he was to receive a plough and harrow. Each Chief was to receive a cow and a male and female of the smaller kinds of animals bred upon a farm. There was to be a bull for the general use of each reserve. In addition to this, each Chief was to receive a dress, a flag and a medal, as marks of distinction; and each Chief, with the exception of Bozawequare, the Chief of the Portage band, was to receive a buggy, or light spring waggon. Two councillors and two braves of each band were to receive a dress, somewhat inferior to that provided for the Chiefs, and the braves and councillors of the Portage band excepted, were to receive a buggy. Every Indian was to receive a gratuity of three dollars, which, though given as a payment for good behaviour, was to be understood to cover all dimensions for the past.

On this basis the treaty was signed by myself and the several Chiefs, on behalf of themselves and their respective bands, on the 3rd of August, 1871, and on the following day the payment commenced.

The three dollars gratuity, above referred to, will not occur in the ordinary annual payments to the Indians of Manitoba, and, though doubling the amount paid this year, may now properly be regarded as belonging to a previous year, but only now liquidated.

A large number of Indians, entitled to share in the treaty, were absent on the 3rd August, and in the belief that I should, almost immediately, be able to obtain a more accurate knowledge than I possessed of the numbers of the several bands, I paid to each person present only three dollars—the gratuity—postponing for a short time the first annual payment. Having completed this disbursement, I prepared to start for Manitoba Post, to open negotiations with the Indians on the immediate north and north-west borders of the Province of Manitoba, promising however to visit the several bands of the first treaty, in their own districts, and to there pay them. By this means the necessity for their leaving their own homes, and for the Government's feeding them while they were being paid, and during their journey home, was avoided.

After completing the treaty at Manitoba Post, of which mention is hereinafter made, I visited Portage la Prairie, the Indian settlement at St. Peter's, Rivière Marais, and the Town of Winnipeg, according to my promise, and at each place, with the exception of Rivière Marais, found the Indians satisfied with the treaty, and awaiting their payment. At Rivière Marais, which was the rendezvous appointed by the bands living in the neighborhood of Pembina, I found that the Indians had either misunderstood the advice given them by parties in the settlement, well disposed towards the treaty, or, as I have some reason to believe, had become unsettled by the representations made by persons in the vicinity of Pembina, whose interests lay elsewhere than in the Province of Manitoba; for, on my announcing my readiness to pay them, they demurred at receiving their money until some further concessions had been made by me.

With a view to inducing the Indians to adopt the habits and labors of civilization, it had been agreed, at the signing of the treaty as before mentioned, to give certain animals as a nucleus for stocking the several reserves, together with certain farming implements; and it was now represented to me by the spokesman of the bands, that as the Queen had, with that kindness of heart which distinguished her dealings with her red children, expressed a desire to see the Indians discard their former precarious mode of living and adopt the agricultural pursuits of the white man, they were desirous of acceding to the wish of their great Mother, and were now prepared to receive the gifts she had been good enough to speak of, through her Commissioner, in full. But, as it could make no difference whatever to their great Mother whether these things were given in kind or in money value, her red children of the Pembina bands were resolved to receive them in the latter form. I had put a valuation upon all the articles mentioned in the supplement to the treaty, and could go no further in the matter unless I was prepared to pay them for all these articles at the rates they would now proceed to mention. I declined to comply with the request, and they declined to receive their first annual payment, whereupon I broke up my camp and returned to Winnipeg. As I foresaw at the time, this determination on their part was shortly repented, and a number of their leading men were subsequently paid at Winnipeg; while at the request of the Indians, the money for the remainder, together with a pay sheet, was forwarded to the officer in charge of the Hudson's Bay Company's Post at Pembina, with instructions to, pay the Indians as per list as each might present himself. At Portage la Prairie, although the number paid at the Stone Fort was largely increased, there still remained many who, from absence or other causes, were not paid, and by the request of the Chief the money was left for these with the officers in charge of the Hudson's Bay Company's Post, in the same manner as was done for the Pembina bands.

As I was unable to proceed to Fort Alexander, the payments for the Indians, or for such of them as were present at the signing of the treaty, were sent in like manner to the officer in charge of the Hudson's Bay Company's Post at Fort Alexander; but it may be as well to mention that the number so paid will fall far short of the total number belonging to that place. The latter remark will apply to the Pembina band, for their payment was sent as per gratuity list, and there must necessarily have been others who did not receive payment. All these must receive their back payments during the course of next year.

During the payment of the several bands, it was found that in some, and most notably in the Indian settlement and Broken Head River Band, a number of those residing among the Indians, and calling themselves Indians, are in reality half-breeds, and entitled to share in the land grant under the provisions of the Manitoba Act. I was most particular, therefore, in causing it to be explained, generally and to individuals, that any person now electing to be classed with Indians, and receiving the Indian pay and gratuity, would, I believed, thereby forfeit his or her right to another grant as a half-breed; and in all cases where it was known that a man was a half-breed, the matter, as it affected himself and his children, was explained to him, and the choice given him to characterize himself. A very few only decided upon taking their grants as half-breeds. The explanation of this apparent sacrifice is found in the fact that the mass of these persons have lived all their lives on the Indian reserves (so called), and would rather receive such benefits as may accrue to them under the Indian treaty, than wait the realization of any value in their half-breed grant.

The Lieutenant-Governor of Manitoba having expressed a desire to be present at the negotiation of the treaty at Manitoba Post, His Honor, accompanied by the Hon. James McKay, proceeded thither with me, in company with Mr. Molyneux St. John, the Clerk of the Legislative Assembly of Manitoba, who had assisted me in the duties connected with the former treaty and payments. I left Winnipeg on the 13th August, but owing to adverse winds on Lake Manitoba did not arrive until two days after the time appointed. I found that, in the meanwhile, the officer in charge of the Hudson's Bay Company's Post had been obliged to give some provisions to the Indians pending my arrival; but on my speaking to the leading men of the bands assembled, it was evident that the Indians of this part had no special demands to make, but having a knowledge of the former treaty, desired to be dealt with in the same manner and on the same terms as those adopted by the Indians of the Province of Manitoba.

4

The negotiation with these bands therefore occupied little time, and on the 21st August, 1871, a treaty was concluded by which a tract of country three times as large as the Province of Manitoba was surrendered by the Indians to the Crown. Payment in full, that is to say, the gratuity and the first payment, was at once made; and I have since written to the officers in charge of the Hudson's Bay Company's Posts within the tract above referred to, requesting them to procure for me a reliable census of the Indians, parties to this treaty.

I have referred to the cost of effecting these treaties, and remarked that it will prove to be exceptional. It may be regarded as entirely so, as far as the Indians with whom the dealings were held are concerned. In the future the annual payment will be only one-half to each Indian of the amount paid this year, for the gratuity was the same as the payment, and the heavy expense of feeding the Indians while at the place of meeting and on their journey home, will be avoided by the payment being made at or near their own reserves.

All the collateral expenses, therefore, of this year, including dresses, medals, presents to the Indians, etc., etc., will not appear in the expenses attending during future payments.

But it is to be remembered that a large number of Indians, whose lands were ceded by the second treaty, were not present. The distance from the hunting grounds of some to Manitoba Post is very great; but while their absence was to be regretted for some reasons, it effected a very considerable saving in the item of provisions.

During the ensuing season, these persons will probably be found at the place where the payments will be made, and will then require their payments as if they had been present at the signing of the treaty.

Of the land ceded in the Province of Manitoba, it will be hardly necessary for me to speak, as His Excellency the Governor-General is already in possession of accurate information touching its fertility and resources; but I may observe that, valuable as are these lands, they are fully equalled if not exceeded by the country of which the Government now comes into possession, by virtue of the treaty concluded at Manitoba Post. Already, settlers from the Provinces in Canada and elsewhere are pushing their way beyond the limits of the Province of Manitoba; and there is nothing but the arbitrary limits of that Province, and certain wood and water advantages found in the territory beyond it, to distinguish one part of the country from the other. The fertility that is possessed by Manitoba is shared by the country and its confines. The water courses of the Province are excelled by those of the territory; and the want of wood which threatens serious difficulty in the one, is by no means so apparent in the other.

The Indians of both parts have a firm belief in the honor and integrity of Her Majesty's representatives, and are fully impressed with the idea that the amelioration of their present condition is one of the objects of Her Majesty in making these treaties. Although many years will elapse before they can be regarded as a settled population—settled in the sense of following agricultural pursuits—the Indians have already shown a disposition to provide against the vicissitudes of the chase by cultivating small patches of corn and potatoes. Moreover, in the Province of Manitoba, where labor is scarce, Indians give great assistance in gathering in the crops. At Portage la Prairie, both Chippawas and Sioux were largely employed in the grain field; and in other parishes I found many farmers whose employés were nearly all Indians.

Although serious trouble has from time to time occurred across the boundary line, with Indians of the same tribes, and indeed of the same bands as those in Manitoba, there is no reason to fear any trouble with those who regard themselves as subjects of Her Majesty. Their desire is to live at peace with the white man, to trade with him, and, when they are disposed, to work for him; and I believe that nothing but gross injustice or oppression will induce them either to forget the allegiance which they now claim with pride, or molest the white subjects of the sovereign whom they regard as their Supreme Chief.

The system of an annual payment in money I regard as a good one, because the recipient is enabled to purchase just what he requires when he can get it most cheaply, and it also enables him to buy articles at second hand, from settlers and others, that are quite as useful to him as are the same things when new. The sum of three dollars does not appear to be large enough to enable an Indian to provide himself with many of his winter necessaries; but as he receives the same amount for his wife or wives, and for each of his children, the aggregate sum is usually sufficient to procure many comforts for his family which he would otherwise be compelled to deny himself.

* * * * * * * * *

I take this opportunity of acknowledging the assistance afforded me in successfully completing the two treaties, to which I have referred, by His Honor the Lieutenant-Governor of Manitoba, the Hon. James McKay, and the officers of the Hudson's Bay Company. In a country where transport and all other business facilities are necessarily so scarce, the services rendered to the Government by the officers in charge of the several Hudson's Bay Posts has been most opportune and valuable.

I have, etc.,

WEMYSS M. SIMPSON,
Indian Commissioner.

CHAPTER V.

TREATY NUMBER THREE, OR THE NORTH-WEST ANGLE TREATY.

IN the year 1871 the Privy Council of Canada issued a joint commission to Messrs. W. M. Simpson, S. J. Dawson and W. J. Pether, authorizing them to treat with the Ojibbeway Indians for the surrender to the Crown of the lands they inhabited—covering the area from the watershed of Lake Superior to the north-west angle of the Lake of the Woods, and from the American border to the height of land from which the streams flow towards the Hudson's Bay. This step had become necessary in order to make the route known as "the Dawson route," extending from Prince Arthur's Landing on Lake Superior to the north-west angle of the Lake of the Woods, which was then being opened up, "secure for the passage of emigrants and of the people of the Dominion generally," and also to enable the Government to throw open for settlement any portion of the land which might be susceptible of improvement and profitable occupation. The Commissioners accepted the appointment, and in July, 1871, met the Indians at Fort Francis.

The tribes preferred claims for right of way through their country. The Commissioners reported "that they had admitted these to a limited extent and had made them presents in provisions and clothing and were also to pay them a small amount in money, it being fully and distinctly understood by the Indians that these presents and clothing were accepted by them as an equivalent for all past claims whatever." The Commissioners having explained to them fully the intentions of the Government as to obtaining a surrender of their territorial rights, and giving in return therefor reserves of land and

annual payments, asked them to consider the proposals c 'nly
and meet the Commissioners the succeeding summer to
come to an arrangement. In 1872, the Indians were found
not to be ready for the making of a treaty and the subject
was postponed. In the year 1873 a commission was issued
to the Hon. Alexander Morris, then Lieutenant-Governor
of Manitoba and the North-West Territories, Lieut.-Col.
Provencher, who had in the interval been appointed Commissioner of Indian Affairs in the place of Mr. Simpson, who
had resigned, and Lindsay Russell, Esq., but the latter being
unable to act, Mr. Dawson, now M.P. for Algoma, was appointed Commissioner in his stead. These Commissioners having accepted the duty confided to them, met the Indians at the
north-west angle of the Lake of the Woods in the end of September, 1873, and, after protracted and difficult negotiations,
succeeded in effecting a treaty with them. A copy of the
treaty will be found in the Appendix, and a brief record
of the utterances of the Indians and of the Commissioners,
which was taken down in short hand by one of the soldiers
of the militia force, is hereto subjoined. This treaty was one of
great importance, as it not only tranquilized the large Indian
population affected by it, but eventually shaped the terms of
all the treaties, four, five, six and seven, which have since been
made with the Indians of the North-West Territories—who
speedily became apprised of the concessions which had been
granted to the Ojibbeway nation. The closing scenes were
striking and impressive. The chief speaker, Mawe-do-pe-nais,
thus winding up the conference on the part of the Indians, in his
final address to the Lieutenant-Governor and his fellow Commissioners :

" Now you see me stand before you all : what has been done
here to-day has been done openly before the Great Spirit and
before the nation, and I hope I may never hear any one say that
this treaty has been done secretly : and now in closing this
council, I take off my glove, and in giving you my hand I

deliver over my birthright and lands : and in taking your hand
I hold fast all the promises you have made, and I hope they
will last as long as the sun rises and the water flows, as you
have said."

The conference then adjourned, and on re-assembling, after
the treaty had been read and explained, the Commissioners signed
it and the Lieutenant-Governor called on an aged hereditary
Chief, Kee-ta-kay-pi-nais, to sign next. The Chief came forward,
but declined to touch the pen, saying, "I must first have the
money in my hand." The Lieutenant-Governor immediately held
out his hand, and directed the interpreter to say to the chief,
"Take my hand and feel the money in it. If you cannot trust
me for half an hour, do not trust me forever." When this was
repeated by the interpreter, the Chief smiled, took the out-
stretched hand, and at once touched the pen, while his mark
was being made, his last lingering distrust having been effect-
ively dispelled by this prompt action and reply. The other
Chiefs followed, and then the interpreter was directed to tell
Kee-ta-kay-pi-nais, the Chief, that he would be paid forthwith,
but the Chief at once replied, "Oh no, it is evening now, and
I will wait till to-morrow." The payments were duly made
next day, and so was closed, a treaty, whereby a territory
was enabled to be opened up, of great importance to Canada,
embracing as it does the Pacific Railway route to the North-
West Territories—a wide extent of fertile lands, and, as is
believed, great mineral resources. I now quote the official
despatch of the Lieutenant-Governor, dated the 14th October,
1873, in which will be found, a full narrative of the proceedings, connected with the treaty, and a statement of the
results thereby effected. I also submit a short-hand report
of the negotiations connected with the treaty.

GOVERNMENT HOUSE,
FORT GARRY, *October 14th, 1873.*

SIR,—I have the honor to enclose copy of a treaty made by myself, Lieut.-Col. Provencher, Indian agent, and S. J. Dawson, Esq., Commissioner, acting on behalf of Her Majesty, of the one part, and the Salteaux tribe of Ojibbeway Indians on the other, at the North-West Angle of the Lake of the Woods, on the 3rd of October, for the relinquishment of the Indian title to the tract of land therein described, and embracing 55,000 square miles. In the first place, the holding of the negotiation of the treaty had been appointed by you to take place at the North-West Angle before you requested me to take part therein, and Mr. Dawson had obtained the consent of the Indians to meet there on the 10th of September, but they afterwards changed their minds, and refused to meet me unless I came to Fort Francis. I refused to do this, as I felt that the yielding to the demand of the Indians in this respect, would operate injuriously to the success of the treaty, and the results proved the correctness of the opinion I had formed. I therefore sent a special agent (Mr. Pierre Levaillier) to warn them that I would meet them as arranged at the North-West Angle on the 25th, or not at all this year, to which they eventually agreed.

I left here for the Angle on the 23rd September, and arrived there on the 25th, when I was joined by Messrs. Provencher and Dawson, the last named of whom I was glad to find had been associated with the Commissioners in consequence of the resignation of Mr. Lindsey Russell, thereby giving us the benefit as well of his knowledge of the country to be dealt with, as of the several bands of Indians therein. Mr. Pether, of Fort Francis, was also in attendance, and Mr. Provencher was accompanied by Mr. St. John, of his department.

On arriving, the Indians, who were already there, came up to the house I occupied, in procession, headed by braves bearing a banner and a Union Jack, and accompanied by others beating drums. They asked leave to perform a dance in my honor, after which they presented to me the pipe of peace. They were then supplied with provisions and returned to their camp. As the Indians had not all arrived, and for other reasons, the 26th, 27th and 28th were passed without any progress, but on the 29th I sent them word that they must meet the Commissioners next morning. Accordingly, on the the 30th, they met us in a tent, the use of which I had obtained from the military authorities. I explained to them the object of the meeting, but as they informed me that they were not ready to confer with us, I adjourned the meeting until next day. On the 1st October they again assembled. The principal cause of the delay was divisions and jealousies among themselves. The nation had not met for many years, and some of them had never before been assembled together. They were very jealous of each other, and dreaded any of the Chiefs having individual communications with me, to prevent which they had guards on the approaches to my house and Mr. Dawson's tent. On the 2nd October they again assembled, when I again explained the object of the meeting, through Mr. McPherson, an intelligent half-breed trader, whose services I secured. M. Chatelan, the Government interpreter, was also present. They had selected three spokesmen, and had also an Indian reporter, whose duty was to commit to memory all that was said. They had also secured the services of M. Joseph Nolin, of Point du Chene, to take notes in French of the negotiations, a copy of which notes I obtained from him and herewith enclose. The spokesmen informed me they would not treat as to the land until we settled with them as to the Dawson route, with regard to which they alleged Mr. Dawson had made promises which had not been kept, and that they had not been paid for the wood used in building the steamers, nor for the use of the route itself. Mr. Dawson explained that he had paid them for cutting wood, but had always asserted a common right to the use of wood and the water way. He asked them what promise had not been kept, and pointed out that the Government had twice before endeavored to treat with them for a settlement of all matters. He referred them to me as to the general question of the use of the route. They were unable to name any promises which had not been kept. Thereupon I told them I came on behalf of the Queen and the Government of the Dominion of Canada to treat with them with regard to the lands and all other matters, but that they refused to hear what I had to say ; they had closed my mouth ; and as we would not treat except for the settlement of all matters past and future I could not speak unless they asked me to do so. They conferred among themselves, and seeing that we were quite firm, the spokesman came forward and said that they would not close my mouth, after which they would make their demands. The Commissioners had had a conference and agreed, as they found there was no hope of a treaty for a less sum, to offer five dollars per head, a present of ten dollars, and reserves of farming and other lands not exceeding one square mile per family of five, or in that proportion, sums within the limits of our instructions, though I had private advices if possible not to give the maximum sum named, as the Government had been under a misapprehension as to amounts given to the bands in the United States. The Chiefs heard my proposal, and the meeting adjourned until next day. On the 3rd October the Chiefs again assembled and made a counter proposition, of which I enclose a copy, being the demand they have urged since 1869. I also enclose an estimate I had made of the money value of the demand, amounting to $125,000 per annum. On behalf of the Commissioners I at once peremptorily refused the demand. The spokesmen returned to the Chiefs, who were arranged on benches, the people sitting on the ground behind them, and on their return they informed me that the Chiefs, warriors and braves were of one mind, that they would make a treaty only if we acceded to their demand. I told them if so the conference was over, that I would return and report that they had refused to make a reasonable treaty, that hereafter I would treat with those bands who were willing to treat, but that I would advise them to return to the council and reconsider their determination before next morning, when, if not, I should certainly leave. This brought matters to a crisis. The Chief of the Lac Seul band came forward to speak. The others tried to prevent him, but he was secured a hearing. He stated that he represented four hundred people in the north ; that they wished a treaty ; that they wished a school-master to be sent them to teach their children the knowledge of the white man ; that they had begun to cultivate the soil and were growing potatoes and Indian corn, but wished other grain for seed and some agricultural implements and cattle. This Chief spoke under evident apprehension as to the course he was taking in resisting the other Indians, and displayed much good sense and moral courage. He was followed by the Chief ''Blackstone,'' who urged the other Chiefs to return to the council and consider my proposals, stating that he was ready to treat, though he did not agree to my proposals nor to those made to me. I then told them that I had known all along they were not united as they had said ; that they ought not to allow a few Chiefs to prevent a treaty, and that I wished to treat with them as a nation and not with separate bands, as they would otherwise compel me to do ; and therefore urged them to return to their council, promising to remain another day to give them time for consideration. They spent the night in council, and next morning having received a message from M. Charles Nolin, a French half-breed, that they were becoming more amenable to reason, I requested the Hon. James McKay (who went to the Angle three times to promote this treaty), Charles Nolin and Pierre Levaillier to go down to the Indian Council, and as men of their own blood, give them friendly advice. They accordingly did so, and were received by the Indians, and in about half an hour afterwards were followed by Messrs. Provencher and St. John, who also took part in the interview with the Council of Chiefs. The Chiefs were summoned to the conference by the sound of a bugle and again met us, when they told me that the determination to adhere to their demands had been so strong a bond that they did not think it could be broken, but they had now determined to see if I would give them anything more.

The Commissioners had had a conference, and agreed previously to offer a small sum for ammunition and twine for nets, yearly—a few agricultural implements and seeds, for any band actually farming or commencing to farm, and to increase the money payment by two dollars per head if it should be found necessary in order to secure a treaty, maintaining a permanent annuities at the sum fixed. The Indians on the other hand had determined on asking fifteen dollars, with some other demands. In fixing the ten dollars the Commissioners had done so as a sum likely to be accepted in view of three dollars per head having been paid the Indians the first year the Dawson route was used, and that they had received nothing since. In reply to the Indians, I told them I was glad that they had reconsidered their decision, and that as they had done so, being desirous of inducing them to practice agriculture and to have the means of getting food if their fishing and hunting failed, we would give them certain implements, cattle and grain, once for all, and the extra two dollars per head of a money payment. This proposal was received favorably, but the spokesmen again came forward and said they had some questions to ask before accepting my proposal. They wanted suits of clothing every year for all the bands, and fifty dollars for every Chief annually. This I declined, but told them that there were some presents of clothing and food which would be given them this year at the close of treaty. They then asked free passes forever over the Canada Pacific Railway, which I refused. They then asked that no "fire-water" should be sold on their reserves, and I promised that a regulation to this effect should be introduced into the treaty. They then asked that they should not be sent to war, and I told them the Queen was not in the habit of employing the Indians in warfare. They asked that they should have power to put turbulent men off their reserves, and I told them the law would be enforced against such men. They asked what reserves would be given them, and were informed by Mr. Provencher that reserves of farming and other lands would be given them as previously stated, and that any land actually in cultivation by them would be respected. They asked if the mines would be theirs; I said if they were found on their reserves it would be to their benefit, but not otherwise. They asked if an Indian found a mine would he be paid for it, I told them he could sell his information if he could find a purchaser like any other person. They explained that some of their children had married in the States, and they wished them to return and live among them, and wanted them included in the treaty. I told them the treaty was not for American Indians, but any *bona fide British Indians* of the class they mentioned who should *within two* years be found *resident* on British soil would be recognized.

They said there were some ten to twenty families of half-breeds who were recognized as Indians, and lived with them, and they wished them included. I said the treaty was not for whites, but I would recommend that those families should be permitted the option of taking either status as Indians or whites, but that they could not take both. They asked that Mr. Charles Nolin should be employed as an Indian Agent, and I stated that I would submit his name to the Government with favorable mention of his services on that occasion. They asked that the Chiefs and head men, as in other treaties, should get an official suit of clothing, a flag, and a medal, which I promised. Mawedopenais produced one of the medals given to the Red River Chiefs, said it was not silver, and they were ashamed to wear it, as it turned black, and then, with an air of great contempt, struck it with his knife. I stated that I would mention what he had said, and the manner in which he had spoken. They also stated the Hudson Bay Company had staked out ground at Fort Francis, on part of the land they claimed to have used, and to be entitled to, and I promised that enquiry would be made into the matter. They apologized for the number of questions put me, which occupied a space of some hours, and then the principal spokesman, Mawe-dopenais, came forward and drew off his gloves, and spoke as follows : "Now you see me stand before you all. What has been done here to-day, has been done openly before the Great Spirit, and before the nation, and I hope that I may never hear any one say that this treaty has been done secretly. And now, in closing this council, I take off my glove, and in giving you my hand, I deliver over my birthright, and lands, and in taking your hand I hold fast all the promises you have made, and I hope they will last as long as the sun goes round, and the water flows, as you have said." To which I replied as follows: "I accept your hand, and with it the lands, and will keep all my promises, in the firm belief that the treaty now to be signed will bind the red man and the white man together as friends forever." The conference then adjourned for an hour to enable the text of the treaty to be completed, in accordance with the understanding arrived at. At the expiration of that period the conference was resumed, and after the reading of the treaty, and an explanation of it in Indian by the Hon. James McKay, it was signed by the Commissioners and by the several Chiefs, the first signature being that of a very aged hereditary Chief. The next day the Indians were paid by Messrs. Pether and Graham, of the Department of Public Works; the latter of whom kindly offered his services, as Mr. Provencher had to leave to keep another appointment. The negotiation was a very difficult and trying one, and required on the part of the Commissioners, great patience and firmness. On the whole I am of opinion that the issue is a happy one. With the exception of two bands in the Shebandowan District, whose adhesion was secured in advance, and the signatures of whose Chiefs Mr. Dawson left to secure, the Indian title has been extinguished over the vast tract of country comprising 55,000 square miles lying between the upper boundary of the Lake Superior treaty, and that of the treaty made by Mr. Commissioner Simpson at Manitoba Post, and embracing within its bounds the Dawson route, the route of the Canada Pacific Railway, and an extensive lumber and mineral region.* It is fortunate, too, that the arrangement has been effected, as the Indians along the lakes and rivers were dissatisfied at the use of the waters, which they considered theirs, having been taken without compensation, so much so indeed that I believe if the treaty had not been made, the Government would have been compelled to place a force on the line next year.

Before closing this despatch, I have much pleasure in bearing testimony to the hearty co-operation and efficient aid the Commissioners received from the *Metis* who were present at the Angle, and who, with one accord, whether of French or English origin, used the influence which their relationships to the Indians gave them, to impress them with the necessity of their entering into the treaty. I must also express my obligations to the detachment of

---

* Mr. Dawson succeeded in obtaining the adhesion to the treaty of the Chiefs in question.

troops under the command of Captain Macdonald, assigned me as an escort, for their soldierly bearing and excellent conduct while at the Angle. Their presence was of great value, and had the effect of deterring traders from bringing articles of illicit trade for sale to the Indians; and moreover exercised a moral influence which contributed most materially to the success of the negotiations. I have further to add, that it was found impossible, owing to the extent of the country treated for, and the want of knowledge of the circumstances of each band, to define the reserves to be granted to the Indians. It was therefore agreed that the reserves should be hereafter selected by officers of the Government, who should confer with the several bands, and pay due respect to lands actually cultivated by them. A provision was also introduced to the effect that any of the reserves, or any interest in them, might hereafter be sold for the benefit of the Indians by the Government with their consent. I would suggest that instructions should be given to Mr. Dawson to select the reserves with all convenient speed; and, to prevent complication, I would further suggest that no patents should be issued, or licenses granted, for mineral or timber lands, or other lands, until the question of the reserves has been first adjusted.

I have the honor to be, Sir,

Your obedient servant,

ALEXANDER MORRIS,

Lieut.-Governor.

Attention is called to the ensuing report of the proceedings connected with the treaty, extracted from the *Manitoban* newspaper of the 18th October, 1873, published at Winnipeg. The reports of the speeches therein contained were prepared by a short-hand reporter and present an accurate view of the course of the discussions, and a vivid representation of the habits of Indian thought.

NORTH-WEST ANGLE,

September 30, 1873.

The Lieutenant-Governor and party, and the other Commissioners appointed to negotiate a treaty with the Indians, arrived here on Thursday, 24th inst., having enjoyed delightful weather during the entire trip from Fort Garry. The Governor occupies the house of the officer in charge of the H. B. Post. The grounds around it have been nicely graded and cleared of brush, and surrounded by rows of evergreens planted closely, so as to completely screen the house from wind, and at the same time contribute much to relieve the monotony of the scenery. Immediately west of this, and likewise enclosed by walls of evergreens, is the large marquee used as a Council House, by the contracting parties; and immediately sur-rounding it to the north and west are the tents of the other officers of the Commission and the officers and men of the Volunteers on detachment duty.

Situated to the eastward, and extending all along the river bank, are the tents of the Indians to the number of a hundred, with here and there the tent of the trader, attracted thither by the prospect of turning an honest penny by exchanging the necessaries of Indian life for such amounts of the price of their heritage as they can be induced to spend.

The natives now assembled here number about 800 all told, and hail from the places given below. Among them are many fine physically developed men, who would be considered good looking were it not for the extravagance with which they be-smear their faces with pigments of all colors.

It was at first thought probable that the serious business of the meeting would be begun on Friday, but owing to the non-arrival of a large body of Rainy River and Lac Seul repre-sentatives, it was decided to defer it until next day. Saturday came, and owing to the arrival of a messenger from the Lac Seul band asking the Governor to wait for their arrival, pro-ceedings have further stayed until Monday. But "hope de-ferred maketh the heart sick;" so the advent of Monday brought nothing but disappointment, and this, coupled with the disagreeable wet and cold weather that prevailed, made every one ill at ease if not miserable. The Chiefs were not ready to treat—they had business of their own to transact, which must be disposed of before they could see the Governor; and so another delay was granted. But Monday did not find them ready, and they refused to begin negotiations. An inti-mation from the Governor that unless they were ready on the following day he would leave for home on Wednesday, hurried them up a little—they did wait on him to-day, Tuesday, but only to say they had not yet finished their own business, but that they would try and be ready to treat on Wednesday. And so the matter stands at present—if the Indians agree amongst themselves, the treaty will be opened to-morrow; otherwise the Governor will strike camp and return to Fort Garry.

Divisions and local jealousies have taken possession of the Indian mind. The difficulties are the inability of the Indians to select a high or principal chief from amongst themselves, and as to the matter and extent of the demands to be made.

It is many years since these people had a general council, and in the interval many head men have died, while others have grown to man's estate, and feel ambitious to take part in the proceedings. But the fiat has gone forth, that unless a conclusion is arrived at to-morrow negotiations will be broken off for this year.

BOUNDARIES OF THE LANDS TO BE CEDED.

Beginning at the North-West Angle eastward, taking in all the Lake of the Woods, including White Fish Bay, Rat Portage and north to White Dog in English River; up English River to Lake Seul, and then south-east to Lake Nepigon; westward to Rainy River and down it to Lake of the Woods, and up nearly to Lac des Mille Lacs; then beginning at the 49th parallel to White Mouth River, thence down it to the north, along the eastern boundary of the land ceded in 1871, embracing 55,000 square miles.

In the neighborhood of Lac des mille Lacs and Shebandowan are several bands, who have sent word that they cannot come as far as this point, but will accept the terms made at this treaty and ratify it with any one commissioner who will go there to meet them.

The whole number of Indians in the territory is estimated at

14,000, and are represented here by Chiefs of the following bands:

1. North-West Angle.
2. Rat Portage.
3. Lake Seul.
4. White Fish Bay on Lake of the Woods.
5. Sha-bas-kang, or Grassy Narrows.
6. Rainy River.
7. Rainy Lake.
8. Beyond Kettle Falls, southward.
9. Eagle Lake.
10. Nepigon.
11. Shoal Lake (three miles to the north of this point).

NORTH-WEST ANGLE,
October 1, 1873.

The assembled Chiefs met the Governor this morning, as per agreement, and opened the proceedings of the day by express-ing the pleasure they experienced at meeting the Commissioners on the present occasion. Promises had many times been made to them, and, said the speaker, unless they were now fulfilled they would not consider the broader question of the treaty.

Mr. S. J. Dawson, one of the Commissioners, reciprocated the expression of pleasure used by the Chiefs through their spokesman. He had long looked forward to this meeting, when all matters relating to the past, the present, and the future, could be disposed of so as to fix permanently the friendly rela-tions between the Indians and the white men. It was now, he continued, some years since the white men first came to this country—they came in the first place at the head of a great military expedition; and when that expedition was passing through the country all the chiefs showed themselves to be true and loyal subjects—they showed themselves able and willing to support their Great Mother the Queen. Subsequently, when we began to open up the road, we had to call upon the Indians to assist us in doing so, and they always proved themselves very happy to help in carrying out our great schemes.   He was, he continued, one of the Commission employed by the Government to treat with them and devise a scheme whereby both white men and Indians would be benefitted.   We made to the Indians the proposals we were authorized to make, and we have carried out these proposals in good faith.   This was three years ago.   What we were directed to offer we did offer, but the Indians thought it was too little, and negotiations were broken off.   Since this I have done what was in my power to bring about this meeting with new terms, and consider it a very happy day that you should be assembled to meet the Governor of the Territory as representative of Her Majesty.   He would explain to them the proposals he had to make.   He had lived long amongst them and would advise them as a friend to take the opportunity of making arrangements with the Governor. When we arrange the general matters in question, should you choose to ask anything, I shall be most happy to explain it, as I am here all the time.

The Chief in reply said his head men and young men were of one mind, and determined not to enter upon the treaty until the promises made in the past were fulfilled, they were tired of waiting.   What the Commissioners called "small matters" were great to them, and were what they wished to have settled.

The route that had been built through the country proved this, and the Commissioners promised something which they now wanted.

This was taking the Commissioners on a new tack, but Mr. Dawson promptly undertook to answer the objections.   He said all these questions had been discussed before; but if he had made any promises that remained unfulfilled, he would be happy to learn their nature.   The Chief replied that all the houses on the line, and all the big boats on the waters, were theirs, and they wanted to be recompensed for them.

Mr. Dawson continued, saying he was glad they had now come to a point on which they could deal. The Indians questioned the right of the Government to take wood for the steamers. This was a right which the speaker had all along told them was common to all Her Majesty's subjects. He then referred them to the Governor if they had anything more to say on that subject. Wood on which Indians had bestowed labor was always paid for; but wood on which we had spent our own labor was ours.

His Excellency then addressed them at some length. He understood that they wanted to have the questions in which they were interested treated separately. This was not what he came there for. Wood and water were the gift of the Great Spirit, and were made alike for the good of both the white man and red man. Many of his listeners had come a long way, and he, too, had come a long way, and he wanted all the questions settled at once, by one treaty. He had a message from the Queen, but if his mouth was kept shut, the responsibility would rest on the Indians, and not with him if he were prevented from delivering it. He had authority to tell them what sum of money he could give them in hand now, and what he could give them every year; but it was for them to open his mouth. He concluded his remarks, which were forcibly delivered, with an emphatic "I have said."

The Chief reiterated that he and his young men were determined not to go on with the treaty until the first question was disposed of. What was said about the trees and rivers was quite true, but it was the Indian's country, not the white man's. Following this the Governor told the Council that unless they would settle all the matters, the big and little, at once, he would not talk. He was bound by his Government, and was of the same mind to treat with them on all questions, and not on any one separately.

On seeing His Excellency so firm, and feeling that it would not do to allow any more time to pass without coming to business the Chief asked the Governor to open his mouth and tell what propositions he was prepared to make.

His Excellency then said—" I told you I was to make the treaty on the part of our Great Mother the Queen, and I feel it will be for your good and your children's. I should have been very sorry if you had shut my mouth, if I had had to go home without opening my mouth. I should not have been a true friend of yours if I had not asked you to open my mouth. We are all children of the same Great Spirit, and are subject to the same Queen. I want to settle all matters both of the past and the present, so that the white and red man will always be friends. I will give you lands for farms, and also reserves for your own use. I have authority to make reserves such as I have described, not exceeding in all a square mile for every family of five or thereabouts. It may be a long time before the other lands are wanted, and in the meantime you will be permitted to fish and hunt over them. I will also establish schools whenever any band asks for them, so that your children may have the learning of the white man. I will also give you a sum of money for yourselves and every one of your wives and children for this year. I will give you ten dollars per head of the population, and for every other year five dollars a-head. But to the chief men, not exceeding two to each band, we will give twenty dollars a-year for ever. I will give to each of you this year a present of goods and provisions to take you home, and I am sure you will be satisfied.

After consultation amongst themselves, the Councillors went to have a talk about the matter and will meet the Governor to-morrow morning, when it is expected the bargain will be concluded. Of course the Indians will make some other demands.

Immediately after the adjournment as above, the Governor presented an ox to the people in camp; and the way it disappeared would have astonished the natives of any other land. Half-an-hour after it was led into encampment, it was cut up and boiling in fifty pots.

THIRD DAY.

Proceedings were opened at eleven o'clock by the Governor announcing that he was ready to hear what the Chiefs had to say. The Fort Francis Chief acted as spokesman, assisted by another Chief, Powhassan.

MA-WE-DO-PE-NAIS—"I now lay down before you the opinions of those you have seen before. We think it a great thing to meet you here. What we have heard yesterday, and as you represented yourself, you said the Queen sent you here, the way we understood you as a representative of the Queen. All this is our property where you have come. We have understood you yesterday that Her Majesty has given you the same power and authority as *she* has, to act in this business; you said the Queen gave you her goodness, her charitableness in your hands. This is what we think, that the Great Spirit has planted us on this ground where we are, as you were where you came from. We think where we are is our property. I will tell you what he said to us when he he planted us here; the rules that we should follow—us Indians—He has given us rules that we should follow to govern us rightly. We have understood you that you have opened your charitable heart to us like a person taking off his garments and throwing them to all of us here. Now, first of all, I have a few words to address to this gentleman (Mr. Dawson). When he understood rightly what was my meaning yesterday, he threw himself on your help. I think I have a right to follow him to where he flew when I spoke to him on the subject yesterday. We will follow up the subject from the point we took it up. I want to answer what we heard from you yesterday, in regard to the money that you have promised us yesterday to each individual. I want to talk about the rules that we had laid down before. It is four years back since we have made these rules. The rules laid down are the rules that they wish to follow—a council that has been agreed upon by all the Indians. I do not wish that I should be required to say twice what I am now going to lay down. We ask fifteen dollars for all that you see, and for the children that are to be born in future. This year only we ask for fifteen dollars; years after ten dollars; our Chiefs fifty dollars per year for every year, and other demands of large amounts in writing, say $125,000 yearly."

ANOTHER CHIEF—"I take my standing point from here. Our councillors have in council come to this conclusion, that they should have twenty dollars each; our warriors, fifteen dollars; our population, fifteen dollars. We have now laid down the conclusion of our councils by our decisions. We tell you our wishes are not divided. We are all of one mind." (Paper put in before the Governor for these demands.)

CHIEF—" I now let you know the opinions of us here. We would not wish that anyone should smile at our affairs, as we think our country is a large matter to us. If you grant us what is written on that paper, then we will talk about the reserves; we have decided in council for the benefit of those that will be born hereafter. If you do so the treaty will be finished, I believe."

GOVERNOR—"I quite agree that this is no matter to smile at. I think that the decision of to-day is one that affects yourselves and your children after, but you must recollect that this is the third time of negotiating. If we do not shake hands and make our Treaty to-day, I do not know when it will be done, as the Queen's Government will think you do not wish to treat with her. You told me that you understood that I represented the Queen's Government to you and that I opened my heart to you, but you must recollect that if *you* are a council there is another great council that governs a great Dominion, and they hold their councils the same as you hold yours. I wish to tell you that I am a servant of the Queen. I cannot do my own will ; I must do hers. I can only give you what she tells me to give you. I am sorry to see that your hands were very wide open when you gave me this paper. I thought what I promised you was just, kind and fair between the Qeeen and you. It is now three years we have been trying to settle this matter. If we do not succeed to-day I shall go away feeling sorry for you and for your children that you could not see what was good for you and for them. I am ready to do what I promised you yesterday. My hand is open and you ought to take me by the hand and say, "yes, we accept of your offer." I have not the power to do what you ask of me. I ask you once more to think what you are doing, and of those you have left at home, and also of those that may be born yet, and I ask you not to turn your backs on what is offered to you, and you ought to see by what the Queen is offering you that she loves her red subjects as much as her white. I think you are forgetting one thing, that what I offer you is to be while the water flows and the sun rises. You know that in the United States they only pay the Indian for twenty years, and you come here to-day and ask for ever more than they get for twenty years. Is that just? I think you ought to accept my offer, and make a treaty with me as I ask you to do. I only ask you to think for yourselves, and for your families, and for your children and children's children, and I know that if you do that you will shake hands with me to-day."

CHIEF—"I lay before you our opinions. Our hands are poor but our heads are rich, and it is riches that we ask so that we may be able to support our families as long as the sun rises and the water runs."

GOVERNOR—"I am very sorry; you know it takes two to make a bargain; you are agreed on the one side, and I for the Queen's Government on the other. I have to go away and report that I have to go without making terms with you. I doubt if the Commissioners will be sent again to assemble this nation. I have only one word more to say; I speak to the Chief and to the head men to recollect those behind them, and those they have left at home, and not to go away without accepting such liberal terms and without some clothing."

CHIEF—" My terms I am going to lay down before you; the decision of our Chiefs; ever since we came to a decision you push it back. *The sound of the rustling of the gold is under my feet where I stand;* we have a rich country; it is the Great Spirit who gave us this; where we stand upon is the Indians' property, and belongs to them. If you grant us our requests you will not go back without making the treaty."

ANOTHER CHIEF—" We understood yesterday that the Qneen had given you the power to act upon, that you could do what you pleased, and that the riches of the Queen she had filled your head and body with, and you had only to throw them round about; but it seems it is not so, but that you have only half the power that she has, and that she has only half filled your head."

GOVERNOR—"I do not like to be misunderstood. I did not say yesterday that the Queen had given me all the power; what I told you was that I was sent here to represent the Queen's Government, and to tell you what the Queen was willing to do for you. You can understand very well; for instance, one of your great chiefs asks a brave to deliver a message, he represents you, and that is how I stand with the Queen's Government."

CHIEF—"It is your charitableness that you spoke of yesterday—Her Majesty's charitableness that was given you. It is our chiefs, our young men, our children and great grandchildren, and those that are to be born, that I represent here, and it is for them I ask for terms. The white man has robbed us of our riches, and we don't wish to give them up again without getting something in their place."

GOVERNOR—" For your children, grandchildren, and children unborn, I am sorry that you will not accept of my terms. I shall go home sorry, but it is your own doing; I must simply go back and report the fact that you refuse to make a treaty with me."

CHIEF—" You see all our chiefs before you here as one mind;

we have one mind and one mouth. It is the decision of all of us; if you grant us our demands you will not go back sorrowful; we would not refuse to make a treaty if you would grant us our demands."

GOVERNOR—"I have told you already that I cannot grant your demands; I have not the power to do so. I have made you a liberal offer, and it is for you to accept or refuse it as you please."

CHIEF—"Our chiefs have the same opinion; they will not change their decision."

GOVERNOR—"Then the Council is at an end."

CHIEF (of Lac Seule)—"I understand the matter that he asks; if he puts a question to me as well as to others, I say so as well as the rest. We are the first that were planted here; we would ask you to assist us with every kind of implement to use for our benefit, to enable us to perform our work; a little of everything and money. We would borrow your cattle; we ask you this for our support; I will find whereon to feed them. The waters out of which you sometimes take food for yourselves, we will lend you in return. If I should try to stop you—it is not in my power to do so; even the Hudson's Bay Company—that is a small power—I cannot gain my point with it. If you give what I ask, the time may come when I will ask you to lend me one of your daughters and one of your sons to live with us; and in return I will lend you one of my daughters and one of my sons for you to teach what is good, and after they have learned, to teach us. If you grant us what I ask, although I do not know you, I will shake hands with you. This is all I have to say,"

GOVERNOR—"I have heard and I have learned something. I have learned that you are not all of one mind. I know that your interests are not the same—that some of you live in the north far away from the river; and some live on the river, and that you have got large sums of money for wood that you have cut and sold to the steamboats; but the men in the north have not this advantage. What the Chief has said is reasonable ; and should you want goods I mean to ask you what amount you would have in goods, so that you would not have to pay the traders' prices for them. I wish you were all of the same mind as the Chief who has just spoken. He wants his children to be taught. He is right. He wants to get cattle to help him to raise grain for his children. It would be a good thing for you all to be of his mind, and then you would not go away without making this treaty with me."

BLACKSTONE (Shebandowan)—"I am going to lay down before you the minds of those who are here. I do not wish to interfere with the decisions of those who are before you, or yet with your decisions. The people at the height of land where the waters came down from Shebandowan to Fort Frances, are those who have appointed me to lay before you our decision. We are going back to hold a Council."

Mr. Dawson—"I would ask the Chief who has just spoken, did the band at Shebandowan—did Rat McKay, authorize him to speak for them ? Ke-ha-ke-ge-nen is Blackstone's own Chief; and I am perfectly willing to think that he authorized him. What I have to say is that the Indians may not be deceived by representations made to them, and that the two bands met me at Shebandowan and said they were perfectly willing to enter into a treaty."

GOVERNOR—"I think the nation will do well to do what the Chief has said. I think he has spoken sincerely, and it is right for them to withdraw and hold a Council among themselves."

Blackstone here handed in a paper which he alleged gave him authority as Chief, but which proved to be an official acknowledgement of the receipt of a letter by the Indian Department at Ottawa.

The Governor here agreed with the Council that it would be well for the Chiefs to have another meeting amongst themselves. It was a most important day for them and for their children, and His Excellency would be glad to meet them again.

The Council broke up at this point, and it was extremely doubtful whether an agreement could be come to or not. The Rainy River Indians were careless about the treaty, because they could get plenty of money for cutting wood for the boats, but the northern and eastern bands were anxious for one. The Governor decided that he would make a treaty with those bands that were willing to accept his terms, leaving out the few disaffected ones. A Council was held by the Indians in the evening, at which Hon. James McKay, Pierre Léveillée, Charles Nolin, and Mr. Genton were present by invitation of the Chiefs. After a very lengthy and exhaustive discussion, it was decided to accept the Governor's terms, and the final meeting was announced for Friday morning. Punctually at the appointed time proceedings were opened by the Fort Francis Chiefs announcing to His Excellency that they were all of one mind, and would accept his terms, with a few modifications. The discussion of these terms occupied five hours, and met every possible contingency so fully that it would be impossible to do justice to the negotiators otherwise than by giving a full report of the speeches on both sides ; but want of space compels us to lay it over until next week.

The treaty was finally closed on Friday afternoon, and signed on Saturday ; after which a large quantity of provisions, ammunition and other goods were distributed.

When the council broke up last (Thursday) night, 3rd October, it looked very improbable that an understanding could be arrived at, but the firmness of the Governor, and the prospect that he would make a treaty with such of the bands as were willing to accept his terms, to the exclusion of the others, led them to reconsider their demands. The Hon. James McKay, and Messrs. Nolin, Genton, and Léveillée were invited in to their council, and after a most exhaustive discussion of the circumstance in which they were placed, it was resolved to accept the Governor's terms, with some modifications. Word was sent to this effect, and at eleven o'clock on Friday, conference was again held with His Excellency.

The Fort Francis Chief opened negotiations by saying:— "We present our compliments to you, and now we would tell you something. You have mentioned our councillors, warriors and messengers—every Chief you see has his councillors, warriors and messengers."

GOVERNOR—"I was not aware what names they gave me—they gave their chief men. I spoke of the subordinates of the head Chiefs; I believe the head Chiefs have three subordinates —I mean the head Chief and three of his head men."

CHIEF—"I am going to tell you the decision of all before you. I want to see your power and learn the most liberal terms that you can give us."

GOVERNOR—"I am glad to meet the Chiefs, and I hope it will be the last time of our meeting. I hope we are going to under-derstand one-another to-day. And that I can go back and re-port that I left my Indian friends contented, and that I have put into their hands the means of providing for themselves and their families at home; and now I will give you my last words. When I held out my hands to you at first, I intended to do what was just and right, and what I had the power to do *at once*,—not to go backwards and forwards, but at once to do what I believe is just and right to you. I was very much pleased yesterday with the words of the Chief of Lac Seul. I was glad to hear that he had commenced to farm and to raise things for himself and family, and I was glad to hear him ask me to hold out my hand. I think we should do everything to help you by giving you the means to grow some food, so that if it is a bad year for fishing and hunting you may have some-thing for your children at home. If you had not asked it the Goverment would have done it all the same, although I had not said so before. I can say this, that when a band settles down and actually commences to farm on their lands, the Goverment

will agree to give two hoes, one spade, one scythe, and one axe
for every family actually settled; one plough for every ten families; five harrows for every twenty families; and a yoke of
oxen, a bull and four cows for every band; and enough barley,
wheat and oats to plant the land they have actually broken
up. This is to enable them to cultivate their land, and it is
to be given them on their commencing to do so, once for all.
There is one thing that I have thought over, and I think it is
a wise thing to do. That is to give you ammunition, and twine
for making nets, to the extent of $1,500 per year, for the whole
nation, so that you can have the means of procuring food.—
Now, I will mention the last thing that I can do. I think
that the sum I have offered you to be paid after this year for
every man, woman and child now, and for years to come, is
right and is the proper sum. I will not make any change in
that, but we are anxious to show you that we have a great
desire to understand you—that we wish to do the utmost in our
power to make you contented, so that the white and the red
man will always be friends. This year, instead of ten dollars we
will give you twelve dollars, to be paid you at once as soon as we
sign the treaty. This is the best I can do for you. I wish you to
understand we do not come here as traders, but as representing
the Crown, and to do what we believe is just and right. We
have asked in that spirit, and I hope you will meet me in that
spirit and shake hands with me-day and make a treaty for
ever. I have no more to say."

CHIEF—"I wish to ask some points that I have not properly
understood. We understand that our children are to have two
dollars extra. Will the two dollars be paid to our principal
men as well? And these things that are promised will they
commence at once and will we see it year after year?"

GOVERNOR—"I thought I had spoken fully as to everything,
but I will speak again. The ammunition and twine will be got
at once for you, *this year*, and that will be for every year. The
Commissioner will see that you get this at once; with regard

to the things to help you to farm, you must recollect, in a very few days the river will be frozen up here and we have not got these things here now.   But arrangements will be made next year to get these things for those who are farming, it cannot be done before as you can see yourselves very well.   Some are farming, and I hope you will all do so."

CHIEF—"One thing I did not say that is most necessary— we want a cross-cut saw, a whip saw, grindstone and files."

GOVERNOR—"We will do that, and I think we ought to give a box of common tools to each Chief of a Band."

CHIEF—"Depending upon the words you have told us, and stretched out your hands in a friendly way, I depend upon that. One thing more we demand—a suit of clothes to all of us."

GOVERNOR—"With regard to clothing, suits will be given to the Chiefs and head men, and as to the other Indians there is a quantity of goods and provisions here that will be given them at the close of the treaty.   The coats of the Chiefs will be given every three years."

CHIEF—"Once more ; powder and shot will not go off without guns.   We ask for guns."

GOVERNOR—"I have shewn every disposition to meet your view, but what I have promised is as far as I can go."

CHIEF—"My friends, listen to what I am going to say, and you, my brothers.   We present you now with our best and our strongest compliments.   We ask you not to reject some of our children who have gone out of our place ; they are scattered all over, a good tasted meat hath drawn them away, and we wish to draw them all here and be contented with us."

GOVERNOR—"If your children come and live here, of course they will become part of the population, and be as yourselves."

CHIEF—"I hope you will grant the request that I am going to lay before you.   I do not mean those that get paid on the other side of the line, but some poor Indians who may happen to fall in our road.   If you will accept of these little matters, the treaty will be at an end.   I would not like that one of my children should not eat with me, and receive the food that you are going to give me."

GOVERNOR—"I am dealing with British Indians and not American Indians ; after the treaty is closed we will have a list of the names of any children of British Indians that may come in during two years and be ranked with them ; but we must have a limit somewhere."

CHIEF—"I should not feel happy if I was not to mess with some of my children that are around me—those children that we call the Half-breed—those that have been born of our women of Indian blood. We wish that they should be counted with us, and have their share of what you have promised. We wish you to accept our demands. It is the Half-breeds that are actually living amongst us—those that are married to our women."

GOVERNOR—"I am sent here to treat with the Indians. In Red River, where I came from, and where there is a great body of Half-breeds, they must be either white or Indian. If Indians, they get treaty money ; if the Half-breeds call them selves white, they get land. All I can do is to refer the matter to the Government at Ottawa, and to recommend what you wish to be granted."

CHIEF—"I hope you will not drop the question ; we have understood you to say that you came here as a friend, and represented your charitableness, and we depend upon your kindness. You must remember that our hearts and our brains are like paper ; we never forget. There is one thing that we want to know. If you should get into trouble with the nations, I do not wish to walk out and expose my young men to aid you in any of your wars."

GOVERNOR—"The English never call the Indians out of their country to fight their battles. You are living here and the Queen expects you to live at peace with the white men and your red brothers, and with other nations."

ANOTHER CHIEF—"I ask you a question—I see your roads

here passing through the country, and some of your boats—useful articles that you use for yourself.   Bye and bye we shall see things that run swiftly, that go by fire—carriages—and we ask you that us Indians may not have to pay their passage on these things, but can go free."

GOVERNOR—" I think the best thing I can do is to become an Indian.   I cannot promise you to pass on the railroad free, for it may be a long time before we get one; and I cannot promise you any more than other people."

CHIEF—"I must address myself to my friend here, as he is the one that has the Public Works."

MR. DAWSON—" I am always happy to do anything I can for you.   I have always given you a passage on the boats when I could.   I will act as I have done though I can give no positive promise for the future."

CHIEF—" We must have the privilege of travelling about the country where it is vacant."

MR. McKAY—" Of course, I told them so."

CHIEF—"Should we discover any metal that was of use, could we have the privilege of putting our own price on it ?"

GOVERNOR—" If any important minerals are discovered on any of their reserves the minerals will be sold for their benefit with their consent, but not on any other land that discoveries may take place upon ; as regards other discoveries, of course, the Indian is like any other man.   He can sell his information if he can find a purchaser."

CHIEF—" It will be as well while we are here that everything should be understood properly between us.   All of us—those behind us—wish to have their reserves marked out, which they will point out, when the time comes.   There is not one tribe here who has not laid it out."

COMMISSIONER PROVENCHER (the Governor being temporarily absent)—" As soon as it is convenient to the Government to send surveyors to lay out the reserves they will do so, and they will try to suit every particular band in this respect."

CHIEF—"We do not want anybody to mark out our reserves, we have already marked them out."

COMMISSIONER—"There will be another undertaking between the officers of the Government and the Indians among themselves for the selection of the land; they will have enough of good farming land, they may be sure of that."

CHIEF—"Of course, if there is any particular part wanted by the public works they can shift us. I understand that; but if we have any gardens through the country, do you wish that the poor man should throw it right away?"

COMMISSIONER—"Of course not."

CHIEF—"These are matters that are the wind-up. I begin now to see how I value the proceedings. I have come to this point, and all that are taking part in this treaty and yourself. I would wish to have all your names in writing handed over to us. I would not find it to my convenience to have a stranger here to transact our business between me and you. It is a white man who does not understand our language that is taking it down. I would like a man that understands our language and our ways. We would ask your Excellency as a favor to appoint him for us."

GOVERNOR—"I have a very good feeling to Mr. C. Nolin, he has been a good man here; but the appointment of an Agent rests with the authorities at Ottawa and I will bring your representation to them, and I am quite sure it will meet with the respect due to it."

CHIEF—"As regards the fire water, I do not like it and I do not wish any house to be built to have it sold. Perhaps at times if I should be unwell I might take drop just for medicine; and shall any one insist on bringing it where we are, I should break the treaty."

GOVERNOR—"I meant to have spoken of that myself, I meant to put it in the treaty. He speaks good about it. The Queen and her Parliament in Ottawa have passed a law prohibiting the use of it in this territory, and if any shall be brought in for the use of you as medicine it can only come in by my permission."

CHIEF—"Why we keep you so long is that it is our wish that everything should be properly understood between us."

GOVERNOR—"That is why I am here. It is my pleasure, and I want when we once shake hands that it should be forever."

CHIEF—"That is the principal article. If it was in my midst the fire water would have spoiled my happiness, and I wish it to be left far away from where I am. All the promises that you have made me, the little promises and the money you have promised, when it comes to me year after year—should I see that there is anything wanting, through the negligence of the people that have to see after these things, I trust it will be in my power to put them in prison."

GOVERNOR—"The ear of the Queen's Government will always be open to hear the complaints of her Indian people, and she will deal with her servants that do not do their duty in a proper manner."

CHIEF—"Now you have promised to give us all your names. I want a copy of the treaty that will not be rubbed off, on parchment."

GOVERNOR—"In the mean time I will give you a copy on paper, and as soon as I get back I will get you a copy on parchment."

CHIEF—"I do not wish to be treated as they were at Red River—that provisions should be stopped as it is there. Whenever we meet and have a council I wish that provisions should be given to us. We cannot speak without eating."

GOVERNOR—"You are mistaken. When they are brought together at Red River for their payments they get provisions."

CHIEF—"We wish the provisions to come from Red River."

GOVERNOR—"If the Great Spirit sends the grasshopper and there is no wheat grown in Red River, we cannot give it to you."

CHIEF—"You have come before us with a smiling face, you

have shown us great charity—you have promised the good things ; you have given us your best compliments and wishes, not only for once but for ever ; let there now for ever be peace and friendship between us. It is the wish of all that where our reserves are peace should reign, that nothing shall be there that will disturb peace. Now, I will want nothing to be there that will disturb peace, and will put every one that carries arms,—such as murderers and thieves—outside, so that nothing will be there to disturb our peace."

GOVERNOR—"The Queen will have policemen to preserve order, and murderers and men guilty of crime will be punished in this country just the same as she punishes them herself."

CHIEF—"To speak about the Hudson's Bay Company. If it happens that they have surveyed where I have taken my reserve, if I see any of their signs I will put them on one side."

GOVERNOR—"When the reserves are given you, you will have your rights. The Hudson's Bay Company have their rights, and the Queen will do justice between you."

CHIEF OF FORT FRANCIS—"Why I say this is, where I have chosen for my reserve I see signs that the H. B. Co. has surveyed. I do not hate them. I only wish they should take their reserves on one side. Where their shop stands now is my property ; I think it is three years now since they have had it on it."

GOVERNOR—"I do not know about that matter ; it will be enquired into. I am taking notes of all these things and am putting them on paper."

CHIEF—I will tell you one thing. You understand me now, that I have taken your hand firmly and in friendship. I repeat twice that you have done so, that these promises that you have made, and the treaty to be concluded, let it be as you promise, as long as the sun rises over our head and as long as the water runs. One thing I find, that deranges a little my kettle. In this river, where food used to be plentiful for our subsistence,

I perceive it is getting scarce.   We wish that the river should be left as it was formed from the beginning—that nothing be broken."

GOVERNOR—"This is a subject that I cannot promise."

MR. DAWSON—"Anything that we are likely to do at present will not interfere with the fishing, but no one can tell what the future may require, and we cannot enter into any engagement."

CHIEF—"We wish the Government would assist us in getting a few boards for some of us who are intending to put up houses this fall, from the mill at Fort Francis."

GOVERNOR—"The mill is a private enterprise, and we have no power to give you boards from that."

CHIEF—"I will now show you a medal that was given to those who made a treaty at Red River by the Commissioner. *He* said it was silver, but *I* do not think it is.   I should be ashamed to carry it on my breast over my heart.   I think it would disgrace the Queen, my mother, to wear her image on so base a metal as this.   [Here the Chief held up the medal and struck it with the back of his knife.   The result was anything but the 'true ring,' and made every man ashamed of the petty meanness that had been practised.]   Let the medals you give us be of silver—medals that shall be worthy of the high position our Mother the Queen occupies."

GOVERNOR—"I will tell them at Ottawa *what* you have said, and *how* you have said it."

CHIEF—"I wish you to understand you owe the treaty much to the Half-breeds."

GOVERNOR—"I know it.   I sent some of them to talk with you, and I am proud that all the Half-breeds from Manitoba, who are here, gave their Governor their cordial support."

The business of the treaty having now been completed, the Chief, Mawedopenais, who, with Powhassan, had with such wonderful tact carried on the negotiations, stepped up to the Governor and said :—

" Now you see me stand before you all ; what has been done here to-day has been done openly before the Great Spirit, and before the nation, and I hope that I may never hear any one say that this treaty has been done secretly; and now, in closing this Council, I take off my glove, and in giving you my hand, I deliver over my birth-right and lands ; and in taking your hand, I hold fast all the promises you have made, and I hope they will last as long as the sun goes round and the water flows, as you have said."

The Governor then took his hand and said:

"I accept your hand and with it the lands, and will keep all my promises, in the firm belief that the treaty now to be signed will bind the red man and the white together as friends for ever."

A copy of the treaty was then prepared and duly signed, after which a large amount of presents, consisting of pork, flour, clothing, blankets, twine, powder and shot, etc., were distributed to the several bands represented on the ground.

On Saturday, Mr. Pether, Local Superintendent of Indian Affairs at Fort Francis, and Mr. Graham of the Government Works, began to pay the treaty money—an employment that kept them busy far into the night. Some of the Chiefs received as much as one hundred and seventy dollars for themselves and families.

As soon as the money was distributed the shops of the H. B. Co., and other resident traders were visited, as well as the tents of numerous private traders, who had been attracted thither by the prospect of doing a good business. And while these shops all did a great trade—the H. B. Co. alone taking in $4,000 in thirty hours—it was a noticeable fact that many took home with them nearly all their money. When urged to buy goods there, a frequent reply was : " If we spend all our money here and go home and want debt, we will be told to get our debt where we spent our money. " Debt " is used by them instead of the word " credit." Many others deposited money with white men and Half-breeds on whose honor they could depend, to be called for and spent at Fort Garry when "the ground froze."

One very wonderful thing that forced itself on the attention of every one was the perfect order that prevailed throughout the camp, and which more particularly marked proceedings in the council. Whether the demands put forward were granted by the Governor or not, there was no petulance, no ill-feeling, evinced; but everything was done with a calm dignity that was pleasing to behold, and which might be copied with advantage by more pretentious deliberative assemblies.

On Sunday afternoon, the Governor presented an ox to the nation, and after it had been eaten a grand dance was indulged in. Monday morning the river Indians took passage on the steamer for Fort Francis, and others left in their canoes for their winter quarters.

The Governor and party left on Monday morning, the troops, under command of Captain McDonald, who had conducted themselves with the greatest propriety, and had contributed, by the moral effect of their presence, much to the success of the negotiation, having marched to Fort Garry on Saturday morning.

CHAPTER VI.

THE QU'APPELLE TREATY, OR NUMBER FOUR.

THIS treaty, is, so generally called, from having been made at the Qu'Appelle Lakes, in the North-West Territories. The Indians treated with, were a portion of the Cree and Saulteaux Tribes, and under its operations, about 75,000 square miles of territory were surrendered. This treaty, was the first step towards bringing the Indians of the Fertile Belt into closer relations with the Government of Canada, and was a much-needed one. In the year 1871, Major Butler was sent into the North-West Territories by the Government of Canada, to examine into and report, with regard to the state of affairs there. He reported, to Lieutenant-Governor Archibald, that "law and order are wholly unknown in the region of the Saskatchewan, in so much, as the country is without any executive organization, and destitute of any means of enforcing the law." Towards remedying this serious state of affairs, the Dominion placed the North-West Territories under the rule of the Lieutenant-Governor and Council of the Territories, the Lieutenant-Governor of Manitoba, being, *ex officio*, Governor of the Territories. This body, composed of representative men, possessed executive functions, and legislative powers. They entered upon their duties with zeal, and discharged them with efficiency. Amongst other measures, they passed a prohibitory liquor law, which subsequently was practically adopted by a Statute of the Dominion. They proposed the establishment of a Mounted Police Force, a suggestion which was given force to by the Dominion Cabinet, and they recommended, that, treaties should be made, with the Indians at Forts Qu'Appelle, Carlton

and Pitt, recommendations, which, were all, eventually, carried
out. In the report of the Minister of the Interior, for the
year 1875, he states "that it is due to the Council to record the
fact, that the legislation and valuable suggestions, submitted
to your Excellency, from time to time, through their official
head, Governor Morris, aided the Government not a little in
the good work of laying the foundations of law and order, in
the North-West, in securing the good will of the Indian tribes,
and in establishing the *prestige* of the Dominion Government,
throughout that vast country." In accordance with these suggestions, the Government of the Dominion, decided, on effecting a treaty, with the plain Indians, Crees and Chippawas, who
inhabit the country, of which, Fort Qu'Appelle, was a convenient
centre, and entrusted the duty, to the Hon. Alexander Morris
then Lieutenant-Governor of Manitoba and the North-West
Territories, the Hon. David Laird, then Minister of the
Interior, and now Lieutenant-Governor of the North-West
Territories, and the Hon. W. J. Christie, a retired factor of
the Hudson's Bay Company, and a gentleman of large experience, among the Indian tribes.

In pursuance of this mission, these gentlemen left Fort
Garry in August, 1874, and journeyed to Lake Qu'Appelle (the
calling or echoing lake), where they met the assembled Indians,
in September. The Commissioners, had an escort of militia,
under the command of Lieut.-Col. Osborne Smith, C.M.G. This
force marched to and from Qu'Appelle, acquitted themselves
with signal propriety, and proved of essential service. Their
return march was made in excellent time. The distance, three
hundred and fifty miles having been accomplished in sixteen
and a half days.

The Commissioners encountered great difficulties, arising,
from the excessive demands of the Indians, and from the jealousies, existing between the two Nations, Crees and Chippawas, but by perseverance, firmness and tact, they succeeded
in overcoming the obstacles, they had to encounter, and

eventually effected a treaty, whereby the Indian title was extinguished in a tract of country, embracing 75,000 square
miles of territory. After long and animated discussions the
Indians, asked to be granted the same terms as were accorded
to the Indians of Treaty Number Three, at the North-West
Angle, hereinbefore mentioned. The Commissioners assented
to their request and the treaty was signed accordingly.

On the return, of the Commissioners to Fort Ellice, they met
there, the Chippawas of that vicinage, and made a supplementary treaty with them. These Indians were included in
the boundaries of Treaty Number Two, but had not been
treated with, owing to their distance from Manitoba House,
where that treaty was made. In 1875, the Hon. W. J.
Christie, and Mr. M. G. Dickieson, then of the Department of
the Interior, and subsequently, Assistant Superintendent of
Indian affairs, in the North-West Territories, were appointed
to make the payments of annuities, to the Indians, embraced
in the Treaty Number Four, and obtain the adhesion of other
bands, which had not been present at Qu'Appelle, the previous
year. They met, the Indians, at Qu'Appelle (where six Chiefs
who had been absent, accepted the terms of the treaty) and at
Fort Pelly and at Shoal River, where two other Chiefs, with
their bands, came into the treaty stipulations. A gratifying
feature connected with the making of this, and the other,
North-Western Treaties, has been the readiness, with which
the Indians, who were absent, afterwards accepted the terms
which had been settled for them, by those, who were able to
attend. I close these observations, by annexing, the reports of
Lieutenant-Governor Morris, to the Honorable the Secretary
of State of Canada, of date 17th October, 1874, giving, an
account, of the making of the treaties at Qu'Appelle and Fort
Ellice, and an extract, from that of Messrs. Christie and Dickieson, dated 7th October, 1875, describing its further completion,
and I also insert, accurate short-hand reports of the proceedings
at Qu'Appelle and Fort Ellice, which, were made, at the time,

by Mr. Dickieson, who, was present, at the treaty, as secretary to the Commissioners. These will be found to be both interesting and instructive.

———

GOVERNMENT HOUSE,
FORT GARRY, MANITOBA, *October 17, 1874.*

SIR,—I have the honor to inform you that in compliance with the request of the Government, I proceeded to Lake Qu'Appelle in company with the Hon. David Laird, in order to act with him and W. J. Christie, Esq., as Commissioners to negotiate a treaty with the tribes of Indians in that region.

Mr. Laird and I left Fort Garry on the 26th of August, and arrived at Lake Qu'Appelle on the 8th of September, Mr. Christie having gone in advance of us to Fort Pelly.

We were accompanied on arriving by the escort of militia under the command of Lieut.-Col. W. Osborne Smith, who had preceded us, but whom we had overtaken.

The escort took up their encampment at a very desirable situation on the edge of the lake, the Indians being encamped at some distance.

The Commissioners were kindly provided with apartments by W. J. McLean, Esq., the officer in charge of the Hudson Bay Company's Post.

After our arrival, the Commissioners caused the Indians to be summoned, to meet them, in a marquee tent adjoining the encampment of the militia.

The Crees came headed by their principal Chief "Loud Voice," and a number of Saulteaux followed, without their Chief, Coté. The Commissioners, having decided that it was desirable that there should be only one speaker on behalf of the Commissioners, requested me owing to my previous experience with the Indian tribes and my official position as Lieutenant-Governor of the North-West Territories, to undertake the duty, which I agreed to do. Accordingly, I told the Indians the object of our coming and invited them to present to us their Chiefs and headmen. "Loud Voice" stated that they were not yet ready and asked for a delay till next day, to which we assented.

On the 9th, four Indian soldiers were sent to the Commissioners to ask for two days delay, but we replied that when they met us in conference they could prefer any reasonable request, but that we expected them to meet us as agreed on the previous day, and further that the Saulteaux had not conducted themselves with proper respect to the Commissioners, as representatives of the Crown, as their principal Chief Coté had not met us. Eventually, both the Crees and the Saulteaux met us, with their Chiefs, when I addressed them. They asked time to deliberate and we appointed the 11th at ten o'clock for the next conference.

The Crees then left the tent suddenly, under constraint of the Indian soldiers, who compelled the Chiefs to go.

On the 11th we sent a bugler round to summon the Indians to the appointed conference, but they did not come.

Instead the Saulteaux sent word that they could not meet us except in their own soldiers tent, distant about a mile from the militia encampment, but we refused to do so.

The Crees were ready to proceed to the marquee, but were prevented by the Saulteaux, a section of whom displayed a turbulent disposition and were numerically the strongest party. We sent our interpreter Charles Pratt, a Cree Indian, who was educated at St. John's College here, and who is a catechist of the Church of England, to tell the Indians that they must meet us as agreed upon.

In consequence, about four o'clock in the afternoon, the Crees led by " Loud Voice," came to the conference, but the Saulteaux kept away, though a number were sent to hear and report. On behalf of the Commissioners, I then explained to the Crees the object of our mission and made our proposals for a treaty, but as they were not ready to reply, we asked them to return to their tents and meet us next day.

On the 12th the Crees and Saulteaux sent four men from the soldiers tent or council, which they had organized, to ask that the encampment of the militia and the conference tents should be removed half way, towards their encampment.

In consequence, we requested Lieut.-Col. Smith to proceed to the Indian encampment and ascertain the meaning of this demand, authorizing him, if necessary, to arrange for the pitching of the conference tent nearer the Indians, if that would give them any satisfaction.

He reported, on his return, that the Indians wished the militia to encamp with them, and that they objected to meet us anywhere on the reserve of the Hudson Bay Company, as they said they could not speak freely there.

He refused to remove the militia camp, as it was a very desirable place where it had been placed, but with the assent of the Indians selected a spot adjoining the reserve and at a suitable distance from the Indian tents, on which the conference tent was to be daily erected, but to be removed after the conferences closed.

We then summoned the Indians to meet us at one o'clock, which they did at the appointed place.

After the formal hand shaking, which ceremony they repeat at the beginning and close of every interview, the Commissioners submitted their terms for a treaty, which were in effect similar to those granted at the North-West Angle, except that the money present offered was eight dollars per head, instead of twelve dollars as there.

The Indians declined, however, to talk about these proposals, as they said there was something in the way. They objected to the reserve having been surveyed for the Hudson Bay Company, without their first having been consulted, and claimed that the £300,000 paid to the Company should be paid to them. They also objected to the Company's trading in the Territory, except only at their posts. The Commissioners refused to comply with their demands, and explained to them how the Company had become entitled to the reserve in question, and the nature of the arrangement, that had resulted in the payment by the Government of Canada of the £300,000.

The conference adjourned to Monday the 14th, on which day the Commissioners again met them, but the Cree Chief "Loud Voice" asked for another day to consider the matter, and "Coté" or "Meemay" the Saulteaux Chief, from Fort Pelly, asked to be treated with, at his own place. They demanded, that the Company should only be allowed to trade at their own posts, and not to send out traders into the Territory—which was of course refused, it being explained to them that all Her Majesty's subjects had equal right of trading. The Commissioners then agreed to grant a final delay of another day, for further consideration. Up to this period the position was very unsatisfactory.

The Crees were from the first ready to treat, as were the Saulteaux from Fort Pelly, but the Saulteaux of the Qu'Appelle District were not disposed to do so and attempted to coerce the other Indians.

They kept the Chiefs "Loud Voice" and "Coté" under close surveillance, they being either confined to their tents or else watched by "soldiers," and threatened if they should make any overtures to us.

The Saulteaux cut down the tent over the head of one of the Cree Chiefs and conducted themselves in such a manner, that "Loud Voice" applied to the Commissioners for protection, and the Crees purchased knives and armed themselves.

The Saulteaux, one day went the length of placing six "soldiers," armed with rifles and revolvers, in the conference tent to intimidate the other Indians, a step which was promptly counteracted by Lieut.-Col. Smith, calling in six of the militiamen who were stationed in the tent. In this connection, I must take the opportunity of stating that the results proved the wisdom of the course taken by the Commissioners in obtaining the escort of the militia, as their presence exerted great moral influence, and I am persuaded, prevented the jealousies and ancient feud between the Crees and Saulteaux culminating in acts of violence.

The conduct of the whole force was excellent and, whether on the march or in the encampment ground, they conducted themselves in a most creditable manner.

Resuming, however, my narrative, on the 15th of September, the Commissioners again met the Indians at eleven o'clock in the forenoon.

The Crees had, in the interval, decided to treat with us independently, and the Saulteaux, finding this, came to a similar conclusion. After a protracted interview, the Indians asked to be granted the same terms as were given at the North-West Angle. The Commissioners took time to consider and adjourned the conference until three o'clock.

In the interval, the Commissioners, being persuaded that a treaty could not otherwise be made, determined on acceding to the request of the Indians.

The Indians, having again met the Commissioners in the afternoon, presented their Chiefs to them, when they asked to be informed what the terms granted at the North-West Angle were. These were fully and carefully explained to them, but after a request that all the Indians owed to the Hudson Bay Company should be wiped out and a refusal of the Commissioners to entertain their demands, they then asked that they should be paid fifteen dollars per annum per head, which was refused, and they were informed that the proposals of the Commissioners were final, and could not be changed.

The Chiefs then agreed to accept the terms offered and to sign the treaty, having first asked that the Half-breeds should be allowed to hunt, and having been assured that the population in the North-West would be treated fairly and justly, the treaty was signed by the Commissioners and the Chiefs, having been first fully explained to them by the interpreter.

Arrangements were then made to commence the payments and distribution of the presents the next day, a duty which was discharged by Mr. Christie and Mr. Dickieson, Private Secretary of the Hon. Mr. Laird.

I forward you to form an appendix to this despatch, a report marked "A" and "B" extended from notes taken in short hand, by Mr. Dickieson, of the various conferences and of the utterances of the Commissioners and the Indians.

It is obvious that such a record will prove valuable, as it enables any misunderstanding on the part of the Indians, as to what was said at the conference, to be corrected, and it, moreover, will enable the council better to appreciate the character of the difficulties that have to be encountered in negotiating with the Indians.

On the 1ʼ. th I left for Fort Ellice, in company with Mr. Laird, Mr. Christie and Mr. Dickieson remaining to complete the payments, which were satisfactorily disposed of.

Before leaving, the Chiefs "Loud Voice" and Coté called on us to tender their good wishes, and to assure us that they would teach their people to respect the treaty.

The Commissioners received every assistance in their power from Mr. McDonald of Fort Ellice, in charge of the Hudson Bay Company District of Swan River, and from Mr. McLean, in charge of the Qu'Appelle Post, —I also add, that the Half-breed population were I believe generally desirous of seeing the treaty concluded and used the influence of their connection with the Indians in its favor.

I forward in another despatch a copy of an address I received from the *Metis,* or Half-breeds, together with my reply thereto.

The treaty was taken charge of by the Hon. Mr. Laird, and will be by him placed on record in his Department and submitted to council for approval.

I enclose herewith, however, a printed copy of it, marked "C," to accompany this despatch.

The supplementary treaty made at Fort Ellice will form the subject of another despatch.

Trusting that the efforts of the Commissioners to secure a satisfactory understanding with the Western Indians will result in benefit to the race, advantage to the Dominion, and meet the approval of the Privy Council,

I have the honor to be, Sir,

Your obedient servant,

ALEXANDER MORRIS,

Lieut.-Gov. N. W. T.

GOVERNMENT HOUSE,

FORT GARRY, MANITOBA, *October 17th, 1874.*

SIR,—Referring to my despatch of the 17th inst., (No. 211) I have the honor to report that Mr. Laird and I arrived at Fort Ellice from Qu'Appelle Lakes, on Saturday the 19th of September.

On Monday, we met the band of Saulteaux Indians, who make their headquarters at Fort Ellice, and who had remained there, instead of going to Qu'Appelle at our request.

This band have been in the habit of migrating between the region covered by the Second Treaty and that comprehended in the Fourth, but had not been treated with.

We proposed to them to give their adhesion to the Qu'Appelle Treaty and surrender their claim to lands, wherever situated, in the North-West Territories, on being given a reserve and being granted the terms on which the treaty in question was made. We explained fully these terms and asked the Indians to present to us their Chief and headmen. As some of the band were absent, whom the Indians desired to be recognized as headmen, only the Chief and one headman were presented. These, on behalf of the Indians accepted the terms and thanked the Queen and the Commissioners for their care of the Indian people. A supplement to the treaty was then submitted and fully explained to them, by our acting interpreter, Joseph Robillard, after which it was signed by Mr. Laird and myself, and by the Chief and head man.

The original of the supplementary treaty will be submitted for approval by Mr. Laird, but I annex a printed copy of it, as an appendix to this despatch.

I also annex, notes of the conference with these Indians, extended from the short hand report taken of the proceedings by Mr. Dickieson, Private. Secretary to the Hon. Mr. Laird.

In the afternoon, Mr. Christie and Mr. Dickieson arrived from Lake

Qu'Appelle, and shortly afterwards proceeded to make the payments to the Indians, under the treaty.

It was satisfactory to have this band dealt with, as they asserted claims in the region covered by the Manitoba Post Treaty, but had not been represented at the time it was made.

On the 22nd of September the Commissioners left Fort Ellice and arrived at Fort Garry on the afternoon of the 26th of that month, having been absent a little over a month.

I have the honor to be, Sir,

Your obedient Servant,

ALEXANDER MORRIS,

Lieut.-Gov. N. W. T.

THE HONORABLE
    THE SECRETARY OF STATE FOR THE PROVINCES,

Ottawa.

WINNIPEG, MANITOBA, *7th October, 1875.*

SIR,—We have now the honor to submit, for your information, our final report in connection with our missions to the Indians included in Treaty No. 4.

As former reports have made you fully acquainted with the arrangements that had been entered into previous to our departure from this place, any further reference to them is unnecessary.

Having left Winnipeg on the 19th August, we arrived at Fort Ellice on the 24th, the day appointed for the meeting the Indians of that place. The same evening we had an interview with, and fully explained the terms and conditions of the treaty to some of the Indians who were not present when the treaty was concluded last year. Next morning, by appointment, we met all the Indians and explained to them the object of our mission, and, after considerable discussion, made arrangements to commence paying the annuities next day. This, however, was prevented by heavy rains, which continued more or less to retard our operations on the two following days, the 27th and 28th, but everything was satisfactorily concluded with this band on the evening of the latter day, and on the following morning we started for the Qu'Appelle Lakes, accompanied by an escort of fifteen men of the Mounted Police Force, under the command of Sub-Inspector McIllree, which had arrived at Fort Ellice on the evening of the 26th, and reached our desination on the forenoon of the 2nd September.

As you are aware, we had heard before leaving Winnipeg, that the number of Indians assembled at the Qu'Appelle Lakes would be very large, but we did not anticipate that so many as we found (nearly five hundred lodges) would be congregated.

We at once saw that the funds at our disposal to pay the annuities and gratuities would be inadequate, and availed ourselves of the opportunity presented by the return of Major Irvine to Winnipeg, to forward a telegram on the 5th September, requesting a further amount of six thousand dollars to be placed to our credit ; and we may state here, though out of the order of time, as we found after the first two days payments that we had still under-estimated the number of Indians present, we transmitted a telegram to Winnipeg by special messenger, on the 9th September, for a further credit of fifteen thousand dollars.

On the 3rd September we met the Indians and explained the object of our mission, and, for the benefit of those who were absent last year, the terms and conditions of the treaty, and stated that we were now ready to fulfil so many of the obligations therein contained as the Government were bound to execute this year. The Indians declined saying anything on this occasion, but wished to meet and confer with us the following day, as they had something they wished to speak about. They accordingly met us on the 4th, and made several demands, one of which was that the annuities be increased to twelve dollars per head. We replied that the treaty concluded last year was a covenant between them and the Government, and it was impossible to comply with their demands; that all we had to do was to carry out the terms of the treaty in so far as the obligations of the same required. An idea seemed prevalent among the Indians who were absent last year that no treaty had been concluded then; that all which had been done at that time was merely preliminary to the making of the treaty in reality, which they thought was to be performed this year. The prevalence of this opinion amongst them operated very prejudicially to the furthering of our business, and we saw that until this was done away with it would be impossible to do anything towards accomplishing the real object of our mission. After a great deal of talking on their part, and explanation on ours, the meeting adjourned until Monday morning, as it was necessary that provisions should be issued to the different bands that evening for the following day.

On Monday (the 6th) we again met the Indians, and as they evidently wished to have another day's talking to urge the same demands they had made on Saturday, we assured them all further discussion on the subject was useless; that if they declined to accept the terms of the treaty we must return and report to the Government that they had broken the promise made last year. They then asked that we should report to the Government what they had demanded. This we agreed to do. After some further explana-tion to those Chiefs who had not signed the treaty, the payment of the annuities and gratuities was commenced and continued by Messrs. Dickieson and Forsyth on this and the three following days until completed, during which time Mr. Christie conferred with the Chiefs as to the locality of their reserves.

Six Chiefs who had not been present last year when the treaty was con-cluded, agreed to accept the terms of the same, and signed their adhesion previous to being paid. The instruments thus signed by them are transmitted herewith.

The suits of clothes, flags, medals and copies of the treaty were given to the Chiefs and headmen as they were paid, and on the 10th the ammunition and twine were distributed, also provisions to each band for the return journey to their hunting grounds.   *   *   *   *   *   *

We have the honor to be, Sir,

Your obedient servants,

W. J. CHRISTIE,
Indian Commissioner.

M. G. DICKIESON.

Report of the proceedings at the Conference between the Hon. Alexander Morris, Lieut.-Governor of the North-West Territories, the Hon. David Laird, Minister of the Interior, and W. J. Christie, Esq., the Commissioners appointed by Order in Council to treat with the Indians inhabiting the country described in the said Order in Council, the first conference having been held at Qu'Appelle, September 8th, 1874 :

FIRST DAY'S CONFERENCE.

At four o'clock the Commissioners entered the marquee erected for the accommodation of themselves, and the Indians, who in in a short time arrived, shook hands with the Commissioners, the officers of the guard, and other gentlemen who were in the tent, and took their seats.

It having been noticed that Cote, " the Pigeon," a leading Chief of the Saulteaux tribe, had not arrived but that several of his band were present and claimed that they had been sent to represent him, His Honor the Lieut.-Governor instructed the (acting) interpreter, William Daniel, to enquire why their Chief had not come to meet the Commissioners, the white chiefs ?

To this question they answered, that he had given no reason. His Honor, through the interpreter, told them that the

Queen had sent him and the other Commissioners to see their Chief and their nation, and that the least a loyal subject could do would be to meet the messengers of the Queen.

His Honor then addressed the Crees as follows: " The Commissioners having agreed that as Lieut.-Governor he should speak to them, as we are sent here by the Queen, by the Great Mother—the Queen has chosen me to be one of her Councillors, and has sent me here to represent her and has made me Governor of all her Territories in the North-West. She has sent another of her Councillors who has come all the way from Ottawa. She has also sent with us Mr. Christie, whom you all know, who has lived for a long time in this country, but who had gone away from it to live in another part of the Dominion of Canada. The Queen loves her Red children; she has always been friends with them ; she knows that it is hard for them to live, and she has always tried to help them in the other parts of the Dominion. Last year she sent me to see her children at the Lake of the Woods. I took her children there by the hand, and the white man and the red man made friends for ever. We have come here with a message from the Queen and want to tell you all her mind. We want to speak to you about the land and what the Queen is willing to do for you, but before we tell you, we want you to tell us, who your Chiefs and headmen are who will speak for you, while we speak for the Queen, and we want to know what bands of Crees are here and who will speak for them. We wish to know if the Crees are ready to speak with us now ?"

RA-KU-SHI-WAY, THE LOUD VOICE,—Said in reply : " I do not wish to tell a lie. I cannot say who will speak for us ; it will only be known after consultation."

HIS HONOR THE LIEUT.-GOV.—" By to-morrow you will probably have chosen whom you will have to speak for you and the Commissioners will be glad to meet you after you have chosen your spokesmen, and will meet you at ten o'clock. We want you to tell us openly what you want and we will speak to you for the Queen in the same way. The Colonel will send a man round to sound a bugle at ten o'clock to let you know."

To the Saulteaux His Honor said: "We are here with a message from the Great Mother and want you to open my mouth so that I can tell you what I have to say. If you and your Chiefs will meet together in council and talk it over we will be glad to meet you, if you bring your Chief to-morrow. You must also choose your speakers who will come with your Chief and speak for you."

LOUD VOICE—"I will tell the message that is given me to tell. I have one thing to say, the first word that came to them was for the Saulteaux tribe to choose a place to pitch their tents."

HIS HONOR—"This place was chosen because it is a good place for my men—for the soldiers—there is plenty of water and grass, and I will meet you here to-morrow. That is all at present."

After the departure of the main body of Cree Indians, Saulteaux, from the Cypress Hills, entered the tent saying that they had no Chief, and did not want to go with the main body of the nation, that they had plenty of friends on the plains.

His Honor said they would hear the Queen's message with the rest of the Indians.

SECOND DAY'S CONFERENCE.

September 9, 1874.

The Indians, both Crees, Saulteaux and their Chiefs having arrived, His Honor Lieut.-Governor Morris said: "I am glad to see so many of the Queen's red children here this morning, I told those I saw yesterday that I was one of the Queen's councillors, and had another councillor with me from Ottawa and that the Queen had sent Mr. Christie who used to live amongst you to help us. Yesterday the Cree nation with their Chief were here, the Saulteaux did not come to meet the

7

Queen's servants, their Chief was not here. I thought that
the Saulteaux could not have understood that the Queen had
sent her servants to see them, or they would have come to
meet them. If Loud Voice or any other Chief came down
to Fort Garry to see me, and I sent one of my servants to
meet them instead of shaking hands with them, would they
be pleased? I wanted you to meet me here to-day because I
wanted to speak to you before the Great Spirit and before the
world. I want both Crees and Saulteaux to know what I say.
I told those who were here yesterday that we had a message
from the Queen to them. Last year I made a treaty with the
Indians, 4,000 in number, at the Lake of the Woods. To-day
the Queen sends us here. I told you yesterday that she loves
her red children, and they have always respected her and
obeyed her laws. I asked you yesterday, and ask you now, to
tell me who would speak for you, and how many bands of each
nation are represented here. I have heard that you are not
ready to speak to me yet but do not know it, and I want you
to say anything you have to say before all, and I will speak in
the same way. What I have to talk about concerns you, your
children and their children, who are yet unborn, and you must
think well over it, as the Queen has thought well over it. What
I want, is for you to take the Queen's hand, through mine, and
shake hands with her for ever, and now I want, before I say
any more, to hear from the Chiefs if they are ready with their
men to speak for them, and if they are not ready if they will
be ready to-morrow."

CAN-A-HAH-CHA-PEW, THE MAN OF THE BOW,—"We are not
ready yet, we have not gathered together yet. That is all I
have to say."

PEICHETO'S SON—O-TA-HA-O-MAN, THE GAMBLER—"My dear
friends, do you want me to speak for you to these great men?"
(the Indians signified their consent.) "I heard you were to
come here, that was the reason that all the camps were collected
together, I heard before-hand too where the camp was to be

placed, but I tell you that I am not ready yet. Every day there are other Indians coming and we are not all together. Where I was told to pitch my tent that is where I expected to see the great men in the camp. That is all."

HIS HONOR—"With regard to the camp, the Queen sent one of her chief men of our soldiers with us, and he selected the best place for the men, the place where we are now, and I think it is a good place. At first he thought to have encamped across the river, but he thought this was better ground and chose it. I think it just as well that our tents should be at a little distance from your braves and your camp. 1 want to say to the Indian children of the Queen that if their people are coming in, that our men have walked a long way here, and must go back again to Fort Garry, and I have other things to do. Mr. Laird has to go back again to look after other things for the Queen at Ottawa. I want to ask the Chiefs when they will be ready to meet us to-morrow."

PEI-CHE-TO'S SON—"I have said before, we are not ready."

HIS HONOR—"Let them send me word through their Chiefs when they are ready."

THIRD DAY'S CONFERENCE.

September 11, 1874.

The Crees and their Chiefs met the Commissioners. The Saulteaux Chief was not present, though most of the tribe were present.

An Indian, "the Crow," advised the assembled Crees, the Saulteaux not having arrived, to listen attentively to what words he said.

His Honor the Lieut.-Governor then arose and said : "I am glad to meet you here to-day. We have waited long and began to wonder whether the Queen's red children were not coming to meet her messengers. All the ground here is the Queen's and you are free to speak your mind fully. We want you to speak to me face to face. I am ready now with my friends here to give you the Queen's message. Are your ears open to hear? Have you chosen your speakers?"

THE LOUD VOICE—"There is no one to answer."

HIS HONOR—"You have had time enough to select your men to answer and I will give you the Queen's message. The Queen knows that you are poor; the Queen knows that it is hard to find food for yourselves and children; she knows that the winters are cold, and your children are often hungry; she has always cared for her red children as much as for her white. Out of her generous heart and liberal hand she wants to do something for you, so that when the buffalo get scarcer, and they are scarce enough now, you may be able to do something for yourselves."

THE LOUD VOICE (to the Indians)—"I wonder very much at your conduct. You understand what is said and you understand what is right and good. You ought to listen to that and answer it, every one of you. What is bad you cannot answer."

HIS HONOR—"What the Queen and her Councillors would like is this, she would like you to learn something of the cunning of the white man. When fish are scarce and the buffalo are not plentiful she would like to help you to put something in the land; she would like that you should have some money every year to buy things that you need. If any of you would settle down on the land, she would give you cattle to help you; she would like you to have some seed to plant. She would like to give you every year, for twenty years, some powder, shot, and twine to make nets of. I see you here before me to-day. I will pass away and you will pass away. I will go where my fathers have gone and you also, but after me and after you will come our children. The Queen cares for you and for your children, and she cares for the children that are yet to be born. She would like to take you by the hand and do as I did for her at the Lake of the Woods last year. We promised them and we are ready to promise now to give five dollars to every man, woman and child, as long as the sun shines and water flows. We are ready to promise to give $1,000 every year, for twenty years, to buy powder and shot and twine, by the end of which time I hope you will have your little farms. If you will settle down we would lay off land for you, a square mile for every family of five. Whenever you go to a Reserve, the Queen will be ready to give you a school and schoolmaster, and the Government will try to prevent fire-water from being sent among you. If you shake hands with us and make a treaty, we are ready to make a present at the end of the treaty, of eight dollars for every man, woman and child in your nations. We are ready also to give calico, clothing and other presents. We are ready to give every recognized Chief, a present of twenty-five dollars, a medal, and a suit of clothing. We are also ready to give the Chief's soldiers, not exceeding four in each band, a present of ten dollars, and next year and every year after, each chief will be paid twenty-five dollars, and his chief soldiers not exceeding four in each band, will receive ten dollars. Now I think that you see that that the Queen loves her red children, that she wants to do you good, and you ought to show that you think so. I cannot believe that you will be the first Indians, the Queen's subjects, who will not take her by the hand. The Queen sent one of her councillors from Ottawa, and me, her Governor, to tell you her mind. I have opened my hands and heart to you. It is for you to think of the future of those who are with you now, of those who are coming after you, and may the Great Spirit guide you to do what is right. I have only one word more to say. The last time I saw you I was not allowed to say all I wanted to say until you went away. What I wanted to say is this, I have put before you our message, I want you to go back to your tents and think over what I have said and come and meet me to-morrow. Recollect that we cannot stay very long here. I have said all."

September 12, 1874.

In the morning four Indians, two Crees and two Saulteaux, waited on the Commissioners and asked that they should meet the Indians half way, and off the Company's reserve, and that the soldiers should remove their camps beside the Indian encampment, that they would meet the Commissioners then and confer with them; that there was something in the way of their speaking openly where the marquee had been pitched. Their request was complied with as regarded the place of meeting only, and the spot for the conference selected by Col. Smith and the Indians.

The meeting was opened by the Lieut.-Governor, who said, "Crees and Saulteaux,—I have asked you to meet us here to-day. We have been asking you for many days to meet us and this is the first time you have all met us. If it was not my duty and if the Queen did not wish it, I would not have taken so much trouble to speak to you. We are sent a long way to give you her message. Yesterday I told the Crees her message, and I know that the Saulteaux know what it was, but that there may be no mistake, I will tell it to you again and I will tell you more. When I have given my message understand that you will have to answer it, as I and my friends will have to leave you. You are the subjects of the Queen, you are her children, and you are only a little band to all her other children. She has children all over the world, and she does right with them all. She cares as much for you as she cares for her white children, and the proof of it is that wherever her name is spoken her people whether they be red or white, love her name and are ready to die for it, because she is always just and true. What she promises never changes. She knows the condition of her people here; you are not her only red children; where I come from, in Ontario and in Quebec, she has many red children, and away beyond the mountains she has other red children, and she

wants to care for them all. Last year I was among the Saulteaux ; we have the Saulteaux where I came from. They were
my friends. I was the son of a white Chief who had a high
place among them, they told him they would do his work, they
called him Shekeisheik. I learned from him to love the red man,
and it was a pleasant duty and good to my heart when the
Queen told me to come among her Saulteaux children and I
expect the Crees and the Saulteaux to take my hand as they did
last year. In our hands they feel the Queen's, and if they take
them the hands of the white and red man will never unclasp.
In other lands the white and red man are not such friends as
we have always been, and why ? Because the Queen always
keeps her word, always protects her red men. She learned last
winter that bad men from the United States had come into her
country and had killed some of her red children, What did
she say ? This must not be, I will send my men and will not
suffer these bad men to hurt my red children, their lives are
very dear to me. And now I will tell you our message. The
Queen knows that her red children often find it hard to live.
She knows that her red children, their wives and children, are
often hungry, and that the buffalo will not last for ever and she
desires to do something for them. More than a hundred years
ago, the Queen's father said to the red men living in Quebec
and Ontario, I will give you land and cattle and set apart
Reserves for you, and will teach you. What has been the
result ? There the red men are happy; instead of getting fewer
in number by sickness they are growing in number ; their children have plenty. The Queen wishes you to enjoy the same
blessings, and so I am here to tell you all the Queen's mind,
but recollect this, the Queen's High Councillor here from
Ottawa, and I, her Governor, are not traders ; we do not come
here in the spirit of traders ; we come here to tell you
openly, without hiding anything, just what the Queen will do
for you, just what she thinks is good for you, and I want you
to look me in the face, eye to eye, and open your hearts to me

as children would to a father, as children ought to do to a
father, and as you ought to the servants of the great mother of
us all.   I told my friends yesterday that things changed here,
that we are here to-day and that in a few years it may be we
will not be here, but after us will come our children.   The
Queen thinks of the children yet unborn.   I know that there
are some red men as well as white men who think only of to-
day and never think of to-morrow.   The Queen has to think of
what will come long after to-day.   Therefore, the promises we
have to make to you are not for to-day only but for to-morrow,
not only for you but for your children born and unborn, and
the promises we make will be carried out as long as the sun
shines above and the water flows in the ocean.   When you are
ready to plant seed the Queen's men will lay off Reserves so as
to give a square mile to every family of five persons, and on
commencing to farm the Queen will give to every family cultivating the soil two hoes, one spade, one scythe for cutting the
grain, one axe and plough, enough of seed wheat, barley, oats
and potatoes to plant the land they get ready.   The Queen
wishes her red children to learn the cunning of the white man
and when they are ready for it she will send schoolmasters on
every Reserve and pay them.   We have come through the
country for many days and we have seen hills and but little
wood and in many places little water, and it may be a long
time before there are many white men settled upon this land,
and you will have the right of hunting and fishing just as you
have now until the land is actually taken up.   (His Honor
repeated the offers which had been given to the Saulteaux on the
previous day.)   I think I have told you all that the Queen is
willing to do for you.   It ought to show you that she has
thought more about you than you have about her.   I will be
glad now to have those whom you have selected speak for you
and I again ask you to keep nothing back.   This is the first
time you have had white chiefs, officers of the Queen, so high
in her Councils, so trusted by her among you.   We have no

object but your good at heart, and therefore we ask you to speak out to us, to open your minds to us, and believe that we are your true and best friends, who will never advise you badly, who will never whisper bad words in your ears, who only care for your good and that of your children. I have told you the truth, the whole truth, and now we expect to hear from the two nations and any other tribe who may be represented here. My friend Mr. Laird reminds me that he has come from an Island in the far off sea, that he has go back to Ottawa and then go to his own home, that he was asked specially to help me in speaking to you and advising me. He is obliged to go away as I am, and therefore we want you to answer us."

COTE, or MEE-MAY (Saulteaux Chief)—"I cannot say anything to you. It is that man (pointing to Loud Voice) will speak."

LOUD VOICE (Cree Chief)—"If I could speak, if I conld manage to utter my feelings there is reason why I should answer you back; but there is something in my way, and that is all I can tell you. This man (the Gambler) will tell you.

O-TA-KA-O-NAN, OR THE GAMBLER.—"This morning I saw the chief of thc soldiers, who asked me what is in your way that you cannot come and meet the Queen's messengers; then I told him what was in the way. And now that I am come in, what do I see? You were rather slow in giving your hand. You said that the Queen spoke through you and spoke very plainly, but I cannot speak about what you said at present; the thing that is in the way that is what I am working at."

LIEUT.-GOV. MORRIS—"We have come here for the purpose of knowing what is in your mind. I held out my hand but you did not do as your nation did at the Angle. When I arrived there the Chief and his men came and gave me the pipe of peace and paid me every honor. Why? Because I was the servant of the Queen. I was not slow in offering my hand, I gave it freely and from my heart, and whenever we found I could please you by coming here, we sent the chief of the soldiers to select a suitable place to meet you. You tell me there is something in your mind. If there is anything standing between us, how can we take it away or answer you unless we know what it is?"

THE GAMBLER—"I told the soldier master you did not set your camp in order, you came and staid beyond over there, that is the reason I did not run in over there. Now when you have come here, you see sitting out there a mixture of Half-breeds, Crees, Saulteaux and Stonies, all are one, and you were slow in taking the hand of a Half-breed. All these things are many things that are in my way. I cannot speak about them."

LIEUT.-GOV. MORRIS—Why are you here to-day? because we asked you to come, because it was a good place to speak with them the reason we wished to see them. I am now quite willing to tell you all about Fort Pelly. The Queen heard that Americans had come into the country and were treating her Indian children badly. I myself sent her word that twenty-five of her Indian children, men, women and children, had been shot down by the American traders, then she resolved to protect her red children, for that reason she has determined to have a body of men on horses as policemen to keep all bad people, white or red, in order. She will not allow her red children to be made drunk and shot down again as some of them were a few months ago. Now you ought to be glad that you have a Queen who takes such an interest in you. What are they doing now up at Fort Pelly? The men must have some place to live in this winter, they cannot live out of doors, and some men have gone to Fort Pelly to build houses for them, and the Queen expects that you will do all you can to help them because they are your friends. There was a treaty before and Indians are paid under it, but we were told as we passed Fort Ellice that there were a few Indians there who were not included in that treaty, and had never been paid, and they agreed to meet us when we go back. I do not quite understand another point. We have here Crees, Saulteaux,

Assiniboines and other Indians, they are all one, and we have another people, the Half-breeds, they are of your blood and my blood. The Queen cares for them, one of them is here an officer with a Queen's coat on his back. At the Lake of the Woods last winter every Half-Breed who was there with me was helping me, and I was proud of it, and glad to take the word back to the Queen, and her servants, and you may rest easy, you may leave the Half-breeds in the hands of the Queen who will deal generously and justly with them. There was a Half-breed came forward to the table. He was only one of many here. I simply wanted to know whether he was authorized by you to take any part in the Council, as it is the Indians alone we are here to meet. He told me you wanted him here as a witness. We have plenty of witnesses here, but when I heard that, I welcomed him as I had done you, and shook hands with him, and he ought to have told you that. I have given our answer and I have always found this that it is good for men to try to understand each other, and to speak openly, if they do that and both are earnest, if their hearts are pure, they will and can understand each other."

THE GAMBLER—"I have understood plainly before what he (the Hudson Bay Company) told me about the Queen. This country that he (H. B. Co.) bought from the Indians let him complete that. It is that which is in the way. I cannot manage to speak upon anything else, when the land was staked off it was all the Company's work. That is the reason I cannot speak of other things."

LIEUT.-GOV. MORRIS—"We don't understand what you mean. Will you explain?

THE GAMBLER—"I know what I have to tell you. Who surveyed this land? Was it done by the Company? This is the reason I speak of the Company, why are you staying in the Company's house?"

LIEUT.-GOVERNOR MORRIS—"The Company have a right to have certain lands granted them by the Queen, who will do what is fair and just for the Company, for the Indians, for the Half-breeds, and for the whites. She will make no distinction. Whatever she promises she will carry out. The Company are are nothing to her except that they are carrying on trade in this country, and that they are subjects to her just as you are· You ask then why I went to the Company's house? I came here not at my own pleasure. I am not so strong as you are. I never slept in a tent in my life before and was only too glad to find a home to go to."

THE GAMBLER—"I understand now. And now this Company man. This is the Company man (pointing to Mr. McDonald). This is the thing I cannot speak of. The Cree does not know, the Saulteaux does not know. It was never known when this was surveyed, neither by the Cree nor the Saulteaux."

LIEUT.-GOV. MORRIS—"The Company are trading in this country and they require to have places to carry out their trade. If the Queen gives them land to hold under her she has a perfect right to do it, just as she will have a perfect right to lay off lands for you if you agree to settle on them. I am sorry for you; I am afraid you have been listening to bad voices who have not the interests of the Indians at heart. If because of these things you will not speak to us we will go away with hearts sorry for you and for your children, who thus throw back in our faces the hand of the Queen that she has held out to you."

THE GAMBLER—"It is very plain who speaks; the Crees are not speaking, and the Saulteaux is speaking, if the Queen's men came here to survey the land. I am telling you plainly. I cannot speak any other thing till this is cleared up. Look at these children that are sitting around here and also at the tents, who are just the image of my kindness. There are different kinds of grass growing here that is just like those sitting around here. There is no difference. Even from the American· land they are here, but we love them all the same, and when the white skin comes here from far away I love him all the same. I am telling you what our love and kindness is. This is what I did when the white man came, but when he came back he paid no regard to me how he carried on."

LIEUT.-GOV. MORRIS—"I did not know till I came here that any survey had been made because I had nothing to do with it; but my friend, one of the Queen's Councillors, tells me it was done by the authority of the Queen."

THE GAMBLER—"I want to tell you the right story. I waited very much for the Queen's messenger when I saw what the Company did. Perhaps he may know why he did so. Perhaps if I were to ask him now he would say. That is what I would think. This is the reason. I am so pleased at what I see here I cannot manage to speak because of the Company.

LIEUT.-GOV. MORRIS—"We cannot see why you cannot speak to the Queen's messengers because of the Company. The Company is no greater in her sight than one of those little children is in yours, and whatever she promises, either to the Company or the little child, she will do. The Company ought not to be a wall between you and us; you will make a mistake if you send us away with a wall between us, when there should be none."

THE GAMBLER—"I do not send you away; for all this I am glad. I know this is not the Queen's work. He (H. B. Co.) is the head; he does whatever he thinks all around here, that is the reason I cannot say anything."

LIEUT.-GOV. MORRIS—"I am very sorry that you cannot answer."

THE GAMBLER—"The Company have stolen our land. I heard that at first. I hear it is true. The Queen's messengers never came here, and now I see the soldiers and the settlers and the policemen. I know it is not the Queen's work, only the Company has come and they are the head, they are foremost; I do not hold it back. Let this be put to rights; when this is righted I will answer the other."

LIEUT.-GOV. MORRIS—"The Company have not brought their soldiers here. This man is not an officer of the Company. I am not an officer of the Company.   We did not come at the request of the Company, but at that of the Queen.   I told you that the Queen had sent her policemen here.   You see the flag there, then know that we are the Queen's servants, and not the Company's, and it is for you to decide on the message I have delivered to you."

THE GAMBLER—" When one Indian takes anything from another we call it stealing, and when we see the present we say pay us.   It is the Company I mean."

LIEUT.-GOV. MORRIS—"What did the Company steal from you?"

THE GAMBLER—" The earth, trees, grass, stones, all that which I see with my eyes."

LIEUT.-GOV. MORRIS—" Who made the earth, the grass, the stone, and the wood?   The Great Spirit.   He made them for all his children to use, and it is not stealing to use the gift of the Great Spirit.   The lands are the Queen's under the Great Spirit.   The Chippewas were not always here.   They come from the East.   There were other Indians here and the Chippewas came here, and they used the wood and the land, the gifts of the Great Spirit to all, and we want to try and induce you to believe that we are asking for the good of all.   We do not know how the division between us is to be taken away.   We do not know of any lands that were stolen from you, and if you do not open your mouths we cannot get the wall taken away.   You can open your mouths if you will; we are patient but we cannot remain here always.

THE GAMBLER—" I cannot manage to speak of anything else. It is this I am speaking.   All the Indians know how the Company set their land in order long ago.   The Company is making it more and that is the reason I am speaking."

LIEUT.-GOVERNOR MORRIS—" Many, many years ago, before we were born, one of the Kings gave the Company certain rights to trade in this country.   The Queen thought that this was not just neither to the white nor the red man.   She considered that all should be equal; but when the Queen's father's father's hand had been given she could not take it back without the Company's consent; therefore she told the Company that the time had come when they should no longer be the great power in this country, that she would plant her own flag, that she would send her own Governor and soldiers, and that they must cease to have the only right to trade here (and I am glad to know that some of you are good traders), the Queen then told the Company that she would govern the country herself, and she told them she would give them some land. They had their forts, their places of trade where they raised cattle and grain, and she told them they could keep them, and she will no more break with them than she will with you. There is no reason why you should not talk to us. The Company have no more power, no more authority to govern this country than you have, it rests with the Queen."

THE GAMBLER—"This is the reason I waited for the Queen's messengers to come here because I knew the Company was strong and powerful, and I knew they would set everything in order. Truly since the Company came here they have brought me many things which are good, but the Company's work is in my way and I cannot utter my words."

LIEUT.-GOV. MORRIS—"What do you complain of? I can not tell."

THE GAMBLER—"The survey. This one (pointing to an Indian) did not say so, and this Saulteaux and he was never told about it. He should have been told beforehand that this was to have been done and it would not have been so, and I want to know why the Company have done so. This is the reason I am talking so much about it."

LIEUT.-GOV. MORRIS—"I have told you before that the Queen had promised to give the Company certain lands around the forts and she gave them land around this fort. I have told you that what she promised she will do. She has taken all the lands in this country to manage ; they were hers ; they were her fathers ; if she gives you reserves they will be yours and she will let no one take them from you unless you want to sell them yourselves. It will be a sorry thing if this nation and that nation scattered all over the country are to suffer because of this little piece of land I see around me. What good is it going to do to raise up a question of this kind and block the way to our understanding each other when the Queen's hand, full of love and generosity is held out to you ? The blame rests with you ; it is time for you to talk, to open your mouth, because I cannot take away what shuts it, you must do it yourselves."

THE GAMBLER—"This is my chief, the Queen never told this man. If this had been told him, I would not have said what I said just now. The Company's store was only there at first. I do not push back the Queen's hand. Let this be cleared up.'

LIEUT.-GOV. MORRIS—"Once for all we tell you, whatever number of acres the Queen has promised to the Company at this post, they will receive no more and no less. We will ascertain what was promised, and will take care to see that what was promised and that only will be performed with regard to the land around this Fort. We can give you no other answer."

THE GAMBLER—"I am telling you and reporting what 1 had to tell. The Company have no right to this earth, but when they are spoken to they do not desist, but do it in spite of you. He is the head and foremost. These Indians you see sitting around report that they only allowed the store to be put up. That is the reason I was very glad when I heard you were coming. The Indians were not told of the reserves at all I hear now, it was the Queen gave the land. The Indians thought it was they who gave it to the Company, who are now all over the country. The Indians did not know when the land was given."

LIEUT.-GOV. MORRIS—"I am weary hearing about the

country. You might understand me now. You are stronger than that little boy over there, and the Company is stronger than a single trader, but the Company has its master, the Queen, and will have to obey the laws as well as all others. We have nothing to do with the Company. We are here to talk with you about the land, I tell you what we wish to do for your good, but if you will talk about the Company I cannot hinder you, I think it is time now you should talk about what concerns you all."

THE GAMBLER—"That is the reason I waited so long. I cannot speak of anything else, my mind is resting on nothing else. I know that you will have power and good rules and this is why I am glad to tell you what is troubling me."

LIEUT.-GOV. MORRIS—" I have told you before and tell you again that the Queen cannot and will not undo what she has done. I have told you that we will see that the Company shall obey what she has ordered, and get no more and no less than she has promised. We might talk here all the year and I could not give you any other answer, and I put it to you now face to face—speak to me about your message, don't put it aside, if you do the responsibility will rest upon your nation, and during the winter that is coming, many a poor woman and child will be saying, how was it that our councillors and our braves shut their ears to the mouth of the Queen's messengers and refused to tell them their words. This Company, I have told you is nothing to us, it is nothing to the Queen, but their rights have to be respected just as much as those of the meanest child in the country. The Queen will do right between you and them. I can say no more than what I have said and if the Indians will not speak to us we cannot help it, and if the Indians wont answer our message, we must go back and tell the Queen that we came here and did everything we could to show the Indians we were in earnest in proving her love for them and that when there was a little difficulty, I came at once to meet them half way. What prevents you from coming

8

out and speaking openly. I cannot take away the difficulty you speak of, and if you will not answer us, there is no use in talking."

THE GAMBLER—"I told the chief of the soldiers what was in our way, what was troubling us and now we are telling you. It is that I am working at."

LIEUT.-GOV. MORRIS—" What is troubling you ?"

PIS-QUA (the plain) pointing to Mr. McDonald, of the Hudson's Bay Company—" You told me you had sold your land for so much money, £300,000. We want that money."

LIEUT.-GOV. MORRIS—"I wish our Indian brother had spoken before what was in his mind. He has been going here and there, and we never knew what he meant. I told you that many years ago the Queen's father's father gave the Company the right to trade in the country from the frozen ocean to the United States boundary line, and from the Atlantic Ocean to the Pacific. The Company grew strong and wanted no one to trade in the country but themselves. The Queen's people said, "no, the land is not yours, the Queen's father's father gave you rights to trade, it is time those rights should stop." You may go on and trade like any other merchant, but as it was worth money to you to say to this trader you shall not buy furs at any post, the Queen would not act unjustly to the Company. She would not take rights away from them any more than from you ; and to settle the question, she took all the lands into her own hands and gave the Company a sum of money in place of the rights which she had taken from them. She is ready to deal with you justly. We are here to-day to make to you her good offers. We have nothing to hide, nothing to conceal. The Queen acts in daylight. I think it is time you are going to talk with us about the offers we have made. "

THE GAMBLER—" I have made up about no other article. I suppose, indeed, I would make the thing very little and very small. When I get back I will think over it."

LIEUT.-GOV. MORRIS—"I have a word to say to you. In our land we worship the Great Spirit, and do not work on Sunday. I am glad to see that you are going back into council, and I will only ask you to think of these things with single hearts desiring only to do what is right and trusting my words. On Monday morning we will be glad to meet you here and hope we will find then that your heart has come to ours, that you will see that it is for your children's good, to take our hands and the promises we have given. As I told you before we would be glad to stay longer with you, but we are obliged to go away. We ask you then to meet us on Monday morning and Mr. Pratt will tell you so that there may be no mistake as to what we have promised. He has it written down so that it may not be rubbed out."

The conference then ended.

FIFTH DAY'S CONFERENCE.

September 14.

Both nations, Crees and Saulteaux, having assembled, His Honor Lieut.-Governor Morris again addressed them :—

"Children of our Great Mother, I am glad to see you again after another day. How have you come to meet us ? I hope you have come to us with good thoughts, and hearts ready to meet ours. I have one or two words to say to you. It is twenty days to-day since we left the Red River. We want to turn our faces homewards. You told me on Saturday that some of you could eat a great deal. I have something to say to you about that. There are Indians who live here, they have their wives and children around them. It is good for them to be here, and have plenty to eat, but they ought to think of their brothers ; they ought to think that there are men here who have come from a distance, from Fort Pelly and beyond, whose wives and children are not here to eat, and they want to be at home with them. It is time now that we began to understand

each other, and when there is something troubles us, I believe
in telling it.   When you told us you were troubled about the
situation of this tent, we had it moved.   Now we want you to
take away our trouble, or tell us what you mean.   We are
troubled about this.   We are servants of the Queen ; we have
been here many days giving you our message, and we have not
yet heard the voice of the nations.   We have two nations here.
We have the Crees, who were here first, and we have the
Ojibbeways, who came from our country not many suns ago.
We find them here ; we won't say they stole the land and the
stones and the trees ; no, but we will say this, that we believe
their brothers, the Crees, said to them when they came in here :
"The land is wide, it is wide, it is big enough for us both ; let
us live here like brothers ;" and that is what you say, as you
told us on Saturday, as to the Half-breeds that I see around.
You say that you are one with them ; now we want all to be
one.   We know no difference between Crees and Ojibbeways.
Now we want to ask you are you wiser, do you know more,
than the Ojibbeway people that I met last year ?   You are a
handful compared with them ; they came to me from the Lake
of the Woods, from Rainy Lake, from the Kaministiquia, and
from the Great Lake.   I told them my message, as I have
told you ; they heard my words and they said they were good,
and they took my hand and I gave them mine and the presents ;
but that is not all.   There was a band of Ojibbeways who
lived at Lake Seul, to the north of the Lake of the Woods,
400 in number, and just before we came away we sent our
messenger to them.   He told them I had shaken hands for
the Queen with all the Ojibbeways down to the Great Lake.
He told them what we had done for these, and asked them if
they found it good to take the Queen's hand through our
messenger ; they were pleased ; they signed the treaty ; they
put their names to it, saying, We take what you promised to
the other Saulteaux ; and our messenger gave them the money,
just as our messengers will give your brothers who are not

here the money if we understand each other. Now, we ask you again, are you wiser than your brothers that I have seen before? I do not think that you will say you are, but we want you to take away our last trouble. What I find strange is this : we are Chiefs ; we have delivered the message of our great Queen, whose words never change, whose tongue and the tongues of whose messengers are never forked ; and how is it that we have not heard any voice back from the Crees or Saulteaux, or from their Chiefs? I see before me two Chiefs ; we know them to be Chiefs, because we see you put them before you to shake hands with us. They must have been made Chiefs, not for anything we are talking about to-day, not for any presents we are offering to you, not because of the land ; then why are they chiefs? Because I see they are old men ; the winds of many winters have whistled through their branches. I think they must have learned wisdom ; the words of the old are wise ; why then, we ask ourselves—and this is our trouble—Why are your Chiefs dumb? They can speak. One of them is called "Loud Voice." He must have been heard in the councils of the nation. Then I ask myself, why do they not answer? It cannot be that you are afraid ; you are not women. In this country, now, no man need be afraid. If a white man does wrong to an Indian, the Queen will punish them. The other day at Fort Ellice, a white man, it is said, stole some furs from an Indian. The Queen's policemen took him at once ; sent him down to Red River, and he is lying in jail now ; and if the Indians prove that he did wrong, he will be punished. You see then that if the white man does wrong to the Indian he will punished ; and it will be the same if the Indian does wrong to the white man. The red and white man must live together, and be good friends, and the Indians must live together like brothers with each other and the white man. I am afraid you are weary of my talking. Why do I talk so much? Because I have only your good at heart. I do not want to go away with my head down, to send word to the Queen, " Your red children could not see that your heart was good towards them ; could not see as you see that it was for the good of themselves and their children's children to accept the good things you mean for them." I have done. Let us hear the voice of the people. Let us hear the voice of your old wise men."

COTE—" The same man that has spoken will speak yet."

KA-KIE-SHE-WAY (Loud Voice)—This is the one who will speak ; after he speaks I will show what I have to say."

LIEUT.-GOV. MORRIS—" Understand me, what I want to know is, does he speak for the nations. If you prefer to speak by the voice of an orator I am glad. All we want is to hear the voice of the people, and I asked you at first to choose among yourselves those who would speak for you ; therefore I am glad to hear the man you have chosen, and I am glad to hear that after he has done the Chief will speak to us."

THE GAMBLER—" Saturday we met, we spoke to each other, we met at such a time as this time, and again we said we would tell each other something ; now, then, we will report to each other a little again. This Company man that we were speaking about, I do not hate him ; as I loved him before I love him still, and I also want that the way he loved me at first he should love me the same ; still, I wish that the Company would keep at his work the same as he did ; that I want to be signed on the paper. I want you to put it with your own hands. After he puts that there it is given to the Indians, then there will be another article to speak about. The Indians want the Company to keep at their post and nothing beyond. After that is signed they will talk about something else."

LIEUT.-GOV. MORRIS—" I told you on Saturday that I had nothing to do with the Company. The Company have a right to trade. I cannot make them buy goods and bring them here, or stop them from bringing them. I dare say some of you are traders ; you do not ask me whether you shall buy

goods and sell them again, and I do not stop you. It is the
same way with the Company. If they make money in bringing goods here they will bring them just as they used to do ;
and I want you to understand it fully, the Company may have
a little more money than the white traders, or the Half-
breeds, or the Indians, but they have no more right, they have
no more privileges, to trade than the Indians, or the Half-
breeds, or the whites ; and that is written with a higher hand
than ours, and we have no power to write anything, or to add
anything, to what is written and remains in the Queen's house
beyond the sea."

THE GAMBLER—" I do not want to drive the Company anywhere. What I said is, that they are to remain here at their
house. Supposing you wanted to take them away, I would
not let them go. I want them to remain here to have nothing
but the trade. I do not hate them ; we always exchange with
them, and would die if they went away."

LIEUT.-GOV. MORRIS—" I do not know whether we rightly
understand or not. I think you have spoken wise words ; the
Company helps you to live, and they have a right to sell goods
as other traders. I do not know that I understand you rightly,
that you do not want them to sell goods anywhere except at
the posts ; to keep at their posts there. If that is what you
mean, I cannot say yes to that ; they have the same right to
sell goods anywhere that you have. They are no longer as
they were once. The Government of the country, I think I
told you that before—understand me distinctly—the Government have nothing to do with the Company, but the Company
and all their servants are subjects of the Queen and love and
obey her laws. The day has gone past when they made the
laws. They have to hear the laws the Queen makes, and like
good subjects submit to them.

THE GAMBLER—" The Company is not to carry anything out
into the country, but are to trade in the Fort. That is what we
want signed on the paper ; then we will talk on other subjects."

LIEUT.-GOV. MORRIS—"I have told you before, and I tell you again, that the Company as traders have the right to sell goods anywhere they please, just as you have, just as the whites have, just as the Half-breeds have, and we have no power to take it away from them. If the Company were to ask me to say to you that you were not to trade anywhere except in their Fort by the lake, you would think it very hard, and I would say to the Company, No, you shall not interfere with the Indians throughout our land. I would like to give you pleasure but I cannot do wrong ; we won't deceive you with smooth words. We will tell you the simple truth what we can do and what we cannot do, but we cannot interfere as you ask us."

THE GAMBLER—"Cannot you sign such a paper?"

LIEUT.-GOV. MORRIS—"No ; the Queen has signed the great paper, and the Company have no more rights than any one else, but they have the same."

KA-KIE-SHE-WAY (Loud Voice)—"I would not be at a loss, but I am, because we are not united—the Crees and the Salteaux—this is troubling me. I am trying to bring all together in one mind, and this is delaying us. If we could put that in order, if we were all joined together and everything was right I would like it. I would like to part well satisfied and pleased. I hear that His Excellency is unwell, and I wish that everything would be easy in his mind. It is this that annoys me, that things do not come together. I wish for one day more, and after that there would not be much in my way."

COTE—"You wanted me to come here and I came here. I find nothing, and I do not think anything will go right. I know what you want ; I cannot speak of anything here concerning my own land until I go to my own land. Whenever you desire to see me I will tell you what you are asking me here. Now I want to return."

LIEUT-.GOV. MORRIS—"We asked the Chief to come here.

He has as much right to be here as another Indian. We
cannot go there and ask the people of the two great tribes to
meet in one place as they have done when they were asked to
meet us. You have had many days to talk together. If the
Saulteaux are determined that they want an agreement to prevent the Company from trading, it cannot be given. I think
the Chief here spoke wisely. He says he is in trouble because
you do not understand each other. Why are you not of one
mind ? Have you tried to be of one mind ? Must we go back
and say we have had you here so many days, and that you
had not the minds of men—that you were not able to understand each other ? Must we go back and tell the Queen that
we held out our hands for her, and her red children put them
back again ? If that be the message that your conduct to-day
is going to make us carry back, I am sorry for you, and fear it
will be a long day before you again see the Queen's Councillors
here to try to do you good. The Queen and her Councillors
may think that you do not want to be friends, that you do not
want your little ones to be taught, that you do not want when
the food is getting scarce to have a hand in yours stronger
than yours to help you. Surely you will think again before
you turn your backs on the offers ; you will not let so little a
question as this about the Company, without whom you tell me
you could not live, stop the good we mean to do. I hope that
I am perfectly understood ; when we asked the chief here we
wanted to speak with him about his lands at his place ; when
we asked "Loud Voice " here we wanted to speak with him
about the land at his place ; so when we asked the other
chiefs here we wanted to speak with them about the lands at
their places. Why ? because we did not want to do anything
that you would not all know about, that there might be no
bad feelings amongst you. We wanted you to be of one mind
and heart in this matter, and that is the reason you are here
to-day. Now it rests with you ; we have done all we could.
Have you anything more to say to us, or are we to turn our

backs upon you, and go away with sorry hearts for you and your children? It remains for you to say."

THE GAMBLER—"We do not understand you and what you are talking about. I do not keep it from you; we have not chosen our Chiefs; we have not appointed our soldiers and councillors; we have not looked around us yet, and chosen our land, which I understand you to tell us to choose. We do not want to play with you, but we cannot appoint our Chiefs and head men quickly; that is in the way. Now it is near mid-day, and we cannot appoint our Chiefs. This Chief who got up last—the Queen's name was used when he was appointed to be Chief—he wants to know where his land is to be and see it, what like it is to be, and to find the number of his children; that is what is in his mind. He says he came from afar, he had a good mind for coming, and he takes the same good mind away with him. I have not heard him say to the Saulteaux to keep back their land."

LIEUT.-GOV. MORRIS—"I think I understand you. We do not want to separate in bad feeling, or to avoid any trouble in coming to an understanding with you; because I do not believe that if we do not agree it will ever be my good fortune to endeavor to do so again. "Loud Voice," the Chief, has told us he wants a day to think it over. The Chief "Cote," from the north, would like to go home, but I am sure he will stop a day and try to understand his brothers, and agree as the others did at the Lake of the Woods. I put my name, and the Chiefs and the head men put theirs, and I gave the Chief a copy, and I told him when I went home to Red River I would have it all written out, a true copy made on skin, that could not be rubbed out, that I would send a copy to his people so that when we were dead and gone the letter would be there to speak for itself, to show everything that was promised; and that was the right way to do. I did so, and sent a copy of the treaty written in letters of blue, gold, and black to the Chief "Maw-do-pe-nais," whom the people had told to keep it for them. He who speaks for the Saulteaux tells us they have not made up their minds yet about the land—he tells us they have not decided to refuse our hands. I am glad to hear him say that, and if it will please my Indian brethren here we will be glad to wait another day and meet them here to-morrow morning, if they will promise me with the words of men that they will look this matter straight in the face ; that they will lay aside every feeling except the good of their people, and try to see what is right, and that they will come back and say, 'We have done our best, we have tried to be of one mind, and considered what was best for now, and to-morrow, and the years that are to come when we have all passed away. This is our answer. We are very much in earnest about this matter.' The Chief said I was not very well, yet I am here. Why ? Because the duty was laid upon me. I was afraid of the journey ; but when a Chief has a duty to do he tries to do it, and I felt that if I could do you any good, as I believed I could, I ought to be here. I tell you this, trust my words, they come from the heart of one who loves the Indian people, and who is charged by his Queen to tell them the words of truth."

SIXTH DAY'S CONFERENCE.

The Crees having come and shaken hands, His Honor Lieut.-Gov. Morris rose and said :

"My friends, I have talked much ; I would like to hear your voices, I would like to hear what you say."

KA-KU-ISH-MAY, (Loud Voice—a principal chief of the Crees) —"I am very much pleased with that, to listen to my friends, for certainly it is good to report to each other what is for the benefit of each other. We see the good you wish to show us. If you like what we lay before you we will like it too. Let us join together and make the Treaty ; when both join together it is very good."

The Saulteaux arrived at this juncture, when the Lieut.-Governor said :

" I will say to the two tribes what I said to the Crees before the Saulteaux came. You have heard my voice for many days, you know its sound. You have looked in my face, you have seen my mind through my face, and you know my words are true and that they do not change. But I am not here to talk to-day, I am here to listen. You have had our message, you have had the Queen's words. It is time now that you spoke. I am here to listen, my ears are open. It is for you to speak."

KAMOOSES—" Brothers, I have one word and a small one, that is the reason I cannot finish anything that is large. You do not see the whole number of my tribe which is away at my back, that is the reason I am so slow in making ready."

LIEUT.-GOV. MORRIS—" I want to hear the voice of those who are here, they can speak for themselves and for those who are away."

CHE-E-KUK (the Worthy One)—" My ears are open to what you say. Just now the Great Spirit is watching over us; it is good, He who has strength and power is overlooking our doings. I want very much to be good in what we are going to talk about, and our Chiefs will take you by the hand just now."

The Chiefs now rose and shook hands with the Commissioners.

KA-HA-OO-KUS-KA-TOO (he who walks on four claws)—" It is very good to meet together on a fine day, father. When my father used to bring me anything I used to go and meet him, and when my father had given it to me I gave it to my mother to cook it. When we come to join together one half at least will come."

CHE-E-KUK (the Worthy)—" Now I am going to tell you, and you say your ears are open. You see the Qu'Appelle Lake Indians that you wished to see, you hear me speak but there are many far away, and that is the reason I cannot speak for these my children who are away trying to get something to eat ; the Crees my child is not here, the Saulteaux my child is not here, the Young Dogs are not here, the Stonies my children are not here ; this is not the number that you see ; I am only telling you this, I think I have opened my mind."

LIEUT.-Gov. MORRIS—"I know you are not all here. We never could get you all together, but you know what is good for you and for your children. When I met the Saulteaux last year we had not 4,000 there, but there were men like you who knew what was good for themselves, for their wives, for their children, and those not born. I gave to those who were there, and they took my hand and took what was in it, and I sent to those who were away, and I did for them just as I did for those who were present. It is the same to-day. What we are ready to give you will be given to those who are not here. What is good for you, what you think will be good for you will be good for them. It is for you to say, not for us ; we have done all that men who love their red brothers can do ; it is for you now to act, on you rests the duty of saying whether you believe our message or not, whether you want the Queen to help you or not, whether or not you will go away and let the days and the years go on, and let the food grow scarcer, and let your children grow up and do nothing to keep off the hunger and the cold that is before them. It is for you to say that, not for us; if we had not your good at heart we would not have been here, and we would not have labored these many days, if our hearts were not warm towards you, and if we did not believe what we are doing, would be for your good as children of our Queen. I have said all."

KAN-OO-SES—"Is it true you are bringing the Queen's kindness? Is it true you are bringing the Queen's messenger's kindness? Is it true you are going to give my child what he may use? Is it true you are going to give the different bands the Queen's kindness? Is it true that you bring the Queen's hand? Is it true you are bringing the Queen's power?"

LIEUT.-GOV. MORRIS—" Yes, to those who are here and those who are absent, such as she has given us."

KAMOOSES—"Is it true that my child will not be troubled for what you are bringing him ?"

LIEUT.-GOV. MORRIS—"The Queen's power will be around him."

KAMOOSES—" Now, I am going to ask you that the debt that has been lying in the Company's store, I want that to be wiped out.   I ask it from the great men of the Queen."

LIEUT.-GOV. MORRIS—"I told you before we have nothing to do with the Company, we have nothing to do with its debts. I have told you what we will do for you, what the Queen will do for you forever.   But the money that the Indian owes the Company is just like the money that the Indians owe to each other or to any trader and is not due to the Queen.   We have no power to put money in your hands and your children's to pay your debts, and it would not be right for the Queen to come in and take away either what is between you and the Company, or what is between you and the traders, or what is betwen you and each other.   If one of you owes the Chief is it right that the Queen should wipe it out ?   I would be very glad if we had it in our power to wipe out your debts, but it is not in our power.   All we can do is to put money in your hands and promise to put money in the hands of those who are away, and give you money every year afterwards, and help you to make a living when the food is scarce.   I have told you from the first that whether my words please you or not I will tell you only the truth, and I will only speak as far as the Queen has given us power."

(He who walks on four claws)—" Whenever you give to these my children what they desire, then you will get what you want."

LIEUT.-GOV. MORRIS—"We will give them what we have power to give.   We are ready to hear."

KAMOOSES—" Yes, I understand and my heart also, but it is

not large, it is small, and my understanding is small ; that is the word I tell you."

LIEUT.-GOV. MORRIS—"I have told you what we are ready to do for you. Your understanding is large enough to know what is good for you. We have talked these many days, and I ask you now to talk straight, to tell me your mind, to tell me whether you wish to take our offers or not, it is for you to say."

KEE-E-KUK—"Twenty dollars we want to be put in our hand every year, this we have heard from the others. Twenty-five dollars to each chief."

LIEUT.-GOV. MORRIS—"If I understand you aright you are mistaken. The Saulteaux did not get twenty-five dollars per head. They get five dollars every year. We promised them five dollars every year, and a messenger was sent this year to pay them that sum. I may tell you that my children at the Lake of the Woods had big hearts to ask. You say you have small. I told them that if the Queen gave them all they asked I would have to ask her to allow me to become an Indian, but I told them I could not give them what they asked, and when they understood that, and understood the full breadth and width of the Queen's goodness, they took what I offered, and I think if you are wise you will do the same."

(A proposition was made here by an Indian that they should receive five dollars per head every second year for fifty years, but he must have done so without authority as it was not acceded to by the other Indians who expressed their dissent strongly as soon as the offer was made.)

KAMOOSES—"I am going to speak for Loud Voice and for the other chiefs. Some chiefs are not here, they are absent, hereafter you will see them. I myself will tell them, and my child that is at my back will tell them also. Will you receive that which I am asking? I want to clear up what the Indians and I want to try and put it right, what my child will say. Well, can you give me that. We want the same Treaty you have given to the North-West Angle. This I am asking for."

LIEUT.-GOV. MORRIS—"Who are you speaking for? Is it for the whole of the Indians? (They expressed their assent.) Are you ready to carry it out? (They again assented.) Are your chiefs ready to sign this afternoon if we grant you these terms? (The Indians assented unanimously.) It is now after twelve, we will speak to you this afternoon."

The Conference here ended to allow the Commissioners time to consult.

AFTERNOON CONFERENCE.

The Indians having assembled, presented the Chiefs, whose names appear on the Treaty to the Commissioners as their Chiefs.

KAMOOSES—"To-day we are met together here and our minds are open. We want to know the terms of the North-West Angle Treaty."

LIEUT.-GOV. MORRIS—"Do we understand that you want the same terms which were given at the Lake of the Woods. (The Indians assented.) I have the Treaty here in a book. You must know that the steamboats had been running through their waters, and our soldiers had been marching through their country, and for that reason we offered the Ojibbeways a larger sum than we offered you. Last year it was a present, covering five years; with you it was a present for this year only. I paid the Indians there a present in money down of twelve dollars per head. I have told you why we offered you less, and you will see there were reasons for it. That is the greatest difference between what we offered you and what was paid them, but on the other hand there were some things promised you that were not given at the Lake of the Woods. (His Honor then explained the terms granted in that Treaty.) We promised there that the Queen would spend $1,500 per year to buy shot and powder, ball and twine. There were 4,000 of

them. I offered you $1,000 although you are only one-half
the number, as I do not think you number more than 2,000.
Your proportionate share would be $750 which you shall receive.
Then at the Lake of the Woods each Chief had their head men;
we have said you would have four who shall have fifteen dollars each per year, and as at the Lake of the Woods each Chief
and head man will receive a suit of clothing once in three
years, and each Chief on signing the treaty will receive a medal
and the promise of a flag. We cannot give you the flag now,
as there were none to be bought at Red River, but we have
the medals here. Now I have told you the terms we gave at
the North-West Angle of the Lake of the Woods, and you
will see that the only difference of any consequence between
there and what we offered you is in the money payment that
we give as a present, and I have told you why we made the
difference, and you will see that it was just. We had to speak
with them for four years that had gone away. We speak to
you only for four days. It was not that we came in the spirit of
traders, but because we were trying to do what was just
between you and the Queen, and the other Indians who would
say that we had treated you better than we had treated them
because we put the children of this year on the same footing
as these children through whose land we had been passing and
running our steamboats for four years. You see when you ask
us to tell you everything, we show you all that has been done,
and I have to tell you again that the Ojibbeways at Lake
Seul who number 400, when I sent a messenger this spring
with a copy of those terms made at the North-West Angle
with their nation, took the Queen's hand by my messenger and
made the same treaty. I think I have told you all you want
to know, and our ears are open again."

KAMOOSES—"I want to put it a little light for all my children around me, something more on the top. For my chief
thirty dollars, for my four chief head men twenty dollars, and
each of my young children fifteen dollars a year."

9

LIEUT.-GOV. MORRIS—"I am afraid you are not talking
to us straight; when we went away you asked us to give you
the terms given at the Lake of the Woods; you asked to know
what they were, and the moment I told you, you ask three
times as much for your children as I gave them. That would
not be right; and it is well that you should know that we have
not power to do so ; we can give you no more than we gave
them. We hope you are satisfied. I have one word more to
say, we are in the last hours of the day you asked us for and
we must leave you. The utmost we can do, the furthest we
can go or that we ought to go is, to do what you asked, to give
you the terms granted last year at the Lake of the Woods.
We can do no more, and you have our last words. It is
for you to say whether you are satisfied or not."

KAMOOSES—" We ask that we may have cattle."

LIEUT.-GOV. MORRIS—" We offered you cattle on the first
day, we offered your Chief cattle for the use of his band—not
for himself, but for the use of his band; we gave the same at
the Lake of the Woods. We can give no more here."

KAMOOSES—" We want some food to take us home."

LIEUT.-GOV. MORRIS—" When you sign the treaty, provisions will be given to take you home. Now I ask you, are
you ready to accept the offer, the last offer we can make, you
will see we have put you on the same footing as the Indians
at the Lake of the Woods, and we think it is more than we
ought to give, but rather than not close the matter we have
given it, we have talked long enough about this. It is time
we did something. Now I would ask, are the Crees and
the Saulteaux and the other Indians ready to make the treaty
with us. Since we went away we have had the treaty written
out, and we are ready to have it signed, and we will leave a
copy with any Chief you may select and after we leave we
will have a copy written out on skin that cannot be rubbed
out and put up in a tin box, so that it cannot be wet, so that

you can keep it among yourselves so that when we are dead our children will know what was written."

KAMOOSES—"Yes, we want each Chief to have a copy of the treaty, we ask that the Half-breeds may have the right of hunting."

LIEUT.-GOV. MORRIS—"We will send a copy to each Chief. As to the Half-breeds, you need not be afraid; the Queen will deal justly, fairly and generously with all her children."

The Chiefs then signed the treaty, after having been assured that they would never be made ashamed of what they then did.

One of the Chiefs on being asked to do so signed; the second called on said he was promised the money when he signed, and returned to his seat without doing so. The Lieutenant-Governor called him forward—held out his hand to him and said, take my hand; it holds the money. If you can trust us forever you can do so for half an hour; sign the treaty. The Chief took the Governor's hands and touched the pen, and the others followed. As soon as the treaty was signed the Governor expressed the satisfaction of the Commissioners with the Indians, and said that Mr. Christie and Mr. Dickieson, the Private Secretary of the Minister of the Interior, were ready to advance the money presents, but the Indians requested that the payment should be postponed till next morning, which was acceded to. The Chiefs then formally approached the Commissioners and shook hands with them, after which the conference adjourned, the Commissioners leaving the place of meeting under escort of the command of Lieut.-Col. Smith, who had been in daily attendance.

Report of the interview at Fort Ellice between the Indian
Commissioners and certain Saulteaux Indians not present
at Qu'Appelle, and not included in Treaty Number Two,
the Chief being Way-wa-se-ca-pow, or "the Man proud
of standing upright:"

Lieut.-Governor Morris said he had been here before, and since
that time he had met the Crees and Saulteaux nations, and had
made a treaty with them.　The Indians there were from Fort
Pelly and as far distant as the Cypress Hills.　He wished to
know the number of the Saulteaux to be found in this locality.

The Chief said there were about thirty tents who were not
at Qu'Appelle, and ten who were there.

LIEUT.-GOV. MORRIS—The Commissioners here are representing the Queen.　I made a treaty with the Saulteaux last year at
the Lake of the Woods.　They were not a little handful; but
there were 4,000 of them—and now we have made a treaty
with the Crees and Saulteaux at Qu'Appelle.　There is not much
need to say much—it is good for the Indians to make treaties
with the Queen—good for them and their wives and children.
Game is getting scarce and the Queen is willing to help her
children.　Now we are ready to give you what we gave the
Saulteaux at the Lake of the Woods and the Saulteaux and
Crees at Qu'Appelle.　It will be for you to say whether you
will accept it or not."　His Honor then explained the treaty
to them.

" What we offer will be for your good, as it will help you, and
not prevent you from hunting.

"We are not traders.　I have told you all we can do and all
we will do.　It is for you to say whether you will accept my
hand or not.　I cannot wait long.　I think you are not wiser
than your brothers.　Our ears are open, you can speak to us."

LONG CLAWS—"My father—I shake hands with you, I shake
hands with the Queen."

SHAPONETUNG'S FIRST SON—" I find what was done at Qu'Appelle was good, does it take in all my children ?"

LIEUT.-GOV. MORRIS—" Yes."

SHAPONETUNG'S FIRST SON—" I thank you for coming and bringing what is good for our children."

LIEUT.-GOV. MORRIS—" I forgot to say that we will be able to give you a small present, some powder and shot, blankets and calicoes. Each band must have a Chief and four headmen, but you are not all here to-day. I want to-day to know the Chief and two headmen.

" Now I want to know will you take my hand and what is in it."

The Indians came up and shook hands in token of acceptance.

LIEUT.-GOV. MORRIS—" I am glad to shake hands with you ; the white man and the red man have shaken hands and are friends. You must be good subjects to the Queen and obey her laws."

The Indians introduced as their Chief, Way-wa-se-ca-pow ; and as their headmen, Ota-ma-koo-euin and Shaponetung's first son.

His Honor then explained the memorandum to them, when it was signed.

CHAPTER VII.

THE REVISION OF TREATIES NUMBERS ONE AND TWO.

WHEN Treaties, Numbers One and Two, were made, certain verbal promises were unfortunately made to the Indians, which were not included in the written text of the treaties, nor recognized or referred to, when these Treaties were ratified by the Privy Council. This, naturally, led to misunderstanding with the Indians, and to widespread dissatisfaction among them. This state of matters was reported to the Council by the successive Lieut.-Governors of Manitoba, and by the Superintendent of Indian Affairs. On examination of the original Treaty Number One, the Minister of the Interior reported that a memorandum was found attached to it signed by Mr. Commissioner Simpson, His Hon. Governor Archibald, Mr. St. John and the Hon. Mr. McKay, purporting to contain their understanding of the terms upon which the Indians concluded the treaty. This memorandum was as follows :

Memorandum of things outside of the Treaty which were promised at the Treaty at the Lower Fort, signed the 3rd day of August, A.D. 1871.

For each Chief that signed the treaty, a dress distinguishing him as Chief.

For braves and for councillors of each Chief, a dress : it being supposed that the braves and councillors will be two for each Chief.

For each Chief, except Yellow Quill, a buggy.

For the braves and councillors of each Chief, except Yellow Quill, a buggy.

In lieu of a yoke of oxen for each reserve, a bull for each, and a cow for each Chief ; a boar for each reserve, and a sow for each Chief, and a male and female of each kind of animal raised by farmers ; these when the Indians are prepared to receive them.

A plow and a harrow for each settler cultivating the ground.

These animals and their issue to be Government property, but to be allowed for the use of the Indians, under the superintendence and control of the Indian Commissioner.

The buggies to be the property of the Indians to whom they are given.

The above contains an inventory of the terms concluded with the Indians.

WEMYSS M. SIMPSON,
MOLYNEUX ST. JOHN,
A. G. ARCHIBALD,
JAS. McKAY.

The Privy Council, by Order in Council, agreed to consider this memorandum as part of the original treaties, and instructed the Indian Commissioner to carry out the promises therein contained, which had not been implemented. They also agreed to offer to raise the annuities from three to five dollars per head, to pay a further annual sum of twenty dollars to each chief, and to give a suit of clothing every three years to each chief and head man, allowing four head men to each band, upon the distinct understanding however, that any Indian accepting the increased payment, thereby formally abandoned all claims against the Government, in connection with the verbal promises of the Commissioners, other than those recognized by the treaty and the memorandum above referred to.

The Government then invited Lieut.-Gov. Morris, in conjunction with the Indian Commissioner, Lieut.-Col. Provencher, to visit the several bands interested in the treaties, with a view to submit to them the new terms, and obtain their acceptance of the proposed revision of the treaties. His Honor accordingly placed his services at the disposal of the Government, and was at his request accompanied by the Hon. Mr. McKay, who had been present at the making of the original treaties, and was well versed in the Indian tongues. In October 1875, these gentlemen entered upon the task confided to them, and first proceeded to meet the large and important band of St. Peters, in the Province of Manitoba. The matter was fully discussed with the Indians, the Order in Council,

and memorandum read and explained to them, and their written assent to the new terms obtained. After their return
from St. Peters, owing to the advanced season of the year, it
was decided to divide the work, the Lieutenant-Governor
requesting the Indian Commissioner to proceed to Fort Alexander on Lake Winnipeg, and to the Broken Head and Roseau
Rivers, while Messrs. Morris and McKay, would undertake to
meet the Indians included in Treaty Number Two at Manitoba
House on Lake Manitoba. Colonel Provencher met the
Indians at the places above mentioned, and obtained the
assent of the Indians of the three bands to the revised treaty.
Messrs. Morris and McKay proceeded by carriage to Lake
Manitoba, and thence in a sail boat, where they met the
Indians of the six bands of Treaty Number Two, and after
full discussion, tha Indians cordially accepted the new terms,
and thus was pleasantly and agreeably closed, with all the
bands of Treaties One and Two, except that of the Portage
band, who were not summoned to any of the conferences, a
fruitful source of dissension and difficulty. The experience
derived from this misunderstanding, proved however, of
benefit with regard to all the treaties, subsequent to Treaties
One and Two, as the greatest care was thereafter taken to
have all promises fully set out in the treaties, and to have the
treaties thoroughly aud fully explained to the Indians, and
understood by them to contain the whole agreement between
them and the Crown, The arrangement, however, of the
matter with the Portage band was one of more difficulty. This
band had always been troublesome. In 1870, they had warned
off settlers and Governor MacTavish of the Hudson's Bay Company had been obliged to send the Hon. James McKay to
make terms for three years with them for the admission of
settlers. In 1874, they twice sent messengers with tobacco
(the usual Indian credentials for such messengers) to
Qu'Appelle to prevent the making of the treaty there. Besides
the claims to the outside promises, preferred by the other

Indians, they had an additional grievance, which they pressed with much pertinacity. To obtain their adhesion to Treaty Number One, the Commissioners had given them preferential terms in respect to their reserve, and the wording in the treaty of these terms enhanced the difficulty. The language used was as follows: " And for the use of the Indians of whom Oo-za-we-kwan is Chief, so much land on the south and east side of the Assiniboine, as will furnish one hundred and sixty acres for each family of five, or in that proportion for larger or smaller families, reserving also a further tract enclosing said reserve, to contain an equivalent to twenty-five square miles of equal breadth, to be laid out around the reserve." The enclosure around the homestead reserve led to extravagant demands by them. They did not understand its extent, and claimed nearly half of the Province of Manitoba under it.

The Indians constantly interviewed the Lieutenant-Governor on the subject, and when the Hon. Mr. Laird, then Minister of the Interior, visited Manitoba, they twice pressed their demands upon him. The Government requested the Hon. Messrs. Morris and McKay to endeavor to settle the long pending dispute, and they proceeded to the Round Plain on the river Assiniboine with that view. They met the Indians, some five hundred in number, but without result. The Indians were divided among themselves. A portion of the band had forsaken Chief Yellow Quill and wished the recognition of the Great Bear, grandson of Pee-qual-kee-quash, a former chief of the band. The Yellow Quill band wanted the reserve assigned in one locality ; the adherents of the Bear said that place was unsuited for farming, and they wished it to be placed at the Round Plain, where they had already commenced a settlement. The land to which they were entitled under the treaty was 34,000 acres, but their demands were excessive.

The Chief Yellow Quill was apprehensive of his own followers, and besides the danger of collision between the two sections was imminent. The Commissioners finally intimated to the

band that they would do nothing with them that year, but
would make the customary payment of the annuities under the
original treaty and leave them till next year to make up their
minds as to accepting the new terms, to which the Indians
agreed.

In 1876, the Government again requested Mr. Morris to
meet these Indians and endeavor to arrange the long pending
dispute with them, and in July he travelled to the Long Plain
on the Assiniboine with that object in view. He had previously summoned the band to meet there, and had also summoned a portion of the band known as the White Mud River
Indians, dwelling on the shores of Lake Manitoba, who were
nominally under the chieftainship of Yellow Quill, and were,
as such, entitled to a portion of the original reserve, but did
not recognize the Chief. Mr. Morris was accompanied by
Mr. Graham, of the Indian Department, Secretary and Paymaster. On arrival at his destination, the Lieutenant-Governor
found the Indians assembled, but in three camps. Those
adhering to Yellow Quill, the Bear, and the White Mud River
Indians, being located on different parts of the plains. Mr.
Reid, Surveyor, was also present, to explain the extent and
exact dimensions of the proposed reserve.

The next day the Indians were assembled, and the conference lasted for two days. The Yellow Quill band were still
obstructive, but the other two sections were disposed to accept
the terms. The question of the reserve was the main difficulty.
The Yellow Quill band still desired a reserve for the whole.
The others wished to remain, the Bear's party at the Round
Plain, and the White Mud River Indians at Lake Manitoba,
where they resided and had houses and farms. In the interval
from the previous year, the Bear's band had built several
houses, and made enclosures for farming. Eventually, the
Indians were made to comprehend the extent of land they
were really entitled to, but the Governor intimated that the
land was for all, and that he would divide the band into three,

each with a Chief and councillors, and that he would give each band a portion of the whole number of acres, proportionate to their numbers—the Bear at the Round Plain, the White Mud Indians at their place of residence, and the Yellow Quill band wherever they might select, in unoccupied territory. After long consultations among themselves the Indians accepted the proposal. The Bear was recognized as a Chief, and a Chief selected by the White Mud River band was accepted as such.

The Indians also agreed to accept the revised terms of Treaty Number One, and an agreement in accordance with the understanding was prepared and signed by the Lieutenant-Governor, and the Chief and head men. The Indians preferred a request to receive the two dollars, increased amount, which, as they said, "had slipped through their fingers last year," which was granted, and also that the councillors should be paid yearly, as in the other treaties, subsequently made. This the Governor promised to recommend, and it was eventually granted, being made applicable to all the bands in Treaties Numbers One and Two.

Thus was so far closed, a controversy which had lasted for some years, and had been fruitful of unpleasant feelings, the negotiations terminating in that result having been from a variety of causes more difficult to bring to a satisfactory solution than the actual making of treaties, for the acquisition of large extents of territory. On the leaving of the Lieutenant-Governor, the morning after the conclusion of the arrangement, the Indians assembled and gave three cheers for the Queen and Governor, and fired a *feu de joie.* Mr. Reid at once proceeded to set aside the reserves for the Bear and White Mud bands, but the selection of a reserve by the Yellow Quill band was attended with still further further difficulty, although it was eventually pointed out by them, and surveyed by Mr. Reid, it being in a very desirable locality. The despatches of the Lieutenant-Governor to the Minister of the Interior, giving an account in full of the negotiations for the revision of the

Treaties Numbers One and Two, will complete this record, and will be found to give a clear narrative of them. These are as follows :

GOVERNMENT HOUSE,
FORT GARRY, MANITOBA, *5th October, 1875.*

SIR,—I have the honor to inform you that in pursuance of your request that I should meet the Indians of Treaties Numbers One and Two, with a view to a revision of the terms thereof, and an adjustment of the disputed questions connected therewith, I proceeded to the St. Peter Reserve on the 5th of August and encamped near the Indian tents.

On the 6th I met Chief Prince and his band, being accompanied by the Hon. James McKay, who at my request gave me the benefit of his valuable services, and by Mr. Provencher. I explained to the Indians the terms offered to them by the Government, and obtained their written assent thereto, endorsed on a parchment copy of the Order in Council of date the 30th April, 1875. As however there are in the bands of Treaties Numbers One and Two, four councillors, *i.e.,* head men, and two braves, we were under the necessity of agreeing that they should continue at that number, instead of two, as specified in the report of the Privy Council. We then brought before them your request that the portion of the reserve embraced in the proposed new town near the Pacific Railway crossing should be sold for their benefit, to which they agreed, and the formal instrument of surrender will be enclosed to you by the Indian Commissioner.

The Indians living at Nettley Creek asked to have a reserve assigned them there, and I promised to bring their request under your notice.

I did not bring up the question of the division of the band into two, as my experience with the Portage band, arising from a similar difficulty, led me to fear that complications might arise from the proposal which might prevent the settlement of the more important matter of the disposal of the open questions relating to the treaty. I was therefore of opinion that the division of the band should be postponed to next year, and acted upon that opinion. A party of Norway House Indians were present and asked for a reserve at the Grassy Narrows. I informed them that one could not be granted at that place, and learning from them that the Chief at Norway House was about leaving there with a party of Indians to confer with me, I engaged three of the Indians present to proceed at once to Norway House and inform the Indians that I would meet them there about the middle of September.

I have since learned that they met the Chief after he had left Norway House or Fort Garry, and caused him to return.

I have the honor to be, etc.,

ALEXANDER MORRIS,
Lieut.-Governor.

GOVERNMENT HOUSE,
FORT GARRY, MANITOBA, *4th October,* 1875.

SIR,—I have the honor to inform you that after my return from St. Peters, finding that in view of my contemplated mission to Lake Winnipeg it would be impossible for me to visit all the bands of Indians included in Treaties Numbers One and Two, I requested the Indian Commissioner, Mr. Provencher, to proceed to meet them at Fort Alexander and the Broken Head and Roseau rivers, while I should proceed to Lake Manitoba and meet at Manitoba House the various bands of Indians included in Treaty Number Two. In pursuance of this arrangement, I left here on the 17th of August for Oak Point, on Lake Manitoba, where I was to take a boat for Manitoba Post.

I was accompanied by the Hon. James McKay, whose presence enabled me to dispense with an interpreter, and was of importance otherwise, as he had assisted my predecessor in the making of the treaty originally at Manitoba Post. Mr. Graham, of the Indian Department, also accompanied me to make the payments and distribute the pensions. I reached Oak Point on the afternoon of the 18th, and left there on the afternoon of the 20th, arriving at Manitoba House on the evening of the 21st. The next day being Sunday, nothing of course was done relating to my mission, but on Monday morning I met the Indians at ten o'clock on the lake shore. The six bands included in the treaty were all represented by their Chiefs and head men and a large number of their people.

I explained to them the object of our mission, my remarks being fully interpreted by Mr. McKay, and obtained their assent in writing to the Order in Council of the 30th April last, the terms of which were accepted with cordiality and good feeling by the Indians.

The new medals and uniforms were distributed to the Chiefs and head men, and the payments under the revised treaty were then commenced by Mr. McKay and Mr. Graham, and continued until 12.30 p.m.

On the 24th, the payments were resumed and concluded, but owing to heavy rain and high winds, we were unable to leave Manitoba Post until the 25th. The Indians on our departure again firing their guns in token of their respect and good will. Owing to stormy weather, which obliged us to encamp on Bird Island, we did not return to Oak Point until the afternoon of the 27th.

On the 28th, the Indians residing in that vicinity, and belonging to Sousanye's band, were paid by Messrs. McKay and Graham. I returned to Fort Garry on the 1st September, in the afternoon, my journey having been protracted by unfavorable weather, and by the fact that owing to the prevalence of shoals, the navigation of Lake Manitoba is difficult in stormy weather.

As only a small portion of the Riding House Indians were present, I informed them that Mr. Graham would proceed to the mountains after our return, to make the payments, and that I would send by him a reply to their requests, as to the retention by them of the reserve originally designated in the treaty, and this I have since done affirmatively with your sanction. Mr. Provencher succeeded in obtaining the adhesion of the bands at Fort Alexander, Broken Head and Roseau rivers to the new terms, and has handed me the copies of the Order in Council with their assents endorsed thereon.

You will therefore perceive that with the exception of the Portage band with regard to whom I wrote you fully on the 2nd of August last, the assent of all the Indians interested therein to the proposed mode of settlement of the unrecorded promises made at the conclusion of Treaties Numbers One and Two, has been obtained, and I feel that I have reason to congratulate the Privy Council on the removal of a fruitful source of difficulty and discontent. But I would add, that it becomes all the more important that a better system of Indian administration should be devised so as to secure the prompt and rigid carrying out of the new terms in their entirety.

You are already in possession of my views on this subject, and I trust that local agents will be appointed to be supervised by the Indian Commissioner and that an Indian Council of advice and control, sitting at Fort Garry, will be entrusted with the direction of the Treaties One, Two, and the upper portion of Three, and the new Treaty Number Five, so as to secure prompt and effective administration of Indian Affairs.

Under the system of local agents, the necessity of large gatherings of the Indians will be avoided, and much expense to the Government, and inconvenience to the Indians, avoided. I have further to record my sense of the services rendered to me by Messrs. McKay and Graham. The latter discharged his duties with promptitude and efficiency, and Mr. McKay and he introduced a mode of distribution of the provisions to which I would call your attention.

I have the honor to be, etc.,

ALEXANDER MORRIS,

Lieut.-Governor.

GOVERNMENT HOUSE,

FORT GARRY, MANITOBA, *2nd August, 1875.*

SIR,—In accordance with your request I have commenced my visits to the Indian bands included in Treaties Numbers One and Two, with a view to settling the matters in dispute. I left here on the 22nd inst., and was accompanied by the Hon. James McKay, whom I had invited to accompany me in consequence of his having been present at the making of the treaties, and by the Indian Commissioner.

I reached the Round Plain on the Assiniboine river, where Yellow Quill's band of Saulteaux had assembled on the 26th, and met the Indians next day, explaining to them our mission, and telling them what I was empowered to promise them. This band, as you are aware, has always been dissatisfied, and have been difficult to deal with. I found them in an intractable frame of mind, and the difficulty of the position was enhanced by a division amongst themselves.

The original Chief of the Portage band was Pee-quah-kee-quah, who was a party to the treaty with Lord Selkirk. On his death he was succeeded by his son, who died some years ago, leaving a boy, who has now grown up. Yellow Quill was appointed chief by the Hudson's Bay Company when Pee-quah-kee-quah's son died. The grandson is now grown up and has returned from the plains, where he has been, and claims to be recognized as an hereditary chief, and about half the band have followed his lead. After we had been in conference some time, an Indian rose and told me that when the chief of the Portage died, he charged him to keep the land for his son, and that they wished a reserve at the Portage. Another rose and produced Pee-quah-kee-quah's King George medal, and said the chief had placed it in his keeping and charged him to deliver it to his son, when he was old enough to be a chief, and then placed it round the neck of Kes-kee-maquah, or the Short Bear. They then asked that I should receive him as a chief, in place of Yellow Quill. I told them that could not be done. That Yellow Quill must remain a chief, but that I would report their request on behalf of the young chief to the Government at Ottawa and let them know their decision, but that they could get no reserve at the Portage, as only that mentioned in the treaty would be given, and with this they were satisfied. The conference then went on, the two parties sitting apart and holding no intercourse with each other. I spent two days with them, making no progress, as they claimed that a reserve thirty miles by twenty was promised them, as shewn in the rough sketch enclosed, made at their dictation and marked "A." I produced the plan of the reserve, as proposed to be allotted to them, containing 34,000 acres, but Yellow Quill said it was not in the right place, and was not what was promised, and morever it was not surrounded by the belt of five miles, mentioned in the treaty, but was only partially so, and did not cross the river. I told them they could get no more land than was promised in the treaty. They appealed to Mr. McKay whether the Reserve was not promised to be on both sides of the river, and he admitted that it was. I told them it was not so written in the treaty, and that if the Government should allow it to cross the river, the rights of navigation must be conserved, but I would cousult the Queen's Councillors. They replied that they would go to the "Grand Father" and get him to intercede for them, meaning the "President of the United States." as I afterwards discovered, an American Indian having persuaded them to take this course.

They refused to discuss or accept anything until the Reserve Question was settled, and while I was speaking on the afternoon of the second day, Yellow Quill's Councillors went away, and left him alone, when he followed.

I then left the Council tent, leaving word that I would depart in the morning. Yellow Quill came back and said that he would accept the five dollars, but Mr. McKay told him he had not taken my hand, and that it would not be paid, as my offer was conditioned on a settlement of all questions between them and the Government. About six o'clock, Yellow Quill and his Councillors sent me the following message which had been written for them by Mr. Deputy Sheriff Setter from their dictation.

"They didn't come to see you. You came to see them, and if you choose to come and speak to them again, you can come if you like."

I felt that I must now deal firmly with them, and therefore prepared the following reply :

"It is not right, for they came to see me at my request, as their Governor, and I came to meet them. After spending two days with them, their Chief insulted me by rising and going out while I was speaking, and breaking up the Conference. I represent the Queen, and his action was disrespectful to her. I will not go to meet you again. If you are sorry for the way I have been treated you can come and see me."

I charged Mr. McKay to deliver it to them in their Council, which he did, when they denied having meant to send the message in the terms in which it was, and disclaimed all intended offence. The message had its desired effect, but their disclaimer was not correct, as Mr. Setter informs me that he had originally written a welcome to me, which they caused him to strike out, and to say that "I could come if I chose." Next morning I struck my tents and loaded my waggons and prepared to leave. Seeing this, Yellow Quill and his Councillors came to Mr. McKay, and asked if I would not see them again, to which I consented. On proceeding to Mr. Provencher's pay tent, I met the Chief, Yellow Quill. His spokesman rose, saying "that they were glad to have met me, that they had found my words good ; that they had not desired to offend the Queen or me, and were sorry ; that God had watched us during two days, and He was again looking on." I accepted their apology, and then proceeded to practical business. the whole tone and demeanor of the Indians being changed, having become cordial and friendly. I may mention here, that Yellow Quill reproached his Councillors for their conduct. He also informed Mr. McKay privately, that he could not act otherwise as he was in danger of his life from some of his own "braves." He was guarded all the time by a man armed with a bow and steel-pointed arrows. I promised to state their claims as to the reserve, but told them it would not be granted, but that I would change the location of the reserve, as it had been selected without their approval, and would represent their view as to its locality, and as to crossing the river, the navigation of which, however, could not be interfered with. They asked to be paid three dollars per head or one dollar per year for the following transaction : In 1868 a number of Ontario farmers had settled on Rat Creek. Yellow Quill's band drove them off and trouble was impending. Governor McTavish sent Mr. McKay up to arrange the difficulty, in anticipation of the advent of Canadian power. He made a lease for three years of their rights, assuring them that before that time the Canadian Government would make a treaty with them and recognize the temporary arrangement, and in consquence the settlers were unmolested. The question was not raised at the "Stone Fort" Treaty, and I told them I had not known of it before, but supposed the Government would hold that the treaty had covered it, and that the extra two dollars would compensate for it, but that I would represent their views and give them an answer. They complained of the mode of payment, as my predecessor assured them that their children who were absent should be paid when they presented themselves, and that they only got two years payment instead of the full amount. As these were Mr. Provencher's instructions I promised to report it. They expressed themselves quite satisfied with the arrangements as to the outside promises, and would gladly accept of it, if the reserve question was settled, but that they could not receive that as surveyed. I took the opportunity of explaining to them that the "President of the United States" had no power here, and that the Queen and Her Councillors were the only authorities they had to deal with, and that I would state their wishes as fully as they could do themselves. They asked if I would come back, but I said not this year, but next year either I or some other Commissioner would meet them. Eventually they cheerfully agreed to accept the three dollars annuity as usual, and to defer a final adjustment of the question between us until next year, and promised to accompany any one I sent to select the reserve and agree on its locality. They again thanked me for my kindness and patience with them, and I took leave of them. I regard the result as very satisfactory, as I left the band contented, and you are aware of their intimate relation with the "Plain Indians," and the difficulty their message to Qu'Appelle, "that the white man had not kept his promises," caused us then, and it is very important that they should be satisfied. I returned to the Portage, and Mr. Provencher proceeded to Totogan, and paid the White Mud section of the band, numbering one hundred and thirty, who are nominally included in it, but do not recognize Yellow Quill's authority, the usual annuities, which they accepted without demur.

I would now make the following recommendations :

1st. That you should write to Yellow Quill declining to entertain his demands for the large reserve, but offering to them a reserve including the "Eagle's Nest" on the north side of the river, and laid off in the terms of the treaty, with the land comprised in the one hundred and sixty acres for each family, surrounded by the belt mentioned in the treaty, in the manner suggested in the enclosed rough sketch "B," reserving the rights of navigation and access to the river. The land is of inferior quality to that already offered them.

2nd. I would propose that the young chief should be recognized as head of the section of the band adhering to him. He and his section are ready to accept the terms and the reserve as described in the treaty. They behaved

10

very well and told Mr. McKay that they were glad I had not recognized him then, as it would have led to bloodshed, and they would be content if the recognition came when the reserve was settled. The young chief is an intelligent, well disposed man, aged about twenty-six.

3rd. I would propose that the White Mud Indians, who live there constantly, should be recognized as a distinct band and should elect a Chief.

4th. I would recommend that the arrears due to Indians who have not yet received their annuities, should be paid in full at once, but that a period of two years should be fixed for those *bona fide* members of the band to come in and be paid, and that after that they should only receive one year's payment. If these steps are taken, I think we shall have no more trouble with these Indians.

In conclusion I have to express my obligations to the Hon. Mr. Mckay for the valuable services he rendered me. The Indians told me they would not have come into the Stone Fort Treaty but for him, and I know it was the case.

I have the honor to be, etc.,

ALEXANDER MORRIS,

Lieut.-Governor.

GOVERNMENT HOUSE,

FORT GARRY, MANITOBA, *8th July 1876,*

TO THE HONORABLE THE MINISTER OF THE INTERIOR.

SIR,—I have the honor to inform you that, in compliance with your request, I left this on the 14th ult. with the view of proceeding to the Long Plain on the Assiniboine, in order to meet the Indians of the Portage Band, to arrange the dispute with regard to the reserve, and to settle the outside promises. Mr. Graham, of the Indian Department, and Mr. Reid, P.L.S., also went there at my request, the one to act as paymaster, and the other, as you wished, to survey the reserve. Owing to the prevalence of heavy rain the roads were in so bad a condition that I was four days in reaching the Long Plain, while we were also subjected to incovenience and expense by the detention of the provisions, owing to the same cause. Added to my other discomforts was the presence of mosquitoes in incredible numbers, so that the journey and the sojourn at the Plain were anything but pleasurable. I had taken the precaution to request Mr. Cummings, the interpreter, to summon the White Mud Indians as well as Yellow Quill's band, and those who adhered to the Short Bear.

On my arrival at the Long Plains, which I accomplished on the 17th, I found about five hundred Indians assembled, but camped in three separate encampments. On arriving, I was saluted by a *feu de joie.* At the Portage, Mr. Graham had obtained some provisions, which he had sent forward in carts.

On our way we met some carts sent by the Indians to relieve my waggons of the tents and baggage, the Indian trail being almost impracticable ; but instead of so using them I sent them on toward the Portage to meet the loaded carts, and was thus enabled to get the temporary supply of provisions to the Plain, which was fortunate, as the Indians were without food. The evening of my arrival the Councillors of Yellow Quill came to talk with me, but I declined to do so, telling them that the Chief had not come, and I would only speak with him. I acted thus, in consequence of the conduct of their head men, last year, when they controlled the Chief and coerced the whole band. In a short time Yellow Quill came with them to see me, and finding that they had come about provisions, I referred them to Mr. Graham, who, I informed them, had charge of the provisions and payments. The incident had a marked effect in giving tone to the following negotiations.

On Monday I met the Indians, who ranged themselves in three parties. I explained to them the proposed arrangement of the outside promises very fully, and told them that as they were willing to accept of the settlement last year, I did so for their information only. I then took up the question of the reserve, read the terms in which it was referred to in the Stone Fort Treaty, explained to them that they were getting double the land any other Indians in Treaties Numbers One and Two were doing, but told them the reserve belonged to all of them, and not to Yellow Quill's band alone. I then called on them to speak to me, asking Yellow Quill first. He said he did not understand the extent of the reserve. I then asked Mr. Reid to shew them a diagram of it, and to explain to them its length in ordinary miles, and otherwise, which he did very satisfactorily, and at length they comprehended it. I then called on Short Bear's band to express their views. They said they wanted a reserve at the Long Plain, if it was only a little piece of land ; that they liked the place, that they had built houses and planted gardens, had cut oak to build more houses, and wished to farm there. I then called on the White Mud Indians. They said that they were Christians and had always lived at the White Mud River ; that they did not wish to join either Yellow Quill's or Short Bear's reserve, but desired a reserve at the Big Point. I told them they could not have it there, as there were settlers, and the Government wished them to join one of the other bands, and explained to them that their holdings would be respected, except where inadvertently sold. I took this course, as I had ascertained that the plan of Yellow Quill's head men was to make no settlement this year, and that they had induced the other Indians to agree to act in that way. I accordingly so shaped my opening speech and my dealings with the Indians as to defeat this project, by securing the support of Short Bear's and the White Mud Indians, which I succeeded in doing, though Yellow Quill's spokesman taunted the others with having broken their agreement. As the conference proceeded, Yellow Quill's councillors said they did not want the band broken up, as they wished all to live together. I told Yellow Quill he would have his reserve on both sides of the river, reserving the navigation, and that if they could agree to go to one reserve, I would be pleased; but if not, that I would settle the matter. Yellow Quill said his councillors were willing that the other Indians should have a separate reserve provided they retained the belt of twenty-five miles, in addition to their proportion of the reserve. I informed them this could not be done; the reserve belonged to all. They then asked for an adjournment, in order that they might meet together and have a smoke over it, to assemble again when I hoisted my flag. After a couple of hours interval I again convened them. The Short Bears and White Mud Indians adhered to what they stated to me, but Yellow Quill's band insisted on one reserve for all, but admitted that the objections of Short Bear's band to the place asked by them were well founded, and that it was sandy and unfit for farming, and that they would like to select a reserve higher up the River Assiniboine. I then adjourned the conference until morning, and asked them to meet together and be prepared for settlement.

On Tuesday, the 20th June, the Indians again responded to the hoisting of my flag, and met at 9 o'clock. Yellow Quill told me that his band were now willing to separate from the others, and wished to select a reserve higher up the river. I informed them that I would accede to their request, but that they must do it at once, and on the approval thereof by the Privy Council it would be laid off. Short Bear's band still desired a reserve at the Long Plain, to which I assented. The White Mud River Indians asked for a separate reserve where they could farm, and I informed them that under the discretionary powers I possessed I would have a reserve selected for them, giving them their proportion of the original reserve. The Indians then asked that the two dollars per head, which had, as they said, slipped through their fingers last year, should be paid to them, and I told them that I had been authorized to do so, which gave them much satisfaction. In anticipation of a settlement I had prepared a draft agreement, which was being copied for me by Mr. Graham. I informed them of this, and stated that I would sign it, and that the Chiefs and Councillors must do so likewise, so that there could be no misunderstanding. When the agreement was completed, I asked Mr. Cummings, the Interpreter, to read it to them, which he did. Three Indians, who understood English, and who had at an early period been selected by the Indians to check the interpretation of what was said, standing by, and Mr. Cummings being assisted by Mr. Cook, of St. James, who, at Mr. Cummings' request, I had associated with him, on the Indians choosing their interpreters. I then signed the agreement, and called upon Yellow Quill to do so. He came forward cheerfully and said he would sign it, because he now understood what he never did before, viz., what was agreed to at the Stone Fort. I then called on his Councillors to sign, but they refused, saying they had agreed by the mouth. I then told the Indians that unless the Councillors signed nothing could be done, and that the Councillors who refused would be responsible for the failure of the negotiations.

One of them then signed, but the other persistently refused. I repeated my warning, and at length he reluctantly came forward and said he wished to ask me a question, "Would the head men be paid?" I told him I had no authority to do so, but would report his request. He said he did not expect it this year, but hoped for it next. Eventually he signed the agreement. I then said I would recognize Short Bear as a Chief, and asked him to select his Councillors and braves. He did so at once, making a judicious choice, and came forward to touch the pen, saying, "I thank you for my people." His Councillors promptly followed, one of them asking for a part of the reserve on the other side of the river, which I refused. I then called on the White Mud River Indians to select a Chief and one Councillor, being under the impression at the time that they were the least numerous band, which, however, has turned out not to be the case, which they did at once, and on their being presented to me they signed the agreement. I then gave a medal to Yellow Quill, and promised to send the other two Chiefs medals when procured from Ottawa, the supply here being exhausted. To the Chiefs and Councillors suits of clothing were then distributed, Yellow Quill and his head men having hitherto refused to accept either medals or coats, but now taking them. Yellow Quill then presented me with a skin coat, and said that he parted with the other Indians as friends, and that there would be no hard feelings. The conference then broke up, and thus terminated a difficulty which has existed for several years, and the influence of which was felt as an obstacle, as you are aware, at Qu'Appelle when the treaty was made there. Mr. Graham at once commenced the payments, and during the evening the three Chiefs and their Councillors called on me, evidently being on the most friendly terms with each other, a state of things which had not existed for a considerable period. In the morning, as I was leaving for the Portage, the Indians assembled near my waggon and gave three cheers for the Queen and three for the Governor, and I then drove off amid a salute of firearms from all sections of the encampment. I left Mr. Graham to complete the payments, and here record my sense of the efficient services he rendered me. He understands the Indian character, and gets on well with them. I requested Mr. Reid to visit the White Mud region and ascertain what persons are entitled to holdings under the terms of your instructions, and also to survey Short Bear's reserve.

Yellow Quill is to go without delay to look up a reserve, and as there are no settlers in the region in question, I propose that if Mr. Reid sees no objection to the locality he should at once lay it off, so as to effectually terminate the chronic difficulty with this band. I shall be glad to receive by telegram your approval of his doing so. The interpreters, Mr. Cummings, Mr. Cook, of St. James, a trader, and Kissoway, an Indian trader belonging to the band, rendered me much service ; the latter trades in the west, and was passing the Portage on his way to Fort Garry, and as he belonged to Yellow Quill's band, and is a relative of his, being a son of the deceased

Pecheto, (another of whose sons was the spokesman at Qu'Appelle, as you will recollect) he came to the Long Plains to advise the band to come to terms. He remained at my request until the negotiations were concluded, and exerted a most beneficial influence over Yellow Quill's band. I call your attention to the request of Yellow Quill's Councillors, that they should be paid. As in Treaties Three, Four and Five, they are paid, and as the expense would not be large, I am of opinion that before the Superintendent of Indian Affairs for the Superintendency of Manitoba proceeds to make the payments in Treaties One and Two, he should be authorized to pay the head men. It will be difficult to explain why the difference is made, and it will secure in every band, men who will feel that they are officers of the Crown and remunerated as such. I returned to Fort Garry on the 23rd inst., encountering on the way a very severe thunder storm, which compelled me to take advantage of the very acceptable shelter of the kindly proffered residence of the Hon. Mr. Breland, at White Horse Plains, instead of a tent on the thoroughly-drenched prairie. I congratulate you that with the successful issue of this negotiation is closed, in Treaties One and Two, the vexed question of the open promises. I forward by this mail a copy of the agreement I have above alluded to, retaining the original for the present, and will be pleased to hear of its speedy approval by the Privy Council.

I have the honor to be, etc.,

ALEXANDER MORRIS,
Lieut.-Governor.

CHAPTER VIII.

THE WINNIPEG TREATY, NUMBER FIVE.

THIS treaty, covers an area of approximately about 100,000 square miles. The region is inhabited by Chippewas and Swampy Crees. The necessity for it had become urgent. The lake is a large and valuable sheet of water, being some three hundred miles long. The Red River flows into it and the Nelson River flows from it into Hudson's Bay. Steam navigation had been successfully established by the Hudson's Bay Company on Lake Winnipeg. A tramway of five miles in length was being built by them to avoid the Grand Rapids and connect that navigation with steamers on the River Saskatchewan. On the west side of the lake, a settlement of Icelandic immigrants had been founded, and some other localities were admirably adapted for settlement. Moreover, until the construction of the Pacific Railway west of the city of Winnipeg, the lake and Saskatchewan River are destined to become the principal thoroughfare of communication between Manitoba and the fertile prairies in the west. A band of Indians residing at Norway House, who had supported themselves by serving the Hudson's Bay Company as boatmen on the route from Lake Winnipeg to the Hudson Bay, by way of the Nelson River, but whose occupation was gone, owing to supplies being brought in by way of the Red River, desired to migrate to the western shore of Lake Winnipeg, and support themselves there by farming.

For these and other reasons, the Minister of the Interior reported " that it was essential that the Indian title to all the

territory in the vicinity of the lake should be extinguished so
that settlers and traders might have undisturbed access to its
waters, shores, islands, inlets and tributary streams." The mouth
of the Saskatchewan River especially seemed to be of importance, as presenting an eligible site for a future town.   For
these reasons the Privy Council of Canada, in the year 1875,
appointed Lieut.-Gov. Morris, and the Hon. James McKay, to
treat with these Indians.   It may be here stated that this
remarkable man, the son of an Orkneyman by an Indian
mother, has recently died at a comparatively early age.   Originally in the service of the Hudson's Bay Company, he became
a trader on his own account.   Thoroughly understanding the
Indian character, he possessed large influence over the Indian
tribes, which he always used for the benefit and the advantage
of the Government.

The Hudson's Bay Company, to resume this narrative, kindly
placed their propeller steamer, the *Colville*, at the service of
the Commissioners, and the Board in London, in view of the
public service rendered by its use by the Commissioners, eventually declined to make any charge for its employment.   A
full report of the voyage of the Commissioners, and of the results of their mission, will be found in the despatch of the
Lieutenant-Governor, which will be found at the end of this
chapter.   Suffice it to say, that the Commissioners proceeded
first to Berens River, on the east side of the lake, and made a
treaty with the Indians of that side of the lake, thence they
sailed to the head of Lake Winnipeg, descended the Nelson
River to Norway House, where no steamer had ever before
been, and concluded a treaty with the Indians there.

They also promised the Indians to give those of them who
chose to remove, a reserve on the west side of Lake Winnipeg,
at Fisher's River, about forty miles from the Icelandic settlement.

A considerable number of families have since removed there,
and have formed a very promising settlement.

From Nelson River the Commissioners proceeded to the

mouth of the Great Saskatchewan River, and met the Indians who live there. Their houses were built at the foot of the Grand Rapids, and in the immediate vicinity of the Hudson's Bay, Tramway, some seven miles from the mouth of the river. The river is here deep to the very shore, so that the steamer ran long aside the bank, and was moored by ropes attached to the Chief's house. The Commissioners met the Indians and informed them of the desire of the Government to control the land where they had settled, and to give them a reserve, instead, on the opposite side of the river. They said, they would surrender the locality in question, and go to the south side of the river, if a small sum was given them, to aid them in removing their houses or building others. To this the Commissioners willingly acceded, and promised that the next year a sum of five hundred dollars would be paid them for that purpose. The treaty was then signed, the Commissioners having extended the boundaries of the treaty limits, so as to include the Swampy Cree Indians at the Pas or Wahpahpuha, a settlement on the Saskatchewan River, and recommended that Commissioners should be sent in the ensuing summer to complete the work. The Commissioners then returned to Winnipeg, after a voyage, on and around the lake, of about one thousand miles. The terms of the treaty were identical with those of Treaties Numbers Three and Four, except that a smaller quantity of land was granted to each family, being one hundred and sixty, or in some cases one hundred acres to each family of five, while under Treaties Numbers Three and Four the quantity of land allowed was six hundred and forty acres to each such family. The gratuity paid each Indian in recognition of the treaty was also five dollars per head, instead of twelve dollars the circumstances under which the treaty was made being different. The area covered by these treaties was approximately about 100,000 square miles and has been described as lying north of the territory covered by Treaties Numbers Two and Three, extending west to Cumberland House (on the Saskatchewan

River) and including the country east and west of Lake Winnipeg, and of Nelson River as far north as Split Lake.

In 1876, Lieut.-Gov. Morris, in accordance with his suggestions to that effect, was requested by the Minister of the Interior, to take steps for completing the treaty, and entrusted the duty to the Hon. Thomas Howard, and J. Lestock Reid, Esq., Dominion Land Surveyor. He gave them formal instructions, and directed them to meet the Indians together at Dog Head Point, on the lake, to treat with the Island Indians there and thence to proceed to Berens River to meet the Indians of the rapids of that river who had not been able to be present the previous year, and thereafter directed Mr. Howard to proceed to the mouth of the Saskatchewan and pay the Indians the five hundred dollars for removal of the houses, and thence to go up the Saskatchewan to the Pas and deal with the Indians there, while Mr. Reid was to proceed from Berens River to Norway House, and arrange with the Indians for the removal of such of them as desired it, to Fisher's River, on Lake Winnipeg.

These gentlemen accordingly in July, 1876, proceeded in York boats (large sail boats) to their respective destinations, and were very successful in accomplishing the work confided to them.

I now append the official despatch of Lieut.-Gov. Morris, dated 11th October, 1875, giving an account of the making of the treaty and of the journey, and his despatch of the 17th November, 1876, relating to the completion of the treaty, together with extracts from the reports of Messrs. Howard and Reid.

FORT GARRY, *October 11th, 1875.*

TO THE HONORABLE THE MINISTER OF THE INTERIOR.

SIR,—I have the honor to inform you, that under authority of the Commission of the Privy Council to that effect, I proceeded to Lake Winnipeg for the purpose of making a treaty with the Saulteaux and Swampy Cree Indians, in company with my associate, the Hon. James McKay, leaving Fort Garry for Chief Prince's Landing on the Red River, on the 17th September last, in order to embark on the Hudson's Bay Company's new propeller, the

Colville, which Chief Commissioner Graham had kindly placed at our disposal on advantageous terms. We selected this mode of conveyance, as travelling and conveyance of provisions in York boats would, at the advanced period of the season, have occupied at least eight weeks, if at all practicable.

The steamer left the landing at five o'clock on the 18th September, but owing to the prevalence of a gale of northerly wind was compelled to be anchored at the three channels of the Red River, inside of the bar which obstructs the entrance of the lake. The wind continued during the 18th and 19th, but on the afternoon of the latter day, Captain Hackland, a sailor of much practical experience on the Northern Seas, decided to risk going out, as the water on the bar was running down so fast that he feared that the steamer would be unable to cross over the bar. I may remark that the wind causes the waters of the lake to ebb and flow into the river with great rapidity, and that the bar is so serious an obstruction to an important navigation, that it ought to be examined with a view to ascertain the cost and practicability of its removal. Leaving our anchorage, we crossed the bar at three in the afternoon with difficulty, and proceeded on our voyage; anchored opposite the mouth of the Berens River on Monday, the 20th, at nine a.m., to await the arrival of a pilot, as no steamer had ever before entered the river. Under the pilotage of a Chief and a Councillor, we reached Berens River Post, the Indians greeting us with volleys of firearms, and at once summoned the Indians to meet us in the Wesleyan Mission School House, which the Rev. Mr. Young kindly placed at our disposal. We met the Indians at four o'clock, and explained the object of our visit. The question of reserves was one of some difficulty, but eventually this was arranged, and the Indians agreed to accept our offer, and the indenture of treaty was signed by the Chiefs and head men about eleven p.m. The payment of the present of five dollars per head, provided by the treaty, was immediately commenced by Mr. McKay and the Hon. Thomas Howard, who accompanied me as Secretary and Pay Master, and was continued until one a.m., when the payment was concluded.

The steamer left next day, the 21st, for Norway House, but the captain was obliged to anchor at George's Island in the evening, owing to the stormy weather. The *Colville* remained at anchor all the next day, the 22nd, but left at midnight for Nelson River. We sighted the Mossy and Montreal points, at the mouth of that river, about nine a.m. on the 23rd, and arrived at the old or abandoned Norway House at eleven o'clock, under the guidance of Roderick Ross, Esquire, of the Hudson's Bay Company's Service, at Norway House, who had been engaged for some days in examining the channel, in anticipation of our visit.

The Nelson River expands into Play Green Lake, a large stream of water studded with islands, presenting a remarkable resemblance to the Thousand Islands of the St. Lawrence River. The distance from the mouth of the river to Norway House is twenty miles. We arrived at Norway House at three o'clock and were welcomed there by the Indians, who fired a salute.

On the 24th we met the Indians in a large store-house of the Hudson's Bay Company, and asked them to present their Chiefs and head men. We found that there were two distinct bands of Indians, the Christian Indians of Norway House, and the Wood or Pagan Indians of Cross Lake. Each elected their Chiefs by popular vote in a most business-like manner, and the Chiefs, after consulting the bands, selected the head men. We then accepted the Chiefs, and I made an explanation of the object of our visit in English, and the Hon. James McKay in the Indian dialect. We severed the questions of terms and reserves, postponing the latter till we had disposed of the former. The Indians gratefully accepted of the offered terms, and we adjourned the conference to enable them to consult as to reserves. On re-assembling, the Christian Chief stated that as they could no longer count on employment in boating for the Hudson's Bay Company, owing to the introduction of steam navigation, he and a portion of his band wished to migrate to Lake Winnipeg, where they could obtain a livelihood by farming and fishing. We explained why we could not grant them a reserve for that purpose at the Grassy Narrows as they wished, owing to the proposed Icelandic settlement there, but offered to allot them a reserve at Fisher River, about forty miles north of the Narrows, and this they accepted. It is supposed that some eighty or ninety families will remove there in spring, and it was arranged that those who remain, instead of receiving a reserve, should retain their present houses and gardens. The Chief of the Pagan band, who has, however, recently been baptized, stated that the Wood Indians wished to remain at Cross Lake, and we agreed that a reserve should be allotted them there. The treaty was then signed and the medals and uniforms presented. The Chiefs, on behalf of their people, thanked Her Majesty and her officers for their kindness to the Indian people, which I suitably acknowledged, and the payment of the presents was commenced by Messrs. McKay and Howard, and completed on the 15th.

We left that day at half-past three amidst cheering by the Indians and a salute of fire-arms, and came to anchor in Play Green Lake, at Kettle Island, at half-past five.

The steamer left Kettle Island next morning at six o'clock for the Grand Rapids of the Saskatchewan, which we reached at four o'clock.

The original post of the Hudson's Bay Company, at the mouth of the river, has been abandoned, and a new one established on their reserve, some six miles higher up the river, at the head of the portage, which the river steamer descends to. The *Colville*, at our request ran up to the Chief's house, situated on the shore of a deep bay, and was moored and gangways laid out to the shore. We found an Indian village on the north side, and also the Chief's house, which was built on the only spot where good and inexpensive wharfage can be had, and ascertained afterwards that the Indians claimed the whole north shore for a reserve.

On the 27th we met the Indians near the Chief's house in the open air, at a spot where a large fire had been lighted by them, as the weather was cold. We took a similar course as at Norway House in severing the question of terms of the treaty and reserves, and with like satisfactory results. After a lengthy discussion the Indians agreed to accept the terms, and we then entered upon the difficult question of the reserves. They complained of the Hudson's Bay Campany's reserve, and wished to have the land covered by it, but we explained whatever had been promised the Company would be given just as promises made to them would be kept. They said the Company's reserve should be at the abandoned post at the mouth of the river, and not at the end of the portage. We informed them that we would inquire as to this. They then claimed a reserve on both sides of the river of large extent, and extending up to the head of the Grand Rapids, but this we declined to accede to. Eventually, as the locality they had hitherto occupied is so important a point, controlling as it does the means of communication between the mouth of the river, and the head of the rapids, and where a " tram-way " will no doubt ere long require to be constructed, presenting also deep-water navigation and excellent wharfage, and evidently being moreover the site where a town will spring up, we offered them reserve on the south side of the river. They objected, that they had their houses and gardens on the north side of the river, but said that as the Queen's Government were treating them so kindly, that they would go to south side of the river, if a small sum was given them to assist in removing their houses, or building others, and this as will be seen by the terms of the treaty, we agreed to do, believing it to be alike in the interests of the Government to have the control of so important a point as the mouth of the great internal river of the Saskatchewan, and yet only just to the Indians, who were making what was to them so large a concession to the wishes of the Commissioners. On our agreeing to the proposal, the treaty was cheerfully signed by the Chief and head men, and the payment of the present was made to them, together with a distribution of some provisions. I enclose a tracing of the mouth of the river, copied from a sketch thereof kindly made for me by Mr. Ross, which will enable you to understand the actual position of the locality in question, and the better appreciate our reasons for our action in the matter.

The steamer left the Grand Rapids in the afternoon of the 27th, and the captain took his course for the mouth of the Red River, but anchored, as the night became very dark, between George's Island and Swampy Island.

On the 28th, resuming our course at half-past five a.m., we sighted Berens River Mission House at eight o'clock, and passed into the channel between Black Bear Island and Dog Head or Wapang Point, at 12.30 ; then observing a number of Indians on the shore making signals to us by firing guns, we requested the captain to approach the shore. The water being very deep the steamer went close inshore and anchored—the Indians coming off to us in their canoes. We found them to be headed by Thickfoot, a principal

Indian of the band inhabiting the islands, and some of those and the Jack Head band of the West Shore, and explained to them the object of our visit. They told us they had heard of it, and had been waiting to see us. Thickfoot said the Island Indians at Big Island, Black Island, Wapang and the other islands in the vicinity had no chief; that they numbered one hundred and twenty-eight, and those at Jack-Fish Head sixty. Thickfoot said he had cattle and would like to have a place assigned to his people on the main shore, where they could live by farming and fishing. We suggested Fisher River to them, which they approved of. Eventually we decided on paying these Indians—took Thickfoot's adhesion to the treaty, of which I enclose a copy, and authorized him to notify the Indians to meet at the Dog Head Point next summer, at a time to be intimated to them, and to request them in the mean time to select a Chief and Councillors. Thickfoot expressed gratitude for the kindness of the Government, and his belief that Indians of the various Islands and of Jack Head Point would cheerfully accept the Queen's benevolence and settle on a reserve. After paying this party, and distributing a small quantity of provisions among them, we resumed our voyage, and, owing to the character of the navigation, again came to anchor in George's Channel at seven o'clock, p.m. On the 29th, we left our anchorage at five o'clock a.m., and entered the mouth of the Red River at twelve o'clock, crossing the bar without difficulty, as the weather was calm. We arrived at the Stone Fort at three o'clock in the afternoon, but had to remain there till next day, awaiting the arrival of conveyances from Winnipeg. Mr. McKay and I left the Stone Fort on the 30th at seven a.m. leaving our baggage and a portion of the provisions which had not been used to be forwarded by the steamer *Swallow*, and reached Fort Garry at ten o'clock, thus terminating a journey of over one thousand miles, and having satisfactorily closed a treaty with the Saulteaux and Swampy Crees, which will prove of much importance in view of the probable rapid settlement of the west coast of Lake Winnipeg. The journey, moreover, is of interest, as having been the first occasion on which a steam vessel entered the waters of Berens River and of the Nelson River, the waters of which river fall into the Hudson's Bay, and as having demonstrated the practicability of direct steam navigation through a distance of three hundred and sixty miles from the city of Winnipeg to Norway House. I may mention here that the prevalence of timber suitable for fuel and building purposes, of lime and sandstone, of much good soil, and natural hay lands on the west shore of the lake, together with the great abundance of white fish, sturgeon and other fish in the lake, will ensure, ere long, a large settlement.

The east coast is much inferior to the west coast, as far as I could learn, but appeared to be thickly wooded, and it is understood that indications of minerals have been found in several places.

I now beg to call your attention to the boundaries of the treaty, which, you will observe, vary somewhat from those suggested in your memorandum to the Privy Council. The Commissioners adopted as the southern boundary of the treaty limits, the northern boundary of Treaties Numbers Two and Three. They included in the limits all the territory to which the Indians ceding, claimed hunting and other rights, but they fixed the western boundary as defined in the treaty, for the following reasons :

1st. The extension of the boundary carries the treaty to the western limit of the lands claimed by the Saulteaux and Swampy Cree Tribes of Indians, and creates an eastern base for the treaties to be made with the Plain Crees next year.

2nd. The Swampy Crees at the Pas, on the Saskatchewan, would otherwise have had to be included in the western treaties.

3rd. That the extension of the boundaries will add some six hundred to the number of Indians in the suggested limits, of whom three hundred at Wahpahhuha or the Pas on the Saskatchewan would have had to be treated with owing to the navigation of the Saskatchewan, in any event.

4th. The inclusion of the Norway House Indians in the treaty, and the surrender of their rights, involved a larger area of territory.

5th. That a number of the Norway House Indians came from Moose Lake and the Cumberland region, and possessed rights there which have been included in the boundaries.

6th. Unless the boundaries had been properly defined, in conformity with known geographical points, a portion of the country lying between the territories formerly ceded and those comprised in Treaty Number Five, would have been left with the Indian title unextinguished.

For these reasons, the Commissioners defined the boundaries as they are laid down in the treaty, and it will remain with the Government to send a Commissioner to the Pas to obtain the adhesion of the Indians there to the treaty next summer, or not as they shall decide, though the Commissioners strongly urge that step to be taken as a necessity.

I forward the original of the treaty to you by the Hon. Mr. Christie, and in order to the better understanding of the treaty area, I enclose a very valuable map copied from one made for me at my request on board of the *Colville*, by Roderick Ross, Esq., who accompanied me from Norway House to the Stone Fort, and to whom I was indebted for much valuable assistance and co-operation, as we were in fact to the Company's officers generally. This map is prepared from actual observation, and locates many places not indicated on any existing map, and covering as it does an area of over 100,000 square miles, which, exclusive of the great waters, has been included in the treaty, possesses much value.

I enclose herewith duplicates of the pay sheets, a statement of the cash expenditure, shewing the balance on hand of the credit which was given me for the purposes of the treaty, and statements of the distribution of the provisions and of the clothing, and medals, as given to the chiefs and head men. These statements will shew that every arrangement was made to secure the utmost economy in effecting the treaty, and yet to give satisfaction to the Indians concerned.

I mention here that the Indians were uniformly informed that no back payments of the present would be made to those who did not attend the meetings with the Commissioners, but that next year those not present would receive payment with the others, if they presented themselves.

I have to express my sense of the services rendered to the Government by my associate the Hon. James McKay, and the Hon. Thomas Howard, who acted as Secretary and Pay Master to the Commissioners as well as of the many kind services we received from Captain Hackland, and the other officers of the *Colville*, from the Wesleyan Missionaries, and from the officers of the Hudson's Bay Company.

• I take this opportunity of suggesting that the supervision of Treaty Number Five, and the carrying out of the treaty obligations with the Indians of the St. Peter's Band, and of those of Fort Alexander and the River Roseau and Broken Head, which fall into Lake Winnipeg, should be entrusted to a local agent, stationed at the Stone Fort or in the vicinity of St. Peter's, and who would thence supervise the whole District.

In conclusion, I have only to express the hope that the action of the Commissioners, which in every respect was governed by a desire to promote the public interest, will receive the approval of the Privy Council, and be regarded by them as the satisfactory discharge of an onerous and responsible duty.

I have the honor to be, Sir,

Your obedient servant,

ALEXANDER MORRIS,

Lieut.-Gov. N. W. T.

GOVERNMENT HOUSE,

FORT GARRY, *17th November, 1876.*

TO THE HONORABLE THE MINISTER OF THE INTERIOR.

Sir,—I recommended in my despatch of the 7th June, that measures should be adopted to secure the adhesion of the Indians, who had not been met with when Treaty Number Five was concluded, and was requested by you to entrust the duty to Mr. Graham, of the Indian Department here, or to the Hon. Thomas Howard, Mr. Graham was unable to leave the office. I, therefore entrusted the matter to Mr. Howard and J. Lestock Reid, D.L.S. I gave these gentleman written instructions, a copy of which will be found appended to the report of Mr. Howard, in which I directed them to meet the Island Indians and those of Berens River together, and then to separate, Mr. Reid proceeding to Norway House and Mr. Howard to the Grand Rapids of the Saskatchewan and the Pas, this course being necessary to enable the work to be accomplished during the season. I have pleasure in informing you that these gentlemen discharged their mission most successfully and satisfactorily, as will be seen from the following reports, which I enclose, viz :—

A. Joint report of Messrs. Howard and Reid as to the Island Indians of Lake Winnipeg and those of Berens River.

B. Report of Mr. Howard as to the band at the Grand Rapids, and as to his negotiations with the Indians at the Pas.

C. Report of Mr. Reid with regard to the Norway House Indians.

D. Report of Mr. Howard, submitting the accounts of the expenditure incurred in carrying out my instructions.

1. It will appear from these reports that the Commissioners obtained the assent of the scattered bands among the islands and shores of Lake Winnipeg, and had them united in a band with one Chief and his Councillors.

2. That the Indians of the Grand Rapids of the Berens River accepted the treaty, being received as part of the band of Jacob Berens, and that the latter band wish their reserves to be allotted them and some hay lands assigned.

3. That the Norway House Indians contemplate removal to Fisher's River, on Lake Winnipeg.

4. That the Indians of Grand Rapids have removed, as they agreed to do last year, from the point where they had settled on the Saskatchewan, and which had been set apart as the site of a town.

5. That the Indians of the Pas, Cumberland, and Moose Lake gave their adhesion to the treaty, and, subject to the approval of the Privy Council, have agreed upon the localities for their reserves.

6. That the bands at the Grand Rapids, the Pas, and Cumberland are in a sufficiently advanced position to be allowed the grant for their schools.

I forward herewith the balance sheet of Mr. Howard for the receipts and disbursements connected with the completion of the treaty and the payments, as also the various vouchers in support thereof. I placed the charge of the financial arrangements in the hands of Mr. Howard, on whom also fell the longest period of service in the work entrusted to the Commissioners.

I also forward by parcel post, registered, the original of the assents to the treaty of the various bands.

To prevent complications and misunderstandings, it would be desirable that many of the reserves should be surveyed without delay, and, from Mr. Reid's connection with the treaty, and his fitness for the work, I think that he would be a suitable person to be employed in the duty.

I would remark in conclusion, that I requested Mr. Provencher to obtain the assent to the treaty of the band at the mouth of the Black River, and that he informs me that he obtained their adhesion and has so reported to you. The having obtained the assent of the whole of the Indians within the region treated for so far, is a most satisfactory feature of the year's operations.

I have, &c.,

ALEXANDER MORRIS,
Lieut.-Governor.

A.

WINNIPEG, *October 10th, 1876.*

TO THE HON. ALEXANDER MORRIS,
        Lieutenant-Governor, Fort Garry.

SIR,—Under instructions received from you, dated 14th July last, we were directed to proceed to the Dog Head Point and Berens River, on Lake Winnipeg, and there obtain the adhesion of certain Indians to the treaty that was made and concluded at Norway House last year, and we have now the honor to report . . . . .

With a fair wind and fine weather we reached the Narrows on Monday afternoon, the 24th, at half-past four. Mr. Howard called at the Hudson's Bay Company's post to see about the provisions stored there, where he found Thickfoot and the Jack-Fish Head Indians encamped, about twenty-five families in all, and learned from them that they were desirous to meet and speak to us where they were, and not across the Narrows at the Dog Head ; but as the place of meeting was distinctly fixed, Mr. Howard informed them that they would have to move their camps.

Mr. Reid having, in the meantime, gone to the Dog Head Point, was received with a salute from the Indians there encamped, viz. : the Blood Vein River, Big Island and Sandy Bar bands, and, almost simultaneously with Mr. Howard's arrival there, the Indians belonging to Thickfoot and the Jack-Fish Head arrived also.

We hardly had time to make our camp before being waited upon by a representative from all the bands except Thickfoot's, and they desired to know when we would be prepared to have a conference ; and, having told them that the following day, the 25th, was the day appointed, and that we would meet them at eleven o'clock in the morning, we gave them some provisions and they withdrew. Thickfoot subsequently called upon us and stated that he was prepared at any time to meet us and sign the treaty, that he had learned that it was our intention to make only one Chief for all the Indians gathered there ; that he had felt when the paper was placed in his hands last year by the Governor, that he was making him the Chief ; that he had notified all the Indians that were there as he had agreed, and that they had threatened him with violence for saying he was to be Chief, and that he was afraid now to join them in any way, and that he and his band wished to be spoken to by themselves. Upon hearing this, we informed him that he need not be afraid of violence, that the paper the Governor gave him merely stated that he was a principal Indian, and we would certainly recognize him as such, and if the Indians desired him to be their Chief it would be a great pleasure to us.

The following morning the Indians sent word by a representative from each band, except Thickfoot's, that they desired another day to meet in council before having a conference ; but, feeling they had sufficient time already, yet not wishing to hurry them too much, we extended the hour of meeting to four o'clock on the same day, which satisfied them, and when they promised to be ready.

About three o'clock, we were informed that the Indians had gathered, so we at once proceeded to meet them. The place we had chosen for the conference was on a granite plateau, and at one end our crews had erected a covering with boughs; a more suitable spot for the meeting could not be found.

After inquiring if they had all gathered, and, being assurred that they had, we began to explain the object of our mission, but immediately saw that the bands were determined to be considered distinct and wished to be treated with separately, when we informed them that only one Chief would be allowed, and that before we could proceed any further we would require them all to meet together in council and there select one Chief and three Councillors, and be prepared to present them to us on the following day. This evidently gave great satisfaction to the Island Band, of which Ka-tuk-e-pin-ois was head man, but they all withdrew ; before doing so, agreeing to be ready the next day at noon to meet us.

Before the hour appointed for the meeting the next day, another delegation came over and informed us that the Indians were not yet prepared, that they could not come to any decision as to who should be Chief, and again asked to have the hour of meeting extended to three o'clock, which we did upon the understanding that if they were not then prepared we would return and report the facts to you.

Shortly after, we noticed Thickfoot and his Indians sitting near our tents, and evidently taking no part in the selection of a Chief, so we called him over and found him still disinclined to join the other Indians. He stated that they would not have him as Chief, and that he would therefore remain away. We then explained that he could he head man of his band by being elected a Councillor to whoever would be appointed Chief, and at last prevailing upon him to go with his Indians to the Council tent, we requested the Rev. Mr. Cochrane to proceed to the Indian encampment and state to them that from each band other than the one from which the chief was chosen, a Councillor would have to be taken. By this means we saw our way to satisfy all the bands, and Mr. Cochrane having notified the Indians accordingly, we felt confident the choice of a chief would soon be made ; but in this we were disappointed, as a messenger shortly after arrived and said no choice could be made, as Ka-tuk-e-pin-ais would do nothing unless he was chosen Chief. On hearing this Mr. Cochrane decided to visit the Indians in Council, and, having done so, proposed to them that they should elect a Chief by ballot, and having got them all to agree to this proposition, they proceeded to the election. Several ballots had to be taken, and at last resulted in favor of the chief Indian of the Blood Vein River band, Sa-ha-cha-way-ass, and the Councillors elected were the head men from the Big Island, Doghead and Jack-Fish Head bands.

At three o'clock p.m., we were notified that the Indians had again gathered, when we proceeded to the place of meeting, and were presented to the Chief and two of his Councillors. Ka-tuk-e-pin-ais, the third Councillor, coming forward, said his band did not want him to act as Councillor; that he had seen the Governor the other day, and had been told by him that he would be the Chief of the Island Indians. Whereupon we informed him that no such promise had been made by you, and that we could only recognize the choice of the majority. He then desired to withdraw from the negotiations, and wait until he saw you, before signing the treaty; but as we had learned that out of the twenty-two families that were in his band, all, with one or two exceptions, had received the annuity since 1870, with the St. Peter's Band, we made them sit by themselves, and then explained that by receiving the annuity as a large number of them had done, they had really agreed to the treaty, and that we were there only to deal with those of the band that had at no time received money from the Queen. Ka-tuk-e-pin-ais then said that there were very few of his Indians that had not received money from the Queen, but that he never had; that he was quite prepared to sign the treaty now, only some of his people did not want him to do so, unless we agreed to give them the Big Island for a reserve. This we at once refused, and at the same time told them that unless he and all his band agreed to the terms we offered them without further delay, they might return to their homes. Hearing this, they all withdrew, but soon returned, when Ka-tuk-e-pin-ais said one or two of his people did not want him to sign any treaty, but most of them did, and that he was going to do so. He then took his seat along with the Chiefs and other Councillors, and we proceeded to explain the terms of the treaty. When we came to the clause referring to the reserves, each band was anxious that the places where they are in the habit of living should be granted them as reserves, and the locations of the same mentioned in the treaty; but as our instructions were positive on this point, we refused, but assured them that the names of the places they asked for, we would certainly forward with our report to you, and we stated that with the exception of the location asked for by the Sandy Bar Indians, we felt sure the Government would grant their request, and give them their reserves where they desired. The following were the localities mentioned :—

DOG HEAD BAND.—The point opposite the Dog Head.

BLOOD VEIN RIVER BAND.—At mouth of Blood Vein River.

BIG ISLAND BAND.—At mouth of Badthroat River.

JACK-FISH HEAD BAND.—The north side of Jack Head Point, at the Lobstick, and the

SANDY BAR BAND.—White Mud River, west side of Lake Winnipeg.

It must be remembered that four bands out of the above named, viz.:— Big Island, Jack-Fish Head, Dog Head and Blood Vein River, are distinct bands, those at Sandy Bar really belonging to the St. Peter's Band of Indians and that they have always lived at the different points upon the lake from which they take their names, and they therefore look upon these points as their homes. We would, therefore, beg to recommend that the request of of all, with the exception of the Sandy Bar Indians, be granted, although in doing so we are aware of the desire of the Government that Indians should not be encouraged to break up into small bands, yet we feel sure in this instance it would be impossible to get them all upon any one reserve.

The adhesion we had signed on Wednesday evening, July 26th, and we then arranged to begin the payments of annuities the following morning at nine o'clock, which was done, and the payments completed by four o'clock on the same day. We then distributed the implements, ammunition, twine, and balance of provisions.

As already stated, the Indians at Sandy Bar, were formerly paid with the St. Peter's band. They are now included in the limits of Treaty Five, and desire to receive their annuity with the Island band.

Having distributed the presents, we immediately moved our camp to an island about a quarter of a mile from the Point, and there remained until Saturday morning, the 29th, when, having a favourable wind, we set sail and arrived off the mouth of Berens River, and camped on Lobstick Island the following morning, Sunday, at half-past nine o'clock.

We remained there until Tuesday, and then moved our camp to the Methodist Mission. The next day we went over in one of our boats to the Hudson's Bay Company's post, where we met Mr. Flett, the officer in charge and received from him the provisions that had been previously forwarded and which he had in store, and then returned to our camp.

Mr. Flett informed us that the Indians from the Narrows of Berens River, he expected would arrive that evening, and on Thursday, visited us to say that they had arrived and were then holding a council. The same afternoon the Chief and Councillors called upon us and desired to know when we would be prepared to meet them, and though the 5th was the day appointed, we thought it advisable, as all the Indians were then gathered there, and were anxious to return to their homes, to appoint the following day, the 4th August.

The next morning the Indians came over from where they were encamped near the Hudson's Bay post, in York boats ; and when we learned that they were all in the school-house we proceeded there, and met, in addition to the Berens River band, about thirty Indians from the Grand Rapids of Berens River. We explained the object of our mission, and found the Indians from the Rapids most anxious to accept the Queen's bounty and benevolence, some of them had already accepted the annuity with the Lac Seule Indians we found, so we immediately told them that it was only to those that had not previously received money or presents from the Queen, that the first part of our mission extended, and with whom it was necessary we should first speak. The head man, Num-ak-ow-ah-nuk-wape, then said that he was fully prepared, on behalf of all his Indians, to accept the same terms as given to the Berens

River band, only he wanted his reserve where he then lived, at the Grand Rapids ; upon which we told him that before we could speak further, we must be assured by the band that he was their head man, and this the band at once did. We then thought it advisable to recommend that they should make the Chief of the Berens River band their Chief, and make their head man a Councillor to him, and although our proposition was not at once received satisfactorily, we ultimately prevailed upon them to accept it, and the Chief was at once elected. By this means we saved the expenses necessarily incurred in maintaining one Chief and two Councillors. We then stated that we were prepared to grant them their reserve where they asked for it ; and having explained the treaty to them, clause by clause, and mentioned in the adhesion where the reserve should be, the adhesion was duly signed by the Chief and Councillors. The payment of the annuity was then gone on with and finished that afternoon at four o'clock.

We then distributed the implements, ammunition, twine and provisions. When we had finished, the Chief and Councillors came forward, and thanked us for all that had been done for them ; they said they were well pleased with what they had received, and desired us to inform you of the fact, which we accordingly promised. They then returned in the same boats they had come over in : before leaving the bank, giving three cheers for the Queen and three for the Governor.

We are very much pleased to inform you that the best possible feeling appears to exist between the Indians in this region. They all appeared anxious to farm and settle down, and we heard that a number of houses had been built at Poplar River, and considerable clearing done there since the treaty was made with them last year ; the implements and tools we brought them were therefore most acceptable. As these bands live at a considerable distance from each other, we would recommend that an extra supply of tools be allowed them. We also feel satisfied that the animals promised by the treaty might be furnished, as we certainly consider them in a position to take care of the same.

As you directed, we informed them that their application for hay lands had been forwarded to the Government, and this gave them great satisfaction. The following morning, Saturday, August 5th, Mr. Reid left for Norway House, and during the afternoon of the same day, Mr. Howard sailed for the Stone Fort on the Red River.

Having obtained the adhesion of the Indians at the Dog Head, and at Berens River, our duties as Joint Commissioners under your instructions ceased. . . . .

We were fortunate enough to secure the services of the Rev. Henry Cochrane, who kindly acted as interpreter. Being in the Province on a visit from his mission at the Pas, and desirous of returning, Mr. Howard gave him a passage in his boat, and he rendered us the most valuable assistance throughout.

Having thus referred to the different matters connected with our mission while acting together, and assuring you that our aim and desire was to fulfill it to your entire satisfaction, which we trust we have done,

We have the honor to be, Sir,

Your obedient servants,

THOS. HOWARD,

J. LESTOCK REID,

Commissioners..

B.

WINNIPEG, *October 10th, 1876.*

To THE HONORABLE ALEXANDER MORRIS,

Lieutenant-Governor, Fort Garry.

SIR,—I have the honor to inform you that in compliance with your instructions, a copy of which I hereunto annex, I proceeded, accompanied by Mr. Reid, to the Dog Head and Berens River on Lake Winnipeg, and there successfully secured the adhesion of the Island and Grand Rapids of Berens River Bands of Indians to Treaty Number Five, and, having paid the annuities to the Berens River Indians, returned to the Stone Fort. As mentioned in the joint report submitted to you by Mr. Reid and myself, I had the greatest difficulty in procuring a boat to take me on my mission, and only through the kindness of Mr. Flett, of the Hudson's Bay Company, at the Stone Fort, was I able to obtain even the loan of one as far as Berens River, from where I had to return it. . . . .

I left the Stone Fort for the Grand Rapids, on the morning of the 17th of August, and after a very fast, though rough and dangerous passage, reached the mouth of the Saskatchewan river, early on the morning of the 26th. I found, on entering the river, that the Indians were encamped near its mouth, on the south bank, where I landed, and arranged to meet them at noon that day. As the provisions were stored at the Hudson's Bay Company's post, about a mile and a half up the river, I decided to camp at the foot of the road leading across the four-mile Portage, and having done so, and in the meantime sent the provisions to the Indian camp, I returned there at the time agreed upon.

The band having assembled, I stated to them the object of my mission— that I had been directed to pay them the annuity and deliver some of the tools and implements granted them by the treaty, and also to distribute amongst those that formerly had houses and gardens on the north bank of the river, and had moved to where they were then living, as stipulated in the treaty, the sum of five hundred dollars.

To my surprise, the Chief at once expressed his astonishment at my saying that the treaty had been made last year, and said he had only a talk then with the Governor preliminary to making the treaty this year, and that they were only then prepared to be treated with.   I explained to the band how I had been present myself when it was made, and that I would have it read to them.   I accordingly requested Mr. Cochrane to do so, explaining it thoroughly; yet, it was only after a great deal of talking on their part, during which they made most unreasonable demands, and many explanations on my part, that the Indians were satisfied that a treaty had been made, when they requested me to go on with the payments; at the same time a number of them stated that they had been misled by one of the counsellors, Joseph Atkinson by name.   I then paid the annuity, distributed the provisions, tools, implements, etc., and gave the Chief a copy of the treaty, and, arranging to meet them again on Monday, the 28th, I returned to my camp at midnight.

On Monday, I met them as agreed, and at once began and made inquiries as to who had houses and gardens on the north bank and had moved their houses to the south bank, and I found that all those that had formerly lived on the north bank had removed from there.   I noticed that great feeling existed amongst them all as to the division of the five hundred dollars granted.   All the band congregated round me and the large majority desired that the amount should be divided equally between them all, and claimed that every one belonging to the band was entitled to participate in the division; so I thought it best to leave it to themselves to decide how the amount should be distributed, and they only succeeded in doing so after a great deal of talking, and, I regret to say, quarrelling; but they at last arranged it, and I was requested by the Chief and Councillors to divide it amongst the whole band in such proportions as I thought right, so I proceeded at once to what turned out to be a long and troublesome undertaking; but having as I considered made a fair and equitable distribution of the amount, I paid the same, had the document witnessed by the Chief and Councillors, and only got back to my camp again at midnight.   As I before said, all the Indians had removed to the south bank of the river, but had made no preparations to build, and were merely living in tents.   Close to the encampment, at the mouth of the river, the Church Missionary Society have put up a large building to answer the purposes of a church and school-house.   Care must be taken and strict watch kept over this band. Living as they do on the bank of a navigable river, where people are constantly passing, they can give great trouble and annoyance, and, I am sorry to say, are inclined to do so.   Several complaints were made to me while there, and I spoke to the Indians regarding them.   They promised me to abide faithfully by the terms of the treaty henceforth and not give any further annoyance.

While occupied paying the Indians there, my crew were engaged in taking my boat and supplies across the Portage.   They left the camp early on Monday morning, and with the assistance kindly rendered them by Mr. Matheson, of the Hudson's Bay Company, succeeded in reaching the north end of the Portage on Tuesday evening. That same afternoon I walked over the four-mile Portage and found there a number of buildings belonging to the Hudson's Bay Company. To this point the Saskatchewan River steamer *Northcote* descends and receives the supplies for the different posts belonging to the Company to the West and North-West.

On Wednesday morning, the 30th, I left for the Pas. From the Grand Rapids to the Narrows, before entering Cedar Lake, a distance of eighteen or twenty miles, a continuous rapid extends, and it is only by tracking and poling simultaneously that you are at all able to ascend the river. The first day I made only nine miles on my way and camped at the Demi Charge, and it was late in the evening on the second day when I reached Cedar Lake. This lake is about thirty-five miles in length and is very shallow and dangerous in stormy weather. I was fortunate enough to have very calm weather, and, therefore, crossed it without any delay and entered the Saskatchewan again at the Che-ma-wa-win or "Seining place," early on Saturday morning, September 2nd. Noticing a large encampment of Indians there, I landed and found they were part of the Moose Lake band. They desired that I should treat with them where they were, and not bring them to the Pas, but upon my telling them that I could only treat with them at the appointed place of meeting, they readily assented to follow me up, and having given them some provisions to take them there, and secured the services of one of them to act as guide, I again started on my journey.

I was then three days and two nights ascending the river, and on Tuesday morning, the 5th September, the day appointed for me to meet the Indians, I arrived at the Pas or Devon Mission, on my way up having been passed by the Indians from the Che-ma-wa-win.

On entering the river after leaving Cedar Lake the whole aspect of the country changes, and from there to the Pas, and, I understand, for fully one hundred miles above it, nothing but marsh can be seen; so much so that it was difficult along the bank of the river to find a spot dry enough to camp upon, and I was, consequently, obliged to eat and sleep in my boat. The dreariness of this voyage can hardly be realized, and it was with feelings of delight that I landed at the Mission at the Pas where the Rev. Mr. Cochrane received me.

Mr. Cochrane had accompanied me from the Stone Fort and had been in my boat up to the night before I arrived, when, meeting some Indians that were on the look-out for us, he returned with them in their canoe and reached his home shortly before I arrived.

The Pas or Devon Mission is situated on the south bank of the Saskatchewan, distant, I should say, one hundred and forty miles from Grand Rapids. The Church Missionary Society have a very nice church, schoolhouse and parsonage there; and the Hudson's Bay Company one of their posts. There are also a large number of houses belonging to the Indians of the place; and on the other bank the firm of Kew, Stobart & Co., have erected a store for trading purposes. There are also several dwelling-houses on the north bank.   Altogether, the appearance of the place, on my arrival, was most prepossessing.   The banks were covered with Indians with their canoes, and immediately the boat rounded the point below the Mission and came in view a salute was fired, the like of which, I was subsequently told, had never been heard in the "Ratty Country."

Having landed at the Mission, Mr. Cochrane informed me that he had, as I requested, summoned the Indians to meet in the school-house at three o'clock that afternoon, and when the hour arrived I proceeded there and found upwards of five hundred Indians gathered.   I stated the object of my mission to them, and was at once assured of their desire to accept of, and their gratitude for, the Queen's bounty and benevolence.

I found that the Pas and Cumberland bands of Indians had acknowledged Chiefs, but that the Moose Lake band had none, owing to a division amongst them.   It appeared that the Indians from the Che-ma-wa-win desired to be a distinct band and have their reserves where I had seen them at the entrance of the river from Cedar Lake; but noticing, on my way up, the unfitness of the locality for a reserve, and having learned that at Moose Lake, where part of the band desired to live, a most suitable locality could be had, I had decided before meeting them upon the course I should take, which was, not to encourage the division in the band, and allow only one Chief ; and this I did, and succeeded, without much trouble, in getting the band to unite.   I then requested all the Indians to meet in council and select their Chief and head men, and be prepared the following morning to present them to me, when I would be ready to speak to them.

The next morning at eleven o'clock I met them and found they had done as I requested, and having been presented to the Chiefs and Councillors I proceeded to explain the terms of the treaty that I desired to receive their adhesion to.   The Chiefs immediately stated that they wanted to make a treaty of their own, and it was only after great difficulty that I could make them understand that in reality it was not a new treaty they were about to make.

They had heard of the terms granted the Indians at Carlton, and this acted most prejudicially at one time against the successful carrying out of my mission ; but I at last made them understand the difference between their position and the Plain Indians, by pointing out that the land they would surrender would be useless to the Queen, while what the Plain Indians gave up would be of value to her for homes for her white children.   They then agreed to accept the terms offered if I would agree to give them reserves where they desired; and to their demands I patiently listened, and having at last come to a satisfactory understanding I adjourned the meeting to the following day.

Before proceeding further, I would draw your attention to the localities I granted for reserves, subject to the approval of the Government, and beg to inform you that I made every inquiry as to the extent of farming land in each locality mentioned.

At the Narrows, at Moose Lake, there is considerable good land, and a suitable place for a reserve can be had for the Moose Lake band.

For the Pas and Cumberland Indians I had to mention several localities. At the Pas all the land obtainable is now cultivated, and consists of a vegetable garden and one field attached to the Mission, and a few patches of potatoes here and there. A short distance from the river the marsh begins, and extends to the south for miles ; and the same thing occurs to the north. In fact, on both banks of the river at this point, and from the Che-ma-wa-win up to it, one hundred and fifty acres of land fit for cultivation cannot be found; and about Cumberland the country in every respect is similar.

The following day, Thursday the 7th, I met the Indians at three p.m., and had the adhesion read to them and signed. I then presented the medals and clothing to the Chiefs and Councillors, with which they were greatly pleased, and having congratulated them upon wearing the Queen's uniform, and having in return been heartily thanked by them for what had been done, I proceeded to pay them, and continued to do so up to seven o'clock, when the funds at my disposal being exhausted, I directed them to meet me again the following morning at nine o'clock, which they did, and I completed the payments the same evening at five o'clock. I then distributed the balance of provisions and the ammunition and twine. The implements and tools I had been unable to bring from Grand Rapids, my boat being very heavily laden ; but Mr. Belanger, of the Hudson's Bay Company, kindly promised to have them brought up free of charge in a boat that was going to the Grand Rapids in a few days ; I therefore gave the Chief of the Pas band an order for the chest of tools and the implements.

The following day, Saturday, having again seen all the Chiefs and Councillors and received their thanks, and after many expressions of gratitude from the Indians gathered, I left the Pas at half-past two o'clock p.m., and with rowing and floating alternately during the afternoon and night, reached the Che-ma-wa-win on Sunday evening ; crossed Cedar Lake on Monday, and landed at the head of Grand Rapids on Tuesday morning. I then ran the rapids and hoisted the sail at the mouth of the river at two p.m., having called upon Mr. Matheson and seen the Chief of the Indians there on my way down. I then made all haste to return here, but, owing to contrary winds, only succeeded in reaching the Stone Fort on the 20th September, yet, having made a very quick trip, unprecedented in fact, and in carrying out the mission entrusted to me, travelled in an open boat, thirteen hundred miles.

I would now inform you that three out of the four bands of Indians I met on the Saskatchewan, viz., the Grand Rapids, Pas and Cumberland, are in a position to receive at once from the Government the grant allowed for the maintenance of schools of instruction ; at the Grand Rapids a large school-house is by this time entirely completed ; and at the Pas and Cumberland, schools, under the charge of the Church Missionary Society, have been in existence some years. The Indians belonging to the bands I have named desired that the assistance promised should be given as soon as possible.

I would now mention the very valuable services rendered the Government by the Rev. Mr. Cochrane, who acted as interpreter at the Dog Head, Berens River, Grand Rapids and the Pas, and who was at all times ready to give his advice and assistance; as well as by Mr. A. M. Muckle, who accompanied me and assisted in making the payments; and by Mr. Nursey, who took charge of the boat with supplies for the Pas. To Mr. Matheson, of the Hudson's Bay Company, Grand Rapids, and Mr. Belanger, of Cumberland House, I am deeply indebted, and take this opportunity of tendering these gentlemen my sincere thanks for the assistance rendered me and the many kindnesses I received from them. I enclose herewith the pay-sheet of the different bands I paid, a statement of the cash expenditure, and statements shewing quantities of provisions, implements, etc., received and how distributed, with a statement of clothing, medals, etc., given to the Chiefs and Councillors, and a report I received from Mr. Bedson.

And, trusting that the manner in which I have carried out the mission entrusted to my care, may meet with your approval,

I have the honor to be, Sir,

Your obedient servant,

THOMAS HOWARD,

Commissioner.

Fort Garry, *July 14th, 1876.*

To the Hon. Thos. Howard and J. Lestock Reid, Esq.

Dear Sirs,—Under authority from the Minister of the Interior, I have to request you to proceed to Lake Winnipeg for the purpose of—on behalf of the Privy Council of Canada—securing the adhesion to Treaty Number Five of the Indians who have not yet been dealt with, and to make the necessary payments to the others.

1st. You will, if possible, together proceed to or meet at the following places, being there on the days named, viz.: Dog-Head Point, 25th July, and Berens River on the 5th August.

2nd. Mr. Howard will then proceed to the mouth of the Saskatchewan, so as to reach there on the 25th of August, and then arrive at the Pas on the 5th of September.

3rd. Mr. Reid will proceed from Berens River to Norway House, to arrive there on or before the 25th of August.

4th. You or either of you will secure the adhesion of the Island Indians to the treaty after the form annexed, and will request them to select a Chief and three Councillors, and will be authorized to promise them a reserve of one hundred and sixty acres to each family of five, or that proportion for larger or smaller families, to be selected for them by the person chosen for that end by the Privy Council with their approval,

5th. You or either of you will obtain the adhesion of the Indians of the Grand Rapids of Berens River to the treaty according to the form annexed. You will ask them to select a Chief and three Councillors. A similar provision will be made as to a reserve, but if necessary you can fix the locality at the Sandy Narrows above the rapids on the Berens River, reserving free navigation and access to the shores to all Her Majesty's subjects.

6th. Mr. Reid will pay the Norway House and Cross Lake Indians, and will ascertain the intentions of the Norway House Indians as to the time of their removal to Fisher River, of which I am unadvised.

7th. Mr. Howard will pay the Indians at the mouth of the Saskatchewan, and if the Indians have removed their houses, as agreed by the treaty, will pay them five hundred dollars, but if not and some have removed, will pay such their proportionate share of the five hundred dollars.

8th. You will distribute the implements, tools, etc., sent among the Indians, as also the ammunition and twine. Cattle cannot be given till the Indians are sufficiently settled on the reserves to make it seem that they will be cared for. You will report any cases where you find this to be the case, for future action.

9th. You will inform the Berens River Indians that their application for a hay reserve has been forwarded to the Privy Council by me, and that they will receive a reply hereafter.

10th. Mr. Howard will secure the adhesion of the Indians at the Pas to the treaty providing that reserves of one hundred and sixty acres to each family of five will be granted at places selected for them by an officer of the Privy Council, with their approval ; but it will probably be necessary to give them a reserve at the Pas where they reside, reserving carefully free navigation and access to the shores. As the extent of land there s very narrow, it may be desirable to indicate localities where farming reserves will be granted, subject to the approval of the Privy Council.

11th. The Moose Lake Indians are a distinct band, and will probably desire the recognition of two separate Chiefs and the allotment of separate reserves to them.

12th. The Cumberland House Indians are another band, but very much scattered; the question of a reserve will have to be considered, and, in connection with it, as in other cases, respect for actual, *bona fide*, substantial improvements, and for the rights of settlers.

13th. In all cases the places indicated for reserves to be subject to Her Majesty's approval in Council, and free navigation and access to the shores to be reserved.

14th. In the case of new adhesions to the treaty, which are in fact new treaties, only five dollars is to be paid, but persons belonging to bands treated with last year are to receive last year's payment, if then absent, if necessary.

15th. You will each take with you a suitable person, to be approved of by me, to assist you in the payment.

I have the honor to be,

Your obedient servant,

ALEXANDER MORRIS,

Lieut.-Governor.

C.

WINNIPEG, *October 14th 1876.*

To the Hon. Alexander Morris,
Lieut.-Governor.

Sir,—Referring to your letter of instructions under date of the 14th of July, relative to the payment of the Norway House and Cross Lake bands of Indians, I have the honor to submit the following report :—

Having, in co-operation with the Hon. Thomas Howard, paid the Indians of Berens River and successfully secured the adhesion of the Island and Upper Berens River bands of Indians to Treaty Number Five, on the morning of Saturday, the 5th of August, I left for Norway House, which place, owing to stormy weather and strong head winds, I did not succeed in reaching until the morning of the 12th. On the way I was met by Indians proceeding to inspect their reserve at Fisher's River, who brought a letter from the Chiefs of Norway House and Cross Lake, stating that the Indians were all assembled, and requesting to be paid at the earliest possible date.

On reaching this place, Norway House, after having camp pitched at a short distance from the fort, I dispatched messengers to the several camps and villages, notifying the Indians of my arrival and desiring the Chiefs to meet me on the Monday morning following. On Sunday evening divine service was held within the fort by the Rev. Mr. Ruttan, Wesleyan missionary, at which a large number of Indians were present.

On Monday morning, the Chiefs and most of the Indians of both bands having assembled at my camp, the Cross Lake band requested to be paid there, and the Norway House Chief asked that his people might be paid in the school-house in their village about two miles from the fort. On hearing that all the Indians that could come were assembled, I consented to pay them where they desired, and told the Cross Lake Chief to bring his people at noon to receive their gratuities, the payment of which was satisfactorily completed the same day.

The next day I crossed over to the Indian village and paid the Norway House bands their annuities. . . . .

The following morning, Wednesday, August 16th, the Chiefs and Indians of the two bands having assembled at my camp, I distributed the provisions implements, &c., which were received with the greatest degree of gratification and satisfaction.

On my inquiring of the Chief of Norway House when his band would be prepared to remove to their reserve at the Fisher River, he informed me that he had sent two of his people to that locality to report on the same, and that he could not say anything definite on the matter until their return. I might here state that, on my way back to Winnipeg I met these men returning from Fisher's River, who expressed themselves as highly pleased with the proposed location, and that the band in all probability would remove there in the spring.

Whilst at Norway House I was waited upon by a Chief and four Councillors from the vicinity of Oxford House, who were anxious to know if the same bounties would be extended to them as were being extended to their brethren of Norway House and Cross Lake, and also whether they could obtain a reserve on Lake Winnipeg, as the country in which they were living was totally unfit for cultivation, and that they had the greatest difficulty in procuring a livelihood. I told them that I had no idea what were the intentions of the Government with regard to those Indians living north of the present Treaty, but that I would make known their requests to Your Excellency, and that they would be duly notified of any action the Government might take in the matter.

I left Norway House on my return trip, on the morning of the 18th, arriving at Winnipeg on the afternoon of Saturday the 26th, having that morning paid my boat's crew off at Selkirk.

I would here mention that previous to my departure from Norway House there was a very hearty and apparently sincere expression of gratitude, on the part of all the Indians present, for the liberality extended to them, and a general and spoken wish that their thanks be conveyed to the Queen's Representative in this Province for his kind interest in their welfare.

I cannot conclude without bearing testimony to the kindness of Mr. Ross, Hudson's Bay Company's Factor, and the Rev. Mr. Ruttan, Wesleyan missionary, for services rendered during the few days occupied in my making the payments at Norway House.

I enclose herewith statement of expenditure, &c., &c., with vouchers attached.

I have the honor to be, Sir,

Your obedient servant,

J. LESTOCK REID,
Commissioner.

CHAPTER IX.

THE TREATIES AT FORTS CARLTON AND PITT.

THE treaties made at Forts Carlton and Pitt in the year 1876, were of a very important character.

The great region covered by them, abutting on the areas included in Treaties Numbers Three and Four, embracing an area of approximately 120,000 square miles, contains a vast extent of fertile territory and is the home of the Cree nation. The Crees had, very early after the annexation of the North-West Territories to Canada, desired a treaty of alliance with the Government. So far back as the year 1871, Mr. Simpson, the Indian Commissioner, addressing the Secretary of State in a despatch of date, the 3rd November, 1871, used the following language :

" I desire also to call the attention of His Excellency to the state of affairs in the Indian country on the Saskatchewan. The intelligence that Her Majesty is treating with the Chippewa Indians has already reached the ears of the Cree and Blackfeet tribes.   In the neighborhood of Fort Edmonton, on the Saskatchewan, there is a rapidly increasing population of miners and other white people, and it is the opinion of Mr. W. J. Christie, the officer in charge of the Saskatchewan District, that a treaty with the Indians of that country, or at least an assurance during the coming year that a treaty will shortly be made, is essential to the peace, if not the actual retention, of the country.   I would refer His Excellency, on this subject, to the report of Lieut. Butler, and to the enclosed memoranda of Mr. W. J. Christie, the officer above alluded to."

He also enclosed an extract of a letter from Mr. Christie, then Chief Factor of the Hudson's Bay Company, and subsequently one of the Treaty Commissioners, in which, he forwarded the messages of the Cree Chiefs to Lieut.-Gov. Archibald, " our Great Mother's representative at Fort Garry, Red River Settlement." This extract and messages are as follows :

EDMONTON HOUSE, *13th April, 1871.*

On the 13th instant (April) I had a visit from the Cree Chiefs, representing the Plain Crees from this to Carlton, accompanied by a few followers.

The object of their visit was to ascertain whether their lands had been sold or not, and what was the intention of the Canadian Government in relation to them. They referred to the epidemic that had raged throughout the past summer, and the subsequent starvation, the poverty of their country, the visible diminution of the buffalo, their sole support, ending by requesting certain presents *at once,* and that I should lay their case before Her Majesty's representative at Fort Garry. Many stories have reached these Indians through various channels, ever since the transfer of the North-West Territories to the Dominion of Canada, and they were most anxious to hear from myself what had taken place.

I told them that the Canadian Government had as yet made no application for their lands or hunting grounds, and when anything was required of them, *most likely Commissioners* would be sent beforehand to treat with them, and that until then they should remain quiet and live at peace with all men. I further stated that Canada, in her treaties with Indians, heretofore, had dealt most liberally with them, and that they were now in settled houses and well off, and that I had no doubt in settling with them the same liberal policy would be followed.

As I was aware that they had heard many exaggerated stories about the troops in Red River, I took the opportunity of telling them why troops had been sent ; and if Her Majesty sent troops to the Saskatchewan, it was as much for the protection of the red as the white man, and that they would be for the maintenance of law and order.

They were highly satisfied with the explanations offered, and said they would welcome civilization. As their demands were complied with, and presents given to them, their immediate followers, and for the young men left in camp, they departed well pleased for the present time, with fair promises for the future. At a subsequent interview with the Chiefs alone, they requested that I should write down their words, or messages to their Great Master in Red River. I accordingly did so, and have transmitted the messages as delivered. Copies of the proclamation issued, prohibiting the traffic in spirituous liquors to Indians or others, and the use of strychnine in the destruction of animal life, have been received, and due publicity given to them.   But without any power to enforce these laws, it is almost useless to publish them here ; and I take this opportunity of most earnestly soliciting, on behalf of the Company's servants, and settlers in this district, that protection be afforded to life and property here as soon as possible, and that Commissioners be sent to speak with the Indians on behalf of the Canadian Government.

MEMORANDA :

Had I not complied with the demands of the Indians—giving them some little presents—and otherwise satisfied them, I have no doubt that they would have proceeded to acts of violence, and once that had commenced, there would have been the beginning of an Indian war, which it is difficult to say when it would have ended.

The buffalo will soon be exterminated, and when starvation comes, these Plain Indian tribes will fall back on the Hudson's Bay Forts and settlements for relief and assistance.   If not complied with, or no steps taken to make some provision for them, they will most assuredly help themselves; and there being no force or any law up there to protect the settlers, they must either quietly submit to be pillaged, or lose their lives in the defence of their families and property, against such fearful odds that will leave no hope for their side.

Gold may be discovered in paying quantities, any day, on the eastern slope of the Rocky Mountains.   We have, in Montana, and in the mining settlements close to our boundary line, a large mixed frontier population, who are now only waiting and watching to hear of gold discoveries to rush into the Saskatchewan, and, without any form of Government or established laws up there, or force to protect whites or Indians, it is very plain what will be the result.

I think that the establishment of law and order in the Saskatchewan District, as early as possible, is of most vital importance to the future of the country and the interest of Canada, and also the making of some treaty or settlement with the Indians who inhabit the Saskatchewan District.

W. J. CHRISTIE, *Chief Factor,*
In charge of Saskatchewan District,
Hudson's Bay Company.

Messages from the Cree Chiefs of the Plains, Saskatchewan, to His Excellency Governor Archibald, our Great Mother's representative at Fort Garry, Red River Settlement.

1. The Chief Sweet Grass, The Chief of the country.

GREAT FATHER,—I shake hands with you, and bid you welcome.   We heard our lands were sold and we did not like it ; we don't want to sell our lands ; it is our property, and no one has a right to sell them.

Our country is getting ruined of fur-bearing animals, hitherto our sole support, and now we are poor and want help—we want you to pity us. We want cattle, tools, agricultural implements, and assistance in everything when we come to settle—our country is no longer able to support us.

Make provision for us against years of starvation. We have had great starvation the past winter, and the small-pox took away many of our people, the old, young, and children.

We want you to stop the Americans from coming to trade on our lands, and giving firewater, ammunition and arms to our enemies the Blackfeet.

We made a peace this winter with the Blackfeet. Our young men are foolish, it may not last long.

We invite you to come and see us and to speak with us. If you can't come yourself, send some one in your place.

We send these words by our Master, Mr. Christie, in whom we have every confidence.—That is all.

2. Ki-he-win, The Eagle.

GREAT FATHER,—Let us be friendly. We never shed any white man's blood, and have always been friendly with the whites, and want workmen, carpenters and farmers to assist us when we settle. I want all my brother, Sweet Grass, asks. That is all.

3. The Little Hunter.

You, my brother, the Great Chief in Red River, treat me as a brother, that is, as a Great Chief.

4. Kis-ki-on, or Short Tail.

My brother, that is coming close, I look upon you, as if I saw you ; I want you to pity me, and I want help to cultivate the ground for myself and descendants. Come and see us.

The North-West Council, as already elsewhere stated, had urged the making of treaties with these Indians, and the necessity of doing so, was also impressed upon the Privy Council, by the Lieutenant-Governor of the North-West Territories, and Col. French, then in command of the Mounted Police therein. The Minister of the Interior, the Hon. David Mills, in his Report for the year 1876, thus alluded to this subject :

" Official reports received last year from His Honor Governor Morris and Colonel French, the officer then in command of the Mounted Police Force, and from other parties, showed that a feeling of discontent and uneasiness prevailed very generally amongst the Assiniboines and Crees lying in the unceded

territory between the Saskatchewan and the Rocky Mountains.   This state of feeling, which had prevailed amongst
these Indians for some years past, had been increased by the
presence, last summer, in their territory of the parties engaged
in the construction of the telegraph line, and in the survey of
the Pacific Railway line, and also of a party belonging to the
Geological Survey.   To allay this state of feeling, and to prevent the threatened hostility of the Indian tribes to the parties
then employed by the Government, His Honor Governor
Morris requested and obtained authority to despatch a messenger to convey to these Indians the assurance that Commissioners would be sent this summer, to negotiate a treaty with
them, as had already been done with their brethren further east.

" The Rev. George McDougall, who had been resident as a
missionary amongst these Indians for upwards of fourteen
years, and who possessed great influence over them, was
selected by His Honor to convey this intelligence to the
Indians, a task which he performed with great fidelity and
success : being able to report on his return that although he
found the feeling of discontent had been very general among
the Indian tribes, he had been enabled entirely to remove it
by his assurance of the proposed negotiations during the coming year.

" For the purpose of negotiating this treaty with the Indians,
Your Excellency availed yourself of the services of His Honor
Governor Morris, who had been formerly employed in negotiating Treaties Numbers Three, Four and Five.   With him were
associated the Hon. James McKay and W. J. Christie, Esq.,
both of whom had had considerable experience in such work,
and possessed moreover an intimate acquaintance with the
Indians of the Saskatchewan, their wants, habits and dialects."

With reference to the Rev. George McDougall,* I may here

---

* This faithful missionary came to an untimely death on the plains during
the succeeding winter.   Having missed his way to his camp, he was found
lying dead on the snow, and there in the lonely wilds was closed a most
useful career.

state, that when the application was made to him, to visit the
Indians of the Plains, in the Saskatchewan Valley, he was on
his way, with his family, to his distant mission, among the
Assiniboines, near the Rocky Mountains, after a brief sojourn
in the Province of Ontario, but on the request being made to
him, to explain to the Indians the intentions of the Government, he at once undertook the duty, and leaving his family to
follow him, went upon the long journey, which his mission involved, carrying with him a letter missive from the Lieutenant-
Governor of the North-West Territories, promising the Indians,
that Commissioners would visit them during the ensuing summer, to confer with them as to a treaty.   The result of his tour,
and of the tidings which he bore was very gratifying, as the
Indians were at once tranquilized, and awaited in full confidence, the coming of the Commissioners.   The way in which
he discharged his important duties and the success which followed his exertions, will be best set forth by giving place to his
Report, addressed to the Lieutenant-Governor, of the results of
his arduous mission :

MORLEYVILLE, BOW RIVER, ROCKY MOUNTAINS,
October 23rd, 1875.

To HIS HONOR LIEUTENANT-GOVERNOR MORRIS.

SIR,—In accordance with my instructions, I proceeded with as little
delay as possible to Carlton, in the neighborhood of which place I met with
forty tents of Crees : From these I ascertained that the work I had undertaken would be much more arduous than I had expected, and that the principal camps would be found on the south branch of the Saskatchewan and
Red Deer Rivers.   I was also informed by these Indians that the Crees and
Plain Assiniboines were united on two points: 1st. That they would not
receive any presents from Government until a definite time for treaty was
stated.   2nd. Though they deplored the necessity of resorting to extreme
measures, yet they were unanimous in their determination to oppose the
running of lines, or the making of roads through their country, until a settlement between the Government and them had been effected. I was further
informed that the danger of a collision with the whites was likely to arise
from the officious conduct of minor Chiefs who were anxious to make themselves conspicuous, the principal men of the large camps being much more

moderate in their demands. Believing this to be the fact, I resolved to visit every camp and read them your message, and in order that your Honor may form a correct judgment of their disposition towards the Government, I will give you a synopsis of their speeches after the message was read. Mistahwahsis, head Chief of the Carlton Indians, addressing the principal Chief of the Assiniboines and addressing me, said : "That is just it, that is all we wanted." The Assiniboines addressing me, said : "My heart is full of gratitude, foolish men have told us that the Great Chief would send his young men to our country until they outnumbered us, and that then he would laugh at us, but this letter assures us that the Great Chief will act justly towards us."

Beardy, or the Hairy Man, Chief of the Willow Indians, said : "If I had heard these words spoken by the Great Queen I could not have believed them with more implicit faith than I do now." The Sweet Grass was absent from camp when I reached the Plain Crees, but his son and the principal men of the tribe requested me to convey to the Great Chief, at Red River, their thanks for the presents received, and they expressed the greatest loyalty to the government. In a word, I found the Crees reasonable in their demands, and anxious to live in peace with the white men. I found the Big Bear, a Saulteaux, trying to take the lead in their council. He formerly lived at Jack Fish Lake, and for years has been regarded as a troublesome fellow. In his speech he said : "We want none of the Queen's presents ; when we set a fox-trap we scatter pieces of meat all round, but when the fox gets into the trap we knock him on the head ; we want no bait, let your Chiefs come like men and talk to us." These Saulteaux are the mischief-makers through all this western country, and some of them are shrewd men.

A few weeks since, a land speculator wished to take a claim at the crossing on Battle River and asked the consent of the Indians, one of my Saulteaux friends sprang to his feet, and pointing to the east, said : "Do you see that great white man (the Government) coming?" "No," said the speculator. "I do," said the Indian, "and I hear the tramp of the multitude behind him, and when he comes you can drop in behind him and take up all the land claims you want; but until then I caution you to put up no stakes in our country." It was very fortunate for me that Big Bear and his party were a very small minority in camp. The Crees said they would have driven them out of camp long ago, but were afraid of their medicines, as they are noted conjurers.

The topics generally discussed at their council and which will be brought before the Commissioner are as follows in their own language. "Tell the Great Chief that we are glad the traders are prohibited bringing spirits into our country ; when we see it we want to drink it, and it destroys us ; when we do not see it we do not think about it. Ask for us a strong law, prohibiting the free use of poison (strychnine). It has almost exterminated the animals of our country, and often makes us bad friends with our white neighbors. We further request, that a law be made, equally applicable to the Half-breed and Indian, punishing all parties who set fire to our forest or plain. Not many years ago we attributed a prairie fire to the malevolence of an enemy, now every one is reckless in the use of fire, and every year large numbers of valuable animals and birds perish in consequence. We would further ask that our chiefships be established by the Government. Of late years almost every trader sets up his own Chief and the result is we are broken up into little parties, and our best men are no longer respected." I will state in connection with this, some of the false reports I had to combat in passing through this country, all calculated to agitate th native mind. In the neighborhood of Carlton an interested party went to considerable trouble to inform the Willow Indians that I had $3,000 for each band, as a present from the Government, and nothing in my long journey gave me greater satisfaction than the manner in which these Indians received my explanation of the contents of my letter of instructions. At the Buffalo Lake I found both Indians and Half-breeds greatly agitated. A gentlemen passing through their country had told them that the Mounted Police had received orders to prevent all parties killing buffalo or other animals, except during three months in the year, and these are only samples of the false statements made by parties who would rejoice to witness a con flict of races.

That your Honor's message was most timely, these are ample proofs.

A report will have reached you before this time that parties have been turned back by the Indians, and that a train containing supplies for the telegraph contractors, when west of Fort Pitt, were met by three Indians and ordered to return. Now after carefully investigating the matter and listening to the statements of all parties concerned, my opinion is, that an old traveller amongst Indians would have regarded the whole affair as too trivial to be noticed. I have not met with a Chief who would bear with the responsibility of the act.   ·   ·   ·   ·

Personally I am indebted both to the missionaries, and the Hudson's Bay Company's officials for their assistance at the Indian councils.

Believing it would be satisfactory to your Honor and of service to the Commissioners, I have kept the number of all the tents visited and the names of the places where I met the Indians.*

By reckoning eight persons to each tent, we will have a very close approximate to the number of Indians to be treated with at Carlton, and Fort Pitt. There may have been a few tents in the forest, and I have heard there are a few Crees at Lesser Slave Lake and Lac la Biche, but the number cannot exceed twenty tents.

All of which is respectfully submitted.

G. McDOUGALL.

* The number of Indians, as estimated by Mr. McDougall, as being visited by him, was 3,976.

The Commissioners, in the discharge of their task, had to travel through the prairie district in going to their destination and returning to Winnipeg, a distance of over 1,800 miles. They first met the Indians in the vicinity of Fort Carlton, on the Saskatchewan, in the month of August, 1876, and eventually succeeded on the 23rd day of that month, in effecting a treaty with the Plain and Wood Crees, and on the 28th of the same month with the tribe of Willow Crees. The negotiations were difficult and protracted. The Hon. David Mills, then Minister of the Interior, in his Annual Report thus characterizes them :—" In view of the temper of the Indians of the Saskatchewan, during the past year, and of the extravagant demands which they were induced to prefer on certain points, it needed all the temper, tact, judgment and discretion, of which the Commissioners were possessed, to bring the negotiations to a satisfactory issue." The difficulties were encountered chiefly at Carlton. The main body of the Crees were honestly disposed to treat, and their head Chiefs, Mistowasis and Ah-tuk-uh-koop, shewed sound judgment, and an earnest desire to come to an understanding.

They were embarrassed, however, by the action of the Willow Crees, who, under the guidance of one of their Chiefs, Beardy, interposed every obstacle to the progress of the treaty, and refused to attend the Council, unless it was held at the top of a hill some miles off, where the Chief pretended it had been revealed to him in a vision that the treaty was to be made. The Willow Crees were, moreover, under the influence of a wandering band of Saulteaux, the chief portion of whom resided within the limits of the other treaties, and who were disposed to be troublesome. Before the arrival of the Commissioners, the Saulteaux conceived the idea of forming a combination of the French Half-breeds, the Crees, and themselves, to prevent the crossing of the Saskatchewan by the Lieutenant-Governor, and his entrance into the Indian territories. They made the proposal first to the French Half-breeds, who declined to undertake it, and then to the Crees, who listened to it in silence. One of them at length arose, and pointing to the River Saskatchewan, said, "Can you stop the flow of that river?" The answer was, " No," and the rejoinder was "No more can you stop the progress of the Queen's Chief." When the Commissioners arrived at the Saskatchewan, a messenger from the Crees met them, proffering a safe convoy, but it was not needed. About a hundred traders' carts were assembled at the crossing, and Kissowayis, a native Indian trader, had the right of passage, which he at once waived, in favor of Messrs. Christie and Morris, the Commissioners. The other Commissioner, Mr. McKay, met them at Duck Lake next day, having proceeded by another route, and there they encountered Chief Beardy, who at once asked the Lieutenant-Governor to make the treaty at the hill, near the lake. On his guard, however, he replied, that he would meet the Cree nation wherever they desired, but must first go on and see them at Carlton, as he had appointed. An escort of Mounted Police also met the Commissioners at Duck Lake, having been sent from Carlton, in consequence of the information given by the Crees of the threatened interference with their progress. After several days' delay the Commissioners were obliged to meet the Crees without the Willow Crees. But after the conference had opened, the Beardy sent a message asking to be informed of the terms the Commissioners intended to offer in advance. The reply was that the messenger could sit with the other Indians, and report to his Chief what he heard, as it was his own fault that the Chief was not there to take part in the proceedings. The negotiations then went on quietly and deliberately, the Commissioners giving the Indians all the time they desired. The Indians were apprehensive of their future. They saw the food supply, the buffalo, passing away, and they were anxious and distressed. They knew the large terms granted to their Indians by the United States, but they had confidence in their Great Mother, the Queen, and her benevolence.

They desired to be fed. Small-pox had destroyed them by hundreds a few years before, and they dreaded pestilence and famine.

Eventually the Commissioners made them an offer. They asked this to be reduced to writing, which was done, and they asked time to consider it, which was of course granted. When the conference resumed, they presented a written counter-proposal. This the Commissioners considered, and gave full and definite answers of acceptance or refusal to each demand, which replies were carefully interpreted, two of the Commissioners, Messrs. Christie and McKay, being familiar with the Cree tongue, watching how the answers were rendered, and correcting when necessary. The food question, was disposed of by a promise, that in the event of a *National* famine or *pestilence* such aid as the Crown saw fit would be extended to them, and that for three years after they settled on their reserves, provisions to the extent of $1,000 per annum would be granted them during seed-time.

The other terms were analogous to those of the previous treaties. The Crees accepted the revised proposals. The treaty was interpreted to them carefully, and was then signed, and the payment made in accordance therewith. After the con-clusion of the treaty, the Comissioners were unwilling that the Willow Crees should remain out of the treaty, and sent a letter to them by a messenger, Pierre Levailler, that they would meet them half way, at the camp of the Hon. James McKay, and give them the opportunity of accepting the terms of the treaty already concluded. The letter was translated to the Indians by the Rev. Père André, a Catholic missionary, who, as well as M. Levailler, urged the Indians to accede to the proposal made to them, which they agreed to do. The Commissioners met the Indians accordingly, at the place proposed, and received, after a full discussion, the adhesion of the three Chiefs and head men of the Willow Crees to the treaty, and the payments were then made to them.

The Commissioners then prepared to leave for Fort Pitt, but having been apprised by the Rev. Mr. Scollan, a Catholic missionary, who had been sent by Bishop Grandin, to be present at the making of the treaty, that Sweet Grass, the principal Chief of the Plain Crees, at Fort Pitt, was unaware of the place and time of meeting, they despatched a messenger to apprise him of them, and request him to be present.

The Commissioners crossed the Saskatchewan and journeyed to Fort Pitt. Near it they were met by an escort of Mounted Police, who convoyed them to the fort.

There they found a number of Indians assembled, and, during the day, Sweet Grass arrived. In the evening the Chief and head men waited upon the Commissioners. Delay was asked and granted before meeting. Eventually the conference was opened. The ceremonies which attended it were imposing. The national stem or pipe dance was performed, of which a full narrative will be found hereafter. The conference proceeded, and the Indians accepted the terms made at Carlton with the utmost good feeling, and thus the Indian title was extinguished in the whole of the Plain country, except a comparatively small area, inhabited by the Black Feet, comprising about 35,000 square miles. I regret to record, that the Chief Sweet Grass, who took the lead in the proceedings, met with an accidental death a few months afterwards, by the discharge of a pistol. The Indians, in these two treaties, displayed a strong desire for instruction in farming, and appealed for the aid of missionaries and teachers.

The latter the Commissioners promised, and for the former they were told they must rely on the churches, representatives of whom were present from the Church of England, the Methodist, the Presbyterian and the Roman Catholic Church. The Bishop (Grandin) of the latter Church travelled from Edmonton to Fort Pitt and Battleford to see the Commissioners and assure them of his good will. After the conclusion of the treaty, the Commissioners commenced their long return journey by way of Battleford, and arrived at Winnipeg on the 6th day of October, with the satisfaction of knowing that they had accomplished a work which, with the efficient carrying out of the treaties, had secured the good will of the Cree Nation, and laid the foundations of law and order in the Saskatchewan Valley.

The officers of the Hudson's Bay Company, the missionaries of the various churches, Colonel McLeod of the Mounted Police Force, his officers and men, and the Half-breed population, all lent willing assistance to the commissioners, and were of substantial service.

I now submit the despatch of the Lieutenant-Governor, giving an account of the journey and of the negotiations attending the treaty, and I include a narrative of the proceedings taken down, day by day, by A. G. Jackes, Esq., M.D., Secretary to the Commission, which has never before been published, and embraces an accurate account of the speeches of the Commissioners and Indians. It is satisfactory to be able to state, that Lieut.-Gov. Laird, officers of the police force and Mr. Dickieson have since obtained the adhesion to the treaty, of, I believe, all but one of the Chiefs included in the treaty area, viz.: The Big Bear, while the head men even of his band have ranged themselves under the provisions of the treaty.

GOVERNMENT HOUSE,
FORT GARRY, MANITOBA, 4th December, 1876.

SIR,—I beg to inform you that in compliance with the request of the Privy Council that I should proceed to the west to negotiate the treaties which I had last year, through the agency of the late Rev. George McDougall, promised the Plain Crees, would be undertaken, I left Fort Garry on the afternoon of the 27th of July last, with the view of prosecuting my mission. I was accompanied by one of my associates, the Hon. J. W. Christie, and by A. G. Jackes, Esq., M.D., who was to act as secretary. I selected as my guide Mr. Pierre Levailler. The Hon. James McKay, who had also been associated in the commission, it was arranged, would follow me and meet me at Fort Carlton.

On the morning of the 4th of August, I forded the Assiniboine about five miles from Fort Ellice, having accomplished what is usually regarded as the first stage of the journey to Fort Carlton, about two hundred and twenty miles. After crossing the river, I was overtaken by a party of the Sioux who have settled on the reserve assigned to them at Bird Tail Creek, and was detained the greater part of the day.

I am sanguine that this settlement will prove a success, as these Sioux are displaying a laudable industry in cutting hay for their own use and for sale, and in breaking up ground for cultivation. I resumed my journey in the afternoon, but a storm coming on, I was obliged to encamp at the Springs, having only travelled eight miles in all during the day.

On the 5th I left the Springs, and after traversing much fine country, with excellent prairie, good soil, clumps of wood, lakelets, and hay swamps, in the Little and Great Touchwood Hills and File Mountain region, I arrived at the South Saskatchewan, at Dumont's crossing, twenty miles from Fort Carlton, on the afternoon of the 14th of August.

Here I found over one hundred carts of traders and freighters, waiting to be ferried across the river. The scow was occupied in crossing the carts and effects of Kis-so-wais, an enterprising Chippewa trader, belonging to the Portage la Prairie band, who at once came forward and gave up to me his right of crossing.

I met, also, a young Cree who had been sent by the Crees to hand me a letter of welcome in the name of their nation.

The reason of this step being taken was, that a few wandering Saulteaux or Chippewa, from Quill Lake, in Treaty Number Four, had come to the Crees and proposed to them to unite with them and prevent me from crossing the river and entering the Indian country. The Crees promptly refused to entertain the proposal, and sent a messenger, as above stated, to welcome me.

I also received from their messenger a letter from Lawrence Clarke, Esq., Chief Factor of the Hudson's Bay Company at Carlton, offering the Commissioners the hospitalities of the fort.

I sent replies in advance, thanking the Crees for their action, and accepting the kind offer of Mr. Clarke, to the extent of the use of rooms in the fort.

It was late in the evening before our party crossed the river, so that we encamped on the heights near it.

On the morning of the 15th we left for Fort Carlton, Mr. Christie preceding me to announce my approaching arrival at Duck Lake. About twelve miles from Carlton I found the Hon. James McKay awaiting me, having travelled by way of Fort Pelly.

Here also a Chief, Beardy of the Willow Crees, came to see me.

He said that his people were encamped near the lake, and that as there were fine meadows for their horses they wished the treaty to be made there.

I was at once on my guard, and replied to him, that after I reached Carlton, which was the place appointed, I would meet the Indians wherever the great body of them desired it.

He then asked me to stop as I passed his encampment, and see his people. This I agreed to do; as I was leaving Duck Lake I met Captain Walker with his troop of mounted police, coming to escort me to Carlton which they did.

When I arrived at Beardy's encampment, the men came to my carriage and holding up their right hands to the skies, all joined in an invocation to the deity for a blessing on the bright day which had brought the Queen's messenger to see them, and on the messenger and themselves; one of them shook hands with me for the others.

The scene was a very impressive and striking one, but as will be seen hereafter, this band gave me great trouble and were very difficult to deal with.

Leaving the Indian encampment I arrived at Fort Carlton, where Mr. Christie, Dr. Jackes and myself were assigned most comfortable rooms, Mr. McKay preferring to encamp about four miles from the fort.

In the evening, Mist-ow-as-is and Ah-tuk-uk-koop, the two head Chiefs of the Carlton Crees, called to pay their respects to me, and welcomed me most cordially.

On the 16th the Crees sent me word that they wished the day to confer amongst themselves.

I acceded to their request, learning that they desired to bring the Duck Lake Indians into the negotiations.

I sent a messenger, Mr. Peter Ballenden, to Duck Lake to inform the Indians that I would meet them at the encampment of the Carlton Crees, about two miles from the fort.

On the 17th, on his return, he informed me that the Chief said "He had not given me leave to meet the Indians anywhere except at Duck Lake, and that they would only meet me there." The Carlton Indians, however, sent me word, that they would be ready next morning at ten o'clock.

On the 18th, as I was leaving for the Indian encampment, a messenger came to me from the Duck Lake Indians, asking for provisions. I replied, that Mr. Christie was in charge of the distribution of provisions, but that I would not give any to the Duck Lake Indians, in consequence of the unreasonableness of their conduct, and that provisions would only be given to the large encampment.

I then proceeded to the Indian camp, together with my fellow Commissioners, and was escorted by Captain Walker and his troop.

On my arrival I found that the ground had been most judiciously chosen, being elevated, with abundance of trees, hay marshes and small lakes. The spot which the Indians had left for my council tent overlooked the whole.

The view was very beautiful: the hills and the trees in the distance, and in the foreground, the meadow land being dotted with clumps of wood, with the Indian tents clustered here and there to the number of two hundred.

On my arrival, the Union Jack was hoisted, and the Indians at once began to assemble, beating drums, discharging fire-arms, singing and dancing. In about half an hour they were ready to advance and meet me. This they did in a semicircle, having men on horseback galloping in circles, shouting, singing and discharging fire-arms.

They then performed the dance of the "pipe stem," the stem was elevated to the north, south, west and east, a ceremonial dance was then performed by the Chiefs and head men, the Indian men and women shouting the while.

They then slowly advanced, the horsemen again preceding them on their approach to my tent. I advanced to meet them, accompanied by Messrs. Christie and McKay, when the pipe was presented to us and stroked by our hands.

After the stroking had been completed, the Indians sat down in front of the council tent, satisfied that in accordance with their custom we had accepted the friendship of the Cree nation.

I then addressed the Indians in suitable terms, explaining that I had been sent by the Queen, in compliance with their own wishes and the written promise I had given them last year, that a messenger would be sent to them.

I had ascertained that the Indian mind was oppressed with vague fears; they dreaded the treaty ; they had been made to believe that they would be compelled to live on the reserves wholly, and abandon their hunting, and that in time of war, they would be placed in the front and made to fight.

I accordingly shaped my address, so as to give them confidence in the intentions of the Government, and to quiet their apprehensions. I impressed strongly on them the necessity of changing their present mode of life, and commencing to make homes and gardens for themselves, so as to be prepared for the diminution of the buffalo and other large animals, which is going on so rapidly.

The Indians listened with great attention to my address, and at its close asked an adjournment that they might meet in council to consider my words, which was of course granted.

The Rev. C. Scollen, a Roman Catholic Missionary amongst the Blackfeet, arrived soon after from Bow River, and informed me that on the way he had learned that Sweet Grass, the principal Chief of the Plain Crees, was out hunting and would not be at Fort Pitt, and that he was of opinion that his absence would be a great obstruction to a treaty.

After consulting with my colleagues, I decided on sending a messenger to him, requesting his presence, and succeeded in obtaining, for the occasion, the services of Mr. John McKay, of Prince Albert, who had acccompanied the Rev. George McDougall on his mission last year.

In the evening, Lieut.-Col. Jarvis arrived with a reinforcement of the Mounted Police, and an excellent band, which has been established at the private cost of one of the troops.

On the 19th, the Commissioners, escorted by the Mounted Police, headed by the band, proceeded to the Indian encampment.

The Indians again assembled, following Mist-ow-as-is and Ah-tuk-uk-koop, the recognized leading Chiefs.

I asked them to present their Chiefs; they then presented the two head Chiefs, and the minor ones.

At this juncture, a messenger arrived from the Duck Lake Indians, asking that I should tell them the terms of the Treaty. I replied that if the Chiefs and people had joined the others they would have heard what I had to say, and that I would not tell the terms in advance, but that the messenger could remain and hear what I had to say. He expressed himself satisfied and took his seat with the others. I then fully explained to them the proposals I had to make, that we did not wish to interfere with their present mode of living, but would assign them reserves and assist them as was being done elsewhere, in commencing to farm, and that what was done would hold good for those that were away.

The Indians listened most attentively, and on the close of my remarks Mist-ow-as-is arose, took me by the hand, and said that "when a thing was thought of quietly, it was the best way," and asked "this much, that we go and think of his words."

I acquiesced at once, and expressed my hope that the Chiefs would act wisely, and thus closed the second day.

The 20th being Sunday, the Rev. Mr. John McKay, of the Church of England, conducted divine service at the fort, which was largely attended; the Rev. Mr. Scollen also conducted service.

At noon a messenger came from the Indian camp, asking that there should be a service held at their camp, which Mr. McKay agreed to do; this service was attended by about two hundred adult Crees.

On Monday, 21st, the head Chiefs sent word that, as the previous day was Sunday, they had not met in council, and wished to have the day for consultation, and if ready would meet me on Tuesday morning. I cheerfully granted the delay from the reasonableness of the request; but I was also aware that the head Chiefs were in a position of great difficulty.

The attitude of the Duck Lake Indians and of the few discontented Saulteaux embarrassed them, while a section of their own people were either averse to make a treaty or desirous of making extravagant demands. The head Chiefs were men of intelligence, and anxious that the people should act unitedly and reasonably.

We, therefore, decided to give them all the time they might ask, a policy which they fully appreciated.

On the 22nd the Commissioners met the Indians, when I told them that we had not hurried them, but wished now to hear their Chiefs.

A spokesman, The Pond Maker, then addressed me, and asked assistance when they settled on the land, and further help as they advanced in civilization.

I replied that they had their own means of living, and that we could not feed the Indians, but only assist them to settle down. The Badger, Sohah-moos, and several other Indians all asked help when they settled, and also in case of troubles unforeseen in the future. I explained that we could not assume the charge of their every-day life, but in a time of a great national calamity they could trust to the generosity of the Queen.

The Honourable James McKay also addressed them, saying that their demands would be understood by a white man as asking for daily food, and could not be granted, and explained our objects, speaking with effect in the Cree tongue.

At length the Indians informed me that they did not wish to be fed every day, but to be helped when they commenced to settle, because of their ignorance how to commence, and also in case of general famine; Ah-tuk-uk-koop winding up the debate by stating that they wanted food in the spring when they commenced to farm, and proportionate help as they advanced in civilization, and then asking for a further adjournment to consider our offers.

The Commissioners granted this, but I warned them not to be unreasonable, and to be ready next day with their decision, while we on our part would consider what they had said.

The whole day was occupied with this discussion on the food question, and it was the turning point with regard to the treaty.

The Indians were, as they had been for some time past, full of uneasiness.

They saw the buffalo, the only means of their support, passing away. They were anxious to learn to support themselves by agriculture, but felt too ignorant to do so, and they dreaded that during the transition period they would be swept off by disease or famine—already they have suffered terribly from the ravages of measles, scarlet fever and small-pox.

It was impossible to listen to them without interest, they were not exacting, but they were very apprehensive of their future, and thankful, as one of them put it, "a new life was dawning upon them."

On the 23rd the conference was resumed, an Indian addressed the people, telling them to listen and the interpreter, Peter Erasmus, would read what changes they desired in the terms of our offer. They asked for an ox and a cow each family; an increase in the agricultural implements; provisions for the poor, unfortunate, blind and lame; to be provided with missionaries and school teachers; the exclusion of fire water in the whole Saskatchewan; a further increase in agricultural implements as the band advanced in civilization; freedom to cut timber on Crown lands; liberty to change the site of the reserves before the survey; free passages over Government bridges or scows; other animals, a horse, harness and waggon, and cooking stove for each chief; a free supply of medicines; a hand mill to each band; and lastly, that in case of war they should not be liable to serve.

Two spokesmen then addressed us in support of these modifications of the terms of the Treaty.

I replied to them that they had asked many things some of which had been promised, and that the Commissioners would consult together about

13

what they had asked that day and the day before, and would reply, but before doing so wished to know if that was the voice of the whole people, to which the Indians all assented.

After an interval we again met them, and I replied, going over their demands and reiterating my statements as to our inability to grant food, and again explaining that only in a national famine did the Crown ever intervene, and agreeing to make some additions to the number of cattle and implements, as we felt it would be desirable to encourage their desire to settle.

I closed by stating that, after they settled on the reserves, we would give them provisions to aid them while cultivating, to the extent of one thousand dollars per annum, but for three years only, as after that time they should be able to support themselves.

I told them that we could not give them missionaries, though I was pleased with their request, but that they must look to the churches, and that they saw Catholic and Protestant missionaries present at the conference. We told them that they must help their own poor, and that if they prospered they could do so. With regard to war, they would not be asked to fight unless they desired to do so, but if the Queen did call on them to protect their wives and children, I believed they would not be backward.

I then asked if they were willing to accept our modified proposals.

Ah-tuk-uk-koop then addressed me, and concluded by calling on the people, if they were in favour of our offers, to say so. This they all did by shouting assent and holding up their hands.

The Pond Maker then rose and said he did not differ from his people, but he did not see how they could feed and clothe their children with what was promised. He expected to have received that; he did not know how to build a house nor to cultivate the ground.

Joseph Toma, a Saulteaux, said he spoke for the Red Pheasant, Chief of the Battle River Crees, and made demands as follows: Men to build houses for them, increased salaries to the Chiefs and head men, etc. He said what was offered was too little; he wanted enough to cover the skin of the people, guns, and also ten miles of land round the reserves in a belt.

I asked the Red Pheasant how it was that he was party to the requests of his people, and how, when I asked if that was their unanimous voice he had assented, and yet had now put forward new and large demands.

I said it was not good faith, and that I would not accede to the requests now made ; that what was offered was a gift as they had still their old mode of living.

The principal Chiefs then rose and said that they accepted our offers, and the Red Pheasant repudiated the demands and remarks of Toma, and stated that he had not authorized him to speak for him.

Mist-ow-as-is then asked to speak for the Half-breeds, who wish to live on the reserves.

I explained the distinction between the Half-breed people and the Indian

Half-breeds who lived amongst the Indians as Indians, and said the Commissioners would consider the case of each of these last on its merits.

The treaty was then signed by myself, Messrs. Christie and McKay, Mist-ow-as-is and Ah-tuk-uk-koop, the head Chiefs, and by the other Chiefs and Councillors, those signing, though many Indians were absent, yet representing all the bands of any importance in the Carlton regions, except the Willow Indians.

On the 24th the Commissioners again met the Indians, when I presented the Head Chiefs with their medals, uniforms and flags, and informed them that Mr. Christie would give the other Chiefs and Councillors the same in the evening.

Some half a dozen of Saulteaux then came forward, of whom I found one was from Qu'Appelle, and had been paid there, and the others did not belong to the Carlton region. I told them that I had heard that they had endeavoured to prevent me crossing the river, and to prevent a treaty being made, but that they were not wiser than the whole of their nation, who had already been treated with.

They did not deny the charge, and their spokesman becoming insolent, I declined to hear them further, and they retired, some stating that they would go to Fort Pitt, which I warned them not to do.

Besides these Saulteaux, there were others present who disapproved of their proceedings, amongst them being Kis-so-way-is, already mentioned, and Pecheeto, who was the chief spokesman at Qu'Appelle, but is now a Councillor of the Fort Ellice Band.

I may mention here that the larger part of the Band to whom these other Saulteaux belonged, with the Chief Yellow Quill, gave in their adhesion to Treaty Number Four, at Fort Pelly about the time that their comrades were troubling me at Fort Carlton.

Mr. Christie then commenced the payments, assisted by Mr. McKay, of Prince Albert, and was engaged in so doing during the 24th and 25th. Amongst those paid were the few resident Saulteaux, who were accepted by the Cree Chiefs as part of their bands.

The next morning, the 26th, the whole band, headed by their Chiefs and Councillors, dressed in their uniforms, came to Carlton House to pay their farewell visit to me.

The Chiefs came forward in order, each addressing me a few remarks, and I replied briefly.

They then gave three cheers for the Queen, the Governor, one for the Mounted Police, and for Mr. Lawrence Clarke, of Carlton House, and then departed, firing guns as they went.

Considering it undesirable that so many Indians should be excluded from the treaty, as would be the case if I left the Duck Lake Indians to their own devices, I determined on sending a letter to them. I, therefore, prepared a message, inviting them to meet me at the Hon. Mr. McKay's encampment about three miles from the large Indian encampment about half way to Duck Lake, on Monday, the 28th, if they were prepared then to accept the terms of the treaty I had made with the Carlton Indians. My letter was entrusted to Mr. Levailler, who proceeded to Duck Lake.

On entering the Indian Council room, he found they had a letter written to me by the Rev. Mr. André, offering to accept the terms of the treaty, if I came to Duck Lake.

The Indians sent for Mr. André to read my letter to them, which was received with satisfaction ; both he and Mr. Levailler urged them to accep^t my proposal, which they agreed to do, and requested Mr. Levailler to in- orm me that they would go to the appointed place.

Accordingly, on the 28th, the Commissioners met the Willow Indians.

After the usual handshaking, and short speeches from two of the Chiefs, I addressed them, telling them I was sorry for the course they had pursued, and that I did not go away without giving them this opportunity to be in- cluded in the treaty.

Kah-mee-yes-too-waegs, the Beardy, spoke for the people. He said some things were too little. He was anxious about the buffalo.

Say-sway-kees wished to tell our mother, the Queen, that they were alarmed about the buffalo. It appeared as if there was only one left.

The Beardy again addressed me, and said,—" You have told me what you have done with the others you will do with us. I accept the terms ; no doubt it will run further, according to our numbers ; when I am utterly unable to help myself I want to receive assistance."

I replied to them, explaining, with regard to assistance, that we could not support or feed the Indians, and all that we would do would be to help them to cultivate the soil.

If a general famine came upon the Indians the charity of the Government would come into exercise. I admitted the importance of steps being taken to preserve the buffalo, and assured them that it would be considered by the Governor-General and Council of the North-West Territories, to see if a wise law could be framed such as could be carried out and obeyed.

The three Chiefs and their head men then signed the treaty, and the medals and flags were distributed, when Mr. Christie intimated that he was ready to make the payments.

They then asked that this should be done at Duck Lake, but Mr. Christie informed them that, as we had to leave for Fort Pitt, this was impossible ; and that, moreover, their share of the unexpended provisions and the cloth- ing and presents were at the fort, where they would require to go for them.

They then agreed to accept the payment, which was at once proceeded with.

The persistency with which these Indians clung to their endeavor to com- pel the Commissioners to proceed to Duck Lake was in part owing to super- stition, the Chief, Beardy, having announced that he had a vision, in which it was made known to him that the treaty would be made there.

It was partly, also, owing to hostility to the treaty, as they endeavored to induce the Carlton Indians to make no treaty, and urged them not to sell the land, but to lend it for four years.

The good sense and intelligence of the head Chiefs led them to reject their proposals, and the Willow Indians eventually, as I have reported, accepted the treaty.

The 29th was occupied by Mr. Christie in settling accounts, taking stock of the clothing, and preparing for our departure.

An application was made to me by Toma, the Saulteaux, who took part in the proceedings on the 23rd, to sign the treaty as Chief of the Saulteaux band.

As I could not ascertain that there were sufficient families of these Indians resident in the region to be recognized as a distinct band, and as I had no evidence that they desired him to be their Chief, I declined to allow him to sign the treaty, but informed him that next year, if the Saulteaux were numerous enough, and expressed the wish that he should be Chief, he would be recognized.

He was satisfied with this, and said that next year they would come to the payments.

His daughter, a widow, with her family, was paid, but he preferred to remain until next year, as he did not wish to be paid, except as a Chief.

On the morning of the 31st, the previous day having been wet, Mr. Christie and I left for Fort Pitt, Mr. McKay having preceded us by the other road —that by way of Battle River.

We arrived on the 5th September, the day appointed, having rested, as was our custom throughout the whole journey, on Sunday, the 3rd.

About six miles from the fort we were met by Col. Jarvis and the police, with their band, as an escort, and also by Mr. McKay, the Factor of the Hudson's Bay Company, who informed us that he had rooms ready for our occupation.

We found over one hundred lodges of Indians already there, and received a message from them, that as their friends were constantly arriving, they wished delay until the 7th.

On the morning of the 6th, Sweet Grass, who had come in, in consequence of my message, accompanied by about thirty of the principal men, called to see me and express their gratification at my arrival.

Their greeting was cordial, but novel in my experience, as they embraced me in their arms, and kissed me on both cheeks, a reception which they extended also to Mr. Christie and Dr. Jackes.

The Hon. James McKay arrived from Battle River in the evening, and reported that he had met there a number of Indians, principally Saulteaux, who had been camped there for some time. There had been about seventy lodges in all, but as the buffalo had come near, the poorer Indians had gone after them.

They expressed good feeling, and said they would like to have waited until the 15th, the day named for my arrival there, to see me and accept the treaty, but that the buffalo hunt was of so much consequence to them that they could not wait so long.

This band is a mixed one, composed of Crees and Saulteaux from Jack Fish Lake, their Chief being the Yellow Sky.

On the 7th the Commissioners proceeded to the council tent, which was pitched on the high plateau above the fort, commanding a very fine view, and facing the Indian encampment.

They were accompanied by the escort of the police, with their band.

The Indians approached with much pomp and ceremony, following the lead of Sweet Grass.

The stem dance was performed as at Fort Carlton, but with much more ceremony, there being four pipes instead of one, and the number of riders, singers and dancers being more numerous. After the pipes were stroked by the Commissioners, they were presented to each of them to be smoked, and then laid upon the table to be covered with calico and cloth, and returned to their bearers.

After the conclusion of these proceedings I addressed them, telling them we had come at their own request, and that there was now a trail leading from Lake Superior to Red River, that I saw it stretching on thence to Fort Ellice, and there branching off, the one track going to Qu'Appelle and Cyprus Hills, and the other by Fort Pelly to Carlton, and thence I expected to see it extended, by way of Fort Pitt to the Rocky Mountains; on that road I saw all the Chippewas and Crees walking, and I saw along it gardens being planted and houses built.

I invited them to join their brother Indians and walk with the white men on this road. I told them what we had done at Carlton, and offered them the same terms, which I would explain fully if they wished it.

On closing Sweet Grass rose, and taking me by the hand, asked me to explain the terms of the treaty, after which they would all shake hands with me and then go to meet in council.

I complied with this request, and stated the terms fully to them, both addresses having occupied me for three hours. On concluding they expressed satisfaction, and retired to their council.

On the 8th the Indians asked for more time to deliberate, which was granted, as we learned that some of them desired to make exorbitant demands, and we wished to let them understand through the avenues by which we had access to them that these would be fruitless.

On the 9th, the Commissioners proceeded to the council tent, but the Indians were slow of gathering, being still in council, endeavoring to agree amongst themselves.

At length they approached and seated themselves in front of the tent. I then asked them to speak to me. The Eagle addressed the Indians, telling them not to be afraid, and that I was to them as a brother, and what the Queen wished to establish was for their good.

After some time had passed, I again called on them to tell me their minds and not to be afraid. Sweet Grass then rose and addressed me in a very sensible manner. He thanked the Queen for sending me; he was glad to have a brother and a friend who would help to lift them up above their present condition. He thanked me for the offer and saw nothing to be afraid of. He therefore accepted gladly, and took my hand to his heart. He said God was looking down on us that day, and had opened a new world to them. Sweet Grass further said, he pitied those who had to live by the buffalo, but that if spared until this time next year, he wanted, this my brother (*i.e.* the Governor), to commence to act for him in protecting the buffalo; for himself he would commence at once to prepare a small piece of land, and his kinsmen would do the same.

Placing one hand over my heart, and the other over his own, he said: "May the white man's blood never be spilt on this earth. I am thankful that the white man and red man can stand together. When I hold your hand and touch your heart, let us be as one; use your utmost to help me and help my children so that they may prosper."

The Chief's speech, of which the foregoing gives a brief outline in his own words, was assented to by the people with a peculiar guttural sound which takes with them the place of the British cheer.

I replied, expressing my satisfaction that they had so unanimously approved of the arrangement I had made with the nation at Carlton, and promised that I would send them next year, as I had said to the Crees of Carlton, copies of the treaty printed on parchment.

I said that I knew that some of the Chiefs were absent, but next year they would receive the present of money as they had done.

The Commissioners then signed the treaty, as did Sweet Grass, eight other Chiefs and those of their Councillors who were present, the Chiefs addressing me before signing. James Senum, Chief of the Crees at White Fish Lake, said that he commenced to cultivate the soil some years ago. Mr. Christie, then chief factor of the Hudson's Bay Company, gave him a plough, but it was now broken. He had no cattle when he commenced, but he and his people drew the plough themselves, and made hoes of roots of trees. Mr. Christie also gave him a pit-saw and a grind-stone, and he was still using them. His heart was sore in spring when his children wanted to plough and had no implements. He asked for these as soon as possible, and referring to the Wesleyan mission at that place, he said by following what I have been taught it helps me a great deal.

The Little Hunter, a leading Chief of the Plain Crees, said he was glad from his very heart; he felt in taking the Governor's hand as if it was the Queen's. When I hear her words that she is going to put this country to rights, it is the help of God that put it into her heart. He wished an everlasting grasp of her hand; he was thankful for the children who would prosper. All the children who were settling there, hoped that the Great Spirit would look down upon us as one. Other Chiefs expressed themselves similarly.

Ken-oo-say-oo, or The Fish, was a Chippewayan or mountaineer, a small band of whom are in this region.

They had no Chief, but at my request they had selected a Chief and presented the Fish to me. He said, speaking in Cree, that he thanked the Queen, and shook hands with me ; he was glad for what had been done, and if he could have used his own tongue he would have said more.

I then presented Sweet Grass his medal, uniform, and flag, the band playing "God Save the Queen " and all the Indians rising to their feet.

The rest of the medals, flags, and uniforms, were distributed, as soon as possible, and Mr. Christie commenced to make the payments.

On Sunday, the 10th, the Rev. Mr. McKay conducted the service for the police and others, who might attend, and in the afternoon the Rev. Mr. McDougall had a service in Cree ; Bishop Grandin and the Rev. Mr. Scollen also had services for the Crees and Chippewayans.

On Monday, the 11th, Mr. Christie completed the payments and distribution of provisions. The police commenced crossing the Saskatchewan, with a view to leaving on Tuesday, the 12th, for Battle River. We therefore sent our horses and carts across the river, and had our tents pitched with the view of commencing our return journey, early in the morning. Just as we were about to leave Fort Pitt, however, the Great Bear, one of the three Cree Chiefs who were absent, arrived at the fort and asked to see me. The Commissioners met him, when he told me that he had been out on the plains hunting the buffalo, and had not heard the time of the meeting ; that on hearing of it he had been sent in by the Crees and by the Stonies or Assiniboines to speak for them. I explained to him what had been done at Carlton and Pitt ; he expressed regret that I was going away as he wished to talk to me. I then said we would not remove until the next day, which gratified him much.

On the 13th, Sweet Grass and all the other Chiefs and Councillors came down to the fort with the Great Bear to bid me farewell.

Sweet Grass told me the object of their visit. The Bear said the Indians on the plains had sent him to speak for them, and those who were away were as a barrier before what he would have to say.

Sweet Grass said, addressing him, "You see the representative of the Queen here. I think the Great Spirit put it into their hearts to come to our help. Let there be no barrier, as it is with great difficulty that this was brought about. Say yes and take his hand." The White Fish spoke similarly.

The Bear said, "Stop, my friends. I never saw the Governor before ; when I heard he was to come, I said I will request him to save me from what I most dread—hanging ; it was not given to us to have the rope about our necks." I replied, that God had given it to us to punish murder by death, and explained the protection the police force afforded the Indians.

Big Bear still demanded that there should be no hanging, and I informed him that his request would not be granted. He then wished that the buffalo might be protected, and asked why the other Chiefs did not speak.

The Fish, the Chipewayan replied, " We do not because Sweet Grass has spoken, and what he says we all say."

I then asked the Bear to tell the other two absent Chiefs, Short Tail and Sagamat, what had been done ; that I had written him and them a letter, and sent it by Sweet Grass, and that next year they could join the treaty ; with regard to the buffalo, the North-West Council were considering the question, and I again explained that we would not interfere with the Indian's daily life except to assist them in farming.

I then said I never expected to see them again. The land was so large that another Governor was to be sent, whom I hoped they would receive as they had done me, and give him the same confidence they had extended to me. The Chiefs and Councillors, commencing with Sweet Grass, then shook hands with Mr. Christie and myself, each addressing me words of parting.

The Bear remained sitting until all had shaken hands, he then took mine and holding it, said, " If he had known he would have met me with all his people. I am not an undutiful child, I do not throw back your hand, but as my people are not here I do not sign. I will tell them what I have heard, and next year I will come." The Indians then left, but shortly afterwards the Bear came to see me again, fearing I had not fully understood him, and assured me that he accepted the treaty as if he had signed it, and would come next year with all his people and accept it.

We crossed the river, and left for Battle River in the afternoon, where we arrived on the afternoon of the 15th. We found no Indians there except Red Pheasant and his band, whom we had already met at Carlton.

On the 16th, the Red Pheasant saw the Commissioners. He said he was a Battle River Indian ; his fathers had lived there before him, but he was glad to see the Government coming there, as it would improve his means of living. He wished the claims of the Half-breeds who had settled there before the Government came to be respected, as for himself he would go away and seek another home, and though it was hard to leave the home of his people, yet he would make way for the white man, and surely, he said, " if the poor Indian acts thus, the Queen, when she hears of this, will help him." He asked, that a little land should be given him to plant potatoes in next spring, and they would remove after digging them, to their reserve, which he thought he would wish to have at the Eagle Hills.

I expressed my satisfaction with their conduct and excellent spirit, and obtained the cheerful consent of Mr. Fuller, of the Pacific telegraph line, who is in occupation of a large cultivated field, that the band should use three acres within the fenced enclosure, and which, moreover, Mr. Fuller kindly promised to plough for them gratuitously.

The 17th being Sunday we remained at our camp, and on Monday morning, the 18th, we commenced our long return journey, with the incidents of which I will not trouble you further than to state that, on arriving on the 4th of October at an encampment about thirty miles from Portage la

Prairie, we found it necessary to leave our tents and carts to follow us leisurely (many of the horses having become completely exhausted with the long journey of sixteen hundred miles) and push on to the Portage; on the 5th we reached the Portage, where Mr. Christie and Dr. Jackes remained, their horses being unable to go farther, and I went on to Poplar Point, forty-five miles from Fort Garry, where I found accommodation for the night from Mr. Chisholm, of the Hudson's Bay Company's Post there.

I arrived at Fort Garry on the afternoon of the 6th of October, having been absent for over two months and a half. Mr. McKay, having taken another road, had arrived before me; Mr. Christie and Dr. Jackes reached here subsequently. Having thus closed the narrative of our proceedings, I proceed to deal with the results of our mission, and to submit for your consideration some reflections and to make some practical suggestions.

1st. The Indians inhabiting the ceded territory are chiefly Crees, but there are a few Assiniboines on the plains and also at the slope of the mountains. There are also a small number of Saulteaux and one band of Chippewayans.

2nd. I was agreeably surprised to find so great a willingness on the part of the Crees to commence to cultivate the soil, and so great a desire to have their children instructed. I requested Mr. Christie to confer with the Chief while the payments were going on, as to the localities where they would desire to have reserves assigned to them, and with few exceptions they indicated the places, in fact most of them have already commenced to settle. It is, therefore, important that the cattle and agricultural implements should be given them without delay.

I would, therefore, recommend that provision should be made for forwarding these as soon as the spring opens. I think it probable that cattle and some implements could be purchased at Prince Albert and thus avoid transportation.

3rd. I would further represent that, though I did not grant the request, I thought the desire of the Indians, to be instructed in farming and building, most reasonable, and I would therefore recommend that measures be adopted to provide such instruction for them. Their present mode of living is passing away; the Indians are tractable, docile and willing to learn. I think that advantage should be taken of this disposition to teach them to become self-supporting, which can best be accomplished with the aid of a few practical farmers and carpenters to instruct them in farming and house building.

The universal demand for teachers, and by some of the Indians for missionaries, is also encouraging. The former, the Government can supply; for the latter they must rely on the churches, and I trust that these will continue and extend their operations amongst them. The field is wide enough for all, and the cry of the Indian for help is a clamant one.

4th. In connection with the aiding of the Indians to settle, I have to call attention to the necessity of regulations being made for the preservation of the buffalo. These animals are fast decreasing in numbers, but I am satisfied that a few simple regulations would preserve the herds for many years. The subject was constantly pressed on my attention by the Indians, and I promised that the matter would be considered by the North-West Council. The council that has governed the territories for the last four years was engaged in maturing a law for this purpose, and had our regime continued we would have passed a statute for their preservation. I commend the matter to the attention of our successors as one of urgent importance.

5th. There is another class of the population in the North-West whose position I desire to bring under the notice of the Privy Council. I refer to the wandering Half-breeds of the plains, who are chiefly of French descent and live the life of the Indians. There are a few who are identified with the Indians, but there is a large class of Metis who live by the hunt of the buffalo, and have no settled homes. I think that a census of the numbers of these should be procured, and while I would not be disposed to recommend their being brought under the treaties, I would suggest that land should be assigned to them, and that on their settling down, if after an examination into their circumstances, it should be found necessary and expedient, some assistance should be given them to enable them to enter upon agricultural operations.

If the measures suggested by me are adopted, viz., effective regulations with regard to the buffalo, the Indians taught to cultivate the soil, and the erratic Half-breeds encouraged to settle down, I believe that the solution of all social questions of any present importance in the North-West Territories will have been arrived at.

In.conclusion, I have to call your attention to the report made to me by the Hon. Mr. Christie, which I forward herewith; that gentleman took the entire charge of the payments and administration of matters connected with the treaty, and I have to speak in the highest terms of the value of his services.

Accompanying his report will be found the pay sheets, statements of distribution of provisions and clothing, memoranda as to the localities of the reserves, suggestions as to the times and places of payment next year, and a general balance sheet.

A credit of $60,000 was given to me, and I have placed as a refund to the credit of the Receiver-General, $12,730.55. This arises from the fact that owing to the proximity of the buffalo, many of the Indians did not come into the treaty.

I have to acknowledge the benefit I derived from the services of the Hon. James McKay, camping as he did near the Indian encampment. He had the opportunity of meeting them constantly, and learning their views which his familarity with the Indian dialects enabled him to do. Dr. Jackes took a warm interest in the progress of our work, and kept a record of the negotiations, a copy of which I enclose and which I think ought to be published, as it will be of great value to those who will be called on to administer the treaty, showing as it does what was said by the negotiators and by the Indians, and preventing misrepresentations in the future. The Commissioners are under obligations to Lieut.-Colonel McLeod, and the other officers and men of the police force for their escort.

The conduct of the men was excellent, and the presence of the force as an emblem and evidence of the establishment of authority in the North-West was of great value.

I have to record my appreciation of the kindness of Messrs. Clarke, of Fort Carlton, and McKay of Fort Pitt, and of the other officials of the Hudson's Bay Company, and of the hearty assistance they extended towards the accomplishment of our mission. I have also to mention the interest taken in the negotiations by His Lordship Bishop Grandin, and by the various missionaries, Protestant and Catholic.

On this occasion, as on others, I found the Half-breed population whether French or English generally using the influence of their relationship to the Indians in support of our efforts to come to a satisfactory arrangement with them.

We also had the advantage of good interpreters, having secured the services of Messrs. Peter Ballendine and John McKay, while the Indians had engaged Mr. Peter Erasmus to discharge the same duty. The latter acted as chief interpreter, being assisted by the others, and is a most efficient interpreter.

I transmit herewith a copy of the treaty, and have only in conclusion to express my hope that this further step in the progress of the work of the Dominion amongst the Indian tribes will prove beneficial to them, and of advantage to the realm.

I have the honor to be, Sir,

Your obedient servant,

ALEXANDER MORRIS,

Lieut.-Governor.

Narrative of the proceedings connected with the effecting of the treaties at Forts Carlton and Pitt, in the year 1876, together with a report of the speeches of the Indians and Commissioners, by A. G. Jackes, Esq., M.D., Secretary to the Commission.

The expedition for the proposed Treaty Number Six, reached the South Saskatchewan on the afternoon of August 14th, where they were met by a messenger from the Cree Indians expressing welcome, also a messenger from Mr. L. Clarke, of

Carlton House, offering to the Governor and party the hospitality of the Fort.

The next morning, when about ten miles from Carlton, the
Commissioners were met by a detachment of Mounted Police
under Major Walker, who escorted them to the Fort ; on the
way the Commissioners passed an encampment of Crees whose
Chief had previously seen the Governor at Duck Lake and
asked him to make the treaty there ; he replied that he could
not promise, that he would meet the Indians where the greater
number wished. These Crees joined in an invocation to the
deity for a blessing on the Governor, and deputed one of their
number to welcome him by shaking hands.

Near the Fort were encamped about two hundred and fifty
lodges of Crees, to whom the Commissioners at once served
out two days' allowance of provisions.

On the 16th the Crees reported that they wanted another
day to confer amongst themselves, this was granted and the
Governor requested them to meet him and the Commissioners
on the 18th at 10 a.m., to commence the business of the
treaty.

FIRST DAY.

August 18th.

At half-past ten His Honor Lieut.-Gov. Morris, the Hon.
W. J. Christie and Hon. Jas. McKay, accompanied by an
escort of North-West Mounted Police, left the Fort for the
camp of the Cree Indians, who had selected a site about a mile
and a half from the Hudson's Bay Fort. There were about
two hundred and fifty lodges, containing over two thousand
souls. The Governor's tent was pitched on a piece of rising
ground about four hundred yards from the Indian camp, and
immediately facing it.

As soon as the Governor and party arrived, the Indians
who were to take part in the treaty, commenced to assemble

near the Chief's tents, to the sound of beating drums and the discharge of small arms, singing, dancing and loud speaking, going on at the same time.

In about half an hour they were ready to advance and meet the Governor; this they did in a large semi-circle ; in their front were about twenty braves on horseback, galloping about in circles, shouting, singing and going through various pictur-esque performances. The semi-circle steadily advanced until within fifty yards of the Governor's tent, when a halt was made and further peculiar ceremonies commenced, the most remark-able of which was the " dance of the stem." This was commenced by the Chiefs, medicine men, councillors, singers and drum-beaters, coming a little to the front and seating themselves on blankets and robes spread for them. The bearer of the stem, Wah-wee-kah-nich-kah-oh-tah-mah-hote (the man you strike on the back), carrying in his hand a large and gorgeously adorned pipe stem, walked slowly along the semi-circle, and advancing to the front, raised the stem to the heavens, then slowly turned to the north, south, east and west, presenting the stem at each point ; returning to the seated group he handed the stem to one of the young men, who commenced a low chant, at the same time performing a ceremonial dance accompanied by the drums and singing of the men and women in the background.

This was all repeated by another of the young men, after which the horsemen again commenced galloping in circles, the whole body slowly advancing. As they approached his tent, the Governor, accompanied by the Hon. W. J. Christie and Hon. Jas. McKay, Commissioners, went forward to meet them and to receive the stem carried by its bearer. It was presen-ted first to the Governor, who in accordance with their cus-toms, stroked it several times, then passed it to the Commis-sioners who repeated the ceremony.

The significance of this ceremony is that the Governor and Commissioners accepted the friendship of the tribe.

The interpreter then introduced the Chiefs and principal

men ; the Indians slowly seating themselves in regular order in front of the tent. In a few minutes there was perfect quiet and order, when His Honor the Lieutenant-Governor addressed them as follows :

" My Indian brothers, Indians of the plains, I have shaken hands with a few of you, I shake hands with all of you in my heart. God has given us a good day, I trust his eye is upon us, and that what we do will be for the benefit of his children.

" What I say and what you say, and what we do, is done openly before the whole people. You are, like me and my friends who are with me, children of the Queen. We are of the same blood, the same God made us and the same Queen rules over us.

" I am a Queen's Councillor, I am her Governor of all these territories, and I am here to speak from her to you. I am here now because for many days the Cree nation have been sending word that they wished to see a Queen's messenger face to face. I told the Queen's Councillors your wishes. I sent you word last year by a man who has gone where we will all go by and by, that a Queen's messenger would meet you this year. I named Forts Carlton and Pitt as the places of meeting, I sent a letter to you saying so, and my heart grew warm when I heard how well you received it.

" As the Queen's chief servant here, I always keep my promises ; the winter came and went but I did not forget my word, and I sent a messenger to tell you that I would meet you at Carlton on the 15th of August, and at Fort Pitt on the 5th of September.

" During the winter I went to Ottawa to consult with the other Queen's Councillors about you amongst other matters, and they said to me, ' you promised a Queen's messenger to the Crees, you have been so much with the Indians, that we wish you to go yourself ;' I said 'the journey is long and I am not a strong man, but when a duty is laid upon me I will do it, but,' I said, ' you must give with me two friends and councillors whom I can trust, to help me in the duty;' and now I have with me two friends whom you and I have known long ; one of them is of your own blood, the other has been many years amongst you.

"I will, in a short time, give you a message from the Queen, and my Councillors will tell you that the words are true. Before I do so, there are so many things I want to say to you that I scarcely know where to begin. I have been nearly four years Governor of Manitoba and these territories, and from the day I was sworn, I took the Indian by the hand, and those who took it have never let it go.

" Three years ago I went to the north-west angle of Lake of the Woods, and there I met the Chippewa nation, I gave them a message and they talked with me and when they understood they took my hand. Some were away, next year I sent messengers to them and I made a treaty between the Queen and them ; there are numbered of those altogether four thousand. I then went to Lake Qu'Appelle the year after, and met the Crees and Chippewas there, gave them my message, and they took my hand. Last summer I went to Lake Winnipeg and gave the Queen's message to the Swampy Crees and they and I, acting for the Queen, came together heart to heart; and now that the Indians of the east understand the Queen and her Councillors, I come to you. And why is all this done ? I will tell you ; it is because you are the subjects of the Queen as I am. She cares as much for one of you as she does for one of her white subjects. The other day a party of Iroquois Indians were taken to England across the ocean ; the Queen heard of it and sent to them, saying, 'I want to see my red children,' took their hands and gave each of them her picture, and sent them away happy with her goodness.

" Before I came here I was one of the Queen's Councillors at Ottawa. We have many Indians there as here, but for many years there has been friendship between the British, and the Indians. We respect the Indians as brothers and as men.

Let me give you a proof it. Years ago there was war between the British and the Americans; there was a great battle ; there were two brave Chief warriors' on the British side, one wore the red coat, the other dressed as you do, but they fought side by side as brothers ; the one was Brock and the other was Tecumseth whose memory will never die ; the blood of both watered the ground ; the bones of Tecumseth were hid by his friends ; the remains of Brock by his, and now a great pile of stone stands up toward heaven in his memory. And now the white man is searching for the remains of Tecumseth, and when found they will build another monument in honour of the Indian.

" I hope the days of fighting are over, but notwithstanding the whites are as much your friends in these days of peace, as in war.

" The many Indians in the place that I have left are happy, prosperous, contented and growing in numbers. A meeting of the Grand Council of the Six Nation Indians was held a month ago; they now number six thousand souls. They met to thank the Queen and to say that they were content, and why are they content ? Because many years ago the Queen's Councillors saw that the Indians that would come after, must be cared for, they saw that the means of living were passing away from the Indians, they knew that women and children were sometimes without food ; they sent men to speak to the Indians, they said your children must be educated, they must be taught to raise food for themselves. The Indians heard them, the Councillors gave them seed, land, food, taught their children and let them feel that they were of one blood with the whites. Now, what we have found to work so well where I came from we want to have here in our territories, and I am happy to say that my heart is gladdened by the way the Indians have met me.

" We are not here as traders, I do not come as to buy or sell horses or goods, I come to you, children of the Queen, to try to help you ; when I say yes, I mean it, and when I say no, I mean it too.

14

" I want you to think of my words, I want to tell you that what we talk about is very important. What I trust and hope we will do is not for to-day or to-morrow only ; what I will promise, and what I believe and hope you will take, is to last as long as that sun shines and yonder river flows.

" You have to think of those who will come after you, and it will be a remembrance for me as long as I live, if I can go away feeling that I have done well for you. I believe we can understand each other, if not it will be the first occasion on which the Indians have not done so. If you are as anxious for your own welfare as I am, I am certain of what will happen.

"The day is passing. I thank you for the respectful reception you have given me. I will do here as I have done on former occasions. I hope you will speak your minds as fully and as plainly as if I was one of yourselves.

" I wish you to think of what I have said. I wish you to present your Chiefs to me to-day if you are ready, if not then we will wait until to-morrow."

Here the Indians requested an adjournment until next day in order that they might meet in council ; this was granted, and the first day's proceedings terminated.

Late in the evening the escort of Mounted Police was reinforced by a detachment, accompanied by their band, under command of Col. Jarvis, making a force of nearly one hundred men and officers.

SECOND DAY.

August 19th.

The Lieutenant-Governor and Commissioners, with the Mounted Police escort, headed by their band, proceeded to the camp to meet the Indians at 10:30 a.m. The Indians having assembled in regular order with their two leading Chiefs, Mistah-wah-sis and Ah-tuck-ah-coop seated in front, the Governor said :

" My friends, we have another bright day before us, and I trust that when it closes our faces will continue as bright as the day before us. I spoke yesterday as a friend to friends, as a brother to brothers, as a father to his children. I did not want to hurry you, I wanted you to think of my words, and now I will be glad if you will do as I asked you then, present your Chiefs to me, and I shall be glad to hear the words of the Indians through the voice of their Chiefs, or whoever they may appoint.

The head men then brought forward Mis-tah-wah-sis, of the Carlton Indians, representing seventy-six lodges. Ah-tuck-ah-coop, of the Wood Indians, representing about seventy lodges. These were acknowledged as the leading Chiefs, after them came James Smith, of the Fort-a-la-Corne Indians, fifty lodges. John Smith, of the Prince Albert and South Branch Indians, fifty lodges. The Chip-ee-wayan, of the Plain Indians, sixty lodges. Yah-yah-tah-kus-kin-un, of the Fishing or Sturgeon lake Indians, twenty lodges. Pee-yahan-kah-mihk-oo-sit, thirty lodges. Wah-wee-kah-nich-kah-oh-tah-mah-hote, of the River Indians, fifty lodges.

Here a messenger came from the Indians under Chief Beardy, camped at Duck Lake, eight miles from the main camp. He shook hands with the Governor and said," I am at a loss at this time what to say, for the Indians' mind cannot be all the same, that is why I came to tell the Governor the right of it ; with a good heart I plead at this time, it is not my own work, I would like to know his mind just now and hear the terms of the treaty."

The Governor said in reply : " If your Chief and his people had been in their places here, they would have heard with the rest what I had to say. You refused to meet me here, yet you sent and asked me to give you provisions, but I refused to do so unless you joined the others; and now I will not tell my message to this messenger until I tell all the rest ; he can hear with the rest and take back my words to his chief." The messenger expressed himself satisfied, and took his seat with the others.

On the Indians expressing themselves ready to hear the message, the Governor said :

" First I wish to talk to you about what I regard as something affecting the lives of yourselves and the lives of your children. Often when I thought of the future of the Indian my heart was sad within me. I saw that the large game was getting scarcer and scarcer, and I feared that the Indians would melt away like snow in spring before the sun. It was my duty as Governor to think of them, and I wondered if the Indians of the plains and lakes could not do as their brothers where I came from did. And now, when I think of it, I see a bright sky before me. I have been nearly four years working among my Indian brothers, and I am glad indeed to find that many of them are seeking to have homes of their own, having gardens and sending their children to school.

" Last spring I went to see some of the Chippewas, this year I went again and I was glad to see houses built, gardens planted and wood cut for more houses. Understand me, I do not want to interfere with your hunting and fishing. I want you to pursue it through the country, as you have heretofore done ; but I would like your children to be able to find food for themselves and their children that come after them. Sometimes when you go to hunt you can leave your wives and children at home to take care of your gardens.

" I am glad to know that some of you have already begun to build and to plant ; and I would like on behalf of the Queen to give each band that desires it a home of their own ; I want to act in this matter while it is time. The country is wide and you are scattered, other people will come in. Now unless the places where you would like to live are secured soon there might be difficulty. The white man might come and settle on the very place where you would like to be. Now what I and my brother Commissioners would like to do is this : we wish to give each band who will accept of it a place where they may live ; we wish to give you as much or more land than you need ; we wish to send a man that surveys the land to mark it off, so you will know it is your own, and no one will interfere with you. What I would propose to do is what we have done in other places. For every family of five a reserve to themselves of one square mile. Then, as you may not all have made up your minds where you would like to live, I will tell you how that will be arranged : we would do as has been done with happiest results at the North-West Angle. We would send next year a surveyor to agree with you as to the place you would like.

"There is one thing I would say about the reserves. The land I name is much more than you will ever be able to farm, and it may be that you would like to do as your brothers where I came from did.

"They, when they found they had too much land, asked the Queen to it sell for them ; they kept as much as they could want, and the price for which the remainder was sold was put away to increase for them, and many bands now have a yearly income from the land.

"But understand me, once the reserve is set aside, it could not be sold unless with the consent of the Queen and the Indians ; as long as the Indians wish, it will stand there for their good ; no one can take their homes.

"Of course, if when a reserve is chosen, a white man had already settled there, his rights must be respected. The rights and interests of the whites and half-breeds are as dear to the Queen as those of the Indians. She deals justly by all, and I am sure my Indian brothers would like to deal with others as they would have others to deal with them. I think you can now understand the question of homes.

"When the Indians settle on a reserve and have a sufficient number of children to be taught, the Queen would maintain a school. Another thing, that affects you all, some of you have temptations as the white men have, and therefore the fire-

water which does so much harm will not be allowed to be sold
or used in the reserve.   Then before I leave the question of
reserves I will tell you how we will help you to make your
homes there.   We would give to every family actually cultivating the soil the following articles, viz., two hoes, one spade,
one scythe, one axe, and then to help in breaking the land,
one plough and two harrows for every ten families ; and to help
you to put up houses we give to each Chief for his band, one
chest of carpenter's tools, one cross-cut saw, five hand saws, one
pit saw and files, five augers and one grindstone.   Then if a
band settles on its reserves the people will require something to
aid them in breaking the soil.   They could not draw the ploughs
themselves, therefore we will give to each Chief for the use of
his band one or two yokes of oxen according to the number in
the band.   In order to encourage the keeping of cattle we would
give each band a bull and four cows ; having all these things we
would give each band enough potatoes, oats, barley and wheat
for seed to plant the land actually broken.   This would be done
once for all to encourage them to grow for themselves.

"Chiefs ought to be respected, they ought to be looked up
to by their people ; they ought to have good Councillors ; the
Chiefs and Councillors should consult for the good of the
people ; the Queen expects Indians and whites to obey her
laws ; she expects them to live at peace with other Indians
and with the white men ; the Chiefs and Councillors should
teach their people so, and once the Queen approves a Chief or
Councillor he cannot be removed unless he behaves badly.

"The Chiefs and head men are not to be lightly put aside.
When a treaty is made they become servants of the Queen ;
they are to try and keep order amongst their people.   We will
try to keep order in the whole country.

"A Chief has his braves ; you see here the braves of our
Queen, and why are they here ?   To see that no white man
does wrong to the Indian.   To see that none give liquor to
the Indian.   To see that the Indians do no harm to each

other. Three years ago some Americans killed some Indians ; when the Queen's Councillors heard of it they said, we will send men there to protect the Indians, the Queen's subjects shall not be shot down by the Americans ; now you understand why the police force is in this country, and you should rejoice.

" I have said a Chief was to be respected ; I wear a uniform because I am an officer of the Queen, the officers of the police wear uniforms as servants of the Queen. So we give to Chiefs and Councillors good and suitable uniform indicating their office, to wear on these and other great days.

" We recognize four head men to each large band and two to each small one.

" I have always been much pleased when Indians came to me and showed me medals given to their grandfathers and transmitted to them ; now we have with us silver medals that no Chief need be ashamed to wear, and I have no doubt that when the Chiefs are gone, they will be passed on to their children. In addition each Chief will be given a flag to put over his lodge to show that he is a Chief.

" I told you yesterday that I and my brother Commissioners were not here as traders.

" There is one thing I ought to have mentioned in addition to what I have already named, that is, if a treaty is made here and at Fort Pitt, we will give every year to the Indians included in it, one thousand five hundred dollars' worth of ammunition and twine.

" You think only for yourselves, we have to think of the Indians all over the country, we cannot treat one better than another, it would not be just, we will therefore do this, and what I tell you now is the last.

" When the treaty is closed, if it be closed, we will make a present to every man, woman and child, of twelve dollars, the money being paid to the head of a family for his wife, and children not married.

"To each Chief, instead of twelve, we give twenty-five dollars, and to each head man fifteen dollars, their wives and children getting the same as the others. I told you also that what I was promising was not for to-day or to-morrow only, but should continue as long as the sun shone and the river flowed. My words will pass away and so will yours, so I always write down what I promise, that our children may know what we said and did. Next year I shall send copies of what is written in the treaty, printed on skin, so that it cannot rub out nor be destroyed, and one shall be given to each Chief so that there may be no mistakes.

"Then I promise to do as we have done with all before from Cypress Hills to Lake Superior, the Queen will agree to pay yearly five dollars per head for every man, woman and child. I cannot treat you better than the others, but I am ready to treat you as well.

"A little thing I had forgotten, and I have done. The Chiefs' and head men's coats will wear out, they are meant to be worn when it is necessary to show that they are officers of the Queen, and every third year they will be replaced by new ones.

"And now, Indians of the plains, I thank you for the open ear you have given me; I hold out my hand to you full of the Queen's bounty and I hope you will not put it back. We have no object but to discharge our duty to the Queen and towards you. Now that my hand is stretched out to you, it is for you to say whether you will take it and do as I think you ought—act for the good of your people.

"What I have said has been in the face of the people. These things will hold good next year for those that are now away. I have done. What do you say?"

MIS-TAH-WAH-SIS here came forward, shook hands with the Governor, and said :—" We have heard all he has told us, but I want to tell him how it is with us as well; when a thing is thought of quietly, probably that is the best way. I ask this much from him this day that we go and think of his words."

The Governor and Commissioners agreed to the request and asked the Indians to meet them Monday morning at ten o'clock with as little delay as possible.

Before parting, the Governor said to the Indians, "This is a great day for us all. I have proposed on behalf of the Queen what I believe to be for your good, and not for yours only, but for that of your children's children, and when you go away think of my words. Try to understand what my heart is towards you. I will trust that we may come together hand to hand and heart to heart again. I trust that God will bless this bright day for our good, and give your Chiefs and Councillors wisdom so that you will accept the words of your Governor. I have said."

Sunday, August 20th.

Divine service, which was largely attended, was held in the square of Fort Carlton, by the Rev. John McKay, at half-past ten a.m.

At noon a message came from the encampment of Indians requesting the Rev. Mr. McKay to hold service with them, which he did in the afternoon, preaching in their own tongue to a congregation of over two hundred adult Crees.

Monday, August 21st.

The principal Chief sent a message that as the Indians had held no Council on Sunday, they wished to have Monday to themselves and would if ready meet the Commissioners on Tuesday morning.

THIRD DAY.

August 22nd.

The Governor and Commissioners having proceeded as usual to the camp, the Indians soon assembled in order, when the Lieutenant-Governor said :

" Indian children of the Queen, it is now a week to-day since

I came here on the day I said I would ; I have to go still further after I leave here, and then a long journey home to Red River.

"I have not hurried you, you have had two days to think ; I have spoken much to you, and now I wish to hear you, my ears are open and I wish to hear the voices of your principal Chiefs or of those chosen to speak for them. Now I am waiting."

Oo-PEE-TOO-KERAH-HAN-AP-EE-WEE-YIN (the Pond-maker) came forward and said :— "We have heard your words that you had to say to us as the representative of the Queen. We were glad to hear what you had to say, and have gathered together in council and thought the words over amongst us, we were glad to hear you tell us how we might live by our own work. When I commence to settle on the lands to make a living for myself and my children, I beg of you to assist me in every way possible—when I am at a loss how to proceed I want the advice and assistance of the Government ; the children yet unborn, I wish you to treat them in like manner as they advance in civilization like the white man. This is all I have been told to say now, if I have not said anything in a right manner I wish to be excused; this is the voice of the people."

GOVERNOR—"I have heard the voice of the people; I am glad to learn that they are looking forward to having their children civilized, that is the great object of the Government, as is proved by what I have offered. Those that come after us in the Government will think of your children as we think of you. The Queen's Councillors intend to send a man to look after the Indians, to be chief superintendent of Indian affairs, and under him there will be two or three others to live in the country, that the Queen's Councillors may know how the Indians are prospering.

"I cannot promise, however, that the Government will feed and support all the Indians ; you are many, and if we were to try to do it, it would take a great deal of money, and some of you would never do anything for yourselves. What I have offered does not take away your living, you will have it then as you have now, and what I offer now is put on top of it. This I can tell you, the Queen's Government will always take a deep interest in your living."

THE BADGER—"We want to think of our children; we do not want to be too greedy; when we commence to settle down on the reserves that we select, it is there we want your aid, when we cannot help ourselves and in case of troubles seen and unforeseen in the future."

Sak-ah-moos and several other Indians in order repeated what The Badger had said.

GOVERNOR—"I have told you that the money I have offered you would be paid to you and to your children's children. I know that the sympathy of the Queen, and her assistance, would be given you in any unforeseen circumstances. You must trust to her generosity. Last winter when some of the Indians wanted food because the crops had been destroyed by grasshoppers, although it was not promised in the treaty, nevertheless the Government sent money to buy them food, and in the spring when many of them were sick a man was sent to try and help them. We cannot foresee these things, and all I can promise is that you will be treated kindly, and in that extraordinary circumstances you must trust to the generosity of the Queen. My brother Commissioner, Mr. McKay, will speak to you in your own language."

MR. MCKAY—"My friends, I wish to make you a clear explanation of some things that it appears you do not understand. It has been said to you by your Governor that we did not come here to barter or trade with you for the land. You have made demands on the Governor, and from the way you have put them a white man would understand that you asked for daily provisions, also supplies for your hunt and for your pleasure excursions. Now my reasons for explaining to you are based on my past experience of treaties, for no sooner will the Governor and Commissioners turn their backs on you than some of you will say this thing and that thing was promised and the promise not fulfilled; that you cannot rely on the Queen's representative, that even he will not tell the truth, whilst among yourselves are the falsifiers. Now before we rise from here it must be understood, and it must be in writing, all that you are promised by the Governor and Commissioners, and I hope you will not leave until you have thoroughly understood the meaning of every word that comes from us. We have not come here to deceive you, we have not come here to rob you, we have not come here to take away anything that belongs to you, and we are not here to make peace as we would to hostile Indians, because you are the children of the Great Queen as we are, and there has never been anything but peace between us. What you have not understood clearly we will do our utmost to make perfectly plain to you."

GOVERNOR—"I have another word to say to the Indians on this matter: last year an unforeseen calamity came upon the people of Red River, the grasshoppers came and ate all their crops. There is no treaty between the people of Red River and the Queen except that they are her subjects. There was no promise to help them, but I sent down and said that unless help came some of the people would die from want of food, and that they had nothing wherewith to plant. The Queen's Councillors at once gave money to feed the people, and seed that they might plant the ground; but that was something out of and beyond every-day life, and therefore I say that some great sickness or famine stands as a special case. You may rest assured that when you go to your reserves you will be followed by the watchful eye and sympathetic hand of the Queen's Councillors."

THE BADGER—"I do not want you to feed me every day; you must not understand that from what I have said. When we commence to settle down on the ground to make there our own

living, it is then we want your help, and that is the only way
that I can see how the poor can get along."

GOVERNOR—"You will remember the promises which I have
already made; I said you would get seed; you need not concern
yourselves so much about what your grand-children are going
to eat ; your children will be taught, and then they will be as
well able to take care of themselves as the whites around
them."

MIS-TAH-WAH-SIS (one of the leading Chiefs)—"It is well
known that if we had plenty to live on from our gardens we
would not still insist on getting more provision, but it is in case
of any extremity, and from the ignorance of the Indian in commencing to settle that we thus speak ; we are as yet in the
dark; this is not a trivial matter for us.

"We were glad to hear what the Governor was saying to us
and we understood it, but we are not understood, we do not
mean to ask for food for every day but only when we commence and in case of famine or calamity.   What we speak of
and do now will last as long as the sun shines and the river
runs, we are looking forward to our children's children, for we
are old and have but few days to live."

AH-TAHK-AH-COOP (the other leading Chief)—"The things
we have been talking about in our councils I believe are for
our good.   I think of the good Councillors of the Queen and
of her Commissioners ; I was told the Governor was a good
man, and now that I see him I believe he is ; in coming to see
us, and what he has spoken, he has removed almost all obstacles
and misunderstandings, and I hope he may remove them all.
I have heard the good things you promise us, you have told us
of the white man's way of living and mentioned some of the
animals by which he gets his living, others you did not.   We
want food in the spring when we commence to farm ; according
as the Indian settles down on his reserves, and in proportion as
he advances, his wants will increase."

The Indians here asked for the afternoon to hold further

council. To this the Governor said, " I grant the request of the Indians but I give them a word of warning, do not listen to every voice in your camp, listen to your wise men who know something of life, and do not come asking what is unreasonable, it pains me to have to say no, and I tell you again I cannot treat you with more favor than the other Indians. To-morrow, when we meet, speak out your minds openly, and I will answer, holding nothing back. Be ready to meet me to-morrow, as soon as my flag is raised, for remember I have a long journey before me and we ought to come to a speedy understanding. I trust the God who made you will give you wisdom in considering what you have to deal with."

FOURTH DAY.

August 23rd.

Shortly after the business had commenced, proceedings were interrupted by the loud talking of a Chippewa, who was addressing the Indians gathered in front of the tent. The Governor said, " There was an Indian, a Chippewa, stood and spoke to you, he did not speak to his Governor as he should have done : I am willing to hear what any band has to say, but they must speak to me. I have been talking to the Crees for several days. I wish to go on with the work ; if the Chippewas want to talk with me I will hear them afterwards. They are a little handful of strangers from the east, I have treated with their whole nation, they are not wiser than their people.

" There are many reasons why business should go on ; I hear that the buffalo are near you and you want to be off to your hunt ; there are many mouths here to feed and provisions are getting low ; now my friends I am ready to hear you."

Tee-tee-quay-say—" Listen to me, my friends, all you who are sitting around here, and you will soon hear what the interpreter has to say for us."

The interpreter then read a list of the things the Indians

had agreed in council to ask, viz. :—One ox and cow for each family. Four hoes, two spades, two scythes and a whetstone for each family. Two axes, two hay forks, two reaping hooks, one plough and one harrow for every three families. To each Chief one chest of tools as proposed. Seed of every kind in full to every one actually cultivating the soil. To make some provision for the poor, unfortunate, blind and lame. To supply us with a minister and school teacher of whatever denomination we belong to. To prevent fire-water being sold in the whole Saskatchewan.

As the tribe advances in civilization, all agricultural implements to be supplied in proportion.

When timber becomes scarcer on the reserves we select for ourselves, we want to be free to take it anywhere on the common. If our choice of a reserve does not please us before it is surveyed we want to be allowed to select another. We want to be at liberty to hunt on any place as usual. If it should happen that a Government bridge or scow is built on the Saskatchewan at any place, we want passage free. One boar, two sows, one horse, harness and waggon for each Chief. One cooking stove for each Chief. That we be supplied with medicines free of cost. That a hand-mill be given to each band. Lastly in case of war occurring in the country, we do not want to be liable to serve in it.

Tee-tee-quay-say then continued—"When we look back to the past we do not see where the Cree nation has ever watered the ground with the white man's blood, he has always been our friend and we his; trusting to the Giver of all good, to the generosity of the Queen, and to the Governor and his councillors, we hope you will grant us this request."

Wah-wee-kah-nihk-kah-oo-tah-mah-hote (the man you strike in the back)—"Pity the voice of the Indian, if you grant what we request the sound will echo through the land; open the way; I speak for the children that they may be glad; the land is wide, there is plenty of room. My mouth is full of

milk, I am only as a sucking child; I am glad; have com-
passion on the manner in which I was brought up; let our
children be clothed; let us now stand in the light of day to see
our way on this earth; long ago it was good when we first
were made, I wish the same were back again. But now the
law has come, and in that I wish to walk. What God has
said, and our mother here (the earth), and these our brethren,
let it be so."

To this the Governor replied—"Indians, I made you my
offer. You have asked me now for many things, some of
which were already promised. You are like other Indians I
have met, you can ask very well. You are right in asking,
because you are saying what is in your minds. I have had
taken down a list of what you have asked, and I will now consult with my brother Commissioners and give you my answer
in a little while."

After consultation, the Governor again had the Indians
assembled, and said—"I am ready now to answer you, but
understand well, it is not to be talked backwards and forwards.
I am not going to act like a man bargaining for a horse for
you. I have considered well what you have asked for, and
my answer will be a final one. I cannot grant everything you
ask, but as far as I can go I will, and when done I can only
say you will be acting to your own interests if you take my
hand.

"I will speak of what you asked yesterday and to-day. I
told you yesterday that if any great sickness or general famine
overtook you, that on the Queen being informed of it by her
Indian agent, she in her goodness would give such help as she
thought the Indians needed. You asked for help when you
settled on your reserves during the time you were planting.
You asked very broadly at first. I think the request you make
now is reasonable to a certain extent; but help should be given
after you settle on the reserve for three years only, for after
that time you should have food of your own raising, besides

all the things that are given to you; this assistance would only be given to those actually cultivating the soil. Therefore, I would agree to give every spring, for three years, the sum of one thousand dollars to assist you in·buying provisions while planting the ground. I do this because you seem anxious to make a living for yourselves, it is more than has been done anywhere else; I must do it on my own responsibility, and trust to the other Queen's councillors to ratify it.

" I will now answer what you had written down and asked to-day. I expect you to be reasonable, none of us get all our own way. You asked first for four hoes, two spades, two scythes and whetstone, two axes, two hay forks and two reaping hooks for every family. I am willing to give them to every family actually cultivating the soil, for if given to all it would only encourage idleness. You ask a plough and harrow for every three families; I am willing to give them on the same conditions. The carpenters' tools, as well as the seed grain, were already promised. I cannot undertake the responsibility of promising provision for the poor, blind and lame. In all parts of the Queen's dominions we have them; the poor whites have as much reason to be helped as the poor Indian ; they must be left to the charity and kind hearts of the people. If you are prosperous yourselves you can help your unfortunate brothers.

" You ask for school teachers and ministers. With regard to ministers I cannot interfere. There are large societies formed for the purpose of sending the gospel to the Indians. The Government does not provide ministers anywhere in Canada. I had already promised you that when you settled down, and there were enough children, schools would be maintained. You see missionaries here on the ground, both Roman Catholic and Protestant; they have been in the country for many years. As it has been in the past, so it will be again, you will not be forgotten.

" The police force is here to prevent the selling or giving of

15

liquor to the Indians.   The Queen has made a strong law against the fire-water; and the councillors of the country have made a law against the use of poison for animals.

"You can have no difficulty in choosing your reserves; be sure to take a good place so that there will be no need to change ; you would not be held to your choice until it was surveyed.

"You want to be at liberty to hunt as before.   I told you we did not want to take that means of living from you, you have it the same as before, only this, if a man, whether Indian or Half-breed, had a good field of grain, you would not destroy it with your hunt.   In regard to bridges and scows on which you want passage free, I do not think it likely that the Government will build any, they prefer to leave it to private enterprise to provide these things.

"In case of war you ask not to be compelled to fight.   I trust there will be no war, but if it should occur I think the Queen would leave you to yourselves.   I am sure she would not ask her Indian children to fight for her unless they wished, but if she did call for them and their wives and children were in danger they are not the men I think them to be, if they did not come forward to their protection.

"A medicine chest will be kept at the house of each Indian agent, in case of sickness amongst you.   I now come to two requests which I shall have to change a little, you have to think only of yourselves, we have to think of all the Indians and of the way in which we can procure the money to purchase all these things the Indians require.   The Queen's Councillors will have to pay every year to help the Indians a very large sum of money.

"I offered you to each band, according to size, two or four oxen, also one bull and four cows, and now you ask for an ox and a cow for each family.   I suppose in this treaty there will be six hundred families, so it would take very much money to grant these things, and then all the other Indians would want them, so we cannot do it: but that you may see it that we are anxious to have you raise animals of your own we will give you for each band four oxen, one bull, six cows, one boar and two pigs. After a band has settled on a reserve and commenced to raise grain, we will give them a hand-mill.

"At first we heard of only two Chiefs, now they are becoming many. You ask a cooking-stove for each, this we cannot give; he must find a way of cooking for himself. And now, although I fear I am going too far, I will grant the request that each Chief be furnished with a horse, harness, and waggon.

"I have answered your requests very fully, and that there may be no mistake as to what we agree upon, it will be written down, and I will leave a copy with the two principal Chiefs, and as soon as it can be properly printed I will send copies to the Chiefs so that they may know what is written, and there can be no mistake.

"It now rests with you, my friends, and I ask you without any hesitation to take what I have offered you."

AH-TUCK-AH-COOP—"I never sent a letter to the Governor; I was waiting to meet him, and what we have asked we considered would be for the benefit of our children. I am not like some of my friends who have sent their messages down, even stretched out their hands to the Queen asking her to come; I have always said to my people that I would wait to see the Governor arrive, then he would ask what would benefit his children; now I ask my people, those that are in favour of the offer, to say so."

They all assented by holding up their hands and shouting.

OO-PEE-TOO-KORAH-HAIR-AP-EE-WEE-YIN (The Pond-maker)— "I do not differ from my people, but I want more explanation. I heard what you said yesterday, and I thought that when the law was established in this country it would be for our good. From what I can hear and see now, I cannot understand that I shall be able to clothe my children and feed them as long as

sun shines and water runs. With regard to the different
Chiefs who are to occupy the reserves, I expected they would
receive sufficient for their support, this is why I speak. In the
presence of God and the Queen's representative I say this, because I do not know how to build a house for myself, you see
how naked I am, and if I tried to do it my naked body would
suffer; again, I do not know how to cultivate the ground for
myself, at the same time I quite understand what you have
offered to assist us in this."

JOSEPH THOMA proposed to speak for The Red Pheasant,
Chief of Battle River Indians—"This is not my own desire
that I speak now, it is very hard we cannot all be of one
mind. You know some were not present when the list of
articles mentioned was made, there are many things overlooked
in it; it is true that what has been done this morning is good.
What has been overlooked I will speak about. The one that
is next to the Chief (first head man) should have had a horse
as well. I want the Governor to give us somebody to build
our houses, we cannot manage it ourselves, for my own part
you see my crippled hand. It is true the Governor says he
takes the responsibility on himself in granting the extra
requests of the Indians, but let him consider on the quality of
the land he has already treated for. There is no farming land
whatever at the north-west angle, and he goes by what he has
down there. What I want, as he has said, is twenty-five dollars
to each Chief and to his head men twenty dollars. I do not
want to keep the lands nor do I give away, but I have set the
value. I want to ask as much as will cover the skin of the
people, no more nor less. I think what he has offered is too
little. When you spoke you mentioned ammunition, I did
not hear mention of a gun; we will not be able to kill anything
simply by setting fire to powder. I want a gun for each Chief
and head man, and I want ten miles around the reserve where
I may be settled. I have told the value I have put on my
land."

GOVERNOR—" I have heard what has been said on behalf of the Red Pheasant. I find fault that when there was handed me a list from the Indians, the Red Pheasant sat still and led me to believe he was a party to it. What I have offered was thought of long before I saw you; it has been accepted by others more in number than you are. I am glad that so many are of our mind. I am surprised you are not all. I hold out a full hand to you, and it will be a bad day for you and your children if I have to return and say that the Indians threw away my hand. I cannot accede to the requests of the Red Pheasant. I have heard and considered the wants of Mist-ow-asis and Ah-tuck-ah-coop, and when the people were spoken to I understood they were pleased. As for the little band who are not of one mind with the great body, I am quite sure that a week will not pass on leaving this before they will regret it. I want the Indians to understand that all that has been offered is a gift, and they still have the same mode of living as before."

Here the principal Chiefs intimated the acceptance of the proposal of the Commissioners, the Red Pheasant repudiating the demands and remarks of Joseph Thoma.

GOVERNOR—" I am happy at what we have done; I know it has been a good work; I know your hearts will be glad as the days pass. This will be the fourth time that I have done what we are going to do to-day. I thank you for your trust in me. I have had written down what I promised. For the Queen and in her name I will sign it, likewise Mr. McKay and Mr. Christie. Then I will ask the Chiefs and their head men to sign it in the presence of the witnesses, whites and *Metis*, around us, some of whom I will also ask to sign. What we have done has been done before the Great Spirit and in the face of the people.

" I will ask the interpreter to read to you what has been written, and before I go away I will have a copy made to leave with the principal Chiefs. The payments will be made to-morrow, the suits of clothes, medals and flags given also, besides which a present of calicoes, shirts, tobacco, pipes and other articles will be given to the Indians."

MIS-TOW-ASIS—" I wish to speak a word for some Half-breeds who wish to live on the reserves with us, they are as poor as we are and need help."

GOVERNOR—" How many are there?"

MIS-TOW-ASIS—"About twenty."

GOVERNOR—"The Queen has been kind to the Half-breeds of Red River and has given them much land; we did not come as messengers to the Half-breeds, but to the Indians. I have heard some Half-breeds want to take lands at Red River and join the Indians here, but they cannot take with both hands. The Half-breeds of the North-West cannot come into the Treaty. The small class of Half-breeds who live as Indians and with the Indians, can be regarded as Indians by the Commissioners, who will judge of each case on its own merits as it comes up, and will report their action to the Queen's Councillors for their approval.

The treaty was then signed by the Lieutenant-Governor, Hon. James McKay, Hon. W. J. Christie, Mist-ow-asis, Ah-tuck-ah-coop, and the remainder of the Chiefs and the Councillors.

August 24th.

Immediately on meeting at ten a.m., the Governor called up Mis-tow-asis and Ah-tuck-ah-coop, the two principal Chiefs, and presented their uniforms, medals and flags; after them the lesser Chiefs, their medals and flags, and told them they and their Councillors would get their uniforms in the evening from the stores. The Governor then told them that Mr. Christie would commence payments as soon as he had finished talking with the few Saulteaux; he expected the Chiefs and Councillors to assist in every way possible; if any of the Chiefs had decided where they would like to have their reserves, they could tell Mr. Christie when they went to be paid. " Now, I have only to say farewell; we have done a good work; we will never all of us meet again face to face, but I go on to my other work, feeling that I have, in the Queen's hands, been instrumental to your good. I pray God's blessing upon you to make you happy and prosperous, and I bid you farewell."

The Indians intimated their pleasure by a general shout of approval, and thus broke up the conference which resulted in the Treaty with the Carlton Crees.

The Lieutenant-Governor then met the few Chippewas who came forward, and told them that they must be paid at the place where they belonged, that they could not be paid at Fort Pitt, and said, "If what I have heard is true I shall not be well pleased. I am told you are of a bad mind ; you proposed to prevent me from crossing the river ;* if you did it was very foolish ; you could no more stop me than you could the river itself. Then I am told you tried to prevent the other Indians from making the treaty. I tell you this to your faces so if it is not true you can say so ; but whether it is or not it makes no difference in my duty. The Queen has made treaties with the whole Chippewa nation except two or three little wandering bands such as you ; you have heard all that has been said and done these many days ; I would like to see you helped as well as the other Indians ; I do not think you are wiser than the Chippewas from Lake Superior to the North-West Angle ; I went there with Mr. McKay, and we made a treaty with twenty Chiefs and four thousand Chippewas."

Nus-was-oo-wah-tum—" When we asked the Cree bands what they intended to do with regard to the treaty they would not come to us ; it is true we told them 'do not be in a hurry in giving your assent ;' you ought to be detained a little while ; all along the prices have been to one side, and we have had no say. He that made us provided everything for our mode of living ; I have seen this all along, it has brought me up and I am not tired of it, and for you, the white man, everything has been made for

---

* South Saskatchewan.

your maintenance, and now that you come and stand on this our earth (ground) I do not understand; I see dimly to-day what you are doing, and I find fault with a portion of it; that is why I stand back; I would have been glad if every white man of every denomination were now present to hear what I say; through what you have done you have cheated my kinsmen."

GOVERNOR—"I will not sit here and hear such words from the Chippewas. Who are you? You come from my country and you tell me the Queen has cheated you; it is not so. You say we have the best of the bargains; you know it is not so. If you have any requests to make in a respectful manner I am ready to hear."

CHIPPEWA—"The God that made us and who alone is our master, I am afraid of Him to deviate from his commandment."

The Chippewas, about half a dozen in all, being from Quill Lake chiefly, left, and Mr. Christie proceeded with the payments, which occupied the remainder of the 24th and all the 25th. He paid in all, Chiefs, 13; head men, 44; men, 262; women, 473; boys, 473; girls, 481; from Treaty Number Four, 41; total, 1,787. A large number of the tribe absent at the hunt will be paid next year.

Next morning, the 26th, the whole Cree camp, headed by their Chiefs and head men, wearing their uniforms and medals, came to Carlton House and assembled in the square to pay their farewell visit to the Governor; the Chiefs came forward in order and shook hands, each one making a few remarks expressive of their gratitude for the benefits received and promised, and of their good will to the white man.

The Governor briefly replied, telling them that he was much gratified with the manner in which they had behaved throughout the treaty; he had never dealt with a quieter, more orderly and respectful body of Indians; he was pleased with the manner in which they had met him and taken his advice; he was glad to hear that they were determined to go to work and help themselves : he hoped their Councils would always be wisely conducted, and that they would do everything in their power to maintain peace amongst themselves and with their neighbors ; he hoped the Almighty would give them wisdom and prosper them. They then gave three cheers for the Queen, the Governor, the mounted police and Mr. Lawrence Clarke, of Carlton House.

On the 27th a message was received from Duck Lake from the Willow Indians, the band which had hitherto held aloof, in reply to a message sent to them by the Governor, that they would meet the Governor and Commissioners at the place designated by the Governor, the camp of the Hon. James McKay, about five miles from Carlton House. Accordingly, the next morning the Commissioners met them, and after the usual ceremonial hand-shaking,

SAY-SWAY-PUS—" God has given us a beautiful day for which I feel very grateful. In grasping your hand I am grasping that of our Mother, the Queen. If it is your intention to honor me with a Chief's clothing, I wish you would give me one that would correspond with the sky above. I hope we will be able to understand each other."

CHIN-UN-US-KUT (The Stump)—" I feel very grateful that I am spared by the Great Spirit to see this day of his, may we be blessed in whatever we do this day."

GOVERNOR—"Crees, my brother children of the Great Queen, I am glad to meet you here to-day. I say as you said the first day I saw you, ' it is a bright day and I hope God will bless us.' I have been sorry for you for many days. I took you by the hand on the first day, but a wall rose up between us, it seemed as if you were trying to draw away but I would not let your hand go. I talked for many days with the great body of the Indians here but you refused to meet me; the others and I understood each other. I was going away to-day, but I thought pity of you who had not talked with me. I was sent here to make you understand the Queen's will. I received your letter last night and was glad to learn that you wanted to accept the terms I had offered, and which had been accepted by the other Indians. Before I received your letter I had sent you one asking you to meet me here where we are now, and I am glad you have come, as I could not otherwise have met you.

"One of you made a request that if he were accepted as a Chief, he should have a blue coat. I do not yet know who the Chiefs are. To be a Chief he must have followers. One man came forward as a Chief and I had to tell him unless you have twenty tents you cannot continue as a Chief.

"The color of your Chief's coat is perhaps a little thing; red is the color all the Queen's Chiefs wear. I wear this coat, but it is only worn by those who stand as the Queen's Councillors; her soldiers and her officers wear red, and all the other Chiefs of the Queen wear the coats we have brought, and the good of this is that when the Chief is seen with his uniform and medal every one knows he is an officer of hers. I should be sorry to see you different from the others, and now that you understand you would not wish it."

KAH-MEE-YIS-TOO-WAYS (The Beardy)—"I feel grateful for this day, and I hope we will be blessed. I am glad that I see something that will be of use; I wish that we all as a people may be benefitted by this. I want that all these things should be preserved in a manner that they might be useful to us all; it is in the power of men to help each other. We should not act foolishly with the things that are given us to live by. I think some things are too little, they will not be sufficient for our wants. I do not want very much more than what has been promised, only a little thing. I will be glad if you will help me by writing my request down; on account of the buffalo I am getting anxious. I wish that each one should have an equal share, if that could be managed; in this I think we would be doing good. Perhaps this is not the only time that we shall see each other. Now I suppose another can say what he wishes.

SAY-SWAY-KUS—" What my brother has said, I say the same, but I want to tell him and our mother the Queen, that although we understand the help they offer us, I am getting alarmed when I look at the buffalo, it appears to me as if there was only one. I trust to the Queen and to the Governor, it is only through their aid we can manage to preserve them. I want to hear from the Governor himself an answer to what I have said, so I may thoroughly understand."

THE BEARDY—"Those things which the Almighty has provided for the sustenance of his children may be given us as well ; where our Father has placed the truth we wish the same to be carried out here, I do not set up a barrier to any road that my children may live by : I want the payment to exist as long as the sun shines and the river runs : if we exercise all our good, this surely will happen : all of our words upon which we agree, I wish to have a copy written on skin as promised ; I want my brother to tell me where I can get this. He has said, ' what I have done with the others I will do with you :' I accept the terms, no doubt it will run further according to our number. When I am utterly unable to help myself I want to receive assistance. I will render all the assistance I can to my brother in taking care of the country. I want from my brother a suit of clothing in color resembling the sky so that he may be able when he sees me to know me ; I want these two (sitting by him) to be Chiefs in our place with me and to have six Councillors (two each) in all."

GOVERNOR—" I will speak to you in regard to food as I have spoken to the other Indians ; we cannot support or feed the Indians every day, further than to help them to find the means of doing it for themselves by cultivating the soil. If you were to be regularly fed some of you would do nothing at all for your own support ; in this matter we will do as we have agreed with the other Indians, and no more. You will get

your share of the one thousand dollars' worth of provisions
when you commence to work on your reserves.

"In a national famine or general sickness, not what happens
in every day life, but if a great blow comes on the Indians,
they would not be allowed to die like dogs.

"What occurred in Red River last year from the destruction
of crops by the grasshoppers, affected our whole people, and
without being bound to do anything, the charity and humanity
of the Government sent means to help them.

"I cannot give the Chief a blue coat : he must accept the
red one and he must not suffer so small a matter as the color
of a coat to stand between us.   I accept the three Chiefs with
two Councillors for each.   With regard to the preservation of
the buffalo, it is a subject of great importance, it will be considered by the Lieutenant-Governor and Council of the North-
West Territories to see if a wise law can be passed, one that
will be a living law that can be carried out and obeyed.   If
such a law be passed it will be printed in Cree as well as in
English and French ; but what the law will be I cannot tell—
you held councils over the treaty, you did not know before the
councils closed what you would decide as to the treaty—no
more can I tell what the North-West Council will decide."

A request was then made that the treaty should include the
Half-breeds, to which the Governor replied : "I have explained
to the other Indians that the Commissioners did not come to
the Half-breeds : there were however a certain class of Indian
Half-breeds who had always lived in the camp with the Indians
and were *in fact* Indians, would be recognized, but no others."

. The Chiefs and head men then signed the treaty in the presence of witnesses, the medals and flags were distributed, payments and distribution of clothing proceeded with and finished,
and the conference came to an end.

The Lieutenant-Governor and party started from Carlton
House on the 31st of August at noon, for Fort Pitt, and when
within about six miles of that post came up with a detachment

of Mounted Police under Inspectors Jarvis and Walker, who escorted them to the fort, arriving on the day appointed (5th September) at an early hour.

There were already assembled near the fort and on the banks of the Saskatchewan over one hundred lodges, and as more were immediately expected they requested postponement of negotiations until the 7th September.

On the morning of the 6th, Sweet Grass, one of the oldest and most respected of the Cree Chiefs, with about thirty of his chief men, who had left their hunt and come in to Fort Pitt purposely to attend the treaty negotiations, called on the Governor to express their satisfaction at his coming and their pleasure in seeing him; the greeting which was certainly affectionate, consisted in the embrace of both arms about the neck and a fraternal kiss on either cheek ; after a short conversation the Governor told them he expected them to be ready to meet him at his tent in the morning; time was rapidly passing and he had a long journey yet before him ; he trusted their Councils would be wise and the results would be beneficial to them.

The Hon. Jas. McKay arrived from Battle River in the evening, and reported that he had met there a number of Indians, principally Saulteaux, who had been in camp at that place for some time. They said there had been about seventy lodges altogether, but as the buffalo were coming near, the poorer ones had started out to hunt, leaving only about ten lodges there. The remaining ones expressed good feeling and said they would like to have waited until the time appointed (September 15th) to meet the Governor and take the treaty, yet as the buffalo hunt was of so much importance to them they could not afford to lose the time, knowing that the Governor had to go to Fort Pitt and return before they could see him, consequently the whole band went out to the plains. This band was composed, it was afterwards ascertained, of the Saulteaux of Jack Fish Lake and of some Crees under the Yellow Sky Chief, and were favorably disposed though unable to remain. They numbered in all sixty-seven tents.

At ten in the morning the Governor and Commissioners, escorted by the Mounted Police, proceeded to the treaty tent a short distance from the fort. About eleven o'clock the Indians commenced to gather, as at Carlton, in a large semicircle. In front were the young men, galloping about on their horses, then the Chiefs and head men, followed by the main body of the band to the number of two or three hundred. As they approached the manœuvres of the horsemen became more and more excited and daring, racing wildly about so rapidly as to be barely distinguishable; unfortunately, from some mischance, two horses and their riders came into collision with such tremendous force as to throw both horses and men violently to the ground; both horses were severely injured and one of the Indians had his hip put out of joint; fortunately, Dr. Kittson of the police, was near by and speedily gave relief to the poor sufferer. The ceremonies, however, still went on; four pipestems were carried about and presented to be stroked in token of good feeling and amity (during this performance the band of the Mounted Police played " God save the Queen), blessings invoked on the whole gathering, the dances performed by the various bands, and finally the pipes of peace smoked by the Governor and Commissioners in turn. The stems, which were finely decorated, were placed with great solemnity on the table in front of the Governor, to be covered for the bearers with blue cloth.

The Chiefs and head men now seated themselves in front of the tent, when the Governor addressed them :

"Indians of the plains, Crees, Chippewayans, Assiniboines and Chippewas, my message is to all. I am here to-day as your Governor under the Queen. The Crees for many days have sent word that they wanted to see some one face to face. The Crees are the principal tribe of the plain Indians, and it is for me a pleasant duty to be here to-day and receive the welcome I have from them. I am here because the Queen and her Councillors have the good of the Indian at heart, because you are the Queen's children and we must think of you for to-day and to-morrow; the condition of the Indians and their future has given the Queen's Councillors much anxiety. In the old provinces of Canada from which I came we have many Indians, they are growing in numbers and are as a rule happy and prosperous; for a hundred years red and white hands have been clasped together in peace. The instructions of the Queen are to treat the Indians as brothers, and so we ought to be. The Great Spirit made this earth we are on. He planted the trees and made the rivers flow for the good of all his people, white and red; the country is very wide and there is room for all. It is six years since the Queen took back into her own hands the government of her subjects, red and white, in this country; it was thought her Indian children would be better cared for in her own hand. This is the seventh time in the last five years that her Indian children have been called together for this purpose; this is the fourth time that I have met my Indian brothers, and standing here on this bright day with the sun above us, I cast my eyes to the East down to the great lakes and I see a broad road leading from there to the Red River, I see it stretching on to Ellice, I see it branching there, the one to Qu'Appelle and Cypress Hills, the other by Pelly to Carlton; it is a wide and plain trail. Anyone can see it, and on that road, taking for the Queen, the hand of the Governor and Commissioners I see all the Indians. I see the Queen's Councillors taking the Indian by the hand saying we are brothers, we will lift you up, we will teach you, if you will learn, the cunning of the white man. All along that road I see Indians gathering, I see gardens growing and houses building; I see them receiving money from the Queen's Commissioners to purchase clothing for their children; at the same time I see them enjoying their hunting and fishing as before, I see them retaining their old mode of living with the Queen's gift in addition.

"I met the Crees at Carlton, they heard my words there, they read my face, and through that my heart, and said my words were true, and they took my hand on behalf of the Queen. What they did I wish you to do; I wish you to travel on the road I have spoken of, a road I see stretching out broad and plain to the Rocky Mountains. I know you have been told many stories, some of them not true; do not listen to the bad voices of men who have their own ends to serve, listen rather to those who have only your good at heart. I have come a long way to meet you; last year I sent you a message that you would be met this year, and I do not forget my promises.

"I went to Ottawa, where the Queen's Councillors have their council chamber, to talk, amongst other things, about you.

"I have come seven hundred miles to see you. Why should I take all this trouble? For two reasons, first, the duty was put upon me as one of the Queen's Councillors, to see you with my brother Commissioners, Hon. W. J. Christie and Hon. Jas. McKay. The other reason is a personal one, because since I was a young man my heart was warm to the Indians, and I have taken a great interest in them; for more than twenty-five years I have studied their condition in the present and in the future. I have been many years in public life, but the first words I spoke in public were for the Indians, and in that vision of the day I saw the Queen's white men understanding their duty; I saw them understanding that they had no right to wrap themselves up in a cold mantle of selfishness, that they had no right to turn away and say, 'Am I my brother's keeper?' On the contrary, I saw them saying, the Indians are our brothers, we must try to help them to make a living for themselves and their children. I tell you, you must think of those who will come after you. As I came here I saw tracks leading to the lakes and water-courses, once well beaten, now grown over with grass; I saw bones bleaching by the wayside; I saw the places where the buffalo had been, and I thought what will become of the Indian. I said to myself, we must teach the children to prepare for the future; if we do not, but a few suns will pass and they will melt away like snow before the sun in spring-time. You know my words are true; you see for yourselves and know that your numbers are lessening every year. Now the whole burden of my message from the Queen is that we wish to help you in the days that are to come, we do not want to take away the means of living that you have now, we do not want to tie you down; we want you to have homes of your own where your children can be taught to raise for themselves food from the mother earth. You may not all be ready for that, but some, I have no doubt, are, and in a short time others will follow. I am here to talk plainly, I have nothing to hide; I am here to tell you what we are ready to do. Your tribe is not all here at the present time, some of the principal Chiefs are absent, this cannot be avoided, the country is wide and when the buffalo come near you must follow them; this does not matter, for what I have to give is for the absent as well as for the present. Next year if the treaty is made, a Commissioner will be sent to you, and you will be notified of the times and places of meeting, so that you will not have long journeys; after that, two or three servants of the Queen will be appointed to live in the country to look after the Indians, and see that the terms of the treaty are carried out.

" I have not yet given you my message. I know you have heard what your brothers did at Carlton, and I expect you to do the same here, for if you do not you will be the first Indians who refused to take my hand. At Carlton I had a slight difficulty; one of the Chiefs dreamt that instead of making the treaty at the camp of the great body of the Indians, I made it at his, and so his people stood aside. I was sorry for him and his people. I did not wish to go and leave them out. I sent him word after I had made the treaty, and brought him in with the others. When I went to North-West Angle I met

16

the Chippewa nation; they were not all present, but the absent ones were seen the next year.   I told them the message from the Queen, and what she wished to do for them; in all four thousand Indians accepted the Treaty, and now, I am glad to say, many of them have homes and gardens of their own.   The next year I went to Qu'Appelle and saw the Crees and Chippewas, and there five thousand understood us and took our hands. Last summer I went with Mr. McKay to Lake Winnipeg, and there all the Swampy Crees accepted the Queen's terms.   Now I have stroked the pipe with your brothers at Carlton as with you.

"Three years ago a party of Assiniboines were shot by American traders; men, women and children were killed; we reported the affair to Ottawa; we said the time has come when you must send the red-coated servants of the Queen to the North-West to protect the Indian from fire-water, from being shot down by men who know no law, to preserve peace between the Indians, to punish all who break the law, to prevent whites from doing wrong to Indians, and they are here to-day to do honor to the office which I hold.   Our Indian Chiefs wear red coats, and wherever they meet the police they will know they meet friends.   I know that you have been told that if war came you would be put in the front, this is not so.   Your brothers at Carlton asked me that they might not be forced to fight, and I tell you, as I assured them, you will never be asked to fight against your will; and I trust the time will never come of war between the Queen and the great country near us.

"Again, I say, all we seek is your good; I speak openly, as brother to brother, as a father to his children, and I would give you a last advice, hear my words, come and join the great band of Indians who are walking hand-in-hand with us on the road I spoke of when I began—a road, I believe in my heart, will lead the Indian on to a much more comfortable state than he is in now.   My words, when they are accepted, are written down, and they last, as I have said to the others, as long as the sun shines and the river runs. I expect you are prepared for the message I have to deliver, and I will wait to see if any of the Chiefs wish to speak before I go further."

Sweet Grass, the principal Cree Chief, rose, and taking the Governor by the hand, said, "We have heard what the Governor has said, and now the Indians want to hear the terms of the treaty, after which they will all shake hands with the Governor and Commissioners, we then want to go to our camp to meet in council."

The Governor then very carefully and distinctly explained the terms and promises of the treaty as made at Carlton; this was received by the Indians with loud assenting exclamations.

On the 8th the Indians sent a message that they required further time for deliberation, and the meeting was put off until the 9th.

On the morning of the 9th the Indians were slow in gathering, as they wished to settle all difficulties and misunderstandings amongst themselves before coming to the treaty tent, this was apparently accomplished about eleven a.m., when the whole body approached and seated themselves in good order, when the Governor said:—

"Indian children of the Great Queen, we meet again on a bright day; you heard many words from me the other day; I delivered you my message from the Queen; I held out my hand in the Queen's name, full of her bounty. You asked time to consult together; I gave it to you very gladly, because I did not come here to surprise you. I trust the Great Spirit has put good thoughts into your hearts, and your wise men have found my words good. I am now ready to hear whether you are prepared to do as the great body of the Indian people have done; it is now for the Indians to speak through those whom they may choose; my heart is warm to you, and my ears are open."

Ku-ye-win (The Eagle) addressed the Indians, telling them not to be afraid, that the Governor was to them as a brother;

that what the Queen wished to establish through him was for their good, and if any of them wished to speak to do so.

After waiting some time the Governor said, "I had hoped the Indians would have taken me at my word, and taken me as a brother and a friend. True, I am the Queen's Governor; that I am here to-day shows me to be your friend. Why can you not open your hearts to me? I have met many Indians before, but this is the first time I have had all the talking to do myself. Now, cast everything behind your backs, and speak to me face to face. I have offered as we have done to the other Indians. Tell me now whether you will take my hand and accept it; there is nothing to be ashamed of, nothing to be afraid of; think of the good of your children and your children's children. Stand up now like wise men and tell me if you will take what I offered. I cannot believe it to be possible that you would throw my hand back. Speak and do not be afraid or ashamed.

WEE-KAS-KOO-KEE-SAY-YIN (Sweet Grass)—"I thank you for this day, and also I thank you for what I have seen and heard, I also thank the Queen for sending you to act for our good. I am glad to have a brother and friend in you, which undoubtedly will raise us above our present condition. I am glad for your offers, and thank you from my heart. I speak this in the presence of the Divine Being. It is all for our good, I see nothing to be afraid of, I therefore accept of it gladly and take your hand to my heart, may this continue as long as this earth stands and the river flows. The Great King, our Father, is now looking upon us this day, He regards all the people equal with one another; He has mercy on the whole earth; He has opened a new world to us. I have pity on all those who have to live by the buffalo. If I am spared until this time next year I want this my brother to commence to act for me, thinking thereby that the buffalo may be protected. It is for that reason I give you my hand. If spared, I shall commence at once to clear a small piece of land for myself,

and others of my kinsmen will do the same. We will commence hand in hand to protect the buffalo. When I hold
your hand I feel as if the Great Father were looking on us
both as brothers. I am thankful. May this earth here never
see the white man's blood spilt on it. I thank God that we
stand together, that you all see us; I am thankful that I can
raise up my head, and the white man and red man can stand
together as long as the sun shines. When I hold your hands
and touch your heart, as I do now (suiting his action to the
words), let us be as one. Use your utmost to help me and
help my children, so that they may prosper."

The Chief's remarks were assented to by the Indians by
loud ejaculations.

GOVERNOR—"I rise with a glad heart; we have come
together and understood each other. I am glad that you have
seen the right way. I am glad you have accepted so unanimously the offer made. I will tell the Queen's Councillors
what good hearts their Indian children have; I will tell them
that they think of the good of their children's children.

" I feel that we have done to-day a good work; the years will
pass away and we with them, but the work we have done
to-day will stand as the hills. What we have said and done
has been written down; my promises at Carlton have been
written down and cannot be rubbed out, so there can be no
mistake about what is agreed upon. I will now have the
terms of the treaty fully read and explained to you, and before
I go away I will leave a copy with your principal Chief.

"After I and the Commissioners, for the Queen, have signed
the treaty, I will call upon your Chief and Councillors to do
the same; and before the payments are made by Mr. Christie,
I will give the Chiefs the medals of the Queen and their flags.

"Some of your Chiefs and people are away; next year we
will send men near to where their bands live, notice will be
given, and those who are away now will receive the present of
money we are going to give you, the same as if they had been

here, and when you go back to the plains I ask you to tell your brothers what we have done."

The Governor and Commissioners then signed the treaty on the part of the Queen, and nine Chiefs and as many of their Councillors as were with them signed on behalf of the Indians·

James Seenum, Chief of White Fish Lake Crees, said that when he commenced to cultivate the soil some years ago, Mr. Christie, then chief factor of the Hudson Bay Company, gave him a plough that he had used but it was now broken. When he commenced he and his brothers drew the plough themselves, and they pulled up roots and used them for hoes. Mr. Christie also gave me a pit-saw and a grindstone, and I am using them yet. I feel my heart sore in the spring when my children want to plough—when they have no implements to use, that is why I am asking them now to have them sent as soon as possible. By following what I have been taught I find it helps me a great deal.

The Little Hunter—"I am here alone just now; if I am spared to see next spring, then I will select my Councillors, those that I think worthy I will choose. I am glad from my very heart. I feel in taking the Governor's hand as if I was taking the Queen's. When I hear her words that she is going to put to rights this country, it is the help of God that has put it in her heart to come to our assistance. In sending her bounty to us I wish an everlasting grasp of her hand, as long as the sun moves and the river flows. I am glad that the truth and all good things have been opened to us. I am thankful for the children for they will prosper. All the children who are sitting here hope that the Great Spirit will look down upon us as one."

See-kahs-kootch (The Cut Arm)—"I am glad of the goodness of the great Queen. I recognize now that this that I once dreaded most is coming to my aid and doing for me what I could not do for myself."

Tus-tuk-ee-skuais—"I am truly glad that the Queen has

made a new country for me. I am glad that all my friends and children will not be in want of food hereafter. I am glad that we have everything which we had before still extended to us."

PEE-QUAY-SIS—" I need not say anything; I have been well pleased with all that I have heard, and I need not speak as we are all agreed."

KIN-OO-SAY-OO (The Fish), Chief of the Chippewayans—" I shake hands with the Queen, and I am glad for what she is doing and what she is to do for us. If I could have used my own language I would then be able to say more."

The Governor then called on Sweet Grass and placed the Queen's medal around his neck, the band of the Police playing "God save the Queen." The rest of the Chiefs' medals, flags and uniforms were given as soon as possible, and Mr. Christie proceeded to make the payments and distribute the presents.

September 13th.

The Chiefs and head men came to pay their respects to the Commissioners in the morning, at Fort Pitt.

SWEET GRASS—" We are all glad to see you here, and we have come to say good-bye before you leave."

THE BIG BEAR—" I find it difficult to express myself, because some of the bands are not represented. I have come off to speak for the different bands that are out on the plains. It is no small matter we were to consult about. I expected the Chiefs here would have waited until I arrived. The different bands that are out on the plains told me that I should speak in their stead ; the Stony Indians as well. The people who have not come, stand as a barrier before what I would have had to say ; my mode of living is hard."

SWEET GRASS, to Big Bear —" My friend, you see the representative of the Queen here, who do you suppose is the maker of it. I think the Great Spirit put it into their hearts to

come to our help ; I feel as if I saw life when I see the representative of the Queen ; let nothing be a barrier between you
and him ; it is through great difficulty this has been brought to
us. Think of our children and those to come after, there is
life and succor for them ; say yes and take his hand."

The White Fish Lake Chief said, " We have all taken it, and
we think it is for our good."

BIG BEAR—" Stop, stop, my friends, I have never seen the
Governor before ; I have seen Mr. Christie many times. I
heard the Governor was to come and I said I shall see him ;
when I see him I will make a request that he will save me
from what I most dread, that is : the rope to be about my neck
(hanging), it was not given to us by the Great Spirit that the
red man or white man should shed each other's blood."

GOVERNOR—" It was given us by the Great Spirit, man
should not shed his brother's blood, and it was spoken to us
that he who shed his brother's blood, should have his own spilt.

" No good Indian has the rope about his neck. If a white
man killed an Indian, not in self defence, the rope would be
put around his neck. He saw red-coats, they were here to protect Indians and whites.

" If a man tried to kill you, you have a right to defend ; but
no man has a right to kill another in cold blood, and we will
do all we can to punish such. The good Indian need never be
afraid ; their lives will be safer than ever before. Look at the
condition of the Blackfeet. Before the red-coats went, the
Americans were taking their furs and robes and giving them
whiskey—we stopped it, they have been able to buy back two
thousand horses—before that, robes would have gone to Americans for whiskey."

BIG BEAR—" What we want is that we should hear what
will make our hearts glad, and all good peoples' hearts glad.
There were plenty things left undone, and it does not look well
to leave them so."

GOVERNOR—" I do not know what has been left undone !"

BIG BEAR said he would like to see his people before he acted. " I have told you what I wish, that there be no hanging."

GOVERNOR—" What you ask will not be granted, why are you so anxious about bad men?

" The Queen's law punishes murder with death, and your request cannot be granted."

BIG BEAR—"Then these Chiefs will help us to protect the buffalo, that there may be enough for all. I have heard what has been said, and I am glad we are to be helped; but why do these men not speak?"

The Chief of the Chippewayans said, "We do not speak, because Sweet Grass has spoken for us all. What he says, we all say."

GOVERNOR—"I wish the Bear to tell Short Tail and See-yah-kee-maht, the other Chiefs, what has been done, and that it is for them, as if they had been here. Next year they and their people can join the treaty and they will lose nothing. I wish you to understand fully about two questions, and tell the others. The North-West Council is considering the framing of a law to protect the buffaloes, and when they make it, they will expect the Indians to obey it. The Government will not interfere with the Indian's daily life, they will not bind him. They will only help him to make a living on the reserves, by giving him the means of growing from the soil, his food. The only occasion when help would be given, would be if Providence should send a great famine or pestilence upon the whole Indian people included in the treaty. We only looked at something unforseen and not at hard winters or the hardships of single bands, and this, both you and I, fully understood.

" And now I have done, I am going away. The country is large, another Governor will be sent in my place; I trust you will receive him as you have done me, and give him your con- fidence. He will live amongst you. Indians of the plains, I bid you farewell. I never expect to see you again, face to face. I rejoice that you listened to me, and when I go back to my home

beyond the great lakes, I will often think of you and will rejoice to hear of your prosperity. I ask God to bless you and
your children. Farewell."

The Indians responded by loud ejaculations of satisfaction,
and the Chiefs and Councillors, commencing with Sweet Grass,
each shook hands with the Governor, and addressed him in
words of parting, elevating his hand, as they grasped it, to
heaven, and invoking the blessings of the Great Spirit.

The Bear remained sitting until all had said good-bye to the
Governor, and then he rose and taking his hand, said, "I am
glad to meet you, I am alone ; but if I had known the time, I
would have been here with all my people. I am not an undutiful child, I do not throw back your hand ; but as my
people are not here, I do not sign. I will tell them what I have
heard, and next year I will come." About an hour afterwards
the Big Bear came to the Fort Pitt House to see the Governor,
and again repeated that he accepted the treaty as if he had
signed it, and would come next year, with all his people, to
meet the Commissioners and accept it.

The Governor and party left Fort Pitt for Battle River, on
the 13th at one o'clock, and arrived there on the 15th. There
were no Indians there, except the Red Pheasant's band, who
had been treated with at Battle River.

On the 16th the Red Pheasant and his Councillors came to
see the Governor and the Commissioners, with the following
result :

THE RED PHEASANT—"I am a Battle River Indian, and I
have chosen this place before, and I am glad to see the Government here too, as I know there is a chance of living. I want
the Half-breed claims at Battle River to be respected, and I do
not wish to turn out any white man ; but I wish to return to
my former mode of life.

"Ever since my grandfather lived at Battle River, it has
been my home. Our houses were swept off by a flood two
years ago, and after that we repaired some old houses that

were built by outsiders (other Indians), and we had fenced in the buildings ; but a short time ago some Canadians arrived, knocked down the fences, and built inside the enclosure."

WAH-TAH-NEE—" We had chosen a point about a mile from the spot where we are now speaking, and got out logs for fences and houses, and when we returned from the plains we found they had all been taken away. There are now twenty families, and ten more to come in from the plains.

" We wish to be remembered to the Queen, and we are thankful to see the Queen's soldiers coming to make their homes on the land that we have been brought up on. I hope that the Queen will look upon our poverty when she hears that we are poor Indians and have welcomed her people to live amongst us. This is my country where I have lived. I want to make way for the Queen's men, and I ask her in return to keep me from want. Next spring I want to plant here, wherever I can get a piece of ground. By that time I may have selected a spot for my reserve. The reason I want to select my reserve is, that I do not want to be cramped up by settlers. In the meantime I do not want any white men to settle on the Eagle Hills.

" When I see that we are numerous, it will be the Eagle Hills I will select as our reserve, although I am very reluctant to leave the place I have been brought up on. If I see that we are not likely to be numerous, I may select some other place across the Saskatchewan River. This man, Peter Ballendine, knows that it is not because settlers are coming here that we speak of this place, Battle River, but because we were here from of old." I wish that the Governor should give us some advice to think over during the winter."

GOVERNOR—" I am glad to give you a word of advice. Next summer, Commissioners will come to make payments here, so that you may not have so far to go, and also that other Indians we have not seen, should come here also, to whom it may be convenient, and I hope that then you will be able to talk with them where you want your reserve. I will speak to you frankly, as if I was talking to my own children ; the sooner you select a place for your reserve the better, so that you can have the animals and agricultural implements promised to you, and so that you may have the increase from the animals, and the tools to help you build houses, &c. When you are away hunting and fishing, the heat of the sun and the rain is making your crops to grow. I think you are showing wisdom in taking a place away from here, although it has been your home. It is better for the Indian to be away a little piece from the white man. You will be near enough to bring your furs to a good market, and by and by I hope you will have more potatoes than you require, and have some to dispose of. I am very anxious that you should think over this, and be able to tell the Commissioner next year where you want your reserve.

"I have asked Mr. Fuller to let you have three acres of land to plant your potatoes next spring, and he has replied that he will be very happy to let you do so, and to plough it for you as well, in the field he has enclosed.

"I am much pleased with the conduct of the Battle River Crees, and will report it to the Queen's Councillors. I hope you will be prosperous and happy."

This closed the interview.

The Commissioners left Battle River on the 19th of September. The Lieutenant-Governor arrived at Fort Garry on the 6th of October.

CHAPTER X.

THE making of this treaty, which completed the series of treaties, extending from Lake Superior to the slopes of the Rocky Mountains, was entrusted, by the Privy Council, to the Hon. David Laird (who, after the effecting of the Carlton and Fort Pitt Treaties, had, in 1876, been appointed Lieutenant-Governor of the North-West Territories, subsequently to the erection of these territories into a distinct Government) and Lieut.-Col. McLeod, of the Mounted Police Force. The necessity which had arisen for making the treaty is thus stated by the Hon. the Minister of the Interior, the Hon. David Mills, in his Annual Report for 1877:

" The conclusion, in 1876, of the treaty with the Crees, Assini-boine and Saulteaux Indians (being the sixth of the series of treaties up to that time negotiated with the Indians of the North-West) left but a small portion of the territory lying between the boundary line and the 54th parallel of latitude unsurrendered.

" The unsurrendered portion of the territory, including about fifty thousand square miles, lies at the south-west angle of the territories, north of the boundary line, east of the Rocky Mountains, south of Red River (Treaty Number Six) and west of the Cypress Hills, or Treaty Number Four. This portion of the North-West is occupied by the Blackfeet, Blood, and Sarcees or Piegan Indians, some of the most warlike and intelligent but intractable bands of the North-West. These bands have for years past been anxiously expecting to be treated with, and have been much disappointed at the delay of negotiations.

" In last year's report, I stated that His Honor Lieut.-Gov. Morris, very strongly recommended that no further delay should take place in entering into negotiations with these Indians. His Honor reported, in effect, "that there was a general consent of opinion amongst the missionaries settled in that territory, and others who are acquainted with these Indians, as to the desirableness of having such a treaty made at the earliest possible date, with a view to preserving the present friendly disposition of these tribes, which might easily give place to feelings of an unfriendly or hostile nature, should the treaty negotiations be much longer delayed."

"In view of these facts, and in order to satisfy these important tribes, and to prevent the difficulties which might hereafter arise through the settlement of whites, who are already flocking into Fort McLeod and other portions of this territory, Your Excellency decided that these Indians should be treated with this year, and the Indians were notified accordingly.

"His Honor Mr. Laird, the Lieutenant-Governor of the North-West Territories, and Lieut.-Col. James F. McLeod, C.M.G., were selected by Your Excellency to negotiate the treaty. The former of these gentlemen, had assisted in 1874 in negotiating Treaty Number Four, with the Cree and Saulteaux Indians, and the latter, during his residence for some years past at Fort McLeod, as Commandant of the Mounted Police Force, had acquired the entire confidence and good will of the Indian tribes proposed to be dealt with."

Besides all this, the Chiefs of the Blackfeet, in 1876, sent to the Lieutenant-Governor of the North-West Territories, a letter, with regard to a treaty, and also by a messenger, in whom they had confidence, a message, to a similar effect. The Blackfeet Indians are a bold and warlike race. When the Sioux war with the United States was about being initiated, the Sioux invited them to join in the war, but they promptly refused. They are unlikely to become farmers, but as the country they inhabit presents unusual facilities for that industry, they may be induced to adopt a pastoral life. They already possess large herds of horses, and may be taught to raise cattle also.

I requested the Rev. C. Scollen, who had for many years been a missionary among the Plain Crees, and latterly, for several years, among the Blackfeet, to make a report to me of the character, habits and condition of this nation, with which request he willingly complied. I now give place to this report, which gives a vivid view of the character of this bold and warlike race, and shews the benefits they had, so far back as 1876, derived from the presence of the Mounted Police, the prohibition of liquor, and the establishment of law and order in the North-West Territories, under Canadian rule. I may here remark, that another great benefit has resulted from the judicious steps taken by the Canadian Government, and that is the cessation of warfare between the various tribes, which was before of constant occurrence. An intelligent Ojibbeway Indian trader told me, that the change was wonderful. "Before," he said, "the Queen's Government came, we were never safe, and now," he said, "I can sleep in my tent anywhere, and have no fear. I can go to the Blackfeet, and Cree camps, and they treat me as a friend." The report of Mr. Scollen is as follows:

FORT PITT, *September 8th, 1876.*

To HIS EXCELLENCY THE GOVERNOR OF MANITOBA.

EXCELLENT GOVERNOR,—Having had some years of experience as a missionary amongst the Cree and Blackfeet Indians of the North-West Territory, I humbly undertake to submit to your consideration a few details regarding the latter tribe of Her Majesty's Indian subjects. I do this with all the more confidence as the successful way in which you conducted the treaty with the Carlton Indians (a treaty including no small difficulties), has convinced me of your thorough knowledge of the character of this people. But, although the general character of all the tribes may be nearly the same, yet in their social dispositions they sometimes materially differ, and this, I think, will be found to be the case with the Crees and Blackfeet when compared on that point. The Crees have always looked upon the white man as a friend, or, to use their own language, as a brother. They have never been afraid of him, nor have they given him any cause to be afraid of them. The Blackfeet have acted somewhat differently; they have regarded the white man as a demi-god, far superior to themselves in intelligence, capable of doing them good or evil, according as he might be well or ill-disposed towards them, unscrupulous in his dealings with others, and consequently a person to be flattered, feared and shunned, and even injured, whenever this could be done with impunity. I am not now describing the Blackfeet of the present day, but those of fifteen years ago, when I first saw them. They were then a proud, haughty, numerous people (perhaps ten thousand on the British side of the line), having a regular politico-religious organization by which their thirst for blood and their other barbarous passions were constantly fired to the highest pitch of frenzy. Since that time their number has decreased to less than one half, and their systematic organizations have fallen into decay ; in fact they have been utterly demoralized as a people. This sudden decadence was brought on by two causes : 1. About ten years ago the Americans crossed the line and established themselves on Pelly River, where they carried on to an extraordinary extent the illicit traffic in intoxicating liquor to the Blackfeet. The fiery water flowed as freely, if I may use the metaphor, as the streams running from the Rocky Mountains, and hundreds of the poor Indians fell victims to the white man's craving for money, some poisoned, some frozen to death whilst in a state of intoxication, and many shot down by American bullets. 2. Then in 1870 came that disease so fatal to Indians, the small-pox, which told upon the Blackfeet with terrible effect, destroying between six hundred and eight hundred of them. Surviving relatives went more and more for the use of alcohol ; they endeavoured to drown their grief in the poisonous beverage. They sold their robes and their horses by the hundred for it, and now they began killing one another, so that in a short time they were divided into several small parties, afraid to meet. Fortunately for them the Government were aware of the state of affairs in the country and did not remain indifferent to it ; and, as I have heard yourself explain to the Indians, Her Gracious Majesty has at heart the welfare of even the most obscure of her subjects. In the summer of 1874, I was travelling amongst the Blackfeet. It was painful to me to see the state of poverty to which they had been reduced. Formerly they had been the most opulent Indians in the country, and now they were clothed in rags, without horses and without guns. But this was the year of their salvation ; that very summer the Mounted Police were struggling against the difficulties of a long journey across the barren plains in order to bring them help. This noble corps reached their destination that same fall, and with magic effect put an entire stop to the abominable traffic of whiskey with the Indians. Since that time the Blackfeet Indians are becoming more and more prosperous. They are now well clothed and well furnished with horses and guns. During the last two years I have calculated that they have bought two thousand horses to replace those they had given for whiskey. They are forced to acknowledge that the arrival of the Red Coats has been to them the greatest boon. But, although they are externally so friendly to the Police and other strangers who now inhabit their country, yet underneath this friendship remains hidden some of that dread which they have always had of the white man's intention to cheat them; and here, excellent Governor, I will state my reasons for believing that a treaty should be concluded with them also at the earliest possible date.

1st. The Blackfeet are extremely jealous of what they consider their country, and never allowed any white men, Half-breeds, or Crees to remain in it for any length of time ; the only reason that they never drove the Americans off, apart from their love for whiskey, was their dread of the Henri rifle.

2nd. They have an awful dread of the future. They think that the Police are in the country not only to keep out whiskey traders, but also to protect white people against them, and that this country will be gradually taken from them without any ceremony. This I can certify, for although they may not say so to others yet they do not hide it from me.

3rd. Numbers of people are settling around Fort McLeod and Fort Calgary in order to farm, raise stock, etc. This will probably drive the buffalo away through time from the ordinary hunting grounds, and if so, the Blackfeet, being the most helpless Indians in the country, and unaccustomed to anything else but hunting buffalo, would suffer extremely.

4th. The settlers also are anxious that a treaty be made as soon as possible, so that they may know what portions of land they can hold without fear of being molested.

5th. The Blackfeet themselves are expecting to have a mutual understanding with the Government, because they have been told of it by several persons, and namely by Gen. Smythe last year.

Such are the principal reasons which occur to my mind for making a treaty with the Blackfeet. It remains for you, excellent Governor, to weigh their value. Of course you would find the same prejudices amongst the Blackfeet that you have found amongst the Crees, but you would have no greater difficulty in dispelling them. You would have four clans to treat with, viz.: the Blackfeet, Bloods, and Piegans, all of the same tribe, and the Sarcees, a branch of the Peace River Indians called Beavers. As to the place of rendezvous there would be no difficulty whatever ; the Blackfeet live in large camps under their respective Chiefs, and could go to any point after due notice.

It remains for me now, excellent Governor, to beg you to excuse the many defects of this communication, and to accept the assurance of sincere esteem and profound respect of

Your most humble servant,

CONSTANTINE SCOLLEN,

Priest, O. U. I.

P.S.—I am also aware that the Sioux Indians, now at war with the Americans, have sent a message to the Blackfeet tribe, asking them to make an alliance offensive and defensive against all white people in the country.

C. SCOLLEN.

17

In order to effect a treaty, Lieut.-Gov. Laird, and Lieut-Col. James F. McLeod, met the Blackfeet, at the Blackfoot crossing, on the Bow River, on the 17th day of September, 1877, which day had been selected for the time of meeting. Gov. Laird proceeded from the temporary seat of the Government of the North-West Territories at Swan River, and Col. McLeod from Fort McLeod, the head-quarters of the Mounted Police, to the appointed rendezvous.

The Commissioners met the Indians on that day, and after five days of tedious negotiations, the treaty was satisfactorily concluded, and signed by the Chiefs and head men present.

The total number of the Indians, represented at the making of the treaty, and who were paid the gratuity under it, was four thousand three hundred and ninety-two. The terms of the treaty, were substantially the same as those contained in the North-West Angle and Qu'Appelle treaties, except that as some of the bands were disposed to engage in pastoral pursuits, it was arranged to give them cattle instead of agricultural implements. The Minister of the Interior well observes in his report "that the conclusion of this treaty with these warlike and intractable tribes, at a time when the Indian tribes, immediately across the border, were engaged in open hostilities with the United States troops, is certainly a conclusive proof of the just policy of the Government of Canada toward the aboriginal population," and, I add, of the confidence of the Indians in the promises and just dealing of the servants of the British Crown, in Canada ; a confidence that can only be kept up by the strictest observance of the stipulations of the treaties.

I now append the interesting despatch of Lieut.-Gov. Laird, giving a detailed account of the negotiation of the treaty, and a report of the speeches of the Commissioners and Indians, extracted from a report in the *Globe* newspaper, dated October 4th, 1877, which, though not authentic, I believe, gives a general view of what passed during the negotiations.

GOVERNMENT HOUSE,
BATTLEFORD, NORTH-WEST TERRITORY.

SIR,—I have the honor to inform you that on the 4th August I received at Swan River your telegram dated on the first of that month.

It notified me that a Commission appointing Lieut.-Col. James F. McLeod, C.M.G., and myself, Commissioners to negotiate a treaty with the Blackfeet and other Indians of the unsurrendered parts of the North-West Territories adjoining the United States boundary, had been forwarded to Fort McLeod.

I immediately made preparations for the journey. These occupied me a week, as arrangements had to be made for the removal of furniture and other property to Battle River, where the Government House for the territories, in course of construction, would probably be ready for occupation on my return from the treaty negotiations. On the 11th August I left Swan River for Fort McLeod, *via* Battleford, proposing to go from the latter place by Cypress Hills to my destination. I took the Quill Lake trail and came to the telegraph line, about four miles from Big Stone Lake. Thence I followed that line until I came to the trail at the elbow of the North Saskatchewan leading to Battle River. Where the telegraph crosses the South Saskatchewan I found an excellent ferry scow, and a ferryman placed there by the Public Works Department. I arrived at the ferry about noon on the 20th, and though a high wind rendered it difficult to manage the scow, the horses, with the vehicles and their contents, were safely ferried before sunset. On the following evening I reached the Elbow, and the morning thereafter before leaving camp, Inspector Walker, of Battleford, drove up, on his way to Carlton, to arrange for the distribution of certain of the articles intended for the Indians of Treaty Number Six, which had not arrived when he paid the annuities at that post in the early part of the month. Some of the Indians had not dispersed since they received their payments, and interested parties were causing dissatisfaction among them by reporting that the provisions intended for them, while assembled to receive their annuities, having now arrived, should be distributed to them, as well as the agricultural implements and other articles promised.

I advised Inspector Walker to distribute to those Indians still around Carlton their share of the presents, and to give them a small quantity of provisions from the Government supplies, to enable them to proceed without delay to their hunting grounds. I then continued my journey to Battleford, which I reached on Monday, the 24th, at noon. Here I was happy to meet Major Irvine, who had come straight from Fort McLeod, across the Great Plains, to conduct me on my journey, and to inform me that for satisfactory reasons adduced by Crowfoot, the leading chief of the Blackfeet, Lieut.-Col. McLeod, my associate Commissioner, had consented that the meeting of the treaty should be held at the Blackfoot crossing of the Bow River, instead of at Fort McLeod. Major Irvine had reached Battleford only a few hours before me, and having a Blackfoot Indian as guide, I abandoned my intention of going to Fort McLeod by Cypress Hills, and resolved to take the more direct and much shorter course by which that officer came.

On Friday I had interviews with several parties on business, among whom were Red Pheasant, the Chief of the Battle River Crees, and a portion of his band. He desired explanations about the articles promised in the treaty of last year, and the reason they were so late in being forwarded. I explained that the unusually heavy rains in Manitoba and the eastern portion of the territories had made the travelling so bad that the freighters had not been able to overtake the journey in the time which they expected; that the Government were very sorry at the disappointment, as it was their desire to faithfully carry out all their promises. The officers here had done their best to meet the difficulty and satisfy the Indians, though at no little expense to the country.

The Chief appeared to be quite satisfied with the explanation, and after some further conversation about the reserve, which he desires to be located at Eagle Hills, he and his companions retired to their lodges, situated for the present close to the south side of Battle River, under the bank in front of Government House.

Inspector Walker having kindly given instructions to the non-commissioned officer in charge of the Mounted Police in his absence, that every assistance in his power was to be afforded to me for continuing my journey, I was enabled to leave Battleford for Fort McLeod with Major Irvine, on the 25th August. Besides us two, the party consisted of four police constables, my personal servant and the guide.

For the first day we followed a trail leading southward, but afterwards our course was across the trackless plains until we approached near our destination. On the third day out we first sighted buffalo, and every day subsequently that we travelled, except the last, we saw herds of the animals. Most of the herds, however, were small, and we remarked with regret that very few calves of this season were to be seen. We observed portions of many buffalo carcasses on our route, from not a few of which the peltries had not been removed. From this circumstance, as well as from the fact that many of the skins are made into parchments and coverings for lodges, and are used for other purposes, I concluded that the export of buffalo robes from the territories does not indicate even one-half the number of those valuable animals slaughtered annually in our country.

Antelope, though not very abundant, are widely scattered over the plains. The numerous lakelets abound with water fowl. Some of the pools contain alkali, but we experienced no inconvenience on the journey from scarcity of fresh water. The grass in many places is short and thin, but in the hollows feed for horses is easily obtained. Altogether, though the plains are perfectly treeless, not even a shrub being visible, a journey across them in fine weather, such as we experienced, when the "buffalo chips" are sufficiently dry to make a good camp fire, is not disagreeable.

On the afternoon of the 29th we reached the lowest ford of the Red Deer River, one hundred and sixty-eight miles, by our course, from Battleford. On the north side of the river at this ford there is quicksand. The water too, in mid-stream, was deep enough to flow over the side-boards of our waggons, and at one place the current was dangerously rapid. After repeated trials by some of the men on horseback to find the best footing, we made the attempt, and the whole party got safely across by night-fall. On Saturday evening, the 1st of September, we arrived at the Blackfoot crossing of the Bow River, one hundred and eighteen miles from where we forded the Red Deer River. The Bow River is a noble stream. The current is pretty rapid, but at this "ridge under the water" (which is the literal translation of the Blackfoot name for the ford) the bed of the river is pebbly and the footing consequently good. Though we found the water almost as deep as at the Red Deer River, yet under the guidance of Mr. French, a small trader who lives near the ford, we, without almost any delay, crossed bravely over and camped until Monday morning on the south bank of the river.

At this crossing, where the Indians had latterly been notified to assemble for the treaty, there is a beautiful river bottom on the south side of the river. It extended about one mile back from the river, and is some three miles in length. The river, as far as the eye can reach, is skirted close to the water by a narrow belt of cotton-wood and other trees.

When I surveyed the clear waters of the stream, the fuel and shelter which the wood afforded, the excellent herbage on hill and dale, and the Indians camped in the vicinity crossing and re-crossing the river on the "ridge" with ease and safety, I was not surprised that the Blackfeet were attached to the locality, and desired that such an important event in their history as concluding a treaty with Her Majesty's Commissioners should take place at this spot.

On Saturday evening and Sunday several of the Indians called to shake hands with me, among whom was the Rainy Chief of the North Bloods. Here also I met Monsieur Jean L. Heureux, a French Canadian, who had spent nearly twenty years of his life among the Blackfeet. From him I obtained much valuable information respecting the numbers and wishes of the Indians, together with an elaborate list of the different Chiefs and minor Chiefs of the Blackfeet, Bloods, Piegans, and Sarcees, with the principal families of their respective tribes and clans of divisions. This list the Commissioners found very useful in enabling them to understand the relative influence of the several Chiefs and the strength of their bands.

On our journey, while within the limits of Treaty Number Six, we met scarcely any Indians, but after we crossed Red Deer River we met a few Crees and Half-breeds, and several hunting parties of Blackfeet. The former generally use carts in travelling, but the Blackfeet and their associates are always on horseback.

The Crees appeared friendly, but were not so demonstrative as the Blackfeet, who always rode up at once with a smile on their countenances and shook hands with us. They knew the uniform of the Mounted Police at a distance, and at once recognized and approached them as their friends.

We resumed our journey on Monday and arrived at Fort McLeod on the Old Man's River, on Tuesday the 4th September. The distance between the Blackfoot crossing of the Bow River and the Fort is about seventy-nine miles, thus making the length of our journey from Battleford three hundred and sixty-five miles, as measured by Major Irvine's odometer.

A few miles from Fort McLeod I was met by the Commissioners of the Mounted Police and a large party of the Force, who escorted me into the Fort, while a salute was fired by the artillery company from one of the hills overlooking the line of march. The men, whose horses were in excellent condition, looked exceedingly well, and the officers performed their duties in a most efficient manner. The villagers presented me with an address of welcome, and altogether my reception at Fort McLeod was such as to satisfy the most fastidious lover of display, and more than enough to satisfy the writer.

At Fort McLeod, on my arrival, I received your despatch of first August, covering the Commission relating to the Treaty and a copy of the Order in Council of 12th July, in terms of which the commission was issued. Also your letter of 27th July, informing me that it had been thought desirable to place the services of the Rev. Father Lacombe at the disposal of the Commissioners while negotiating the treaty. A few days afterwards I was sorry to learn by telegraph that the reverend gentleman had been taken by illness on the journey and would be unable to be present at the meeting with the Indians. Here, however, I was happy to meet Rev. Father Scollen, a Roman Catholic missionary, who has labored for some years among the Crees and Blackfeet in the western portion of the territories. He kindly furnished me such information as he possessed, and afterwards went to the treaty, where his assistance was of some value, particularly in dealing with the Crees present.

While at the fort I had interviews with several of the Blood Chiefs, who called upon me to inquire if they could not be treated with there instead of at Bow River. I explained that hereafter the Government would endeavor to pay them their annuities at places most convenient for them, but that on the occasion of making a treaty it was desirable that the several Chiefs and their principal head men should meet together to talk over the matter, so that all might feel that they had been consulted as to the terms of the agreement. They went away satisfied, said they would do as the Great Father advised, and go to Bow River.

I cannot speak too highly of the kind manner in which the officers and men of the Mounted Police at Fort McLeod treat their Indian visitors. Though the red man is somewhat intrusive, I never heard a harsh word employed in asking him to retire. The beneficial effects of this treatment, of the exclusion of intoxicants from the country, and of impartially admin-

istering justice to whites and Indians alike, were apparent in all my interviews with the Indians. They always spoke of the officers of the Police in
the highest terms, and of the Commander of the Force, Lieut.-Col.
McLeod, especially as their great benefactor. The leading Chiefs of the
Blackfeet and kindred tribes, declared publicly at the treaty that had it
not been for the Mounted Police they would have all been dead ere this time.

Having rested a week after my tedious journey of over seven hundred
miles, I then occupied myself for a few days in viewing the surrounding
country. In the village I found some excellent stores, supplied with almost
every article of dry goods, hardware and groceries, that any inland community requires. Notably among these were the stores of J. G. Baker &
Co. and Messrs. T. C. Power & Bro. There is also a good blacksmith's
shop in the village, in which coal is used from the Pelly River, at a place
some twenty miles distant from Fort McLeod. I was told by the propri-
etor of the shop that the coal answers tolerably well for blacksmithing purposes, and in the fort it is extensively used for fuel. It burns nearly as
well in a stove as some varieties of Pictou coal.

The land around the fort, and indeed for almost the whole distance between the Bow and Old Man's Rivers, is well adapted for grazing ; and
where cultivation has been fairly attempted this season, grain and vegetables have been a success. In short, I have very little doubt that this
portion of the territories, before many years, will abound in herds of
cattle, and be dotted with not a few comfortable homesteads.

Lieut.-Col. McLeod having attended to forwarding the supplies to Bow
River, which had been previously delivered at the fort, left for the Black-
foot crossing with some eighty officers and men of the Police Force, on
Wednesday, the 12th September. I followed on Friday, and reached Bow
River on Sunday morning. The Police having arrived on Saturday, the
Commissioners were fully prepared for business on Monday, the 17th, the
day which I had from the first appointed for the opening of the treaty
negotiations.

The Commissioners were visited by Crowfoot, the principal Chief of the
Blackfeet, shortly after their arrival. He desired to know when he and
his people might meet us. We ascertained that most of the Indians on the
ground were Blackfeet and Assiniboines or Stonies, from the upper part of
Bow River. But as the 17th was the day named, the Commissioners determined to adhere to the appointment, and sent a messenger early in the
morning to invite the Indians camped around to meet them at the council
tent at two o'clock, p.m.

Half an hour before the time appointed a gun was fired as a signal for the
Indians to assemble. The meeting was well attended. The Chiefs came
forward first and were introduced to the Commissioners, and their followers,
on being invited, sat up close to the tent.

I addressed them, stating that the Queen's Government had last year
promised that they would this year be visited by Commissioners to invite

them to make a treaty. That months ago I had named this very day to meet them, and that in accordance with the promises made, the Commissioners were now here to discuss the terms of a treaty. Yet as we had learned that very few of the Bloods, Sarcees or Piegans had arrived, we would not unduly press forward the negotiations, but wait until Wednesday to give the others time to arrive.

The Indians listened attentively to what was said, and several of the Chiefs expressed their satisfaction at not being asked to meet us on the morrow. The Commissioners then told them there were rations provided for them by the Government, and that those who were in need of provisions might apply to certain of the Police officers detailed to see to their proper distribution.

The Stonies and one Blood Chief applied for flour, tea, sugar and tobacco, but said they were not then in need of beef. Crowfoot and some other Chiefs under his influence would not accept any rations until they would hear what terms the Commissioners were prepared to offer them. He appeared to be under the impression that if the Indians were fed by the bounty of the Government they would be committed to the proposals of the Commissioners, whatever might be their nature. Though I feared this refusal did not augur well for the final success of the negotiations, yet I could not help wishing that other Indians whom I have seen, had a little of the spirit in regard to dependence upon the Government exhibited on this occasion by the great Chief of the Blackfeet.

Among the visitors at the treaty I was pleased to meet the Rev. John McDougall, Wesleyan missionary at Morley Ville, and son of the late lamented Rev. George McDougall, so well and favourably known in connection with Indian affairs in the North-West. Mr. McDougall was present at the first interview the Commissioners held with the Indians, and acted as interpreter for the Stonies, who do not understand the Blackfoot language. He, as well as the Rev. C. Scollen, rendered the Commissioners all the assistance in their power. Traders, with large supplies of goods, were arriving on the ground. They desired to erect buildings of logs to protect their property, but as some of the Indian Chiefs objected to the trees along the river being cut down for such a purpose until after the treaty, the Commissioners deemed it prudent, to prevent complications, to ask the traders to erect only temporary stanchions sufficient to support canvas coverings. They complied with our wishes, and the Indians gave us no further trouble on the subject.

On the evening of Monday I also received a message from Bobtail, a Cree Chief, who, with the larger portion of the band, had come to the treaty grounds. He represented that he had not been received into any treaty. He, however, had not attended the meeting that day, because he was uncertain whether the Commissioners would be willing to receive him along with the Blackfeet. I asked him and his band to meet the Commissioners separate from the other Indians on the following day.

On Tuesday, at two o'clock, the Cree Chief and his band assembled according to appointment. The Commissioners ascertained from him that he had frequented for some time the Upper Bow River country, and might fairly be taken into the present treaty, but he expressed a wish to have his reserve near Pigeon Lake, within the limits of Treaty Number Six, and from what we could learn of the feelings of the Blackfeet toward the Crees, we considered it advisable to keep them separate as much as possible. We therefore informed the Chief that it would be most expedient for him to give in his adhesion to the treaty of last year, and be paid annually, on the north of Red Deer River, with the other Cree Chiefs. He consented. We then told him that we could not pay him until after the Blackfeet had been dealt with, as it might create jealousy among them, but that in the meantime his band could receive rations. He said it was right that he should wait until we had settled with the Blackfeet, and agreed to come and sign his adhesion to Treaty Number Six at any time I was prepared to receive him.

During Tuesday, several parties of Indians came in, but the principal Blood Chiefs had not yet arrived. According to appointment, however, the Commissioners met the Indians at two o'clock on Wednesday. An outline was given of the terms proposed for their acceptance. We also informed them we did not expect an answer that day, but we hoped to hear from them to-morrow.

That day we again intimated to the Indians that rations would be delivered to such as applied for them. We told them the provisions were a present, and their acceptance would not be regarded as committing the Chiefs to the terms proposed by the Commissioners. Most of the Chiefs at once applied for flour, tea, sugar and tobacco, and in a day or two they also asked for meat. Even Crowfoot, at last thankfully accepted his share of the rations, and the beef cattle began to decrease rapidly.

On Tuesday we met the Indians at the usual hour. We further explained the terms outlined to them yesterday, dwelling especially upon the fact that by the Canadian Law their reserves could not be taken from them, occupied or sold, without their consent. They were also assured that their liberty of hunting over the open prairie would not be interfered with, so long as they did not molest settlers and others in the country.

We then invited the Chiefs to express their opinions. One of the minor Blood Chiefs made a long speech. He told us the Mounted Police had been in the country for four years, and had been destroying a quantity of wood. For this wood he asked the Commissioners should make the Indians a present payment of fifty dollars a head to each Chief, and thirty dollars a head to all others. He said the Blackfeet, Bloods, Sarcees and Piegans were all one; but he asked that the Crees and Half-breeds should be sent back to their own country. The Queen, he remarked, had sent the police to protect them; they had made it safe for Indians to sleep at night, and he hoped she would not soon take these men away.

Crowfoot said he would not speak until to-morrow. Old Sun, another influential Blackfoot Chief, said the same. Eagle Tail, the head Chief of the Piegans, remarked that he had always followed the advice the officers of the Mounted Police gave him. He hoped the promise which the Commissioners made would be secured to them as long as the sun shone and water ran. The Stony Chiefs unreservedly expressed their willingness to accept the terms offered.

Fearing that some of the Indians might regard the demands of the Blood Chief who had spoken, if not promptly refused, as agreed to, I told them he had asked too much. He had admitted the great benefit the Police had been to the Indians, and yet he was so unreasonable as to ask that the Government should pay a large gratuity to each Indian for the little wood their benefactors had used. On the contrary, I said, if there should be any pay in the matter it ought to come from the Indians to the Queen for sending them the Police. Hereupon, Crowfoot and the other Chiefs laughed heartily at the Blood orator of the day.

I also said the Commissioners could not agree to exclude the Crees and Half-breeds from the Blackfoot country ; that they were the Great Mother's children as much as the Blackfeet and Bloods, and she did not wish to see any of them starve. Of course the Crees and Half-breeds could be prosecuted for trespassing on their reserves. In this the Indian Act secured them. The Local Government had passed a law to protect the buffalo. It would have a tendency to prevent numbers from visiting their country in the close season. But to altogether exclude any class of the Queen's subjects, as long as they obeyed the laws, from coming into any part of the country, was contrary to the freedom which she allowed her people, and the Commissioners would make no promise of the kind.

On the following morning there was a rumor that the Indians in their own Councils could not agree, that a small party was opposed to making a treaty. The opposition, however, could not have been very formidable. The principal Chiefs seemed fully to understand the importance of accepting some terms. About noon, Crowfoot, with Mr. L'Heureux, as interpreter, came to my tent and asked for explanations on some points, which I cheerfully gave him. During the forenoon a large party of Bloods came in, among whom was Bad Head, an aged minor Blood Chief, of considerable influence, who attended the meeting in the afternoon.

When the Commissioners intimated that they were ready to hear what the Chiefs had to say, Crowfoot was the first to speak. His remarks were few, but he expressed his gratitude for the Mounted Police being sent to them, and signified his intention to accept the treaty. The Blood Chief who made the large demands on the previous day said he would agree with the other Chiefs. Old Sun, head Chief of the North Blackfeet, said Crowfoot spoke well. We are not going to disappoint the Commissioners. He was glad they were all agreed to the same terms. They wanted cattle, guns, ammunition, tobacco, axes and money. Bull's Head, the principal Chief of the Sarcees, said, we are all going to take your advice. Eagle Head, the Piegan head Chief, remarked, "I give you my hand. We all agree to what Crowfoot says." Rainy Chief, head of the North Bloods, said he never went against the white man's advice. Some of the minor Chiefs spoke to the same effect.

The Commissioners expressed their satisfaction at the unanimity among the Indians, and said they would prepare the treaty and bring it to-morrow for signature. The only difficult matter then to be arranged was the reserves. The Commissioners thought it would take unnecessary time to discuss this question in open meeting, and resolved that one of them should visit the head Chiefs at their camps, and consult them separately as to the localities they might desire to select. Lieut.-Col. McLeod undertook this duty, while I attended to the preparation of the draft treaty. He succeeded so well in his mission that we were able to name the places chosen in the treaty.

On Saturday, 22nd September, we met the Indians to conclude the treaty. Mekasto, or Red Crow, the great Chief of the South Bloods, had arrived the previous evening, or morning, on the ground, and being present, came forward to be introduced to the Commissioners.

The assemblage of Indians was large. All the head Chiefs of the several tribes were now present ; only two Blackfeet and two Blood minor Chiefs were absent. The representation was all that could be expected.

The Commissioners had previously informed the Indians that they would accept the Chiefs whom they acknowledged, and now close in front of the tent sat those who had been presented to the Commissioners as the recognized Chiefs of the respective bands.

The conditions of the treaty having been interpreted to the Indians, some of the Blood Chiefs, who had said very little on the previous day, owing to Red Crow's absence, now spoke, he himself in a few kind words agreeing to accept the treaty. Crowfoot then came forward and requested his name to be written to the treaty. The Commissioners having first signed it, Mr. L'Heureux, being familiar with the Blackfoot language, attached the Chiefs' names to the document at their request and witnessed to their marks.

While the signing was being proceeded with a salute was fired from the field guns in honor of the successful conclusion of the negotiations.

I may mention in this connection that on Saturday also I was waited upon by a deputation of Half-breeds, who presented me with a petition, expressing the hope that the buffalo law might not be stringently enforced during the approaching winter, and praying that they might receive some assistance to commence farming. With respect to the buffalo ordinance, I told them that the notice having been short, the law would not be very strictly enforced for the first winter, and in regard to their prayer for assistance to farm, I said I would make it known at Ottawa.

On Monday, the 24th, the Commissioners met the Indians at ten a.m. Some minor Chiefs who had not remained until the close of the proceedings on Saturday signed the treaty this morning. The Chiefs were then asked to stand up in a body, their names were read over and the Indians once more asked to say whether they were their recognized Chiefs. Heavy Shield, a brother of Old Sun, at the request of the latter, took the place of head Chief of his band. It was, however, ascertained that this arrangement caused dissatisfaction, and Old Sun was restored to his position, and the band adhering to his brother, was called the "Middle Blackfoot Band."

After their names were called over, I gave the head Chiefs of the Blackfeet, Blood, Piegans, and Sarcees their flags and uniforms, and invested them with their medals.

While I was shaking hands with them, acknowledging their Chiefs in the name of the Great Mother, the band played "God Save the Queen." The payments were then immediately begun by the officers of the Mounted Police, one party taking the Blackfeet, and another the Bloods, while a third was detailed to pay the Assiniboines, or Stonies, near their encampment some two miles up the river.

The Commissioners went in the afternoon with the latter party, and before the payments were commenced, presented the Chiefs with their medals, flags and uniforms. The Stonies received us with quite a demonstration. They are a well-behaved body of Indians. The influence of the Christian missionary in their midst is apparent, polygamy being now almost wholly a thing of the past.

On Tuesday I took the adhesion of Robtail, the Cree Chief, and his band, to Treaty Number Six, and they were paid out of the funds which I had brought with me from Swan River.

On the invitation of the Blackfeet, Blood, and kindred Chiefs, the Commisioners went on Wednesday to the Council tent to receive an address of thanks. A large number of Indians were present. Mr. L'Heureux spoke on their behalf, and expressed their gratitude to the Commissioners generally for the kind manner in which they conducted the negotiations, to me personally for having come so far to meet them, and to Lieut.-Col. McLeod for all that he and the Mounted Police had done for them since their arrival in the country.

To this address the Commissioners feelingly replied, and expressed their confidence that the Indians before them would not regret having agreed to the treaty.

The Cree Chief and his band also waited upon us in the evening at my tent, and through Father Scollen, as interpreter, thanked us for the manner in which we had treated them. The presents sent for the Indians were distributed to each band, after payment. On Wednesday also the Commissioners drove to see the coal seam about five miles east of the Blackfoot crossing. Under the guidance of Mr. French, they found an outcrop of the seam at a coulee some three miles south of the river. The seam there is from three to ten feet in thickness, and the coal, some of which was burned every day in the officers' mess tent at the treaty, is of a very fair quality.

About noon on Friday the payments were completed, and the Commissioners proceeded to close the accounts. They found that the number of Indians paid, who had accepted the terms of the new treaty, was as follows :—

Head Chiefs	10	at $25	$250
Minor Chiefs and Councillors	40	at 15	600
Men, women and children	4,342	at 12	52,104
Total	4,392		$52,954

The Crees who gave in their adhesion to Treaty Number Six were only paid the gratuity, this year's annuity being still due them. These were paid from the funds of Treaty Number Six, as follows :—

Chief	1	at $25	$25
Councillors	2	at 15	30
Men, women and children	429	at 12	5,148
Total	432		$5,203

The officers of the Police Force who conducted the payments, discharged this duty in a most efficient manner. Not in regard to the payments alone were the services of the officers most valuable. With respect to the whole arrangements, Lieut.-Col. McLeod, my associate Commissioner, both in that capacity and as Commander of the Police, was indefatigable in his exertions to bring the negotiations to a successful termination. The same laudable efforts were put forth by Major Irvine and the other officers of the Force, and their kindness to me, personally, I shall never fail to remember. The volunteer band of the Police at Fort McLeod deserve more than a passing notice, as they did much to enliven the whole proceedings.

The Commissioners at first had not a good interpreter of the Blackfoot language, but on Wednesday they secured the services of Mr. Bird, a brother of the late Dr. Bird, of Winnipeg. He has been many years among the Piegans and Blackfeet, and is a very intelligent interpreter. Mr. L'Heureux also rendered good service in this respect.

The accounts being closed and certified to by the Commissioners, I commenced my return journey on the evening of the 28th September. I came by a crossing of the Red Deer River some fifteen miles east of the Hand Hills, travelled across the prairies further west than my former route, and arrived at Battleford on the evening of Saturday, the 6th of October.

I transmit herewith the treaty as signed by the Commissioners and Chiefs, and also the adhesion of the Cree Chief to Treaty Number Six.

In conclusion I beg to offer a few observations on the treaty, and subjects connected therewith.

1. With respect to the reserves, the Commissioners thought it expedient to settle at once their location, subject to the approval of the Privy Council. By this course it is hoped that a great deal of subsequent trouble in selecting reserves will be avoided. The object of the ten years' reserve on

the south side of Bow River is to keep hunters from building winter shanties on the river bottom. This practice has a tendency to alarm the buffalo, and keep them from their feeding grounds on the lower part of the river. After ten years it is feared the buffalo will have become nearly extinct, and that further protection will be needless. At any rate by that time the Indians hope to have herds of domestic cattle. The country on the upper part of the Bow River is better adapted for settlement than most of that included in the Blackfeet reserve, consequently the Commissioners deemed it advisable to agree that a belt on the south side of the river should be exempt from general occupation for ten years, particularly as the Indians set great value on the concession.

2. The articles promised in addition to the money payments may to some appear excessive. The Stonies are the only Indians adhering to this treaty who desired agricultural implements and seed. The promises, therefore, respecting these things may be understood as merely applicable to that tribe. The Blackfeet and Bloods asked for nothing of this kind; they preferred cattle, and the Commissioners being fully of opinion that such were likely to be much more serviceable to them than seed and implements, encouraged them in their request. The number of cattle promised may appear large; but when it is considered that cows can be readily purchased at Fort McLeod for twenty or twenty-five dollars per head, and their delivery to the Indians will cost an inconsiderable sum, the total expense of supplying the articles promised by this treaty will, I am convinced, cost less than those under either Treaty Number Four or Number Six.

3. I would urge that the officers of the Mounted Police be entrusted to make the annual payments to the Indians under this treaty. The Chiefs themselves requested this, and I said I believed the Government would gladly consent to the arrangement. The Indians have confidence in the Police, and it might be some time before they would acquire the same respect for strangers.

4. The organization of the Blackfeet bands is somewhat different from that of the Saulteaux and Crees. They have large bands with head and minor Chiefs, and as they preferred that this arrangement should remain unchanged, the Commissioners gladly acceded to their desire, as expense would be saved to the Government in clothing, were councillors and head men not named. The Stonies, however, asked to be allowed councillors and their request was granted to the extent of two to each Chief.

5. Copies of the treaty printed on parchment should be forwarded to Fort McLeod in good time to be delivered to each head and minor Chief at next year's payment of annuities.

I have the honour to be, Sir,

Your obedient servant,.

DAVID LAIRD,

Lieut.-Gov., and Special Indian Commissioner.

Report from correspondence in The Globe newspaper, Toronto.

FORT McLEOD, *October 4, 1877.*

The treaty with the Blackfeet nation has been concluded satisfactorily, and was signed by the Chiefs of the Blackfeet, Blood, Piegan and Sarcee tribes, in the presence of the Commissioners—Governor Laird and Col. McLeod, C.M.G., and of Major Irvine, Assistant Commissioner, North-West Mounted Police, and officers of the Police Force, at the Council House, near "Ridge under the Water," or "The Blackfoot Crossing" the Great Bow River, on the 22nd September last.

On the morning of the 4th of September Col. McLeod received information from the ubiquitous Indian that the Queen's father (Lieut.-Gov. Laird) was at Little Bow River, thirty miles north from McLeod, and was accompanied by the "Buffalo Bull" (Major Irvine), and that they would arrive before the sun sank below the western horizon. At three p.m. the Commissioner left Fort McLeod, accompanied by a guard of honor of one hundred mounted men, to meet and escort the representative of Vice-Royalty to the first white settlement in the Blackfeet country. The Governor was met three miles north of Willow Creek, and expressed his surprise and pleasure at the splendid appearance of the well-mounted, well-equipped, well-drilled body of men who formed the guard of honour. When the head of the column forming the escort wound round the bend of Willow Creek, and the extensive wooded valley on which McLeod is built appeared in view, the guns, which had been unlimbered and placed in position on the highest of the bluffs which girdle the north side of Old Man's River, fired a salute of thirteen guns. On the arrival of the *cortege* at the upper or south end of the village, the police band took the lead and welcomed the Governor with its lively music. The whole white, Half-breed and Indian population of McLeod turned out to obtain a view of the great man who had arrived. At the request of the leading inhabitants of

McLeod the carriage of the Governor was halted in the centre of the village, and the following neatly worded address was read and presented to His Honor by Mr. John C. Bell:

To THE HONORABLE DAVID LAIRD,
Lieutenant-Governor, N.-W. T.

We, the citizens of Fort McLeod, beg to welcome you to this little village, one of the pioneer settlements of this great North-West.

To have so distinguished a visitor in our midst is an honor we all appreciate, as in that visit we feel an assurance of your interest in our welfare and prosperity, which had its dawn with the advent of the Mounted Police in the North-West, and which, through their vigilance and care, has continued to this time.

We trust that your visit here will be as pleasant to you as it will be long remembered by us.

> CHAS. E. CONRAD,
> THOMAS J. BOGY,
> DANIEL SAMPLE,
> LIONEL E. MANNING,
> JOHN C. BELL.

To which the Governor replied —

GENTLEMEN,—I thank you for your kind address, and for the hearty welcome you have extended to me on my first visit to this pioneer settlement of the Canadian North-West. After roughing it for the last twenty-four days on the broad unsettled prairies, you have surprised me by a reception which betokens all the elements of civilization.

It affords me unfeigned pleasure to learn that the advent of the Mounted Police in this country has been fraught with such advantages to you as a community.

Permit me to express the conviction that in return for that diligence and care on the part of the Police Force which you so highly and justly value, you will always be found conducting yourselves as becomes worthy subjects of that illustrious Sovereign whom I have the distinguished honour to represent in these territories.

In conclusion, I would remark that you have taken me so unexpectedly by your address that I feel unequal to making an appropriate reply; but the agreeableness of the surprise will tend to heighten the pleasure of my visit, as well as to render abiding the interest which I undoubtedly feel in your welfare and prosperity.

During his stay at Fort McLeod, which extended to the 14th of the month, the Lieutenant-Governor reviewed the garrison, which consisted of troops C and D, and two divisions of artillery.. They deployed past at a walk, trot and gallop, and His Honor expressed his unqualified admiration of the splendid form of the men. He was especially pleased with the artillery, whose horses and equipments were in beautiful condi-tion, and requested Col. McLeod to convey to the officers and men his surprise and pleasure at finding the force at this post so perfectly drilled and acquainted with their duties.

On the 12th the two troops and the artillery, accompanied by a baggage train of six light waggons, left Fort McLeod *en route* for the scene of the treaty. The Commissioner took command of the detachment, and the Assistant Commissioner remained behind to accompany the Governor on the 14th.

The force accomplished the march in three days, and pitched the tents on ground previously laid out for the encampment by Inspector Crozier, at the head of a magnificently wooded valley, of about a mile in width and extending for several miles along the Big Bow. It is a lovely spot, this " Ridge under the Water," and has always been a favorite camping ground of the Blackfeet nation.

Monday, 17th October.

This was the day appointed for the opening of the Treaty, but as a number of the Indian Chiefs, who had a long distance to come, were absent, it was deferred until the following Wednesday. The Governor, however, addressed a number of the Chiefs who were assembled at the Council House. He said, " Last year a message was sent to you by the Councillors of the Great Mother that they would meet you at an early date, and as her Councillors always keep their promises, they have appointed Col. McLeod and myself to meet you here now. We appointed this day, and I have come a very long distance to keep my promise, and have called you together to discover if you all have responded to my summons, and if any Chiefs are now absent, to learn when they shall arrive. You say that

18

some of the Blood Chiefs are absent, and as it is our wish to speak to them as well as to you, and as they have a very long way to come to reach this place, we shall give them until next Wednesday to come in. On that day I will deliver to you the Queen's message, but if any of the Chiefs would desire to speak now, we will be glad to listen to them. I would tell you now that while you remain provisions will be issued for the use of those who wish to accept them."

CROWFOOT—"I am glad to see the Queen's Chief and Stamixo-tokon (Col. McLeod), who is a great Chief and our friend. I will wait and hold a council with my own children (the Black-feet), and be ready on Wednesday to hear the Great Mother's message."

PIEGAN CHIEF—"My children (the North Piegans) have looked long·for the arrival of the Great Mother's Chief; one day we did not look for him, and he passed us; we have travelled after him for fourteen nights, and now are glad to see and shake hands with the Great Chief."

BEAR'S PAW (Stony Chief)—"We have been watching for you for many moons now, and a long time has gone by since I and my children first heard of your coming. Our hearts are now glad to see the Chief of the Great Mother, and to receive flour and meat and anything you may give us. We are all of one mind, and will say what we think on Wednesday."

On Wednesday the Commissioners met the Chiefs at the great Council House. A guard of honor of fifty mounted men accompanied them, commanded by Major Irvine. The Police band received them, and at one o'clock the guns fired a salute as the Governor and Col. McLeod took their seats. There were present at the opening of the treaty a number of ladies and gentlemen who had come long distances to witness this novel spectacle. Mrs. McLeod, Mrs. Winder, Mrs. Shurt-leff, and a number of other ladies from Morleyville and Edmonton, also the Rev. Messrs. Scollen and McDougall, Mr. De L'Hereux, Mr. Conrad, Mr. Bogy, and the whole white popu-

lation of Fort McLeod. Nearly all of the Chiefs and minor
Chiefs of the Blackfeet, Blood, Piegan, Stony, and Sarcee tribes
were seated directly in front of the Council House; and forming
a semicircle of about one-third of a mile beyond the Chiefs,
about four thousand men, women, and children were squatted
on the grass, watching with keen interest the commencement
of the proceedings. Lieut.-Gov. Laird delivered the following
speech:

"The Great Spirit has made all things—the sun, the moon,
and the stars, the earth, the forests, and the swift running
rivers. It is by the Great Spirit that the Queen rules over
this great country and other great countries. The Great
Spirit has made the white man and the red man brothers, and
we should take each other by the hand. The Great Mother
loves all her children, white man and red man alike; she
wishes to do them all good. The bad white man and the bad
Indian she alone does not love, and them she punishes for
their wickedness. The good Indian has nothing to fear from
the Queen or her officers. You Indians know this to be true.
When bad white men brought you whiskey, robbed you, and
made you poor, and, through whiskey, quarrel amongst your
selves, she sent the Police to put an end to it. You know how
they stopped this and punished the offenders, and how much
good this has done. I have to tell you how much pleased the
Queen is that you have taken the Police by the hands and
helped them, and obeyed her laws since the arrival of the
Police. She hopes that you will continue to do so, and you
will always find the Police on your side if you keep the Queen's
laws. The Great Mother heard that the buffalo were being
killed very fast, and to prevent them from being destroyed her
Councillors have made a law to protect them. This law is for
your good. It says that the calves are not to be killed, so that
they may grow up and increase; that the cows are not to be
killed in winter or spring, excepting by the Indians when they
are in need of them as food. This will save the buffalo, and

provide you with food for many years yet, and it shews you that the Queen and her Councillors wish you well.

"Many years ago our Great Mother made a treaty with the Indians far away by the great waters in the east. A few years ago she made a treaty with those beyond the Touchwood Hills and the Woody Mountains. Last year a treaty was made with the Crees along the Saskatchewan, and now the Queen has sent Col. McLeod and myself to ask you to make a treaty. But in a very few years the buffalo will probably be all destroyed, and for this reason the Queen wishes to help you to live in the future in some other way. She wishes you to allow her white children to come and live on your land and raise cattle, and should you agree to this she will assist you to raise cattle and grain, and thus give you the means of living when the buffalo are no more. She will also pay you and your children money every year, which you can spend as you please. By being paid in money you cannot be cheated, as with it you can buy what you may think proper.

"The Queen wishes us to offer you the same as was accepted by the Crees. I do not mean exactly the same terms, but equivalent terms, that will cost the Queen the same amount of money. Some of the other Indians wanted farming implements, but these you do not require, as your lands are more adapted to raising cattle, and cattle, perhaps, would be better for you. The Commissioners will give you your choice, whether cattle or farming implements. I have already said we will give you money, I will now tell you how much. If you sign the treaty every man, woman and child will get twelve dollars each ; the money will be paid to the head of each family for himself, women and children ; every year, for ever, you, your women and your children will get five dollars each. This year Chiefs and Councillors will be paid a larger sum than this; Chiefs will get a suit of clothes, a silver medal, and flag, and every third year will get another suit. A reserve of land will be set apart for yourselves and your cattle, upon which none others will be permitted to encroach ; for every five persons one square mile will be allotted on this reserve, on which they can cut the trees and brush for firewood and other purposes. The Queen's officers will permit no white man or Half-breed to build or cut the timber on your reserves. If required roads will be cut through them. Cattle will be given to you, and potatoes, the same as are grown at Fort McLeod. The Commissioners would strongly advise the Indians to take cattle, as you understand cattle better than you will farming for some time, at least as long as you continue to move about in lodges.

"Ammunition will be issued to you each year, and as soon as you sign the treaty one thousand five hundred dollars' worth will be distributed amongst the tribes, and as soon as you settle, teachers will be sent to you to instruct your children to read books like this one (the Governor referred to a Bible), which is impossible so long as you continue to move from place to place. I have now spoken. I have made you acquainted with the principal terms contained in the treaty which you are asked to sign.

"You may wish time to talk it over in your council lodges ; you may not know what to do before you speak your thoughts in council. Go, therefore, to your councils, and I hope that you may be able to give me an answer to-morrow. Before you leave I will hear your questions and explain any matter that may not appear clear to you."

A few questions by the Chiefs were answered, and the council was closed for the day.

Thursday, October 19th.

The Governor, on arriving at the Council House, where all the Chiefs were awaiting him, said that he was glad to see them all there, and that he had only a few words to say to them. He said, "I expect to listen to what you have to say to-day, but, first, I would explain that it is your privilege to hunt all over the prairies, and that should you desire to sell any portion of your land, or any coal or timber from off your reserves, the Government will see that you receive just and fair prices, and that you can rely on all the Queen's promises being fulfilled. Your payments will be punctually made. You all know the Police; you know that no promise of theirs to you has ever been broken; they speak and act straight. You have perfect confidence in them, and by the past conduct of the Police towards you, you can judge of the future. I think I have now said all, and will listen to you and explain anything you wish to know; we wish to keep nothing back."

BUTTON CHIEF—"The Great Spirit sent the white man across the great waters to carry out His (the Great Spirit's) ends. The Great Spirit, and not the Great Mother, gave us this land. The Great Mother sent Stamixotokon (Col. McLeod) and the Police to put an end to the traffic in fire-water. I can sleep now safely. Before the arrival of the Police, when I laid my head down at night, every sound frightened me; my sleep was broken; now I can sleep sound and am not afraid. The Great Mother sent you to this country, and we hope she will be good to us for many years. I hope and expect to get plenty; we think we will not get so much as the Indians receive from the Americans on the other side; they get large presents of flour, sugar, tea, and blankets. The Americans gave at first large bags of flour, sugar, and many blankets; the next year it was only half the quantity, and the following years it grew less and less, and now they give only a handful of flour. We want to get fifty dollars for the Chiefs and thirty dollars each for all the others, men, women, and children, and we want the same every year for the future. We want to be paid for all the timber that the Police and whites have used since they first came to our country. If it continues to be used as it is, there will soon be no firewood left for the Indians. I hope, Great Father, that you will give us all this that we ask."

CROWFOOT—"Great Father, what do you think now, what

do you say to that ? What I have to say will be spoken to-morrow. My brother Chiefs will speak now."

EAGLE TAIL—"Great Father, from our Great Mother, Stamixotokon and officers of the Police, the advice and help I received from the Police I shall · never forget as long as the moon brightens the night, as long as water runs and the grass grows in spring, and I expect to get the same from our Great Mother. I hope she will supply us with flour, tea, tobacco and cattle, seed and farming implements. I have done at present."

OLD SUN—"Father and sons, I shall speak to-morrow."

GOVERNOR—"I fear Button Chief is asking too much. He has told us of the great good the Police have done for him and his tribe and throughout the country by driving away the whiskey traders, and now he wants us to pay the Chiefs fifty dollars and others thirty dollars per head, and to pay him for the timber that has been used. Why, you Indians ought to pay us rather, for sending these traders in fire-water away and giving you security and peace, rather than we pay you for the timber used. (Here the Indians indulged in a general hearty laugh at this proposition.) We cannot do you good and pay you too for our protection. Button Chief wants us to prevent the Crees and Half-breeds from coming in and killing the buffalo. They too are the Queen's children, as well as the Blackfeet and Crees. We have done all we can do in preventing the slaying of the young buffalo, and this law will preserve the buffalo for many years. Button Chief wishes to get the same every year ; this we cannot promise. We cannot make a treaty with you every year. We will give you something to eat each year, but not so much as you will receive now. He says the Americans at first gave the Indians many large sacks of flour, and now they only receive a handful. From us you receive money to purchase what you may see fit ; and as your children increase yearly, you will get the more money in the future, as you are paid so much per head.

"(To the Stony Chiefs)—When your reserves will be allotted to you no wood can be cut or be permitted to be taken away from them without your own consent. The reserve will be given to you without depriving you of the privilege to hunt over the plains until the land be taken up."

Bear's Paw said that he was pleased with the treaty, the Police, and the prospect of getting provisions and money, and hoped that the Commissioners would give his tribe (the Stonies) as much as possible, and that as speedily as possible. This Chief appeared by his speech to be of a mercenary bent of mind.

Friday, October 20th.

On this day the Indians accepted the terms of the treaty, and several of the Chiefs made speeches. The first speaker was Crowfoot.

CROWFOOT—" While I speak, be kind and patient. I have to speak for my people, who are numerous, and who rely upon me to follow that course which in the future will tend to their good. The plains are large and wide. We are the children of the plains, it is our home, and the buffalo has been our food always. I hope you look upon the Blackfeet, Bloods and Sarcees as your children now, and that you will be indulgent and charitable to them. They all expect me to speak now for them, and I trust the Great Spirit will put into their breasts to be a good people—into the minds of the men, women and children, and their future generations. The advice given me and my people has proved to be very good. If the Police had not come to the country, where would we be all now? Bad men and whiskey were killing us so fast that very few, indeed, of us would have been left to-day. The Police have protected us as the feathers of the bird protect it from the frosts of winter. I wish them all good, and trust that all our hearts will increase in goodness from this time forward. I am satisfied. I will sign the treaty."

BUTTON CHIEF—"I must say what all the people say, and I agree with what they say. I cannot make new laws. I will sign."

RED CROW—"Three years ago, when the Police first came to the country, I met and shook hands with Stamixotokon (Col. McLeod) at Pelly River. Since that time he made me many promises. He kept them all—not one of them was ever broken. Everything that the police have done has been good. I entirely trust Stamixotokon, and will leave everything to him. I will sign with Crowfoot."

FATHER OF MANY CHILDREN—"I have come a long way, and far behind the rest of the bands. I have travelled with these *traveaux* that you now see outside there with my women and children. I cannot speak much now, but I agree with Crowfoot, and will sign."

OLD SUN—"Crowfoot speaks well. We were summoned to meet the Great Mother's Chiefs here, and we would not disappoint them; we have come, and will sign the treaty. During the past Crowfoot has been called by us our Great Father. The Great Mother's Chief (Governor Laird) will now be our Great Father. Everything you say appears to me to be very good, and I hope that you will give us all we ask—cattle, money, tobacco, guns, and axes, and that you will not let the white man use poison on the prairies. It kills horses and buffalo as well as wolves, and it may kill men. We can ourselves kill the wolves, and set traps for them. We all agree with Crowfoot."

The remainder of the day was consumed by about a dozen other chiefs speaking in favour of the treaty. On the following day all the chiefs and counsellors signed their names under the signatures of the Commissioners, and a salute of thirteen guns announced the final conclusion of the last treaty with the Indians of the North-West.

On Sunday afternoon the Indians fought a sham battle on horseback. They only wore the breech-cloths. They fired off their rifles in all directions, and sent the bullets whistling past

the spectators in such close proximity as to create most unpleasant feelings. I was heartily glad when they defiled past
singly on the way back to their lodges, and the last of their
unearthly yells had died away in the distance.

Monday, Tuesday and Wednesday were occupied in paying
off the different tribes. They were paid by Inspector Winder,
Sub-Inspector Denny, and Sub-Inspector Antrobus, each assisted
by a constable of the Force. It was hard work to find out the
correct number of each family. Many after receiving their
money would return to say that they had made a wrong count;
one would discover that he had another wife, another two more
children, and others that they had blind mothers and lame
sisters. In some cases they wanted to be paid for the babies
that were expected to come soon.

On Wednesday the Chiefs presented an address to the Commissioners, expressing the entire satisfaction of the whole
nation with the treaty, and to the way in which the terms had
been carried out. They tendered their well-wishes to the
Queen, the Governor, Col. McLeod, and the Police Force.
They spoke in the most flattering and enthusiastic manner of
the Commissioner, Assistant-Commissioner, officers, and the
Force in general, and said that it was their firm determination
to adhere to the terms of the treaty, and abide by the laws of
the Great Mother. Potts, the interpreter at Fort McLeod,
said he never heard Indians speak out their minds so freely in
his life before.

In reply, the Lieutenant-Governor said he was much pleased
to receive this address from the Chiefs of the great Blackfeet
nation, which in fact was to the Great Mother, as the Commissioners were merely acting for her, and carrying out her
wishes. He was certain she would be gratified to learn of
the approval of the Chiefs and their acceptance of her offers.
In return the Great Mother only required of them to abide by
her laws.

Lieut.-Col. McLeod said in reply:—"The Chiefs all here

know what I said to them three years ago, when the Police first came to the country—that nothing would be taken away from them without their own consent. You all see to-day that what I told you then was true. I also told you that the Mounted Police were your friends, and would not wrong you or see you wronged in any way. This also you see is true. The Police will continue to be your friends, and be always glad to see you. On your part you must keep the Queen's laws, and give every information to them in order that they may see the laws obeyed and offenders punished. You may still look to me as your friend, and at any time when I can do anything for your welfare, I shall only be too happy to do so. You say that I have always kept my promises. As surely as my past promises have been kept, so surely shall those made by the Commissioners be carried out in the future. If they were broken I would be ashamed to meet you or look you in the face ; but every promise will be solemnly fulfilled as certainly as the sun now shines down upon us from the heavens. I shall always remember the kind manner in which you have to-day spoken of me."

After this there was a great shaking of hands, and the Great Council ended.

On Thursday afternoon the Lieutenant-Governor departed for Battleford. On leaving the grounds the usual honors were paid to him. The Commissioner left the following day for Fort Walsh to attend the Commission that was to meet the Sitting Bull.

The traders were notified that they were to cease trading and move off the reservation not later than the following Tuesday, at ten p.m. By this hour they had all departed, and at noon on the same day the Force commenced its return journey to McLeod, which was accomplished in two days and a half. All were glad to get back to headquarters, as the weather had been for some days intensely cold and the prairies covered with snow.

CHAPTER XI.

THE SIOUX IN THE NORTH-WEST TERRITORIES.

MUCH interest has been awakened with regard to this warlike race, owing to recent events ; namely, the war between them and the United States, the destruction by them of
Captain Custer's command, and their subsequent flight into
British territory, and now prolonged sojourn therein.

Prior, however, to this irruption, a portion of the Sioux tribe
of American Indians, took refuge in the Red River settlement,
after the massacre of the whites by the Indians in Minnesota,
in the year 1862. Their arrival caused great consternation in
the settlement. The main body took up a position at Sturgeon
Creek, about six miles from Fort Garry, now the City of Winnipeg, and others, at Poplar Point, and the Turtle Mountain.
The Governor and Council of Assiniboia then governed the
Province of Assiniboia, under the Hudson's Bay Company, and
was composed of representative men. Their deliberations
were grave and anxious. In December, 1863, the Governor-
in-Chief, Mr. Dallas, reported to the Council, that he had
visited the principal camp of the Sioux at Sturgeon Creek, and
found there about five hundred men, women and children, and
more had since arrived ; that he had found them in great des-
titution and suffering, from want of food and clothing, and
that after consultation with Governor Mactavish, of the Province of Assiniboia, he had offered sufficient provisions to
enable them to remove to such a distance from the settlement
as would place it beyond all danger and apprehension, and also
offered to have the provisions conveyed for them, and ammunition supplied them to procure game, but they had positively

refused to go away—giving as a reason the inability of the old men, women and children, to travel in the winter. The Governor was in consequence authorized by the Council, to offer them the means of transport, for those who were unable to walk. The Indians then removed to White Horse Plains, a distance of twenty miles only from Fort Garry, and camped there. A supply of food was given them, but no ammunition. The United States military authorities in December, 1863, sent an envoy to see the Governor-in-Chief of Rupert's Land, and the North-West Territories, with a view to ordering the Sioux to return to United States territory. The Governor was assured, that, though the American authorities would punish such of the Sioux as had actually been engaged in the massacre, they would furnish the innocent with all needful supplies of food and clothing for the winter, in the event of giving themselves up peaceably. The Council, on hearing this statement, authorized the granting permission to the American authorities to enter into negotiations with the Sioux in the territories, on condition that they adopted no aggressive measures against them, and that in the event of the Americans accepting the proposed permission, they should protect themselves by a sufficient guard to preclude the danger of attack from the Indians, and to ensure the preservation of peace.

In January, 1864, the Council considered a despatch from Major Hatch, in command of the American forces, representing that on the approach of spring, he apprehended a renewal of the barbarous scenes of 1862 and 1863, and asked authority to cross the national boundaries and pursue and capture the murderers, wherever they might be found. The Council accorded the permission asked, but it was never acted on. It is not likely that a permission to cross our borders in pursuit of a flying enemy would ever again be granted. It was conceded in exceptional circumstances by an irresponsible Government, but the growth of the Dominion of Canada has been such, and its relations to the empire have become so intimate, that it would not in my judgment be granted, if at all, except in concert with the Imperal Government. The Governor also reported to the Council, that the main body of the Sioux on the Missouri in the United States, had sent him a message asking his advice as to making peace with the Americans, and expressing a desire to visit Red River in spring, and that he had advised the Sioux to make peace with the Americans, as otherwise, the war would be renewed with increased vigor next summer. He had also counselled them not to visit the Red River country. The Council warned the Sioux not to visit the settlement, but in the summer of 1866, the advice was disregarded. A band of Sioux came to Fort Garry and were leaving quietly, with a number of Saulteaux, but when about a mile from the Fort, they were attacked by a band of Red Lake Saulteaux Indians, who had just come into the settlement from the United States, and five of them were shot. The remainder fled for their lives.

The Council apprehended that the Sioux might congregate in force, and a collision take place between the Sioux and the Saulteaux, and therefore authorized the formation of a body of from fifty to one hundred mounted armed men from among the settlers, to prevent the Sioux from coming into the settlement. Fortunately they did not return and a collision was avoided.

In 1866, the American authorities again opened up communications with the Governor and Council of Assiniboia, through Colonel Adams, who intimated that he had been authorized by Brevet Major-General Corse, commanding the District of Minnesota, "to use every possible means to induce the hostile Sioux to surrender themselves at Fort Abercrombie, and to grant them protection and entire absolution for all past offences in the event of giving themselves up," and asking the aid of the Council, to endeavor to influence the Sioux to accede to the proposals he made. The Council accordingly authorized Judge Black and Mr. McClure to communicate to the Chiefs of the Sioux, the letter of Colonel Adams, and endeavor to induce them to accept of it, and to supply them with what provisions might be necessary to carry the Sioux to Fort Abercrombie.

All efforts having that end in view failed, and the Sioux remained, some in the Province of Assiniboia, and others in the territories beyond, As time went on, in 1870, the country passed under the rule of Canada, and when the Government of Canada was established in the Province of Manitoba, which included the district of Assiniboia, the Sioux were found living quietly in tents, in the parishes of Poplar Point, High Bluff, and Portage la Prairie, in what became the new Province of Manitoba. Immigrants from Ontario, had begun to settle in that section of the Province, and the settlement rapidly increased.

The Sioux were found very useful, and were employed as labourers, cutting grain, making fence-rails, and ploughing for the settlers. They also endeavored to gain a subsistence, by killing game and fur-bearing animals, and by fishing. They frequently applied to Lieut.-Gov. Archibald, to be allowed to settle on a reserve, where they might support themselves by farming, a step which that officer favored. In 1873, they renewed the application to his successor, Lieut.-Gov. Morris, who having obtained authority to do so, promised to give them a reserve; upwards of one hundred of these Sioux, resident within Manitoba, having waited upon him, and represented " that they had no homes or means of living," and asked for land and agricultural implements.

They were informed, that the case was exceptional, and that what would be done, would be as a matter of grace and not of right, which they admitted. They were also told that the reserve would be for themselves alone, and that the Sioux now in the States must remain there. A reserve was proposed to them on Lake Manitoba, but they were unwilling to go there, being afraid of the Saulteaux, and especially the Red Lake Saulteaux.

It is satisfactory to state, that after the treaty at the North-West Angle, the Saulteaux having become bound to live at peace with all people under Canadian authority, sent the aged Chief Kou-croche to see the Lieutenant-Governor at Fort Garry, to acquaint him of their desire to make peace with the Sioux· The Chief said the words he had heard at the Angle were good, he had promised to live at peace with all men, and he now wished to make friends with the Sioux. The distrust between the two tribes had been great, owing to past events. At the Angle, but for the presence of the troops, the Chippewas would have fled, it having been circulated among them, that the Sioux were coming to attack them. Permission was given to the Chief to pay his visit to the Sioux, and messengers were sent to them, in advance, to explain the object of his visit.

The result of the interview was satisfactory, and the ancient feud was buried. In 1874, two reserves were allotted the Sioux, one on the Assiniboine River, at Oak River, and another still further west, at Bird Tail Creek. These reserves were surveyed, the former containing eight thousand and the latter seven thousand acres.

Settlements, were commenced, on both reserves, and cattle, seed and agricultural implements were supplied to them. In 1875, the Lieutenant-Governor finding that a large number still continued their nomadic life, in the vicinity of Poplar Point and Portage la Prairie, visited them, and obtained their promise to remove to the reserves—which the majority eventually did. Kenneth Mackenzie, Esq., M.P.P., a very successful farmer from Ontario, who had largely employed Sioux laborers, kindly agreed to visit the Assiniboine reserve and direct them from time to time as to the agricultural operations. The Church of England undertook the establishment of a mission and erected buildings there, while the Presbyterians opened a mission at Bird Tail Creek, and obtained the services of a native ordained Sioux miinster, from the Presbytery of Dakotah. The number of these Sioux is estimated at about fifteen hundred. Both settlements give promise of becoming self-sustaining, and in view of the rapid settlement of the country, some disposition of them had become necessary.

During their sojourn of thirteen years on British territory, these Indians have on the whole, been orderly, and there was only one grave crime committed among them, under peculiar circumstances—the putting to death of one of their number, which was done under their tribal laws. An indictment was laid before the Grand Jury of Manitoba, and a true bill found against those concerned in this affair, but the chief actors in the tragedy fled. Had they been tried, their defence would probably have been that the act was committed in self-defence. The slain man having, as the Chief represented, killed one of the tribe, cruelly assaulted another, and threatened the lives of others. When the war broke out between the Sioux and the American Government, the American Sioux, endeavored to induce those in Canadian territory to join them, but they refused. Precautionary measures were however taken, and messengers sent to them, by the Lieuten-ant-Governor, to warn them against taking any part. They disclaimed all intention to do so, and said they meant to live peacefully, being grateful for the kindness with which they had been treated. Besides these Manitoban Sioux, there were two other bands in the North-West Territories—one at Turtle Mountains, and another large party in the bounds of the Qu'Appelle Treaty. In 1876 the latter sent their Chiefs to see Lieut.-Gov. Morris and the Hon. Mr. Laird, at Qu'Appelle, and asked to be assigned a home. They were told that their case would be represented to the Canadian authorities. In 1877, the Sioux at the Turtle Mountains, sent two deputations to the Lieutenant-Governor, to ask for a reserve in that region. They said they had lived for fifteen years in British territory, they wanted land to be given them and implements to cultivate the soil, and seed to sow, and scythes and sickles to reap their grain, and some cattle.

19

They were told that they had no claim on the Queen, as they were not British Indians, unless she chose to help them out of her benevolence. This they cheerfully admitted, but hoped that they would be helped. They were further informed, that if a reserve was granted them, it could not be near the boundary line as they wished, and that they must avoid all interference with the American trouble with their nation. This they willingly promised, and said "they had already taken care to have nothing to do with the matter." These Sioux were very intelligent and superior Indians, and were well dressed. A reserve was subsequently allotted to them in the year 1876, in the vicinity of Oak Lake, about fifty miles due north of Turtle Mountains, allowing them the same quantity of land, which had been given the Manitoba Sioux, viz., 80 acres to each band of five persons, and they will doubtless follow the example of their brethren on the other two reserves. With regard to the Sioux to whom reserves have been assigned, the then Minister of the Interior, the Hon. David Mills, thus reported in 1877 : " The report of the Deputy Superintendent-General in 1877 gives some details respecting the operations of the Manitoba Sioux on their reserves, during the past year. He says: ' Upon the whole, they appear to have made fair progress in cultivating the land, and their prospects for the future, had they the advice and assistance of some good farmers, for a few years, would be encouraging. Indeed, the Sioux generally, who are resident in Canada, appear to be more intelligent, industrious, and self-reliant, than the other Indian bands in the North-West.' "

While the authorities were thus successfully dealing with the problem of how to provide a future for these wandering Sioux, a grave difficulty presented itself by the incursion into the North-West Territories of a large body of American Sioux (supposed to be under the lead of what is now an historic name, the Sitting Bull), who had fled from the American troops. The

Minister of the Interior, the Hon. David Mills, in 1877, thus alluded to this difficult subject :

" The presence of Sitting Bull and his warriors in Canada is a source of anxiety both to the Government of Canada and the United States. These Indians harbor feelings of fierce hostility towards, and thorough distrust of, the United States people and Government. These feelings may be traced to two principal causes, the dishonesty of Indian agents and the failure of the Federal authorities to protect the Indian reservations from being taken possession of by an adventurous and somewhat lawless white population. The officers of the North-West Mounted Police have been instructed to impress upon Sitting Bull and his warriors the necessity of keeping the peace towards the people of the United States, and there is no reason for supposing they will not heed the warnings which have been given them. It is not, however, desirable to encourage them to remain on Canadian territory, and Col. McLeod has been accordingly instructed to impress them with their probable future hardships after the failure of the buffalo, should they elect to remain in Canada ; that the President of the United States and his Cabinet are upright men, willing and anxious to do justice to the Indians ; and should they return peacefully they will be properly cared for, and any treaty made with them will be honestly fulfilled. It is desirable that as wards of the United States they should return to that country, upon the Government of which morally devolves the burden and the responsibility of their civilization."

The Sioux have since continued within the borders of Canada, and the Minister of the Interior, Sir John Macdonald, reported in 1878, " That it is only just to them to say, that they have behaved remarkably well ever since they crossed into Canada." Their presence in the North-West Territories has, however, been attended and will be followed, in any event, by serious consequences. The natural food supply of our Canadian

Indians, the Crees, Chippewas, Assiniboines and Blackfeet, of the Plain Country, viz., the buffalo, was rapidly diminishing, and the advent of so large a body of foreign Indians has precipitated its diminution, so that the final extinction of the buffalo is fast drawing near. Already the Government of Canada, in the discharge of a national obligation, which has ever been recognized by all civilized authorities, has been obliged to come to the aid of the Blackfeet and other Indians to avert the danger and suffering from famine. The Sioux are already feeling the hardships of their position, and it will tax the skill and energies of the Government of Canada to provide a remedy. Already, at the instance of the Hon. David Mills, then Minister of the Interior (who visited Washington for the purpose), an effort was made by the American Government to induce the Sioux to return to their homes. Envoys were sent to them from the United States, but they declined to accept the overtures made to them. On the previous occasion of the flight into our territories of the Sioux, the American Government, as has been before recited, after an interval of nearly four years, offered them protection on their return journey from British territory to their homes in the United States and "entire absolution for all past offences." This forms a precedent which should be invoked and would doubtless be accepted by the Sioux if they can be induced to believe in the good faith of the American Government towards them. Every effort should be made to bring about so desirable a result, and the subject will doubtless engage in the future, as it has done in the past, the anxious consideration and wise action of the Canadian Government, who have a right to appeal to the President of the United States and his advisers, to relieve them from the incubus of the presence in our territories of so many of the wards of that Government, and who are without the means or opportunities of obtaining a livelihood for themselves.

CHAPTER XII.

THE ADMINISTRATION OF THE TREATIES—THE HALF-BREEDS— THE FUTURE OF THE INDIAN TRIBES.

HAVING placed before my readers, a history of the treaties of Canada with the Indian tribes, of Manitoba, the North-West Territories and Kee-wa-tin, I now proceed, in conclusion, to deal with the administration of these treaties and to consider the future of these interesting aboriginal races. I remark in the first place that the provisions of these treaties must be carried out with the utmost good faith and the nicest exactness. The Indians of Canada have, owing to the manner in which they were dealt with for generations by the Hudson's Bay Company, the former rulers of these vast territories, an abiding confidence in the Government of the Queen, or the Great Mother, as they style her. This must not, at all hazards, be shaken. It can be easily and fully maintained. The treaties are all based upon the models of that made at the Stone Fort in 1871 and the one made in 1873 at the north-west angle of the Lake of the Woods with the Chippewa tribes, and these again are based, in many material features, on those made by the Hon. W. B. Robinson with the Chippewas dwelling on the shores of Lakes Huron and Superior in 1860.

These may be summarized thus :

1. A relinquishment, in all the great region from Lake Superior to the foot of the Rocky Mountains, of all their right and title to the lands covered by the treaties, saving certain reservations for their own use, and

2. In return for such relinquishment, permission to the In-

dians to hunt over the ceded territory and to fish in the waters thereof, excepting such portions of the territory as pass from the Crown into the occupation of individuals or otherwise.

3. The perpetual payment of annuities of five dollars per head to each Indian—man, woman and child. The payment of an annual salary of twenty-five dollars to each Chief, and of fifteen dollars to each Councillor, or head man, of a Chief (thus making them in a sense officers of the Crown), and in addition, suits of official clothing for the Chiefs and head men, British flags for the Chiefs, and silver medals. These last are given both in the United States and in Canada, in conformity with an ancient custom, and are much prized and cherished by the Chiefs and their families. Frequently the Indians have exhibited to me with pride, old medals issued, with the likeness of the King before the American war of Independence, and which have passed down as heirlooms of their families. On one occasion a young Chief, who had come of age and aspired to be recognized as a Chief, was decorated in my presence with the old King George silver medal, by one of the band, to whom it had been entrusted for safe keeping by the young man's father, who was a Chief, with the charge that on the boy's coming of age, it would be delivered over to him. The Chieftainships were at first partly hereditary, partly won by deeds of daring and of leadership against the foe. They are now generally elective, though the tendency to hereditary succession still largely exists. The power of the Chiefs has been much broken of late, and I am of opinion that it is of importance to strengthen the hands of the Chiefs and Councillors by a due recognition of their offices and respect being shewn them. They should be strongly impressed with the belief that they are officers of the Crown, and that it is their duty to see that the Indians of their tribes obey the provisions of the treaties. The importance of upholding the Chiefs, may be illustrated· by an incident which occurred near Fort Ellice, after the making of the treaty. A party composed of three men and the wife

of one of them, were travelling as freighters ; two of the men were Half-breeds, the other a Canadian. One night, one of the Half-breeds shot the Canadian, and attempted to kill the other Half-breed, who fled to an Indian camp in the vicinity. The Chief of the band was there, and he at once took his young men with him, proceeded to the scene of the murder, and after making the offender a prisoner, took him to the nearest police station and delivered him to the authorities. The culprit was subsequently tried in Manitoba, convicted of murder and hanged. For this action the Chief received the thanks of His Excellency the Earl of Dufferin, then Governor-General of Canada. This case affords an illustration of the value of the recognition of the Chiefs of the various bands, and shews of how much advantage, it is to the Crown to possess so large a number of Indian officials, duly recognized as such, and who can be inspired with a proper sense of their responsibility to the Government and to their bands, as well as to others. In all the negotiations for treaties, the Chiefs took a controlling part, and generally exhibited great common sense and excellent judgment. It is therefore of the utmost importance to retain their confidence and cause their office to be recognized and respected by both whites and Indians.

4. The allotment of lands to the Indians, to be set aside as reserves for them for homes and agricultural purposes, and which cannot be sold or alienated without their consent, and then only for their benefit; the extent of lands thus set apart being generally one section for each family of five. I regard this system as of great value. It at once secures to the Indian tribes tracts of land, which cannot be interfered with, by the rush of immigration, and affords the means of inducing them to establish homes and learn the arts of agriculture. I regard the Canadian system of allotting reserves to one or more bands together, in the localities in which they have had the habit of living, as far preferable to the American system of placing whole tribes, in large reserves, which eventually

become the object of cupidity to the whites, and the breaking
up of which, has so often led to Indian wars and great discontent even if warfare did not result.   The Indians, have a
strong attachment to the localities, in which they and their
fathers have been accustomed to dwell, and it is desirable to
to cultivate this home feeling of attachment to the soil.   Moreover, the Canadian system of band reserves has a tendency to
diminish the offensive strength of the Indian tribes, should
they ever become restless, a remote contingency, if the treaties
are carefully observed.   Besides, the fact of the reserves being
scattered throughout the territories, will enable the Indians to
obtain markets among the white settlers, for any surplus produce they may eventually have to dispose of.   It will be found
desirable, to assign to each family parts of the reserve for their
own use, so as to give them a sense of property in it, but all
power of sale or alienation of such lands should be rigidly prohibited.   Any premature enfranchisement of the Indians, or
power given them to part with their lands, would inevitably
lead to the speedy breaking up of the reserves, and the
return of the Indians to their wandering mode of life, and
thereby to the re-creation of a difficulty which the assignment
of reserves was calculated to obviate.   There is no parallel
between the condition of the North-Western Indians, and that
of the Indians who have so long been under the fostering care
of the Government in the older Provinces of Ontario and
Quebec.

5. A very important feature of all the treaties, is the giving
to the Indian bands, agricultural implements, oxen, cattle (to
form the nuclei of herds), and seed grain.

The Indians are fully aware that their old mode of life is passing away.   They are not " unconscious of their destiny;" on the
contrary, they are harassed with fears as to the future of their
children and the hard present of their own lives.   They are
tractable, docile, and willing to learn.   They recognize the fact
that they must seek part of their living from "the mother

earth," to use their own phraseology. A Chief at Fort Pitt said to me,—"I got a plough from Mr. Christie of the Company twelve years ago. I have no cattle; I put myself and my young men in front of it in the spring, and drag it through the ground. I have no hoes; I make them out of the roots of trees. Surely, when the Great Mother hears of our needs, she will come to our help."* Such a disposition as this should be encouraged. Induce the Indians to erect houses on their farms, and plant their "gardens" as they call them, and then while away on their hunts, their wives and children will have houses to dwell in, and will care for their patches of corn and grain and potatoes. Then, too, the cattle given them will expand into herds. It is true that the number assigned to each band is comparatively limited, and the Government are not bound to extend the number. This was done advisedly, by the successive Governments of Canada, and the Commissioners, acting under their instructions; for it was felt, that it was an experiment to entrust them with cattle, owing to their inexperience with regard to housing them and providing fodder for them in winter, and owing, moreover, to the danger of their using them for food, if short of buffalo meat or game. Besides, it was felt, that as the Indian is, and naturally so, always asking, it was better, that if the Government saw their way safely to increase the number of cattle given to any band, it should be, not as a matter of right, but of grace and favor, and as a reward for exertion in the care of them, and as an incentive to industry. Already, the prospect of many of the bands turning their attention to raising food from the soil is very hopeful. In the reserve of St. Peter's, in Manitoba, the Church of England has for many years had a church and mission, and long before the advent of Canada as ruler of the lands, the Indians of the Indian settlement had their houses and gardens, the produce of which, went to supplement the results of

---

* This band a year ago raised sufficient farm produce to support themselves without hunting.

fishing and hunting.   And so on the shores and islands of the
Lake of the Woods and on Rainy Lake, the Indians had their
gardens.   Since the treaties, the Indians are turning their
attention much more to cultivating the soil.   The Indian district agent in the Qu'Appelle region, reported in November,
1878, that of the twenty-four bands in this treaty, eleven are
gradually turning their attention to farming, and of these
Chief Cote, of Swan River, is the most advanced, having har-
vested that year two hundred and eighty bushels of barley, over
three thousand bushels of potatoes, and a large quantity of
other vegetables.   The increase from the four cows he received
two years since is eleven head.   This may appear large, but
such is the fact.

Lieut.-Gov. Laird reported in 1877, "That some of the bands
within the limits of Treaties Numbers Four and Six sowed
grain and potatoes with good results that year, one band having
about one hundred acres under cultivation."   He also states
that the Indians are very desirous of farming, and that he has
hopes that a much larger quantity of seed will be sown next
year (1879).   He also states that the band at White Fish
Lake, raised enough that year to maintain themselves without
going to hunt.   The Superintendent also reported that in the
Manitoba superintendency "a general desire to be taught
farming, building and other civilized arts exists, and some of
the Indians in Treaty Number Three, living in the vicinity of
Fort Francis, are said to evince enterprise and progress in
their farming operations."   At Lac Seule, also in this treaty,
the progress of the Indians is quite marked.   They have
established two villages in order to have the benefit of schools.

The Indian agent in the Lake Manitoba district makes a similar statement.   One band has eighteen small farms of one
hundred acres in all, on which they raise potatoes, Indian corn
and garden vegetables.   They have twenty-nine houses, twenty-
four horses, and thirty-six head of cattle, of their own.   Another
built during the year a good school-house, nineteen new houses,

and had one hundred and twenty-five acres under cultivation. Another had just begun farming, built six houses, two stables and a barn, and possess seven head of cattle. Still another had twenty-three houses and one hundred and fifty acres under tillage, raising barley, wheat, potatoes and vegetables, and having thirty-six head of cattle. It is unnecessary to multiply instances, of the aptitude, the Indians are exhibiting, within so recent a period after the completion of the treaties, to avail themselves of obtaining their subsistence from the soil. Their desire to do so, should be cultivated to the fullest extent. They are, of course, generally ignorant of the proper mode of farming. In the year 1876, I reported to the Minister of the Interior, the Hon. David Mills, after my return from the negotiation of the treaties at Forts Carlton and Pitt, "that measures ought to be taken to instruct the Indians in farming and building."

I said "that their present mode of living is passing away; the Indians are tractable, docile and willing to learn. I think that advantage should be taken of this disposition to teach them to become self-supporting, which can best be accomplished by the aid of a few practical farmers and carpenters to instruct them in farming and house-building."

This view was corroborated by my successor, Lieutenant-Governor Laird, who in 1878 reported from Battleford "that if it were possible to employ a few good, practical men to aid and instruct the Indians at seed time, I am of opinion that most of the bands on the Saskatchewan would soon be able to raise sufficient crops to meet their most pressing wants."

It is satisfactory to know, that the Government of Canada, decided to act on these suggestions, at least in part, and have during the past summer sent farm instructors into the Plain country. It is to be hoped, that this step may prove as fruit-ful of good results, as the earnest desire of the Indians to farm would lead us to believe it may be.

SCHOOLS.

6. The treaties provide for the establishment of schools, on the reserves, for the instruction of the Indian children. This is a very important feature, and is deserving of being pressed with the utmost energy. The new generation can be trained in the habits and ways of civilized life—prepared to encounter the difficulties with which they will be surrounded, by the influx of settlers, and fitted for maintaining themselves as tillers of the soil. The erection of a school-house on a reserve will be attended with slight expense, and the Indians would often give their labour towards its construction.

7. The treaties all provide for the exclusion of the sale of spirits, or "fire-water," on the reserves. The Indians themselves know their weakness. Their wise men say, "If it is there we will use it, give us a strong law against it." A general prohibitory liquor law, originally enacted by the North-West Council and re-enacted by the Parliament of Canada, is in force in the North-West Territories and has been productive of much benefit, but will, in the near future, be difficult of enforcement owing to the vast extent of the territory.

Such are the main features of the treaties between Canada and the Indians, and, few as they are, they comprehend the whole future of the Indians and of their relations to the Dominion.

MACHINERY OF GOVERNMENT.

To carry them out, the treaty area has been divided into two Superintendencies, that of Manitoba, including Treaties Numbers One, Two Three and Four ; and that of the North-West Territories, including Treaties Numbers Five, Six and Seven. Mr. Dewdney, late a Member of the House of Commons from British Columbia, has recently been appointed to the latter Superintendency as Chief Superintendent, and has spent the summer among the Indian tribes. He has had large experience among Indians, and will prove, I have no doubt, an efficient and able officer. His residence will be in his Superintendency, and he will be able to meet the Indians and supervise his deputies. Under the Superintendents are agents having charge of particular districts and the bands within them, who reside among them. The Chief Superintendents and agents are officers of the Department of the Interior, and are directed by and report to the Deputy Superintendent of Indian Affairs at Ottawa, Lawrence Vankoughnet, Esq., who has had long experience of Indian management in the older Provinces, and his superior, Col. Dennis, Deputy Minister of the Interior, who had a large practical acquaintance with the North-West, and the head of the Department, now the Premier of the Dominion, the Right Hon. Sir John Macdonald. The system of management is thus a complete one, and doubtless, day by day, its mode of management, will be perfected and adapted to the growing exigencies and wants of the native population.

THE HALF-BREEDS.

Ere passing from the subject, I cannot refrain from alluding to the Half-breed population of the North-West Territories. Those people are mainly of French Canadian descent, though there are a few of Scotch blood in the territories. Their influence with the Indian population is extensive. In Manitoba there is a large population of French Metis and Scotch Half-breeds, and they are proud of their mixed blood. This race is an important factor with regard to all North-West questions. His Excellency the Earl of Dufferin, with his keen appreciation of men and facts, astutely seized the position and thus referred to them in his speech at a banquet in his honor, given by the citizens of the whilome hamlet, and now city of Winnipeg, on the occasion of his visit to the Province of Manitoba in the year 1877.

"There is no doubt that a great deal of the good feeling

thus subsisting between the red men and ourselves is due to the influence and interposition of that invaluable class of men the Half-breed settlers and pioneers of Manitoba, who, combining as they do the hardihood, the endurance and love of enterprise generated by the strain of Indian blood within their viens, with the civilization, the instruction, and the intellectual power derived from their fathers, have preached the Gospel of peace and good will, and mutual respect, with equally beneficent results to the Indian chieftain in his lodge and to the British settler in the shanty. They have been the ambassadors between the east and the west; the interpreters of civilization and its exigencies to the dwellers on the prairie as well as the exponents to the white men of the consideration justly due to the susceptibilities, the sensitive self-respect, the prejudices, the innate craving for justice, of the Indian race. In fact they have done for the colony what otherwise would have been left unaccomplished, and have introduced between the white population and the red man a traditional feeling of amity and friendship which but for them it might have been impossible to establish."

For my own part, I can frankly say, that I always had the confidence, support and active co-operation of the Half-breeds of all origins, in my negotiations with the Indian tribes, and I owe them this full acknowledgment thereof. The Half-breeds in the territories are of three classes—1st, those who, as at St. Laurent, near Prince Albert, the Qu'Appelle Lakes and Edmonton, have their farms and homes; 2nd, those who are entirely identified with the Indians, living with them, and speaking their language; 3rd, those who do not farm, but live after the habits of the Indians, by the pursuit of the buffalo and the chase.

As to the first class, the question is an easy one. They will, of course, be recognized as possessors of the soil, and confirmed by the Government in their holdings, and will continue to make their living by farming and trading.

The second class have been recognized as Indians, and have passed into the bands among whom they reside.

The position of the third class is more difficult. The loss of the means of livelihood by the destruction of the buffalo, presses upon them, as upon our Indian tribes ; and with regard to them I reported in 1876, and I have seen no reason to change my views, as follows :

" There is another class of the population in the North-West whose position I desire to bring under the notice of the Privy Council. I refer to the wandering Half-breeds of the plains, who are chiefly of French descent and live the life of the Indians. There are a few who are identified with the Indians, but there is a large class of Metis who live by the hunt of the buffalo, and have no settled homes. I think that a census of the numbers of these should be procured, and while I would not be disposed to recommend their being brought under the treaties, I would suggest that land should be assigned to them, and that on their settling down, if after an examination into their circumstances, it should be found necessary and expedient, some assistance should be given them to enable them to enter upon agricultural operations."

FUTURE OF THE INDIANS.

And now I come, to a very important question, What is to be the future of the Indian population of the North-West? I believe it to be a hopeful one. I have every confidence in the desire and ability of the present administration, as of any succeeding one, to carry out the provisions of the treaties, and to extend a helping hand to this helpless population. That, conceded, with the machinery at their disposal, with a judicious selection of agents and farm instructors, and the additional aid of well-selected carpenters, and efficient school teachers, I look forward to seeing the Indians, faithful allies of the Crown, while they can gradually be made an increasing and self-supporting population.

They are wards of Canada, let us do our duty by them, and repeat in the North-west, the success which has attended our dealings with them in old Canada, for the last hundred years.

But the Churches too have their duties to fulfil. There is a common ground between the Christian Churches and the Indians, as they all believe as we do, in a Great Spirit. The transition thence to the Christian's God is an easy one.

Many of them appeal for missionaries, and utter the Macedonian cry, "come over and help us." The Churches have already done and are doing much. The Church of Rome has its bishops and clergy, who have long been laboring assiduously and actively. The Church of England has its bishops and clergy on the shores of the Hudson's Bay, in the cold region of the Mackenzie and the dioceses of Rupert's Land and Saskatchewan. The Methodist Church has its missions on Lake Winnipeg, in the Saskatchewan Valley, and on the slopes of the Rocky Mountains. The Presbyterians have lately commenced a work among the Chippewas and Sioux. There is room enough and to spare, for all, and the Churches should expand and maintain their work. Already many of the missionaries have made records which will live in history: among those of recent times, Archbishop Taché, Bishop Grandin, Père Lacombe, and many others of the Catholic Church; Bishops Machray, Bompas, Archdeacons Cochran and Cowley of the Church of England; Revs. Messrs. Macdougall of the Wesleyan and Nisbet of the Presbyterian Churches, have lived and labored, and though some of them have gone to their rest, they have left and will leave behind them a record of self-denial, untiring zeal, and many good results. Let the Churches persevere and prosper.

And now I close. Let us have Christianity and civilization to leaven the mass of heathenism and paganism among the Indian tribes; let us have a wise and paternal Government faithfully carrying out the provisions of our treaties, and doing its utmost to help and elevate the Indian population, who have been cast upon our care, and we will have peace, progress, and concord among them in the North-West; and instead of the Indian melting away, as one of them in older Canada, tersely put it, " as snow before the sun," we will see our Indian population, loyal subjects of the Crown, happy, prosperous and self-sustaining, and Canada will be enabled to feel, that in a truly patriotic spirit, our country has done its duty by the red men of the North-West, and thereby to herself. So may it be.

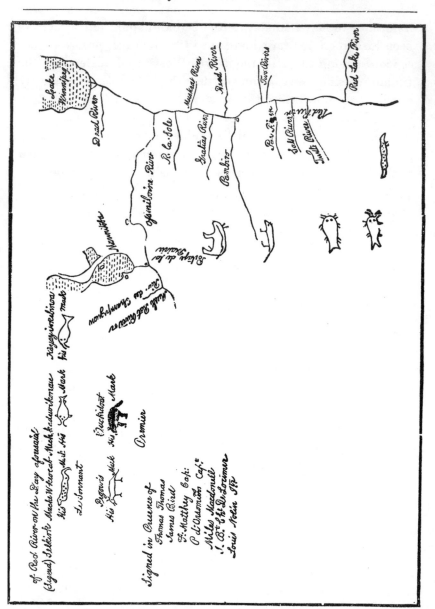

NOTE.—The foregoing represents a copy of the signatures of the contracting parties to the Selkirk Treaty, the Indians signing by their own distinctive marks, and also affixing their signs opposite the tracts of country claimed by them.

APPENDIX.

THE SELKIRK TREATY.

THIS INDENTURE, made on the eighteenth day of July, in the fifty-seventh year of the reign of our Sovereign Lord King George the Third, and in the year of our Lord eighteen hundred and seventeen, between the undersigned Chiefs and warriors of the Chippeway or Saulteaux Nation and of the Killistine or Cree Nation, on the one part, and the Right Honorable Thomas Earl of Selkirk, on the other part :

Witnesseth, that for and in consideration of the annual present or quit rent hereinafter mentioned, the said Chiefs have given, granted and confirmed, and do, by these presents, give, grant and confirm unto our Sovereign Lord the King all that tract of land adjacent to Red River and Ossiniboyne River, beginning at the mouth of Red River and extending along same as far as Great Forks at the mouth of Red Lake River, and along Ossiniboyne River, otherwise called Rivière des Champignons, and extending to the distance of six miles from Fort Douglas on every side, and likewise from Fort Doer, and also from the Great Forks and in other parts extending in breadth to the distance of two English statute miles back from the banks of the said rivers, on each side, together with all the appurtenances whatsoever of the said tract of land, to have and to hold forever the said tract of land and appurtenances to the use of the said Earl of Selkirk, and of the settlers being established thereon, with the consent and permission of our Sovereign Lord the King, or of the said Earl of Selkirk. Provided always, and these presents are under the express condition that the said Earl, his heirs and successors, or their agents, shall annually pay to the Chiefs and warriors of the Chippeway or Saulteaux Nation, the present or quit rent consisting of one hundred pounds weight of good and merchantable tobacco, to be deliver_ ed on or before the tenth day of October at the forks of Ossiniboyne River— and to the Chiefs and warriors of the Killistine or Cree Nation, a like present or quit rent of one hundred pounds of tobacco, to be delivered to them on or before the said tenth day of October, at Portage de la Prairie, on the banks of Ossiniboyne River. Provided always that the traders hitherto established upon any part of the above-mentioned tract of land shall not be molested in the possession of the lands which they have already cultivated and improved, till His Majesty's pleasure shall be known.

In witness whereof the Chiefs aforesaid have set their marks, at the Forks of Red River on the day aforesaid.

(Signed)   SELKIRK.

MACHE WHESEAB,   His x mark.
Le Sonnant.

MECHKADDEWIKONAIE,   " x "
La robe noire.

KAYAJIESKEBINOA,   " x "
L'Homme Noir.

PEGOWIS.   " x "

OUCKIDOAT,   " x "
Le Premier.

Signed in presence of
    THOMAS THOMAS.
    JAMES BIRD.
    F. MATTHEY,
       Captain.
    P. D. ORSONNENS,
       Captain.
    MILES MACDONELL.
    J. BTE. CHARLES DE LORIMIER.
    LOUIS NOLIN,
       Interpreter.

INDENTURE OF SALE FROM THE HUDSON'S BAY COMPANY TO THE EARL OF SELKIRK.

THIS INDENTURE, made the twelfth day of June, in the fifty-first year of the reign of Our Sovereign Lord George the Third, by the grace of God, of the United Kingdom of Great Britain and Ireland, King, Defender of the Faith, and in the year of our Lord one thousand eight hundred and eleven, between the Governor and Company of Adventurers of England, trading into Hudson's Bay, of the one part, and the Right Honorable Thomas Earl of Selkirk, of the other part :

Whereas the said Governor and Company are seized to them and their successors in fee simple, as absolute lords and proprietors of all the lands and territories situate upon the coasts and confines of the seas, streights, bays, lakes, rivers, creeks, and sounds, within the entrance of the streights commonly called Hudson's Streights, in the north-west part of America, and which lands and territories are reputed as one of the plantations or colonies belonging or annexed to the United Kingdom of Great Britain and Ireland, and are called Rupert's Land.

And whereas the said Governor and Company have, for divers good and valuable causes and considerations them thereunto moving, agreed to convey and assure a certain tract or parcel of the said lands and territories hereinafter described, unto and to the use of the said Earl of Selkirk, his heirs and assigns, under and subject to certain conditions hereinafter expressed and contained. Now, therefore, this indenture witnesseth, that in pursuance of such agreement, and in consideration of the sum of ten shillings of lawful money of Great Britain to the said Governor and Company, well and truly paid by the said Earl of Selkirk, at or before the execution of these presents (the receipt whereof is hereby acknowledged), and for divers good and other valuable causes and considerations, them, the said Governor and Company hereunto moving, the said Governor and Company have given, granted, aliened, enfeoffed and confirmed, and by these presents do give, grant, alien, enfeoff, and confirm unto the said Earl of Selkirk, his heirs and assigns, all that tract of land or territory, being within and forming part of the aforesaid lands and territories of the said Governor and Company, bounded by an imaginary line running as follows, that is to say : beginning on the western shore of the Lake Winnipie, otherwise Winnipey, at a point in fifty-two degrees, and thirty north latitude, and thence running due west to the Lake Winnipegoos, otherwise called Little Winnipey, then in a southerly direction through the said lake so as to strike its western shore in latitude fifty-two degrees, then due west to the place where the parallel of fifty-two degrees north latitude intersects the western branch of Red River, otherwise called Assiniboyne River, then due south from that point of intersection to the height of land which separates the waters running into Hudson's Bay, from those of the Missouri and Mississippi, then in an easterly direction along the said height of land to the source of the River Winnipie, or Winnipey (meaning by such last named river, the principal branch of the waters which unite in Lake Saginagus), thence along the main stream of these waters and the middle of the several lakes through which they flow to the mouth of the Winnipie River, and thence in a northerly direction through the middle of Lake Winnipie to the place of beginning.

In witness whereof the said parties to these presents have hereunto set their hands and seals the day and year first above written.

(Signed)   SELKIRK.   [L. S.]

ALEXANDER LEAN,   [L. S.]
Secretary of the Hudson's Bay Company.

Indorsed.—Sealed under the common seal of the within mentioned Governor and Company, and signed and delivered by Alexander Lean, their Secretary, pursuant to their order and appointment, and signed, sealed and delivered by the within mentioned Thomas, Earl of Selkirk (being first duly stamped), in the presence of

ALEXANDER MUNDELL,
Parliament Street, Westminster.

EDWARD ROBERTS,
Hudson's Bay House.

Suit l'attestation écrite et assermentie du premier de ces deux temoins, Alex. Mundell, en presence du Maire de Londres.

Sworn at the Mansion House, London, this twenty-third day of April, 1819, before me, } (Signed)   ALEXANDER MUNDELL.

JOHN AIKINS,   [L. S.]
Mayor.

Puis, Attestation notariée, in testimonium veritatis.

(Signed)   WILLIAM DUFF,
Notary Public.

Be it remembered that on the fourth day of September, in the year 1812, at the Forks of Red River, peaceable possession of the land and hereditaments by the within written indenture, granted and enfeoffed, or otherwise assured or expressed, and intended so to be, was taken, had, and delivered, by the within named William Hillier, one of the attorneys for that purpose appointed, unto the within named Miles Macdonell, Esquire, who was duly authorized to receive the same, to and for the use of the within named Earl of Selkirk, his heirs and assigns, according to the form and effect of the within written indenture in the presence of

(Signed)   JOHN McLEOD,
RODERICK McKENZIE.

THE ROBINSON SUPERIOR TREATY.

THIS AGREEMENT, made and entered into on the seventh day of September, in the year of Our Lord one thousand eight hundred and fifty, at Sault Ste. Marie, in the Province of Canada, between the Honorable William Benjamin Robinson, of the one part, on behalf of Her Majesty the Queen, and Joseph Peandechat, John Iuinway, Mishe-Muckqua, Totomencie, Chiefs, and Jacob Warpela, Ahmutchiwagabou, Michel Shelageshick, Manitoshainse, and Chiginans, principal men of the Ojibewa Indians inhabiting the Northern Shore of Lake Superior, in the said Province of Canada, from Batchewananng Bay to Pigeon River, at the western extremity of said lake, and inland throughout the extent to the height of land which separates the territory covered by the charter of the Honorable the Hudson's Bay Company from the said tract, and also the islands in the said lake within the boundaries of the British possessions therein, of the other part, witnesseth :

That for and in consideration of the sum of two thousand pounds of good and lawful money of Upper Canada, to them in hand paid, and for the further perpetual annuity of five hundred pounds, the same to be paid and delivered to the said Chiefs and their tribes at a convenient season of each summer, not later than the first day of August at the Honorable the Hudson's Bay Company's Posts of Michipicoton and Fort William, they the said Chiefs and principal men do freely, fully and voluntarily surrender, cede, grant and convey unto Her Majesty, Her heirs and successors for-ever, all their right, title and interest in the whole of the territory above described, save and except the reservations set forth in the schedule here-unto annexed, which reservations shall be held and occupied by the said Chiefs and their tribes in common, for the purposes of residence and culti-vation,—and should the said Chiefs and their respective tribes at any time desire to dispose of any mineral or other valuable productions upon the said reservations, the same will be at their request sold by order of the Superintendent-General of the Indian Department for the time being, for their sole use and benefit, and to the best advantage.

And the said William Benjamin Robinson of the first part, on behalf of Her Majesty and the Government of this Province, hereby promises and agrees to make the payments as before mentioned ; and further to allow the said Chiefs and their tribes the full and free privilege to hunt over the ter-ritory now ceded by them, and to fish in the waters thereof as they have heretofore been in the habit of doing, saving and excepting only such por-tions of the said territory as may from time to time be sold or leased to individuals, or companies of individuals, and occupied by them with the consent of the Provincial Government. The parties of the second part further promise and agree that they will not sell, lease, or otherwise dispose of any portion of their reservations without the consent of the Superintend-ent-General of Indian Affairs being first had and obtained ; nor will they at any time hinder or prevent persons from exploring or searching for minerals or other valuable productions in any part of the territory hereby ceded to Her Majesty as before mentioned. The parties of the second part also agree that in case the Government of this Province should before the date of this agreement have sold, or bargained to sell, any mining locations or other property on the portions of the territory hereby reserved for their use and benefit, then and in that case such sale, or promise of sale, shall be perfected, if the parties interested desire it, by the Government, and the amount accruing therefrom shall be paid to the tribe to whom the reserva-tion belongs. The said William Benjamin Robinson on behalf of Her Majesty, who desires to deal liberally and justly with all her subjects, further promises and agrees that in case the territory hereby ceded by the parties of the second part shall at any future period produce an amount which will enable the Government of this Province without incurring loss to increase the annuity hereby secured to them, then, and in that case, the same shall be augmented from time to time, provided that the amount paid to each individual shall not exceed the sum of one pound provincial cur-rency in any one year, or such further sum as Her Majesty may be gra-ciously pleased to order ; and provided further that the number of Indians entitled to the benefit of this treaty shall amount to two-thirds of their present numbers (which is twelve hundred and forty) to entitle them to claim the full benefit thereof, and should their numbers at any future period not amount to two-thirds of twelve hundred and forty, the annuity shall be diminished in proportion to their actual numbers.

Schedule of Reservations made by the above named and subscribing Chiefs and principal men.

First—Joseph Pean-de-chat and his tribe, the reserve to commence about two miles from Fort William (inland), on the right bank of the River Kiministiquia ; thence westerly six miles, parallel to the shores of the lake ; thence northerly five miles, thence easterly to the right bank of the said river, so as not to interfere with any acquired rights of the Honorable Hudson's Bay Company.

Second—Four miles square at Gros Cap, being a valley near the Honorable Hudson's Bay Company's post of Michipicoton, for Totominai and tribe.

Third—Four miles square on Gull River, near Lake Nipigon, on both sides of said river, for the Chief Mishimuckqua and tribe.

(Signed)   W. B. ROBINSON.

JOSEPH PEAN-DE-CHAT.	His x mark.		[L. S.]
JOHN MINWAY.	" x "		[L. S.]
MISHE-MUCKQUA.	" x "		[L. S.]
TOTOMINAI.	" x "		[L. S.]
JACOB WAPELA.	" x "		[L. S.]
AH-MUTCHINAGALON.	" x "		[L. S.]
MICHEL SHELAGESHICK.	" x "		[L. S.]
MANITOU SHAINSE.	" x "		[L. S.]
CHIGINANS.	" x "		[L. S.]

Signed, sealed and delivered at Sault Ste. Marie, the day and year first above written, in presence of—

(Signed)   GEORGE IRONSIDE,
         S. I. Affairs.

    ASTLEY P. COOPER,
         Capt. Com. Rifle Brig.

    H. M. BALFOUR,
         2nd Lieut. Rifle Brig.

    JOHN SWANSTON,
         C. F. Hon. Hud. Bay Co.

    GEORGE JOHNSTON,
         Interpreter.

    F. W. KEATING.

THE ROBINSON HURON TREATY.

THIS AGREEMENT, made and entered into this ninth day of September, in the year of our Lord one thousand eight hundred and fifty, at Sault Ste. Marie, in the Province of Canada, between the Honorable William Benjamin Robinson, of the one part, on behalf of Her Majesty the Queen, and Shinguacouse Nebenaigoching, Keokouse, Mishequonga, Tagawinini, Shabokishick, Dokis, Ponekeosh, Windawtegowinini, Shawenakeshick, Namassin, Naoquagabo, Wabakekik, Kitchepossigun, by Papasainse, Wagemaki, Pamequonaisheung, Chiefs; and John Bell, Paqwatchinini, Mashekyash, Idowekesis, Waquacomick, Ocheek, Metigomin, Watachewana, Minwawapenasse, Shenaoquom, Oningegun, Panaissy, Papasainse, Ashewasega, Kageshewawetung, Shawonebin; and also Chief Maisquaso (also Chiefs Muckata, Mishoquet, and Mekis), and Mishoquetto and Asa Waswanay and Pawiss, principal men of the Ojibewa Indians, inhabiting and claiming the eastern and northern shores of Lake Huron, from Penetanguishene to Sault Ste. Marie, and thence to Batchewanaung Bay, on the northern shore of Lake Superior, together with the Islands in the said Lakes, opposite to the shores thereof, and inland to the height of land which separates the territory covered by the charter of the Honorable Hudson's Bay Company from Canada; as well as all unconceded lands within the limits of Canada West to which they have any just claim, of the other part, witnesseth:

That for and in consideration of the sum of two thousand pounds of good and lawful money of Upper Canada, to them in hand paid, and for the further perpetual annuity of six hundred pounds of like money, the same to be paid and delivered to the said Chiefs and their tribes at a convenient season of each year, of which due notice will be given, at such places as may be appointed for that purpose, they the said Chiefs and principal men, on behalf of their respective tribes or bands, do hereby fully, freely and voluntarily surrender, cede, grant, and convey unto Her Majesty, her heirs and successors forever, all their right, title, and interest to, and in the whole of, the territory above described, save and except the reservations set forth in the schedule hereunto annexed; which reservations shall be held and occupied by the said Chiefs and their tribes in common, for their own use and benefit.

And should the said Chiefs and their respective tribes at any time desire to dispose of any such reservations, or of any mineral or other valuable productions thereon, the same will be sold or leased at their request by the Superintendent-General of Indian Affairs for the time being, or other officer having authority so to do, for their sole benefit, and to the best advantage.

And the said William Benjamin Robinson of the first part, on behalf of Her Majesty and the Government of this Province, hereby promises and agrees to make, or cause to be made, the payments as before mentioned;

and further to allow the said Chiefs and their tribes the full and free privilege to hunt over the territory now ceded by them, and to fish in the waters thereof, as they have heretofore been in the habit of doing ; saving and excepting such portions of the said territory as may from time to time be sold or leased to individuals or companies of individuals, and occupied by them with the consent of the Provincial Government.

The parties of the second part further promise and agree that they will not sell, lease, or otherwise dispose of any portion of their Reservations without the consent of the Superintendent-General of Indian Affairs, or other officer of like authority, being first had and obtained. Nor will they at any time hinder or prevent persons from exploring or searching for minerals, or other valuable productions, in any part of the territory hereby ceded to Her Majesty, as before mentioned. The parties of the second part also agree, that in case the Government of this Province should before the date of this agreement have sold, or bargained to sell, any mining locations, or other property, on the portions of the territory hereby reserved for their use ; then and in that case such sale, or promise of sale, shall be perfected by the Government, if the parties claiming it shall have fulfilled all the conditions upon which such locations were made, and the amount accruing therefrom shall be paid to the tribe to whom the Reservation belongs.

The said William Benjamin Robinson, on behalf of Her Majesty, who desires to deal liberally and justly with all her subjects, further promises and agrees, that should the territory hereby ceded by the parties of the second part at any future period produce such an amount as will enable the Government of this Province, without incurring loss, to increase the annuity hereby secured to them, then and in that case the same shall be augmented from time to time, provided that the amount paid to each individual shall not exceed the sum of one pound Provincial currency in any one year, or such further sum as Her Majesty may be graciously pleased to order ; and provided further that the number of Indians entitled to the benefit of this treaty shall amount to two-thirds of their present number, which is fourteen hundred and twenty-two, to entitle them to claim the full benefit thereof. And should they not at any future period amount to two-thirds of fourteen hundred and twenty-two, then the said annuity shall be diminished in proportion to their actual numbers.

The said William Benjamin Robinson of the first part further agrees, on the part of Her Majesty and the Government of this Province, that in consequence of the Indians inhabiting French River and Lake Nipissing having become parties to this treaty, the further sum of one hundred and sixty pounds Provincial currency shall be paid in addition to the two thousand pounds above mentioned.

Schedule of Reservations made by the above-named subscribing Chiefs and Principal Men.

First—Pamequonaishcung and his band, a tract of land to commence seven miles, from the mouth of the River Maganetawang, and extending six miles east and west by three miles north.

Second—Wagemake and his band, a tract of land to commence at a place called Nekickshegeshing, six miles from east to west, by three miles in depth.

Third—Kitcheposkissegan (by Papasainse), from Point Grondine westward, six miles inland, by two miles in front, so as to include the small Lake Nessinassung—a tract for themselves and their bands.

Fourth—Wabakekik, three miles front, near Shebawenaning, by five miles inland, for himself and band.

Fifth—Namassin and Naoquagabo and their bands, a tract of land commencing near Quacloche, at the Hudson Bay Company's boundary ; thence westerly to the mouth of the Spanish River; then four miles up the south bank of said river, and across to the place of beginning.

Sixth—Shawenakishick and his band, a tract of land now occupied by them, and contained between two rivers, called Whitefish River, and Wanabitaseke, seven miles inland.

Seventh—Windawtegawinini and his band, the Peninsula east of Serpent River, and formed by it, now occupied by them.

Eighth—Ponekeosh and his band, the land contained between the River Mississaga and the River Penebewabecong, up to the first rapids.

Ninth—Dokis and his band, three miles square at Wanabeyakokaun, near Lake Nipissing and the Island near the Fall of Okickandawt.

Tenth—Shabokishick and his band, from their present planting grounds on Lake Nipissing to the Hudson Bay Company's post, six miles in depth.

Eleventh—Tagawinini and his band, two miles square at Wanabitibing, a place about forty miles inland, near Lake Nipissing.

Twelfth—Keokouse and his band, four miles front from Thessalon River eastward, by four miles inland.

Thirteenth—Mishequanga and his band, two miles on the lake shore east and west of Ogawaminang, by one mile inland.

Fourteenth—For Shinguacouse and his band, a tract of land extending from Maskinongé Bay, inclusive, to Partridge Point, above Garden River on the front, and inland ten miles, throughout the whole distance ; and also Squirrel Island.

Fifteenth—For Nebenaigoching and his band, a tract of land extending from Wanabekineyunnung west of Gros Cap to the boundary of the lands ceded by the Chiefs of Lake Superior, and inland ten miles throughout the whole distance, including Batchewanaunng Bay ; and also the small island at Sault Ste. Marie used by them as a fishing station.

Sixteenth—For Chief Mekis and his band, residing at Wasaquesing (Sandy Island), a tract of land at a place on the main shore opposite the Island ; being the place now occupied by them for residence and cultivation, four miles square.

Seventeenth—For Chief Muckatamishaquet and his band, a tract of land on the east side of the River Naishconteong, near Pointe aux Barils, three miles square; and also a small tract in Washauwenega Bay—now occupied by a part of the band—three miles square.

(Signed) W. B. ROBINSON.

SHINGUACOUSE.	His x mark.	[L. S.]
NEBENAIGOCHING.	" x "	[L. S.]
KEOKOUSE.	" x "	[L. S.]
MISHEQUONGA.	" x "	[L. S.]
TAGAWININI.	" x "	[L. S.]
SHABOKESHICK.	" x "	[L. S.]
DOKIS.	" x "	[L. S.]
PONEKEOSH.	" x "	[L. S.]
WINDAWTEGOWININI.	" x "	[L. S.]
SHAWENAKESHICK.	" x "	[L. S.]
NAMASSIN.	" x "	[L. S.]
MUCKATA MISHAQUET.	" x "	[L. S.]
MEKIS.	" x "	[L. S.]
MAISQUASO.	" x "	[L. S.]
NAOQUAGABO.	" x "	[L. S.]
WABOKEKICK.	" x "	[L. S.]
KITCHEPOSSEGUN (by Papasainse).	" x "	[L. S.]
WAGEMAKE.	" x "	[L. S.]
PAMEQUONAISHCUNG.	" x "	[L. S.]
JOHN BELL.	" x "	[L. S.]
PAQWATCHININI.	" x "	[L. S.]
MASHEKYASH.	" x "	[L. S.]
IDOWEKESIS.	" x "	[L. S.]
WAQUACOMICK.	" x "	[L. S.]
MISHOQUETTO.	" x "	[L. S.]
ASA WASWANAY.	" x "	[L. S.]
PAWISS.	" x "	[L. S.]
OCHEEK.	" x "	[L. S.]
METIGOMIN.	" x "	[L. S.]
WATACHEWANA.	" x "	[L. S.]
MIMEWAWAPENASSE.	" x "	[L. S.]
SHENAOQUM.	" x "	[L. S.]
ONINGEGUN.	" x "	[L. S.]
PANAISSY.	" x "	[L. S.]
PAPASAINSE.	" x "	[L. S.]
ASHEWASEGA.	" x "	[L. S.]
KAGISHEWAWETUNG (by Baboncung).	" x. ".	[L. S.]
SHAWONEBIN.	" x "	[L. S.]

Signed, sealed and delivered at Sault Ste. Marie, the day and year first
above written, in presence of

(Signed) ASTLEY P. COOPER,
Capt. Rifle Brig.
GEORGE IRONSIDE,
S. I. Affairs.
F. W. BALFOUR,
Lieut. Rifle Brig.
ALLAN MACDONELL.
GEO. JOHNSON,
Interpreter.
LOUIS CADOTT.
J. B. ASSIKINACK.
T. W. KEATING.
JOS. WILSON.

Witnesses to signatures of Muckata Mishaquet, Mekis, Mishoquetto,
Asa Waswanay, and Pawiss—
T. G. ANDERSON, *S. I. A.*
W. B. HAMILTON.
W. SIMPSON.
ALFRED A. THOMPSON.

THE MANITOULIN ISLAND TREATY.

ARTICLES OF AGREEMENT AND CONVENTION made and concluded at Manitowaning, on the Great Manitoulin Island, in the Province of Canada,
the sixth day of October, Anno Domini 1862, between the Hon.
William McDougall, Superintendent-General of Indian Affairs, and
William Spragge, Esquire, Deputy Superintendeht of Indian Affairs,
on the part of the Crown and Government of said Province, of the
first part, and Mai-she-quong-gai, Oke-mah-be-ness, J. B. Assiginock,
Benjamin Assiginock, Mai-be-nesse-ma, She-no-tah-gun, George Ah-be-
tos-o-wai, Paim-o-quo-waish-gung, Abence, Tai-bose-gai, Ato-wish-
cosh, Nai-wan-dai-ge-zhik, Wan-kan-o-say, Keesh-kewan-bik, Chiefs
and principal men of the Ottawa, Chippewa, and other Indians occupying the said Island, on behalf of the said Indians, of the second part:

Whereas, the Indian title to said Island was surrendered to the Crown
on the ninth August, Anno Domini 1836, under and by virtue of a treaty
made between Sir Francis Bond Head, then Governor of Upper Canada,
and the Chiefs and principal men of the Ottawas and Chippewas then
occupying and claiming title thereto, in order that the same might "be
made the property (under their Great Father's control) of all Indians
whom he should allow to reside thereon;"

And whereas, but few Indians from the mainland whom it was intended to transfer to the Island, have ever come to reside thereon ;

And whereas, it has been deemed expedient (with a view to the improvement of the condition of the Indians, as well as the settlement and improvement of the country), to assign to the Indians now upon the Island certain specified portions thereof, to be held by patent from the Crown, and to sell the other portions thereof fit for cultivation to settlers, and to invest the proceeds thereof, after deducting the expenses of survey and management, for the benefit of the Indians;

And whereas, a majority of the Chiefs of certain bands residing on that portion of the Island easterly of Heywood Sound and the Manitoulin Gulf have expressed their unwillingness to accede to this proposal as respects that portion of the Island, but have assented to the same as respects all other portions thereof; and whereas the Chiefs and principal men of the bands residing on the Island westerly of the said Sound and Gulf have agreed to accede to the said proposal :

Now this agreement witnesseth that in consideration of the sum of seven hundred dollars now in hand paid (which sum is to be hereafter deducted from the proceeds of lands sold to settlers), the receipt whereof is hereby acknowledged, and in further consideration of such sums as may be realized from time to time as interest upon the purchase money of the lands to be sold for their benefit as aforesaid, the parties hereto of the second part have and hereby do release, surrender and give up to Her Majesty the Queen, all the right, title, interest and claim of the parties of the second part, and of the Ottawa, Chippewa and other Indians in whose behalf they act, of, in and to the Great Manitoulin Island, and also of, in and to the Islands adjacent, which have been deemed or claimed to be appertinent or belonging thereto, to have and to hold the same and every part thereof to Her Majesty, her heirs and successors forever.

And it is hereby agreed by and between the parties hereto as follows :

Firstly. A survey of the said Manitoulin Island shall be made as soon as conveniently may be, under the authority of the Department of Crown Lands.

Secondly—The Crown will, as soon as conveniently may be, grant by deed for the benefit of each Indian being the head of a family and residing on the said Island, one hundred acres of land ; to each single person over twenty-one years of age, residing as aforesaid, fifty acres of land ; to each family of orphan children under twenty-one years of age, containing two or more persons, one hundred acres of land ; and to each single orphan child under twenty-one years of age, fifty acres of land ; to be selected and located under the following rules and conditions : Each Indian entitled to land under this agreement may make his own selection of any land on the Great Manitoulin Island :

Provided, 1st. That the lots selected shall be contiguous or adjacent to each other, so that Indian settlements on the Island may be as compact as possible. 2nd. That if two or more Indians claim the same lot of land, the matter shall be referred to the Resident Superintendent, who shall examine the case and decide between them. 3rd. That selections for orphan children may be made by their friends, subject to the approval of the Resident Superintendent. 4th. Should any lot or lots, selected as aforesaid, be contiguous to any bay or harbor, or any stream of water, upon which a mill site shall be found, and should the Government be of opinion that such lot or lots ought to be reserved for the use of the public, or for village or park lots, or such mill site be sold with a view to the erection of a mill thereon, and shall signify such its opinion through its proper agent, then the Indian who has selected, or who wishes to select such lot, shall make another selection; but if he has made any improvements thereon, he shall be allowed a fair compensation therefor. 5th. The selections shall all be made within one year after the completion of the survey, and for that purpose plans of the survey shall be deposited with the Resident Superintendent as soon as they are approved by the Department of Crown Lands, and shall be open to the inspection of all Indians entitled to make selections as aforesaid.

Thirdly—The interests which may accrue from the investment of the proceeds of sales of lands as aforesaid, shall be payable annually, and shall be apportioned among the Indians now residing westerly of the said Sound and Gulf, and their descendants *per capita*, but every Chief lawfully appointed shall be entitled to two portions.

Fourthly—So soon as one hundred thousand acres of the said land is sold, such portion of the salary of the Resident Superintendent, and of the expenses of his office as the Government may deem equitable, shall become a charge upon the said fund.

Fifthly—The deeds or patents for the lands to be selected as aforesaid, shall contain such conditions for the protection of the grantees as the Governor in Council may, under the law, deem requisite.

Sixthly—All the rights and privileges in respect to the taking of fish in the lakes, bays, creeks and waters within and adjacent to the said Island, which may be lawfully exercised and enjoyed by the white settlers thereon, may be exercised and enjoyed by the Indians.

Seventhly—That portion of the Island easterly of Heywood Sound and Manitoulin Gulf, and the Indians now residing there, are exempted from the operation of this agreement as respects survey, sale of lots, granting deeds to Indians, and payment in respect of moneys derived from sales in other parts of the Island. But the said Indians will remain under the protection of the Government as formerly, and the said easterly part or division of the Island will remain open for the occupation of any Indians entitled to reside upon the Island as formerly, subject, in case of dispute, to the approval of the Government.

Eighthly—Whenever a majority of the Chiefs and principal men at a council of the Indians residing easterly of the said Sound and Gulf, to be called and held for the purpose, shall declare their willingness to accede to the present agreement in all respects and portions thereof, and the Indians there shall be entitled to the same privileges in every respect from and after the date of such approval by the Government, as those residing in other parts of the Island.

Ninthly—This agreement shall be obligatory and binding on the contracting parties as soon as the same shall be approved by the Governor in Council.

In witness whereof the said Superintendent-General of Indian affairs, and Deputy Superintendent, and the undersigned Chiefs and principal men of the Ottawa, Chippewa and other Indians have hereto set their hands and seals at Manitowaning, the sixth day of October, in the year first above written.

(Signed)	WM. McDOUGALL.	[L. S.]
	WM. SPRAGGE.	[L. S.]
	J. B. ASSIGINACK.	[L. S.]
	MAISHEGUONG-PAI.	[L. S.]
	OKEMAHBENESS.	[L. S.]
	BENJAMIN ASSIGINACK.	[L. S.]
	WAIBENESSIENNE.	[L. S.]
	SHEWETOGUN.	[L. S.]
	GEORGE WEBETOOSOWN.	[L. S.]
	PAIMOQUONAISHKING.	[L. S.]
	ABENCE.	[L. S.]
	TAIBOSEGAI.	[L. S.]
	ATOWISHCOSTE.	[L. S.]
	WETCOWSAI.	[L. S.]
	KUSHKEWABIE.	[L. S.]
	BAIBONISAI.	[L. S.]
	KEGHIKGODONESS.	[L. S.]
	PALTAHDOGINSHKING.	[L. S.]

Executed in the presence of (having been first read, translated and explained):

(Signed) GEORGE IRONSIDE,
          S. I. Affairs.
       S. PHILLIPS DAY.
       WM. GIBBARD.
       DAVID S. LAYTON.
       JOSEPH WILSON. [L. S.]
       JOHN H. McDOUGALL.
       F. ASSICKINACK.
       PETER JACOBS,
          Church of England Mission.
       McGREGOR IRONSIDE.

The undersigned is one of the Chiefs of the Wequainorekong band, and appends his signature in testimony of his general approval and his assent as an individual to all the terms of the above agreement.

(Signed)　　SIHKUMMEH.　　[L. S.]
　　　　　　RUNIC SAHLENG.　[L. S.]

MANITOWANING, *October 6th, 1862.*

Memorandum from Captain Ironside of Indian settlements on the Manitoulin Island :

Man-a-to-wan-ning.	She-she-gwan-a-sing.
She-qui-ain-dand.	Min-de-moo-ya-se-be.
Y-a-be-je-wong.	Che-to-wai-e-gun-ning (West).
Me-che-co-wed-e-nong.	Weg-wai-me-kong.
Mai-mon-a-ke-kong.	Weg-wai-me-kos-ing.
She-she-gwan-ning.	Ohe-to-wai-e-gun-ning (East.)

TREATIES IN MANITOBA, THE NORTH-WEST TERRITORIES, AND KEE-WA-TIN.

TREATY NUMBER ONE.

ARTICLES OF A TREATY, made and concluded this third day of August, in the year of our Lord, one thousand eight hundred and seventy-one, between Her Most Gracious Majesty the Queen of Great Britain and Ireland, by Her Commissioner Wemyss M. Simpson, Esquire, of the one part, and the Chippewa and Swampy Cree Tribes of Indians, inhabitants of the country within the limits hereinafter defined and described by their Chiefs, chosen and named as hereinafter mentioned, of the other part :

Whereas, all the Indians inhabiting the said country have, pursuant to an appointment made by the said Commissioner, been convened at the Stone Fort, otherwise called Lower Fort Garry, to deliberate upon certain matters of interest to Her Most Gracious Majesty of the one part, and to the said Indians of the other ; and whereas the said Indians have been notified and informed by Her Majesty's said Commissioner, that it is the desire of Her Majesty to open up to settlement and immigration a tract of country bounded and described as hereinafter mentioned, and to obtain the consent thereto of her Indian subjects inhabiting the said tract and to make a treaty and arrangements with them, so that there may be peace and good will between them and Her Majesty, and that they may know and be as-

21

sured of what allowance they are to count upon and receive, year by year, from Her Majesty's bounty and benevolence.

And whereas the Indians of the said tract, duly convened in Council as aforesaid, and being requested by Her Majesty's said Commissioner to name certain Chiefs and head men, who should be authorized on their behalf to conduct such negotiations, and sign any treaty to be founded thereon, and to become responsible to Her Majesty for the faithful performance, by their respective bands, of such obligations as should be assumed by them the said Indians, have thereupon named the following persons for that purpose, that is to say : Mis-koo-kenew, or Red Eagle, (Henry Prince); Ka-ke-ka-penais, or Bird for ever ; Na-sha-ke-penais, or Flying down Bird ; Na-na-wa-nana, or Centre of Bird's Tail ; Ke-we-tayash, or Flying round ; Wa-ko-wush, or Whip-poor-Will ; Oo-za-we-kwun, or Yellow Quill ; and there-upon, in open Council, the different bands have presented their respective Chiefs to His Excellency the Lieutenant-Governor of the Province of Manitoba, and of the North-West Territory, being present at such Council, and to the said Commissioner, as the Chiefs and head men for the purposes aforesaid, of the respective bands of Indians inhabiting the said District, hereinafter described ; and whereas the said Lieutenant-Governor and the said Commissioner, then and there received and acknowledged the persons so presented as Chiefs and head men, for the purpose aforesaid ; and whereas the said Commissioner has proceeded to negotiate a treaty with the said Indians, and the same has finally been agreed upon and concluded as follows, that is to say :

The Chippewa and Swampy Cree Tribes of Indians, and all other the Indians inhabiting the district hereinafter described and defined, do hereby cede, release, surrender, and yield up to Her Majesty the Queen, and her successors for ever, all the lands included within the following limits, that is to say : Beginning at the International boundary line near its junction with the Lake of the Woods, at a point due north from the centre of Roseau Lake, thence to run due north to the centre of Roseau Lake ; thence northward to the centre of White Mouth Lake, otherwise called White Mud Lake ; thence by the middle of the lake and the middle of the river issuing therefrom, to the mouth thereof in Winnipeg River; thence by the Winnipeg River to its mouth ; thence westwardly, including all the islands near the south end of the lake, across the lake to the mouth of the Drunken River ; thence west-wardly, to a point on Lake Manitoba, half way between Oak Point and the mouth of Swan Creek ; thence across Lake Manitoba, on a line due west to its western shore ; thence in a straight line to the crossing of the Rapids on the Assiniboine ; thence due south to the International boundary line, and thence easterly by the said line to the place of beginning ; to have and to hold the same to Her said Majesty the Queen, and her successors for ever ; and Her Majesty the Queen, hereby agrees and undertakes to lay aside and reserve for the sole and exclusive use of the Indians, the following tracts of land, that is to say : For the use of the Indians belonging to the band of which Henry Prince, otherwise called Mis-koo-ke-new, is the Chief, so much of land on both sides of the Red River, beginning at the south line of St. Peter's Parish, as will furnish one hundred and sixty acres for each family of five, or in that proportion for larger or smaller families; and for the use of the Indians of whom Na-sha-ke-penais, Na-na-wa-nanan, Ke-we-tayash, and Wa-ko-wush, are the Chiefs, so much land on the Roseau River, as will furnish one hundred and sixty acres for each family of five, or in that proportion for larger or smaller families, beginning from the mouth of the river; and for the use of the Indians, of which Ka-ke-ka-penais is the Chief, so much land on the Winnipeg River, above Fort Alexander, as will furnish one hundred and sixty acres for each family of five, or in that proportion for larger or smaller families; beginning at a distance of a mile or thereabout above the Fort; and for the use of the Indians, of whom Oo-za-we-Kwun is Chief, so much land on the south and east side of the Assiniboine, about twenty miles above the Portage, as will furnish one hundred and sixty acres for each family of five, or in that proportion for larger or smaller families, reserving also a further tract enclosing said reserve, to comprise an equivalent to twenty-five square miles of equal breadth, to be laid out round the reserve; it being understood, however, that if at the date of the execution of this treaty, there are any settlers within the bounds of any lands reserved by any band, Her Majesty reserves the right to deal with such settlers as she shall deem just, so as not to diminish the extent of land allotted to the Indians.

And with a view to show the satisfaction of Her Majesty with the behaviour and good conduct of her Indians, parties to this treaty, she hereby, through her Commissioner, makes them a present of three dollars for each Indian man, woman and child belonging to the bands here represented.

And further, Her Majesty agrees to maintain a school on each reserve hereby made, whenever the Indians of the reserve should desire it.

Within the boundary of Indian Reserves, until otherwise enacted by the proper legislative authority, no intoxicating liquor shall be allowed to be introduced or sold, and all laws now in force or hereafter to be enacted to preserve Her Majesty's Indian subjects, inhabiting the reserves or living elsewhere, from the evil influence of the use of intoxicating liquors, shall be strictly enforced.

Her Majesty's Commissioner shall, as soon as possible after the execution of this treaty, cause to be taken an accurate census of all the Indians inhabiting the district above described, distributing them in families, and shall in every year ensuing the date hereof, at some period during the month of July in each year, to be duly notified to the Indians, and at or near the respective reserves, pay to each Indian family of five persons the sum of fifteen dollars Canadian currency, or in like proportion for a larger or smaller family, such payment to be made in such articles as the Indians shall require of blankets, clothing, prints (assorted colors), twine or traps, at the current cost price in Montreal, or otherwise, if Her Majesty shall deem the same desirable in the interests of Her Indian people, in cash.

And the undersigned Chiefs do hereby bind and pledge themselves and their people strictly to observe this treaty, and to maintain perpetual peace between themselves and Her Majesty's white subjects, and not to interfere with the property or in any way molest the persons of Her Majesty's white or other subjects.

In witness whereof Her Majesty's said Commissioner and the said Indian Chiefs have hereunto subscribed and set their hand and seal, at the Lower Fort Garry, this day and year herein first above mentioned.

Signed)	WEMYSS M. SIMPSON, *Indian Commissioner.*	[L. S.]
	MIS-KOO-KE-NEW (or Red Eagle) (Henry Prince).	His x mark.
	KA.KE-KA-PENAIS (or Bird Forever) (William Pennefather).	" x "
	NA-SHA-KE-PENAIS (or Flying down Bird).	" x "
	NA-NA-WA-NANAN (or Centre of Bird's Tail).	" x "
	KE-WE-TAY-ASH (or Flying Round).	" x "
	WA-KO-WUSH (or Whip-poor-will).	" x "
	OI-ZA-WE-KWUN (or Yellow Quill).	" x "

Signed, sealed and delivered in the presence of (the same having been first read and explained)—

(Signed) ADAMS G. ARCHIBALD,
          Lieut.-Gov. of Manitoba and the N.-W. Territories.

JAMES McKAY, P.L.C.

A. G. IRVINE,
          Major.

ABRAHAM COWLEY.

DONALD GUNN, M.L.C.

THOMAS HOWARD.

HENRY COCHRANE.

JAMES McARRISTER.

HUGH McARRISTER.

E. ALICE ARCHIBALD.

HENRY BOUTHILLIER.

TREATY NUMBER TWO.

ARTICLES OF A TREATY made and concluded this twenty-first day of August, in the year of our Lord one thousand eight hundred and seventy-one, between Her Most Gracious Majesty the Queen of Great Britain and Ireland, by Her Commissioner, Wemyss M. Simpson. Esquire, of the one part, and the Chippewa tribe of Indians, inhabitants of the country within the limits hereinafter defined and described by their Chiefs, chosen and named as hereinafter mentioned, of the other part :

Whereas, all the Indians inhabiting the said country have, pursuant to an appointment made by the said Commissioner, been convened at a meeting at Manitoba Post, to deliberate upon certain matters of interest to Her Most Gracious Majesty of the one part, and to the said Indians of the other ; and whereas the said Indians have been notified and informed by Her Majesty's said Commissioner, that it is the desire of Her Majesty to open up to settlement and immigration a tract of country bounded and described as hereinafter mentioned, and to obtain the consent thereto of her Indian subjects inhabiting the said tract, and to make a treaty and arrangement with them, so that there may be peace and good will between them and Her Majesty, and that they may know and be assured of what allowance they are to count upon and receive from Her Majesty's bounty and benevolence.

And whereas the Indians of the said tract, duly convened in Council as aforesaid, and being requested by Her Majesty's said Commissioner to name certain Chiefs and head men who should be authorized on their behalf to conduct such negotiations and sign any treaty to be founded thereon, and to become responsible to Her Majesty for the faithful performance by their respective bands of such obligations as shall be assumed by them, the said Indians have thereupon named the following persons for that purpose, that is to say :

For the Swan Creek and Lake Manitoba Indians, Sou-sonse, or Little Long Ears ; for the Indians of Fairford and the neighboring localities, Masah-kee-yash, or, He who flies to the bottom, and Richard Woodhouse, whose Indian name is Ke-wee-tah-quun-na-yash, or, He who flies round the feathers ; for the Indians of Waterhen River and Crane River and the neighboring localities, François, or, Broken Fingers ; and for the Indians of Riding Mountains and Dauphin Lake, and the remainder of the territory hereby ceded, Mekis (the Eagle), or, Giroux. And thereupon, in open Council, the different bands have presented their respective Chiefs to His Excellency the Lieutenant-Governor of Manitoba and of the North-West Territory, being present at such Council, and to the said Commissioner, as the Chiefs and head men for the purposes aforesaid of the respective bands of Indians inhabiting the said district hereinafter described ; and whereas the said Lieutenant-Governor and the said Commissioner then and there received and acknowledged the persons so presented as Chiefs and head men, for the purpose aforesaid, of the respective bands of Indians inhabiting the said district hereinafter described ; and whereas the said Commissioner has proceeded to negotiate a treaty with the said Indians, and the same has finally been agreed upon and concluded as follows, that is to say :—

The Chippewa tribe of Indians, and all other the Indians inhabiting the district hereinafter described and defined, do hereby cede, release, surrender and yield up to Her Majesty the Queen, and her successors forever, all the lands included within the following limits, that is to say :—All that tract of country lying partly to the north and partly to the west of a tract of land ceded to Her Majesty the Queen by the Indians inhabiting the Province of Manitoba, and certain adjoining localities, under the terms of a treaty made at Lower Fort Garry, on the third day of August last past, the land now intended to be ceded and surrendered, being particularly described as follows, that is to say :—Beginning at the mouth of Winnipeg River, on the north line of the lands ceded by said treaty, thence running along the eastern shore of Lake Winnipeg, northwardly as far as the mouth of Berens River ; thence across said lake to its western shore at the north bank of the mouth of the Little Saskatchewan or Dauphin River ; thence up said stream and along the northern and western shores thereof, and of St. Martin's Lake and along the north bank of the stream flowing into St. Martin's Lake from Lake Manitoba by the general course of such stream to such last mentioned lake ; thence by the eastern and northern shores of Lake Manitoba to the mouth of the Waterhen River ; thence by the eastern and northern shores of said river up stream to the northernmost extremity of a small lake known as Waterhen Lake ; thence in a line due west to and across Lake Winnepegosis ; thence in a straight line to the most northerly waters forming the source of the Shell River ; thence to a point west of the same, two miles distant from the river, measuring at right angles thereto ; thence by a line parallel with the Shell River to its mouth and then crossing the Assiniboine River and running parallel thereto and two miles distant therefrom and to the westward thereof to a point opposite Fort Ellice ; thence in a southwesterly course to the northwestern point of the Moose Mountains ; thence by a line due south to the United States frontier ; thence by the frontier eastwardly to the westward line of said tract ceded by treaty as aforesaid ; thence bounded thereby, by the west, northwest and north lines of said tract to the place of beginning at the mouth of Winnipeg River ; to have and to hold the same to Her Majesty the Queen and her successors for ever, and Her Majesty the Queen hereby agrees and undertakes to lay aside and reserve, for the sole and exclusive use of the Indians inhabiting the said tract, the following lots of land, that is to say :

For the use of the Indians belonging to the band of which Mekis is Chief, so much land between Turtle River and Valley River on the south side of Lake Dauphin as will make one hundred and sixty acres for each family of five persons, or in the same proportion for a greater or smaller number of persons. And for the use of the Indians belonging to the band of which François, or Broken Fingers, is Chief, so much land on Crane River running into Lake Manitoba as will make one hundred and sixty acres for each family of five persons, or in the same proportion for a greater or smaller number of persons. And for the use of the band of Indians belonging to the bands of which Ma-sah-kee-yash and Richard Woodhouse are Chiefs, so much land on the river between Lake Manitoba and St. Martin's Lake,—known as " Fairford River," and including the present Indian Mission grounds,— as will make one hundred and sixty acres for each family of five persons, or in the same proportion for a greater or smaller number of persons. And for the use of the Indians of whom Son-sense is Chief, so much land on the east side of Lake Manitoba to be laid off north of the creek near which a fallen elm tree now lies, and about half-way between Oak Point and Manitoba Post, so much land as will make one hundred and sixty acres for each family of five persons, or in the same proportion for a greater or smaller number of persons. Saving, nevertheless, the rights of any white or other settler now in occupation of any lands within the lines of any such reserve.

And with a view to show the satisfaction of Her Majesty with the behaviour and good conduct of her Indians, parties to this treaty, she hereby, through her Commissioner, makes them a present of three dollars for each Indian—man, woman, and child—belonging to the bands here represented.

And further, Her Majesty agrees to maintain a school in each reserve hereby made, whenever the Indians of the reserve shall desire it.

Her Majesty further agrees with her said Indians, that within the boundary of Indian reserves, until otherwise enacted by the proper legislative authority, no intoxicating liquors shall be allowed to be introduced or sold ; and all laws now in force or hereafter to be enacted to preserve her Indian subjects inhabiting the reserves or living elsewhere within her North-West Territories, from the evil influence of the use of intoxicating liquors, shall be strictly enforced.

And further, that Her Majesty's Commissioner shall, as soon as possible after the execution of this treaty, cause to be taken an accurate census of all the Indians inhabiting the tract above described, distributing them in families, and shall in every year ensuing the date hereof, at some period during the month of August in each year, to be duly notified to the Indians, and at or near the respective reserves, pay to each Indian family of five persons, the sum of fifteen dollars, Canadian currency, or in like proportion for a larger or smaller family ; such payment to be made in such articles as the Indians shall require of blankets, clothing, prints (assorted colors), twine or traps, at the current cash price in Montreal, or otherwise, if Her Majesty shall deem the same desirable in the interest of her Indian people, in cash.

And the undersigned Chiefs, on their own behalf, and on behalf of all other Indians inhabiting the tract within ceded, do hereby solemnly promise and engage, to strictly observe this treaty, and also to conduct and behave themselves as good and loyal subjects of Her Majesty the Queen. They promise and engage that they will, in all respects, obey and abide by the law ; that they will maintain peace and good order between each other and also between themselves and other tribes of Indians, and between themselves and others of Her Majesty's subjects, whether Indians or whites, now inhabiting, or hereafter to inhabit, any part of the said ceded tract ;

and that they will not molest the person or property of any inhabitants of such ceded tract ; or the property of Her Majesty the Queen, or interfere with or trouble any person passing or travelling through the said tract, or any part thereof ; and that they will aid and assist the officers of Her Majesty in bringing to justice and punishment, any Indian offending against the stipulations of this treaty, or infringing the laws in force in the country so ceded.

In witness whereof, Her Majesty's said Commissioner and the said Indian Chiefs have hereunto subscribed and set their hands at Manitoba Post, this day and year first above named.

(Signed)   WEMYSS M. SIMPSON,
                    Indian Commissioner.

MEKIS.	His x Mark.
SON-SENSE.	" x "
MA-SAH-KEE-YASH.	" x "
FRANÇOIS.	" x "
RICHARD WOODHOUSE.	

Signed by the Chiefs within named in presence of the following witnesses (the same having been first read and explained)—

(Signed)   ADAMS G. ARCHIBALD,
                 Lieut.-Gov. of Manitoba and the N.-W. Territories.
         JAMES MCKAY, P.C.C.
         MOLYNEUX ST. JOHN.
         E. A. ARCHIBALD.
         LILY ARCHIBALD.
         HENRI BOUTHILLIER.
         PAUL DE LARONDE.
         DONALD MCDONALD.
         ELIZA MCDONALD.
         ALEXANDER MUIR, SR.

THE NORTH-WEST ANGLE TREATY, NUMBER THREE.

ARTICLES OF A TREATY made and concluded this third day of October, in the year of our Lord one thousand eight hundred and seventy-three, between Her Most Gracious Majesty the Queen of Great Britain and Ireland, by her Commissioners, the Hon. Alexander Morris, Lieutenant-Governor of the Province of Manitoba and the North-West Territories; Joseph Albert Norbert Provencher, and Simon James Dawson, of the one part; and the Saulteaux tribe of the Ojibbeway Indians, inhabitants of the country within the limits hereinafter defined and described, by their Chiefs, chosen and named as hereinafter mentioned, of the other part :

Whereas the Indians inhabiting the said country have, pursuant to an appointment made by the said Commissioners, been convened at a meeting at the North-West angle of the Lake of the Woods, to deliberate upon certain matters of interest to Her Most Gracious Majesty, of the one part, and the said Indians of the other ;

And whereas the said Indians have been notified and informed by Her Majesty's said Commissioners, that it is the desire of Her Majesty to open up for settlement, immigration, and such other purposes as to Her Majesty may seem meet, a tract of country bounded and described as hereinafter mentioned, and to obtain the consent thereto of her Indian subjects inhabiting the said tract, and to make a treaty and arrange with them, so that there may be peace and good will between them and Her Majesty, and that they may know and be assured of what allowance they are to count upon and receive from Her Majesty's bounty and benevolence :

And whereas, the Indians of the said tract, duly convened in Council, as aforesaid, and being requested by Her Majesty's said Commissioners to name certain Chiefs and head men, who should be authorized on their behalf to conduct such negotiations, and sign any treaty to be founded thereon, and to become responsible to Her Majesty for the faithful performance by their respective bands of such obligations as shall be assumed by them, the said Indians have thereupon named the following persons for that purpose, that is to say :—Kee-tak-pay-pi-nais (Rainy River), Kitihi-gay-lake (Rainy River), Note-na-qua-hung (North-West Angle), Mawe-do-pe-nais (Rainy River), Pow-wa-sang (North-West Angle), Canda-com-igo-wi-ninie (North-West Angle), Pa-pa-ska-gin (Rainy River), May-no-wah-tau-ways-kung (North-West Angle), Kitchi-ne-ka-be-han (Rainy River), Sah-katch-eway (Lake Seul), Muka-day-wah-sin (Kettle Falls), Me-kie-sies (Rainy Lake, Fort Francis), Oos-con-na-geist (Rainy Lake), Wah-shis-kince (Eagle Lake), Rah-kie-y-ash (Flower Lake), Go-bay (Rainy Lake), Ka-me-ti-ash (White Fish Lake), Nee-sho-tal (Rainy River), Kee-gee-go-kay (Rainy River), Sha-sha-gance (Shoal Lake), Shah-win-na-bi-nais (Shoal Lake), Ay-ash-a-wash (Buffalo Point), Pay-ah-be-wash (White Fish Bay), Rah-tay-tay-pa-o-cutch (Lake of the Woods).

And thereupon in open council the different bands having presented their Chiefs to the said Commissioners as the Chiefs and head men for the purposes aforesaid of the respective bands of Indians inhabiting the said district hereinafter described.

And whereas the said Commissioners then and there received and acknowledged the persons so presented as Chiefs and head men for the purposes aforesaid of the respective bands of Indians inhabiting the said district hereinafter described ;

And whereas the said Commissioners have proceeded to negotiate a treaty with the said Indians, and the same has been finally agreed upon and concluded as follows, that is to say :

The Saulteaux tribe of the Ojibbeway Indians, and all other the Indians inhabiting the district hereinafter described and defined, do hereby cede, release, surrender, and yield up to the Government of the Dominion of Canada, for Her Majesty the Queen and her successors forever, all their rights, titles and privileges whatsoever to the lands included within the following limits, that is to say :

Commencing at a point on the Pigeon River route where the international boundary line between the territories of Great Britain and the United States intersects the height of land separating the waters running to Lake Superior from those flowing to Lake Winnipeg, thence northerly, westerly and easterly, along the height of land aforesaid, following its sinuosities, whatever their course may be, to the point at which the said height of land meets the summit of the water-shed from which the streams flow to Lake Nepigon, thence northerly and westerly, or whatever may be its course along the ridge separating the waters of the Nepigon and the Winnipeg to the height of land dividing the waters of the Albany and the Winnipeg, thence westerly and north-westerly along the height of land dividing the waters flowing to Hudson's Bay by the Albany or other rivers from those running to English River and the Winnipeg to a point on the said height of land bearing north forty-five degrees east from Fort Alexander at the mouth of the Winnipeg ; thence south forty-five degrees west to Fort Alexander at the mouth of the Winnipeg ; thence southerly along the eastern bank of the Winnipeg to the mouth of White Mouth River ; thence southerly by the line described as in that part forming the eastern boundary of the tract surrendered by the Chippewa and Swampy Cree tribes of Indians to Her Majesty on the third of August, one thousand eight hundred and seventy-one, namely, by White Mouth River to White Mouth Lake and thence on a line having the general bearing of White Mouth River to the forty-ninth parallel of north latitude ; thence by the forty-ninth parallel of north latitude to the Lake of the Woods, and from thence by the international boundary line to the place of beginning.

The tract comprised within the lines above described embracing an area of fifty-five thousand square miles, be the same more or less.

To have and to hold the same to Her Majesty the Queen and her successors forever.

And Her Majesty the Queen hereby agrees and undertakes to lay aside reserves for farming lands, due respect being had to lands at present cultivated by the said Indians, and also to lay aside and reserve for the benefit of the said Indians, to be administered and dealt with for them by Her Majesty's Government of the Dominion of Canada, in such a manner as shall seem best, other reserves of land in the said territory hereby ceded, which said reserves shall be selected and set aside where it shall be deemed most convenient and advantageous for each band or bands of Indians, by the officers of the said Government appointed for that purpose, and such selection shall be so made after conference with the Indians : Provided, however, that such reserve whether for farming or other purposes shall in nowise exceed in all one square mile for each family of five, or in that proportion for larger or smaller families, and such selection shall be made if possible during the course of next summer or as soon thereafter as may be found practicable, it being understood, however, that if at the time of any such selection of any reserves as aforesaid, there are any settlers within the bounds of the lands reserved by any band, Her Majesty reserves the right to deal with such settlers as she shall deem just, so as not to diminish the extent of land allotted to Indians; and provided also that the aforesaid reserves of lands or any interest or right therein or appurtenant thereto, may be sold, leased or otherwise disposed of by the said Government for the use and benefit of the said Indians, with the consent of the Indians entitled thereto first had and obtained.

And with a view to show the satisfaction of Her Majesty with the behavior and good conduct of her Indians, she hereby, through her Commissioners, makes them a present of twelve dollars for each man, woman and child belonging to the bands here represented, in extinguishment of all claims heretofore preferred.

And further, Her Majesty agrees to maintain schools for instruction in such reserves hereby made as to her Government of her Dominion of Canada may seem advisable, whenever the Indians of the reserve shall desire it.

Her Majesty further agrees with her said Indians, that within the boundary of Indian reserves, until otherwise determined by the Government of the Dominion of Canada, no intoxicating liquor shall be allowed to be introduced or sold, and all laws now in force, or hereafter to be enacted to preserve her Indian subjects inhabiting the reserves, or living elsewhere within her North-West Territories, from the evil influence of the use of intoxicating liquors shall be strictly enforced.

Her Majesty further agrees with her said Indians, that they, the said Indians, shall have right to pursue their avocations of hunting and fishing throughout the tract surrendered as hereinbefore described, subject to such regulations as may from time to time be made by her Government of her Dominion of Canada, and saving and excepting such tracts as may from time to time be required or taken up for settlement, mining, lumbering or other purposes, by her said Government of the Dominion of Canada, or by any of the subjects thereof duly authorized therefor by the said Government.

It is further agreed between Her Majesty and her said Indians that such sections of the reserves above indicated as may at any time be required for public works or buildings, of what nature soever, may be appropriated for that purpose by Her Majesty's Government of the Dominion of Canada, due compensation being made for the value of any improvements thereon.

And further, that Her Majesty's Commissioners shall, as soon as possible, after the execution of this treaty, cause to be taken an accurate census of all the Indians inhabiting the tract above described, distributing them in families, and shall in every year ensuing the date hereof at some period in each year, to be duly notified to the Indians, and at a place or places to be appointed for that purpose within the territory ceded, pay to each Indian person the sum of five dollars per head yearly.

It is further agreed between Her Majesty and the said Indians, that the sum of fifteen hundred dollars per annum shall be yearly and every year expended by Her Majesty in the purchase of ammunition, and twine for nets for the use of the said Indians.

It is further agreed between Her Majesty and the said Indians, that the following articles shall be supplied to any band of the said Indians who are now actually cultivating the soil, or who shall hereafter commence to cultivate the land, that is to say—two hoes for every family actually cultivating ; also one spade per family as aforesaid ; one plough for every ten families as aforesaid ; five harrows for every twenty families as aforesaid ; one scythe for every family as aforesaid ; and also one axe and one cross-cut saw, one hand saw, one pit saw, the necessary files, one grindstone, one auger for each band, and also for each Chief for the use of his band, one chest of ordinary carpenter's tools ; also for each band, enough of wheat, barley, potatoes and oats to plant the land actually broken up for cultivation by such band ; also for each band, one yoke of oxen, one bull and four cows ; all the aforesaid articles to be given once for all for the encouragement of the practice of agriculture among the Indians.

It is further agreed between Her Majesty and the said Indians, that each Chief, duly recognized as such, shall receive an annual salary of twenty-five dollars per annum, and each subordinate officer, not exceeding three for each band, shall receive fifteen dollars per annum ; and each such Chief and subordinate officer as aforesaid shall also receive, once in every three years, a suitable suit of clothing ; and each Chief shall receive, in recognition of the closing of the treaty, a suitable flag and medal.

And the undersigned Chiefs, on their own behalf and on behalf of all other Indians inhabiting the tract within ceded, do hereby solemnly promise and engage to strictly observe this treaty, and also to conduct and behave themselves as good and loyal subjects of Her Majesty the Queen. They promise and engage that they will, in all respects obey and abide by the law ; that they will maintain peace and good order between each other, and also between themselves and other tribes of Indians, and between themselves and others of Her Majesty's subjects, whether Indians or whites, now inhabiting or hereafter to inhabit any part of the said ceded tract ; and that they will not molest the person or property of any inhabitant of such ceded tract, or the property of Her Majesty the Queen, or interfere with or trouble any person passing or travelling through the said tract or any part thereof ; and that they will aid and assist the officers of Her Majesty in bringing to justice and punishment any Indian offending against the stipulations of this treaty, or infringing the laws in force in the country so ceded.

In witness whereof, Her Majesty's said Commissioners and the said Indian Chiefs have hereunto subscribed and set their hands, at the north-west angle of the Lake of the Woods, this day and year herein first above-named.

(Signed)   ALEXANDER MORRIS,   [L. S.]
Lieutenant-Governor.

J. A. N. PROVENCHER,
Indian Commissioner.

S. J. DAWSON,
Indian Commissioner.

KEE-TA-KAY-PI-NAIS.	His x mark.
KITIHI-GAY-KAKE.	" x "
NO-TE-NA-QUA-HUNG.	" x "
MAWE-DO-PE-NAIS.	" x "
POW-WA-SANG.	" x "
CANDA-COM-IGO-WI-NINIE.	" x "
PA-PA-SKA-GIN.	" x "
MAY-NO-WAH-TAU-WAYS-KUNG.	" x "
KITCHI-NE-KA-BE-HAN.	" x "
SAH-KATCH-EWAY.	" x "
MUKA-DAY-WAH-SIN.	" x "
ME-KIE-SIES.	" x "
OOS-CON-NA-GEIST.	" x "
WAH-SHIS-KINCE.	" x "
RAH-KIE-Y-ASH.	" x "
GO-BAY.	" x "
KA-ME-TI-ASH.	" x "
NEE-SHO-TAL.	" x "
KEE-JEE-GO-KAY.	" x "
SHA-SHA-GANCE.	" x "
SHAH-WIN-NA-BI-NAIS.	" x "
AY-ASH-A-WASH.	" x "
PAY-AH-BEE-WASH.	" x "
RAH-TAY-TAY-PA-O-CUTCH.	" x " .

Signed by the Chiefs within named in presence of the following witnesses, the same having been first read and explained by the Honorable James McKay :—

(Signed) JAMES MCKAY.
MOLYNEUX ST. JOHN.
ROBERT PITHER.
CHRISTINE V. K. MORRIS.
CHARLES NOLIN.
A. MCDONALD,
Captain commanding escort to Lieutenant-Governor.
JAMES F. GRAHAM.
JOSEPH NOLIN.

A. McLEOD.
GEORGE McPHERSON, SEN.
SEDLEY BLANCHARD.
W. FRED. BUCHANAN.
FRANK G. BECHER.
ALFRED CODD, M.D.
GORDON S. CORBAULT.
PIERRE LeVIELLER.
NICHOLAS CHATELAINE.

We hereby certify that the foregoing is a true copy of the original articles of treaty of which it purports to be a copy.

(Signed)   ALEXANDER MORRIS,
                    Lieutenant-Governor.
        J. A. N. PROVENCHER,
                    Indian Commissioner.
        S. J. DAWSON,
                    Indian Commissioner.

We having had communication of the treaty, certified copy whereof is hereto annexe l, but not having been at the Councils held at the north-west angle of the Lake of the Woods, between Her Majesty's Commissioners, and the several Indian Chiefs and others therein named, at which the articles of the said treaty were agreed upon, hereby, for ourselves and the several bands of Indians which we represent, in consideration of the provisions of the said treaty being extended to us and the said bands which we represent, transfer, surrender and relinquish to Her Majesty the Queen, her heirs and successors, to and for the use of her Dominion of Canada, all our right, title and privilege whatsoever, which we, the said Chiefs, and the said bands which we represent, have held, or enjoy, of, in and to the territory described and fully set out in the said articles of treaty and every part thereof, to have and to hold the same unto the use of Her said Majesty the Queen, her heirs and successors for ever.

And we hereby agree to accept the several provisions, payments and reserves of the said treaty as therein stated, and solemnly promise and engage to abide by, carry out and fulfil all the stipulations, obligations and conditions therein contained, on the part of the said Chiefs and Indians therein named to be observed and performed, and in all things to conform to the articles of the said treaty, as if we ourselves, and the bands which we represent had been originally contracting parties thereto, and had been present and attached our signatures to the said treaty.

In witness whereof, Her Majesty's said Commissioners and the said Indian Chiefs have hereunto subscribed and set their hands, this thirteenth day of October, in the year of Our Lord one thousand eight hundred and seventy-three.

For and on behalf of the Commissioners, the Honorable Alexander Morris, Lieutenant-Governor of Manitoba and the North-West Territories, Joseph Albert Norbert Provencher, Esq., and the undersigned :

(Signed)   S. J. DAWSON,
Commissioner.

PAY--BA-MA-CHAS.   His x mark.

RE-BA-QUIN.   " x "

ME-TAS-SO-QUE-NE-SKANK. " x "

Signed by S. J. Dawson, Esq., one of Her Majesty's said Commissioners, for and on behalf, and with the authority and consent of the Honorable Alexander Morris, Lieutenant-Governor of Manitoba and the North-West Territories, and J. A. N. Provencher, Esq., the remaining two Commissioners, and himself, and by the Chiefs within named on behalf of themselves and the several bands which they represent, the same and the annexed certified copy of articles of treaty having been first read and explained in presence of the following witnesses :

(Signed) THOS. A. P. TOWERS.

         JOHN AITKEN.

         A. J. McDONALD.

         UNZZAKI.

         JAS. LOGANOSH, His x mark.

         PINLLSISE.

REPORT OF COMMISSIONER DAWSON.

OTTAWA, *26th December, 1873.*

SIR,—I beg leave to inform you that, after the treaty had been concluded with certain bands of the Saulteaux tribe of the Ojibbeway Indians, at the north-west angle of the Lake of the Woods, by arrangements made with my associate Commissioners, His Honor the Lieutenant-Governor of Manitoba and the North-West Territories, and Mr. Provencher, I came eastward and convened the leading people of the remaining bands at Shebandowan where they also, through their Chiefs, accepted and signed the treaty.

I have much satisfaction in saying that these Indians were most friendly in their bearing, and desired me to convey to the Government their cordial expressions of loyalty to their Great Mother, Her Majesty the Queen.

They took some time to deliberate over the provisions of the treaty and asked me occasionally to explain certain passages, more especially those in relation to the reserves.

Before signing it they comprehended perfectly the nature of the obligations into which they were about to enter, that the surrender of their territorial rights would be irrevocable, and that they were to stand forever afterwards in new relations to the white man.

This, the Chiefs themselves stated with great solemnity to their people, in short but impressive speeches, as they each in turn advanced to touch the pen.

One cause of delay at the Lake of the Woods arose from the circumstance of there being a number of aspirants to the office of Chief; but at Sheban-dowan I had no such difficulty, for the whole of the bands east of the narrows of Rainy Lake, are under three principal Chiefs, whose authority is unquestioned.

The names of these Chiefs and their respective districts are as follows:

Pay-ba-ma-chas, Chief of the country intervening between the narrows of Rainy Lake and Sturgeon Falls, and of the region drained by the River Seine and its tributary streams, between the latter place (Sturgeon Falls) and Lac des Mille Lacs. This is a very extensive district, and in it are many valuable groves of pine.

Ke-ba-quin, Chief of the region intervening between the present line of the Red River route and the United States boundary line, east of Rainy Lake and west of the height of land. The gold bearing country is in this Chief's district.

Metas-so-que-nes-hauk, Chief of Lac des Mille Lacs and the district to the north, lying along the height of land between that lake and the waters of the Nipegon and Lac Seul. This Chief is a very intelligent man, and has already begun, to make his people clear land and grow crops.

Each of these three principal Chiefs will have a staff of Lieutenants or subordinate Chiefs, not exceeding three to their respective bands, as provided for in the treaty, but they preferred not to name them at once, saying that the selection was a matter of some delicacy to them, and requiring a little time.

In regard to the reserves provided for in the treaty, I shall as soon as possible submit a scheme which I think will meet the circumstances, and at the same time draw attention to some experience gained in negotiating with these Indians, which may be of use in similar negotiations in the future.*

---

* In 1874 Mr. Dawson and Mr. Pither were appointed to meet the Indians and arrange the position of the reserves, which they did; but subsequently, the Indians claiming that they had not fully understood the exact location or extent of some of the reserves, Colonel Dennis, then Surveyor-General, now Deputy Minister of the Interior, was instructed to visit the Indians comprised in Treaty Number Three, and finally adjust the question of reserves. Colonel Dennis undertook this duty in 1875 and satisfactorily arranged a scheme of reserves for the different bands of the Lake of the Woods. Colonel Dennis submitted a comprehensive report of the results of his mission, and suggested the appointment of sub-agents, the fixing of a specific day for payment to the Indians of their annuities in each agency district, that the necessary funds and the articles for distribution should be provided and in the agents' hands in good time. He advised that the local agents should have some practical knowledge of agriculture, as he believed that the Indians would succeed in raising quantities of stock, though

The copy of the treaty signed by these Chiefs is enclosed herewith and to it is attached a document signed by the Lieutenant-Governor of Manitoba and the North-West Territories, and Mr. Provencher, empowering me to act for them in their absence, in their capacity of Indian Commissioners.

I have the honor to be, Sir,

Your obedient servant,

(Signed) S. J. DAWSON.

THE HONORABLE THE MINISTER OF THE INTERIOR,
Ottawa.

ADHESION OF LAC SEUL INDIANS.

LAC SEUL, *9th June, 1874.*

We, the Chiefs and Councillors of Lac Seul, Seul, Trout and Sturgeon Lakes, subscribe and set our marks, that we and our followers will abide by the articles of the treaty made and concluded with the Indians at the north-west angle of the Lake of the Woods, on the third day of October, in the year of our Lord one thousand eight hundred and seventy-three, between Her Most Gracious Majesty the Queen of Great Britain and Ireland, by Her Commissioners, Hon. Alexander Morris, Lieutenant-Governor of Manitoba and the North-West Territories, Joseph Albert, N. Provencher and Simon J. Dawson, of the one part, and the Saulteaux tribes of Ojebewas Indians, inhabitants of the country as defined by the Treaty aforesaid.

In witness whereof, Her Majesty's Indian Agent and the Chiefs and Councillors have hereto set their hands at Lac Seul, on the 9th day of June, 1874.

(Signed) R. J. N. PITHER,
Indian Agent.

JOHN CROMARTY, His x mark.
Chief.

ACKEMENCE, " x "

MAINEETAINEQUIRE, " x "

NAH-KEE-JECKWAHE, " x "
Councillors.

The whole treaty explained by R. J. N. Pither.

Witnesses:

(Signed) JAMES McKENZIE.

LOUIS KITTSON.

NICHOLAS CHATELAN. His x mark.

---

the character of the country prevented their general success as farmers. He suggested further the erection of halls at each agency and the employment of young Indians by the builders entrusted with their construction, "as they are so quick in perception and handy in the use of tools that they would speedily become very expert." The author regrets that he did not obtain communication of this valuable report until this work had advanced too far to admit of its being incorporated with it.

THE QU'APPELLE TREATY, NUMBER FOUR.

ARTICLES OF A TREATY made and concluded this fifteenth day of September, in the year of our Lord one thousand eight hundred and seventy-four, between Her Most Gracious Majesty the Queen of Great Britain and Ireland, by Her Commissioners, the Honorable Alexander Morris, Lieutenant-Governor of the Province of Manitoba and the North-West Territories, the Honorable David Laird, Minister of the Interior, and William Joseph Christie, Esq., of Brockville, Ontario, of the one part; and the Cree, Saulteaux and other Indians, inhabitants of the territory within the limits hereinafter defined and described, by their Chiefs and head men, chosen and named as hereinafter mentioned, of the other part;

Whereas, the Indians, inhabiting the said territory have, pursuant to an appointment made by the said Commissioners, been convened at a meeting at Qu'Appelle Lakes, to deliberate upon certain matters of interest to Her Most Gracious Majesty, of the one part, and the said Indians of the other :

And whereas, the said Indians have been notified and informed, by Her Majesty's said Commissioners, that it is the desire of Her Majesty to open up for settlement, immigration, trade and such other purposes as to Her Majesty may seem meet, a tract of country bounded and described as hereinafter mentioned; and to obtain the consent thereto of her Indian subjects inhabiting the said tract; and to make a treaty and arrange with them so that there may be peace and good-will between them and Her Majesty, and between them and Her Majesty's other subjects; and that her Indian people may know and be assured of what allowance they are to count upon and receive from Her Majesty's bounty and benevolence ;

And whereas, the Indians of the said tract, duly convened in councils as aforesaid, and being requested by Her Majesty's said Commissioners to name certain Chiefs and head men who should be authorized on their behalf to conduct such negotiations, and sign any treaty to be founded thereon, and to become responsible to Her Majesty for the faithful performance by their respective bands of such obligations as shall be assumed by them, the said Indians have thereupon named the following persons for that purpose, that is to say : Ka-ki-sha-way, or Loud Voice (Qu'Appelle River); Pis-qua, or The Plain (Leech Lake); Kea-wez-auce, or The Little Boy (Leech Lake); Ka-ke-na-wup, or One that sits like an Eagle (Upper Qu'Appelle Lakes); Kus-kee-tew-mus-coo-mus-qua, or Little Black Bear (Cypress Hills); Ka-ne-on-us-ka-tew, or One that walks on four claws (Little Touchwood Hills); Can-ah-ha-cha-pew, or Making ready the Bow (south side of the south branch of the Saskatchewan); Kii-si-can-ah-chuck, or Day Star (south side of the south branch of the Saskatchewan); Ka-wa-ca-toose, or The Poor Man (Touchwood Hills and Qu'Appelle Lakes) ; Ka-ku-wis-ta-haw, or Him that flies round (towards the Cypress Hills); Cha-ca-chas (Qu'Appelle River); Wah-pii-moose-too-siis, or White Calf, or Pus-coos (Qu'Appelle River); Gabriel Cote, or Mee-may, or The Pigeon (Fort Pelly);

And thereupon in open council the different bands having presented the men of their choice to the said Commissioners as the Chiefs and head men for the purpose aforesaid of the respective bands of Indians inhabiting the said district hereinafter described;

And whereas, the said Commissioners have proceeded to negotiate a treaty with the said Indians, and the same has been finally agreed upon and concluded as follows, that is say :

The Cree and Saulteaux tribes of Indians, and all other the Indians inhabiting the district hereinafter described and defined, do hereby cede, release, surrender and yield up to the Government of the Dominion of Canada for Her Majesty the Queen and her successors forever, all their rights, titles and privileges whatsoever to the lands included within the following limits, that is to say :

Commencing at a point on the United States frontier due south of the north-western point of the Moose Mountains, thence due north to said point of said Mountains, thence in a north-easterly course to a point two miles due west of Fort Ellice, thence in a line parallel with, and two miles westward from, the Assiniboine River to the mouth of the Shell River, thence parallel to the said river, and two miles distant therefrom, to its source ; thence in a straight line to a point on the western shore of Lake Winnipegoosis due west from the most northern extremity of Waterhen Lake, thence east to the centre of Lake Winnipegoosis, thence northwardly through the middle of the said lake (including Birch Island) to the mouth of Red Deer River, thence westwardly and south-westwardly along and including the said Red Deer River and its lakes, Red Deer and Etoimami, to the source of its western branch, thence in a straight line to the source of the northern branch of the Qu'Appelle, thence along and including said streams to the forks near Long Lake, thence along and including the valley of the west branch of the Qu'Appelle, thence along and including said river to the mouth of Maple Creek; thence southwardly along said creek to a point opposite the western extremity of the Cypress Hills ; thence due south to the international boundary ; thence east along said boundary to the place of commencement. Also all their rights, titles and privileges whatsoever to all other lands wheresoever situated within Her Majesty's North-West Territories, or any of them, to have and to hold the same to Her Majesty the Queen and her successors forever.

And Her Majesty the Queen hereby agrees, through the said Commissioners, to assign reserves for said Indians, such reserves to be selected by officers of Her Majesty's Government of the Dominion of Canada appointed for that purpose, after conference with each band of the Indians, and to be of sufficient area to allow one square mile for each family of five, or in that proportion for larger or smaller families.

Provided, however, that it be understood that if, at the time of the selection of any reserves as aforesaid, there are any settlers within the bounds of the lands reserved for any band, Her Majesty retains the right to deal with such settlers as she shall deem just, so as not to diminish the extent of lands allotted to the Indians ; and provided further that the aforesaid reserves of land, or any part thereof, or any interest or right therein, or appurtenant thereto, may be sold, leased or otherwise disposed of by the said Government for the use and benefit of the said Indians, with the consent of the Indians entitled thereto first had and obtained ; but in no wise shall the said Indians, or any of them, be entitled to sell or otherwise alienate any of the lands allotted to them as reserves.

In view of the satisfaction with which the Queen views the ready response which Her Majesty's Indian subjects have accorded to the invitation of her said Commissioners to meet them on this occasion ; and also in token of their general good conduct and behavior, she hereby, through Her Commissioners, makes the Indians of the bands here represented, a present— For each Chief, of twenty-five dollars in cash, a coat, and a Queen's silver medal ; for each head man, not exceeding four in each band, fifteen dollars in cash, and a coat ; and for every other man, woman and child, twelve dollars in cash ; and for those here assembled some powder, shot, blankets, calicoes and other articles.

As soon as possible after the execution of this treaty, Her Majesty shall cause a census to be taken of all the Indians inhabiting the tract hereinbefore described, and shall next year, and annually afterwards, forever, cause to be paid, in cash, at some suitable season to be duly notified to the Indians, and at a place or places to be appointed for that purpose within the territory ceded ; each Chief, twenty-five dollars ; each head man, not exceeding four to a band, fifteen dollars ; and to every other Indian, man, woman and child, five dollars per head ; such payment to be made to the heads of families for those belonging thereto, unless for some special reason it be found objectionable.

Her Majesty also agrees that each Chief, and each head man, not to exceed four in each band, once in every three years during the term of their office, shall receive a suitable suit of clothing, and that yearly and every year, she will cause to be distributed among the different bands included in the limits of this treaty, powder, shot, ball and twine, in all to the value of seven hundred and fifty dollars ; and each Chief shall receive hereafter, in recognition of the closing of the treaty, a suitable flag.

It is further agreed between Her Majesty and the said Indians that the following articles shall be supplied to any band thereof who are now actually cultivating the soil, or who shall hereafter settle on these reserves and commence to break up the land, that is to say—two hoes, one spade, one scythe, and one axe for every family so actually cultivating ; and enough seed, wheat, barley, oats and potatoes to plant such lands as they have broken up ; also one plough and two harrows for every ten families so cultivating as aforesaid; and also to each Chief, for the use of his band as aforesaid, one yoke of oxen, one bull, four cows, a chest of ordinary carpenter's tools, five hand-saws, five augers, one cross-cut saw, one pit saw, the necessary files, and one grindstone; all the aforesaid articles to be given once for all, for the encouragement of the practice of agriculture among the Indians.

Further, Her Majesty agrees to maintain a school in the reserve, allotted to each band, as soon as they settle on said reserve, and are prepared for a teacher.

Further, Her Majesty agrees that within the boundary of the Indian reserves, until otherwise determined by the Government of the Dominion of Canada, no intoxicating liquors shall be allowed to be introduced or sold; and all laws now in force, or hereafter to be enacted to preserve her Indian subjects inhabiting the reserves, or living elsewhere within the North-West Territories, from the evil effects of intoxication, shall be strictly enforced.

And further, Her Majesty agrees that her said Indians shall have right to pursue their avocations of hunting, trapping and fishing throughout the tract surrendered, subject to such regulations as may from time to time be made by the Government of the country acting under the authority of Her Majesty, and saving and excepting such tracts as may be required or taken up from time to time for settlement, mining or other purposes under grant, or other right given by Her Majesty's said Government.

It is further agreed between Her Majesty and her said Indian subjects that such sections of the reserves above indicated as may at any time be required for public works or buildings, of whatever nature, may be appropriated for that purpose by Her Majesty's Government of the Dominion of Canada, due compensation being made to the Indians for the value of any improvements thereon, and an equivalent in land or money for the area of the reserve so appropriated.

And the undersigned Chiefs and head men on their own behalf, and on behalf of all other Indians inhabiting the tract within ceded, do hereby solemnly promise and engage to strictly observe this treaty, and also to conduct and behave themselves as good and loyal subjects of Her Majesty the Queen.

They promise and engage that they will, in all respects, obey and abide by the law: that they will maintain peace and good order between each other, and between themselves and other tribes of Indians, and between themselves and others of Her Majesty's subjects, whether Indians, Half-breeds or whites, now inhabiting, or hereafter to inhabit, any part of the said ceded tract; and that they will not molest the person or property of any inhabitant of such ceded tract, or the property of Her Majesty the Queen, or interfere with or trouble any person passing or travelling through the said tract or any part thereof : and that they will assist the officers of Her Majesty in bringing to justice and punishment any Indian offending against the stipulations of this treaty, or infringing the laws in force in the country so ceded.

In witness whereof, Her Majesty's said Commissioners, and the said Indian Chiefs and head men, have hereunto subscribed and set their hands at Qu'Appelle, this day and year herein first-above written.

    (Signed)   ALEXANDER MORRIS,
            Lieut.-Gov. N.-W. Territories.
        DAVID LAIRD,
            Indian Commissioner.
        WILLIAM J. CHRISTIE.

KA-KII-SHI-WAY.	His x mark.
PIS-QUA.	" x "
KA-WE-ZAUCE.	
KA-KEE-NA-WUP.	" x "
KUS-KEE-TEW-MUS-COO-MUS-QUA.	" x "
KA-NE-ON-US-KA-TEW.	" x "
CAN-AH-HA-CHA-PEW.	" x "
KII-SI-CAW-AH-CHUCK.	" x "
KA-RA-CA-TOOSE.	" x "
KA-KII-NIS-TA-HAW.	" x "
CHA-CA-CHAS.	" x "
WA-PII-MOOSE-TOO-SUS.	" x "
GABRIEL COTE, or MEE-MAY.	" x "

Signed by the Chiefs and head men within named in presence of the following witnesses, the same having been first read and explained by Charles Pratt:

(Signed)   W. OSBORNE SMITH, C. M. G.,
        Lieut.-Col., D. A. G.,
            Commanding Dominion Forces in North-West.
    PASCAL BRELAND.
    EDWARD McKAY.
    CHARLES PRATT.
    PIERRE POITRAS.
    BAPTIST DAVIS.   His x mark.
    PIERRE DENOMME. " x "
    JOSEPH McKAY.
    DONALD McDONALD.
    A. McDONALD,
        Captain Prov. Batt. Infantry.
    G. W. W. STREET,
        Ensign Prov. Batt. Infantry.
    ALFRED CODD, M.D.,
        Surgeon Prov. Batt. Infantry.
    W. M. HERCHMER,
        Captain.
    C. DE CAZES,
        Ensign.
    JOSEPH POITRON.

M. G. DICKIESON,
Private Secretary of the Minister of the Interior.

PETER LAPIERRE.

HELEN H. MCLEAN.

FLORA GARRIOCH.

JOHN COTTON,
Lieutenant Canadian Artillery.

JOHN ALLAN,
Lieutenant Prov. Batt. Infantry.

ADHESION OF THE FORT ELLICE SAULTEAUX INDIANS.

We, members of the Saulteaux tribe of Indians, having had communication of the treaty hereto annexed, made on the 15th day of September instant, between Her Majesty the Queen and the Cree and Saulteaux Indians and other Indians at Qu'Appelle Lakes, but not having been present at the councils held at the Qu'Appelle Lakes between Her Majesty's Commissioners and the several Indian Chiefs and others therein named, at which the articles of the said treaty were agreed upon, hereby for ourselves and the band which we represent, in consideration of the provisions of the said treaty being extended to us and the said band which we represent, transfer, surrender and relinquish to Her Majesty the Queen, her heirs and successors, to and for the use of her Government of her Dominion of Canada, all our right, title and privileges whatsoever which we and the said bands which were present have held or enjoy of, in, and to the territory described and fully set out in the said articles of treaty and every part thereof ; also all our right, title, and privileges whatsoever to all other lands wherever situated, whether within the limit of any treaty formerly made, or hereafter to be made, with the Saulteaux tribe or any other tribe of Indians inhabiting Her Majesty's North-West territories, or any of them, to have and to hold the same unto and to the use of her said Majesty the Queen, her heirs and successors, forever.

And we hereby agree to accept the several provisions, payments and reserves of the said treaty, signed at the Qu'Appelle Lakes as therein stated, and solemnly promise, and engage to abide by, carry out and fulfil all the stipulations, obligations and conditions therein contained, on the part of the said Chiefs and Indians therein named to be observed and performed, and in all things to conform to the articles of the said treaty as if we ourselves and the band which we represent had been originally contracting parties thereto, and had been present and attached our signatures to the said treaty.

In witness whereof, Her Majesty's said Commissioners and the said Indian Chief and head man, have hereunto subscribed and set their hands at Fort Ellice this twenty-first day of September, in the year of our Lord one thousand eight hundred and seventy-four.

(Signed)   ALEXANDER MORRIS,
                Lieut.-Gov. N.-W. Territories.
            DAVID LAIRD,
                Indian Commissioner.
            W. J. CHRISTIE,
                Indian Commissioner.
            WA-WA-SE-CAPOW (or The man
                proud of standing upright). His x mark.
            OTA-MA-KOO-EWIN (or Shapous-
                e-tung's first son—The man
                who stands on the earth).   " x "

Signed by the parties hereto in the presence of the undersigned witnesses, the same having been first explained to the Indians by Joseph Robillard :

(Signed)   ARCH. MCDONALD.
            GEORGE FLETT.
            A. MAXWELL.
            DAVID ARMIT.
            HENRY McKAY.
            ELLEN McDONALD.
            MARY ARMIT.

————

ADHESION OF SAULTEAUX AND ASSINIBOINE INDIANS.

The members of the Saulteaux and Stoney tribes of Indians, having had communication of the treaty hereto annexed, made on the 15th day of September last, between Her Majesty the Queen and the Cree and Saulteaux Indians and other Indians at Qu'Appelle Lakes, but not having been present at the Councils held at the Qu'Appelle Lakes, between Her Majesty's Commissioners and the several Indian Chiefs and others therein named, at which the articles of the said treaty were agreed upon, hereby for ourselves, and the bands which we represent in consideration of the provisions of the said treaty having been extended to us, and the said bands which we represent, transfer, surrender, and relinquish, to Her Majesty the Queen, her heirs and successors, to and for the use of her Government of her Dominion of Canada, all our right, title and privileges whatsoever which we and the said bands which we represent, have, hold or enjoy of, in, and to the territory described and fully set out in the said articles of treaty and every part thereof ; also, all our right, title and privileges whatsoever to all other lands wherever situated, whether within the limit of any treaty formerly made or hereafter to be made with the Saulteaux tribe or any other tribe of Indians inhabiting Her Majesty's North-West Territories, or any of them, to have and to hold the same unto and to the use of her said Majesty the Queen, her heirs and successors forever.

And we hereby agree to accept the several provisions, payments and reserves of the said treaty, signed at the Qu'Appelle Lakes as therein stated, and solemnly promise and engage to abide by, carry out and fulfil all the stipulations, obligations and conditions therein contained on the part of said Chiefs and Indians therein named to be observed and performed, and in all things to conform to the articles of the said treaty as if we ourselves and the bands which we represent had been originally contracting parties thereto, and had been present and attached our signatures to the said treaty.

In witness whereof, Her Majesty's Commissioners and the said Indian Chiefs have hereunto subscribed and set their hands at Qu'Appelle Lakes this eighth day of September, in the year of Our Lord one thousand eight hundred and seventy-five.

(Signed)   W. J. CHRISTIE,
Indian Commissioner.

M. G. DICKIESON,
Acting Indian Commissioner.

W. F. WRIGHT.

CHEECUCK.   His x mark.

Signed by the parties hereto in the presence of the undersigned witnesses, the same having been explained to the Indians by William the Second McKay :—

(Signed)   WILLIAM S. MCKAY.
A. MCDONALD.
PASCAL BRELAND.
WILLIAM WAGNER.

ADHESION OF CREE, SAULTEAUX AND ASSINIBOINE INDIANS.

We, members of the Cree, Saulteaux, and Stonie tribes of Indians, having had communication of the treaty hereto annexed, made on the fifteenth day of September last, between Her Majesty the Queen and the Cree and Saulteaux Indians, and other Indians at Qu'Appelle Lakes, but not having been present at the councils held at the Qu'Appelle Lakes, between Her Majesty's Commissioners, and the several Indian Chiefs and others therein named, at which the articles of the said treaty were agreed upon, hereby for ourselves, and the bands which we represent in consideration of the provisions of the said treaty having been extended to us, and the said bands which we represent, transfer, surrender and relinquish, to Her Majesty the Queen, her heirs and successors, to and for the use of her Government, of her Dominion of Canada, all our right, title, and privileges whatsoever which we and the said bands which we represent, have, hold or enjoy of, in, and to the territory described and fully set out in the said articles of treaty and every part thereof, also, all our right, title and privileges whatsoever to all other lands wherever situated whether within the limit of any treaty formerly made, or hereafter to be made with the Saulteaux tribe or any other tribe of Indians inhabiting Her Majesty's North-West Territories, or any of them. To have and to hold the same, unto and to the use of her said Majesty the Queen, her heirs and successors forever.

And we hereby agree to accept the several provisions, payments, and reserves of the said treaty signed at the Qu'Appelle Lakes as therein stated, and solemnly promise and engage to abide by, carry out, and fulfil all the stipulations, obligations, and conditions therein contained on the part of said Chiefs and Indians therein named to be observed and performed, and in all things to conform to the articles of the said treaty as if we ourselves and the bands which we represent had been originally contracting parties thereto, and had been present and attached our signatures to the said treaty.

In witness whereof Her Majesty's Commissioners and the said Indian Chiefs have hereunto subscribed and set their hands at Qu'Appelle Lakes, this ninth day of September, in the year of Our Lord one thousand eight hundred and seventy-five.

(Signed)	W. J. CHRISTIE, *Indian Commissioner.*
	M. G. DICKIESON, *Acting Indian Commissioner.*
	W. J. WRIGHT.
	WAH-PEE-MAKWA, His x mark.
	(The White Bear).
	O'KANES, " x "
	PAYEPOT, " x "
	LE-CROUP-DE-PHEASANT, " x "
	KITCHI-KAH-ME-WIN, " x "

Signed by the parties hereto in the presence of the undersigned witnesses, the same having been first explained to the Indians by Charles Pratt.

(Signed) CHARLES PRATT.
A. McDONALD.
JOS. READER.
PASCAL BRELAND.

REVISION OF TREATIES NUMBERS ONE AND TWO.

COPY OF A REPORT of a Committee of the Honorable the Privy Council, approved by His Excellency the Governor-General in Council, on the 30th April, 1875.

On a memorandum dated 27th April, 1875, from the Honorable the Minister of the Interior, bringing under consideration the very unsatisfactory state of affairs arising out of the so called "outside promises" in connection with the Indian Treaties Numbers One and Two—Manitoba and North West Territories—concluded, the former on the 3rd August, 1871, and the latter on 21st of the same month, and recommending for the reasons stated :

1st. That the written memorandum attached to Treaty Number One be considered as part of that treaty and of Treaty Number Two, and that the Indian Commissioner be instructed to carry out the promises therein contained in so far as they have not yet been carried out, and that the Commissioner be advised to inform the Indians that he has been authorized so to do.

2nd. That the Indian Commissioner be instructed to inform the Indians, parties to Treaties Numbers One and Two, that, while the Government cannot admit their claim to anything which is not set forth in the treaty and in the memorandum attached thereto, which treaty is binding alike upon the Government and upon the Indians, yet, as there seems to have been some misunderstanding between the Indian Commissioner and the Indians in the matter of Treaties Numbers One and Two, the Government out of good feeling to the Indians and as a matter of benevolence, is willing to raise the annual payment to each Indian under Treaties Numbers One and Two from three dollars to five dollars per annum, and make payment over and above such sum of five dollars, of twenty dollars each and every year to each Chief, and a suit of clothing every three years to each Chief and each head man, allowing two head men to each band; on the express understanding, however, that each Chief or other Indian who shall receive such increased annuity or annual payment shall be held to abandon all claim whatever against the Government in connection with the so called " outside promises" other than those contained in the memorandum attached to the treaty.

The committee submit the foregoing recommendation for Your Excellency's approval.

(Signed)   W. A. HIMSWORTH,
Clerk, Privy Council.

Certified :

W. A. HIMSWORTH,
     Clerk, Privy Council.

ACCEPTANCES THEREOF BY LAKE MANITOBA INDIANS AND THE OTHER BANDS.

We, the undersigned Chiefs and head men of Indian bands representing bands of Indians who were parties to the Treaties Numbers One and Two mentioned in the report of a Committee of the Queen's Privy Council of Canada above printed, having had communication thereof and fully understanding the same, assent thereto and accept the increase of annuities therein mentioned on the condition therein stated and with the assent and approval of their several bands, it being agreed, however, with the Queen's Commissioners, that the number of braves and councillors for each Chief shall be four as at present, instead of two as printed 1875. (Treaty Number Two, 23rd August, 1875.)

Representing East Manitoba or Elm Point:

(Signed)	Son-sonse, *Chief.*	His x mark.
	Na-ka-na-wa-tany.	" x "
	Pa-pa-we-gun-wa-tak, *Councillors.*	" x "

Representing Fairford Prairie:

	Ma-sah-ree-yash, *Chief.*	His x mark.
	David Marsden,	" x "
	Joseph Sumner, *Councillors.*	" x "

Representing Fairford Mission:

	Richard Woodhouse, *Chief.*	His x mark.
	John Anderson,	" x "
	John Thompson, *Councillors.*	" x "

Representing (formerly Crane River and now) Ebb and Flow Lake:

	Oenaise, *Chief.*	His x mark.
	Baptiste (son of deceased Broken Finger),	" x "
	Ka-nee-gua-nash, *Councillors.*	" x "

Representing Waterhen band:

	Ka-tah-kak-wa-na-yaas, *Chief.*	His x mark.
	Wa-wah-ron-wek-ah-pon, *Councillor.*	" x "

Representing the Turtle and Valley Rivers, and Riding Mountain:

	Kee-sick-koo-we-nin (in place of Mekis, dead), *Chief.*	His x mark.
	Kee-say-kee-sick, *Councillor.*	" x "
	Nos-quash,	" x "
	Baptiste, *Braves.*	

Representing the St. Peter's band:

	Mis-koo-ke-neu (or Red Eagle).	His x mark.
	Ma-twa-ka-ke-tooh.	" x "
	I-and-evayway.	" x "
	Ma-ko-me-we-kem.	" x "
	As-sho-ah-mey.	" x "

In presence of the following :

(Signed) ALEX. MORRIS,
Lieut.-Governor.
JAMES McKAY.
JAMES F. GRAHAM.
ISAAC COWIE.
FRANCIS FIELD.
JOHN A. DAVIDSON.
CHARLES WOOD.

We, the undersigned, Chiefs and head men of Indian bands representing bands of Indians who were parties to the Treaties Numbers One and Two, mentioned in the report of a Committee of the Queen's Privy Council of Canada, "as printed on the other side of this parchment," having had communication thereof, and fully understanding the same, assent thereto and accept the increase of annuities therein mentioned on the condition therein stated, and with the assent and approval of their several bands, it being agreed, however, with the Queen's Commissioners, that the number of braves and councillors for each Chief shall be four, as at present, instead of two as printed, 1875.

Signed near Fort Alexander, on the Indian reserve, the twenty-third day of August, in the year of Our Lord one thousand eight hundred and seventy-five.

KA-KE-KE-PENOIS (William Pennefather).	His x mark		
JOSEPH KENT.	"	x	"
PETANAQUAQE (Henry Vane).	"	x	"
PETER HENDERSON.	"	x	"
KAY-PAYAHSINISK.	"	x	"

Witnesses :

(Signed) J. A. N. PROVENCHER,
Indian Commissioner.
J. DUBUC.
A. DUBUC.
JOS. MONKMAN,
Interpreter.
WILLIAM LEUNT.

Signed at Broken Head River, the twenty-eighth day of August, in the year of Our Lord one thousand eight hundred and seventy-five.

(Signed)	J. A. N. PROVENCHER, *Indian Commissioner.*	
	NASHA-KE-PE-NOIS.	His x mark
	AH-KEE-SEEK-WAS-KEMG.	" x "
	NAYWA-BE-BEE-KEE-SIK.	" x "
	MAY-JAH-KEE-GEE-QUAN.	" x "
	PAY-SAUGA.	" x "

Witnesses :
(Signed) J. DUBUC.
        H. S. REYNOLDS.
        DANIEL DEVLIN.
        H. COOK.

Signed on the Reserve at Roseau River, eighth day of September, in the year of Our Lord one thousand eight hundred and seventy-five.

(Signed)	J. A. N. PROVENCHER, *Indian Commissioner.*	
	NA-NA-WA-NA-NAN (or, Centre of Bird's Tail),	His x mark.
	KE-WE-SAY-ASH (or, Flying Round),	" x "
	WA-KO-WASH (or, Whippoorwill), *Chiefs.*	" x "
	OSAH-WEE-KA-KAY,	" x "
	OSAYS-KOO-KOON,	" x "
	SHAY-WAY-ASH,	" x "
	SHE-SKE-PENSE,	" x "
	MA-MEH-TAH-CUM-E-CUP,	" x "
	PAH-TE-CU-WEE-NIUN, *Councillors.*	" x "
	KAK-KA-QUIN-IASH,	" x "
	ANA-WAY-WEE-TIN,	" x "
	TIBIS-QUO-QE-SICK,	" x "
	WE-SHO-TA,	" x "
	NAT-TEE-KEE-GET, *Braves.*	" x "

Witness :
(Signed) JAMES F. GRAHAM.

THE LAKE WINNIPEG TREATY, NUMBER FIVE.

ARTICLES OF A TREATY made and concluded at Berens River the twentieth day of September, and at Norway House the twenty-fourth day of September in the year of Our Lord one thousand eight hundred and seventy-five, between Her Most Gracious Majesty the Queen of Great Britain and Ireland, by her Commissioners, the Honorable Alexander

Morris, Lieutenant-Governor of the Province of Manitoba and the North-West Territories, and the Honorable James McKay, of the one part, and the Saulteaux and Swampy Cree Tribes of Indians, inhabitants of the country within the limits hereinafter defined and described by their Chiefs, chosen and named as hereinafter mentioned, of the other part :

Whereas the Indians inhabiting the said country have, pursuant to an appointment made by the said Commissioners, been convened at meetings at Berens River and Norway House, to deliberate upon certain matters of interest to Her Most Gracious Majesty, of the one part, and the said Indians of the other ;

And whereas the said Indians have been notified and informed by Her Majesty's said Commissioners, that it is the desire of Her Majesty to open up for settlement, immigration, and such other purposes as to Her Majesty may seem meet, a tract of country bounded and described as hereinafter mentioned, and to obtain the consent thereto of her Indian subjects inhabiting the said tract, and to make a treaty and arrange with them, so that there may be peace and good will between them and Her Majesty, and that they may know and be assured of what allowance they are to count upon and receive from Her Majesty's bounty and benevolence ;

And whereas, the Indians of the said tract, duly convened in council as aforesaid, and being requested by Her Majesty's said Commissioners to name certain Chiefs and head men, who should be authorized on their behalf to conduct such negotiations and sign any treaty to be founded thereon, and to become responsible to Her Majesty for the faithful performance by their respective bands of such obligations as shall be assumed by them, the said Indians have thereupon named the following persons for that purpose, that is to say :—For the Indians within the Berens River region and their several bands :

Nah-wee- kee-sick-quah-yash, Chief ; Kah-nah-wah-kee-wee-nin and Nah-kee-quan-nay-yash, Councillors, and Pee-wah-noo-wee-nin, of Poplar River, Councillor ; for the Indians within the Norway House region and their several bands, David Rundle, Chief ; James Cochrane, Harry Constatag and Charles Pisequinip, Councillors ; and Ta-pas-ta-num, or Donald William Sinclair Ross, Chief ; James Garriock and Proud McKay, Councillors ;

And thereupon in open council, the different bands having presented their Chiefs to the said Commissioners as the Chiefs and head men, for the pur_ poses aforesaid, of the respective bands of Indians inhabiting the said district hereinafter described ;

And whereas, the said Commissioners then and there received and acknowledged the persons so presented as Chiefs and head men, for the purposes aforesaid, of the respective bands of Indians inhabiting the said district hereinafter described ;

And whereas, the said Commissioners have proceeded to negotiate a treaty

with the said Indians and the same has been finally agreed upon and concluded as follows, that is to say :

The Saulteaux and Swampy Cree tribes of Indians and all other the
Indians inhabiting the district hereinafter described and defined, do hereby
cede, release, surrender, and yield up to the Government of the Dominion
of Canada, for Her Majesty the Queen and her successors forever, all their
rights, titles and privileges whatsoever to the lands included within the
following limits, that is to say :

Commencing at the north corner or junction of Treaties Numbers One
and Three, thence easterly along the boundary of Treaty Number Three to
the height of land at the north-east corner of the said treaty limits, a point
dividing the waters of the Albany and Winnipeg Rivers, thence due north
along the said height of land to a point intersected by the 53° of north latitude and thence north-westerly to Favourable Lake, thence following the
east shore of said lake to its northern limit, thence north-westerly to the
north end of Lake Winnipegosis, thence westerly to the height of land called
"Robinson's Portage," thence north-westerly to the east end of Cross Lake,
thence north-westerly crossing Fox's Lake, thence north-westerly to the
north end of Split Lake, thence south-westerly to Pipestone Lake, on Burnt-
wood River, thence south-westerly to the western point of John Scott's
Lake, thence south-westerly to the north shore of Beaver Lake, thence
south-westerly to the west end of Cumberland Lake, thence due south to
the Saskatchewan River, thence due south to the north-west corner of the
northern limits of Treaty Number Four, including all territory within the
said limits, and all islands on all lakes within the said limits as above described, and it being also understood that in all cases where lakes form the
treaty limits, ten miles from the shore of the lake should be included in the
treaty ;

And also all their rights, titles and privileges whatsoever to all other
lands wherever situated in the North-West Territories, or in any other
Province or portion of Her Majesty's Dominions situated and being within
the Dominion of Canada ;

The tract comprised within the lines above described embracing an area
of one hundred thousand square miles, be the same, more or less ;

To have and to hold the same to Her Majesty the Queen and her successors forever.

And Her Majesty the Queen hereby agrees and undertakes to lay aside
reserves for farming lands, due respect being had to lands at present cultivated by the said Indians, and other reserves for the benefit of the said
Indians to be administered and dealt with for them by Her Majesty's
Government of the Dominion of Canada ; provided all such reserves shall
not exceed in all one hundred and sixty acres for each family of five, or in
that proportion for larger or smaller families in manner following, that is to
say :—For the band of Saulteaux in the Berens River region now settled,
or who may within two years settle therein, a reserve commencing at the

outlet of Berens River into Lake Winnipeg, and extending along the shores of said lake and up said river and into the interior behind said lake and river, so as to comprehend one hundred and sixty acres for each family of five, a reasonable addition being, however, to be made by Her Majesty to the extent of the said reserve for the inclusion in the tract so reserved of swamps, but reserving the free navigation of the said lake and river, and free access to the shores and waters thereof for Her Majesty and all her subjects, and excepting thereout such land as may have been granted to or stipulated to be held by the Hudson's Bay Company, and also such land as Her Majesty or her successors may in her good pleasure see fit to grant to the mission established at or near Berens River by the Methodist Church of Canada, for a church, school-house, parsonage, burial ground and farm, or other mission purposes ; and to the Indians residing at Poplar River, falling into Lake Winnipeg north of Berens River, a reserve not exceeding one hundred and sixty acres to each family of five, respecting as much as possible their present improvements ; and inasmuch as a number of the Indians now residing in and about Norway House, of the band of whom David Rundle is Chief, are desirous of removing to a locality where they can cultivate the soil, Her Majesty the Queen hereby agrees to lay aside a reserve on the west side of Lake Winnipeg, in the vicinity of Fisher River, so as to give one hundred acres to each family of five, or in that proportion for larger or smaller families, who shall remove to the said locality within "three years," it being estimated that ninety families or thereabout will remove within the said period, and that a reserve will be laid aside sufficient for that or the actual number ; and it is further agreed that those of the band who remain in the vicinity of "Norway House" shall retain for their own use their present gardens, buildings and improvements until the same be departed with by the Queen's Government, with their consent first had and obtained for their individual benefit, if any value can be realized therefor ; and with regard to the band of Wood Indians of whom Ta-pas-ta-num or Donald William Sinclair Ross is Chief, a reserve at Otter Island on the west side of Cross Lake of one hundred and sixty acres for each family of five, or in that proportion for smaller families, reserving however to Her Majesty, her successors, and her subjects, the free navigation of all lakes and rivers, and free access to the shores thereof ; Provided, however, that Her Majesty reserves the right to deal with any settlers within the bounds of any lands reserved for any band as she shall deem fit, and also that the aforesaid reserves of land, or any interest therein, may be sold or otherwise disposed of by Her Majesty's Government for the use and benefit of the said Indians entitled thereto, with their consent first had and obtained ; and with a view to shew the satisfaction of Her Majesty with the behavior and good conduct of her Indians she hereby through her Commissioners makes them a present of five dollars for each man, woman and child belonging to the bands here represented, in extinguishment of all claims heretofore preferred ;

And further, Her Majesty agrees to maintain schools for instruction in

2ᴬ

such reserves hereby made as to her Government of the Dominion of Canada may seem advisable, whenever the Indians of the reserve shall desire it ;

Her Majesty further agrees with her said Indians, that within the boundary of Indian reserves, until otherwise determined by her Government of the Dominion of Canada, no intoxicating liquor shall be allowed to be introduced or sold, and all laws now in force, or hereafter to be enacted, to preserve her Indian subjects inhabiting the reserves or living elsewhere within her North-West Territories, from the evil influence of the use of intoxicating liquors, shall be strictly enforced ;

Her Majesty further agrees with her said Indians that they, the said Indians, shall have right to pursue their avocations of hunting and fishing throughout the tract surrendered as hereinbefore described, subject to such regulations as may from time to time be made by her Government of her Dominion of Canada, and saving and excepting such tracts as may from time to time be required or taken up for settlement, mining, lumbering or other purposes by her said Government of the Dominion of Canada, or by any of the subjects thereof duly authorized therefor by the said Government ;

It is further agreed between Her Majesty and her said Indians, that such sections of the reserves above indicated as may at any time be required for public works or buildings, of what nature soever, may be appropriated for that purpose by Her Majesty's Government of the Dominion of Canada, due compensation being made for the value of any improvement thereon ;

And further, that Her Majesty's Commissioners shall, as soon as possible after the execution of this treaty, cause to be taken an accurate census of all the Indians inhabiting the tract above described, distributing them in families, and shall in every year ensuing the date hereof, at some period in each year, to be duly notified to the Indians, and at a place or places to be appointed for that purpose within the territory ceded, pay to each Indian person the sum of five dollars per head yearly ;

It is further agreed between Her Majesty and the said Indians that the sum of five hundred dollars per annum shall be yearly and every year expended by Her Majesty in the purchase of ammunition and twine for nets for the use of the said Indians, in manner following, that is to say :—In the reasonable discretion as regards the distribution thereof among the Indians inhabiting the several reserves or otherwise included herein, of Her Majesty's Indian Agent having the supervision of this treaty ;

It is further agreed between Her Majesty and the said Indians that the following articles shall be supplied to any band of the said Indians who are now cultivating the soil, or who shall hereafter commence to cultivate the land, that is to say :—Two hoes for every family actually cultivating ; also one spade per family as aforesaid ; one plough for every ten families as aforesaid ; five harrows for every twenty families as aforesaid ; one scythe for every family as aforesaid, and also one axe ; and also one cross-cut saw, one hand saw, one pit saw, the necessary files, one grindstone, and one auger for each band ; and also for each Chief for the use of his band, one chest of ordinary carpenter's tools ; also, for each band, enough of wheat, barley, potatoes and oats to plant the land actually broken up for cultivation by such band ; also, for each band, one yoke of oxen, one bull, and four cows : all the aforesaid articles to be given *once for all* for the encouragement of the practice of agriculture among the Indians.

It is further agreed between Her Majesty and the said Indians, that each Chief, duly recognized as such, shall receive an annual salary of twenty-five dollars per annum, and each subordinate officer, not exceeding three for each band, shall receive fifteen dollars per annum ; and each such Chief and subordinate officer as aforesaid shall also receive, once every three years, a suitable suit of clothing ; and each Chief shall receive, in recognition of the closing of the treaty, a suitable flag and medal.

And the undersigned Chiefs, on their own behalf, and on behalf of all other Indians inhabiting the tract within ceded, do hereby solemnly promise and engage to strictly observe this treaty, and also to conduct and behave themselves as good and loyal subjects of Her Majesty the Queen. They promise and engage that they will, in all respects, obey and abide by the law, and they will maintain peace and good order between each other, and also between themselves and other tribes of Indians, and between themselves and others of Her Majesty's subjects, whether Indians or whites, now inhabiting or hereafter to inhabit any part of the said ceded tracts ; and that they will not molest the person or property of any inhabitant of such ceded tracts, or the property of Her Majesty the Queen, or interfere with or trouble any person passing or travelling through the said tracts or any part thereof : and that they will aid and assist the officers of Her Majesty in bringing to justice and punishment any Indian offending against the stipulations of this treaty, or infringing the laws in force in the country so ceded.

In witness whereof, Her Majesty's said Commissioners and the said Indian Chiefs have hereunto subscribed and set their hands at Berens River, this twentieth day of September, A.D. 1875, and at Norway House, on the twenty-fourth day of the month and year herein first above named.

(Signed) ALEXANDER MORRIS, *Lieut.-Governor.*		[L.S.]
JAMES MCKAY.		[L.S.]
NAH-WEE-KEE-SICK-QUAH-YASH (otherwise Jacob Berens), *Chief.*		His x mark.
KAH-WAH-NAH-KEE-WEE-NIN┊ (otherwise Antoine Gouin),	" x "	
NAH-KEE-QUAN-NAY-YASH,	" x "	
PEE-WAH-ROO-WEE-NIN, *Councillors.*	" x "	

Signed by the Chiefs within named in presence of the following witnesses, the same having been first read and explained by the Honorable James McKay :

(Signed) THOMAS HOWARD.
          A. G. JACKES, M.D.
          CHRISTINE MORRIS.
          E. C. MORRIS.
          ELIZABETH YOUNG.
          EGERTON RYERSON YOUNG.
          WILLIAM McKAY.
          JOHN McKAY.

Signed at Norway House by the Chiefs and Councillors hereunto subscribing in the presence of the undersigned witnesses, the same having been first read and explained, by the Honorable James McKay :

(Signed) ALEXANDER MORRIS,		[L.S.]
Lieut.-Governor.		
JAMES McKAY.		[L.S.]
DAVID RUNDLE,		
Chief.		
JAMES COCHRANE,	His x mark.	
HARRY CONSTATAG,	" x "	
CHARLES PISEQUINIP,	" x "	
Councillors.		
TA-PAS-TA-NUM	" x "	
(or Donald William		
Sinclair Ross),		
Chief.		
GEORGE GARRIOCK,		
PROUD McKAY,	" x "	
Councillors.		

Witnesses :

(Signed) RODERICK ROSS.
          JOHN H. RUTTAN,
             Methodist Minister.
          O. GERMAN,
             Methodist Minister.
          D. C. McTAVISH.
          ALEXANDER SINCLAIR.
          L. C. McTAVISH.
          CHRISTINE V. K. MORRIS.
          E. C. MORRIS.
          A. G. JACKES, M.D.
          THOMAS HOWARD.

ADHESION OF SASKATCHEWAN INDIANS.

We the band of the Saulteaux tribe of Indians, residing at the mouth of the Saskatchewan River, on both sides thereof, having had communication of the foregoing treaty, hereby, and in consideration of the provisions of the said treaty being extended to us, transfer, surrender, and relinquish to Her Majesty the Queen, her heirs and successors, to and for the use of the Government of Canada, all our right, title and privileges whatsoever, which we have or enjoy in the territory described in the said treaty, and every part thereof, to have and to hold to the use of Her Majesty the Queen, and her heirs and successors forever.

And Her Majesty agrees, through the said Commissioners, to assign a reserve of sufficient area to allow one hundred and sixty acres to each family of five, or in that proportion for larger or smaller families—such reserves to be laid off and surveyed next year, on the south side of the River Saskatchewan.

And having regard to the importance of the land where the said Indians are now settled, in respect of the purposes of the navigation of the said river, and transport in connection therewith, and otherwise, and in view of the fact that many of the said Indians have now houses and gardens on the other side of the river, and elsewhere, which they will abandon, Her Majesty agrees, through her said Commissioners, to grant a sum of five hundred dollars to the said band, to be paid in equitable proportions to such of them as have houses, to assist them in removing their houses to the said reserve, or building others. And the said Indians represented herein by their Chief and Councillors, presented as such by the band, do hereby agree to accept the several provisions, payments, and other benefits as stated in the said treaty, and solemnly promise and engage to abide by, carry out and fulfil all the stipulations, obligations and conditions therein contained, on the part of the said Chiefs and Indians therein named, to be observed and performed, and in all things to conform to the articles of the said treaty as if we ourselves had been originally contracting parties thereto.

In witness whereof, Her Majesty's said Commissioners and the said Indian Chief and Councillors have hereunto subscribed and set their hands, at the Grand Rapids, this twenty-seventh day of September, in the year of Our Lord one thousand eight hundred and seventy-five.

(Signed)   ALEXANDER MORRIS,   [L.S.]
                  Lieut.-Governor.

            JAMES McKAY.   [L.S.]

            PETER BEARDY,   His x mark.
                  Chief.

            JOSEPH ATKINSON,   " x "

            ROBERT SANDERSON,   " x "
                  Councillors.

Signed by the parties in the presence of the undersigned witnesses, the same having been first explained to the Indians by the Honorable James McKay:

(Signed) THOMAS HOWARD.

RODERICK ROSS.

E. C. MORRIS.

A. G. JACKES, M.D.

ALEXANDER MATHESON.

JOSEPH HOUSTON.

CHRISTINE V. K. MORRIS.

Memorandum.

The Queen's Indian Commissioners having met Thickfoot and a portion of the Islands band of Indians at Wapang or Dog Head Island, on the twenty-eighth day of September, A.D. 1875, request him to notify the Island Indians and those of Jack Head Point, to meet at Wapang an Indian agent next summer, to receive payments under the treaty which they have made with the Indians of Norway House, Berens River, Grand Rapids and Lake Winnipeg, and in which they are included, at a time of which they will be notified, and to be prepared then to designate their Chief and two Councillors. The Commissioners have agreed to give some of the Norway House Indians a reserve at Fisher Creek, and they will give land to the Island Indians at the same place.

Given at Wapang, this 28th day of September, A.D. 1875, under our hands.

ALEXANDER MORRIS,
Lieut.-Governor.

JAMES McKAY.

I accept payments under the treaty for myself and those who may adhere to me, and accept the same and all its provisions, as a principal Indian, and agree to notify the Indians as above written.

Wapang, September 28th, 1875.

(Signed) THICKFOOT. His x mark.

Witness :

(Signed) THOMAS HOWARD.

RODERICK ROSS.

NOTE.—In 1876 Messrs. Howard and Reid obtained the adhesions to the Winnipeg Treaty of the Indians of the Dog Head, Bloodvein River, Big Island, and Jack Fish Head bands on Lake Winnipeg, and of the Island and Grand Rapids of the Berens River band, and of the Pas, Cumberland and Moose Lake bands on the Saskatchewan River, as will be found stated in Chapter VIII.

THE TREATIES AT FORTS CARLTON AND PITT, NUMBER SIX.

ARTICLES OF A TREATY made and concluded near Carlton, on the twenty-third day of August, and on the twenty-eighth day of said month, respectively, and near Fort Pitt on the ninth day of September, in the year of Our Lord one thousand eight hundred and seventy-six, between Her Most Gracious Majesty the Queen of Great Britain and Ireland, by her Commissioners, the Honorable Alexander Morris, Lieutenant-Governor of the Province of Manitoba and the North-West Territories, and the Honorable James McKay and the Honorable William Joseph Christie, of the one part, and the Plain and the Wood Cree Tribes of Indians, and the other Tribes of Indians, inhabitants of the country within the limits hereinafter defined and described, by their Chiefs, chosen and named as hereinafter mentioned, of the other part.

Whereas the Indians inhabiting the said country have, pursuant to an appointment made by the said Commissioners, been convened at meetings at Fort Carlton, Fort Pitt and Battle River, to deliberate upon certain matters of interest to Her Most Gracious Majesty, of the one part, and the said Indians of the other ;

And whereas the said Indians have been notified and informed by Her Majesty's said Commissioners that it is the desire of Her Majesty to open up for settlement, immigration and such other purposes as to Her Majesty may seem meet, a tract of country, bounded and described as hereinafter mentioned, and to obtain the consent thereto of her Indian subjects inhabiting the said tract, and to make a treaty and arrange with them, so that there may be peace and good will between them and Her Majesty, and that they may know and be assured of what allowance they are to count upon and receive from Her Majesty's bounty and benevolence ;

And whereas the Indians of the said tract, duly convened in council as aforesaid, and being requested by Her Majesty's Commissioners to name certain Chiefs and head men, who should be authorized, on their behalf, to conduct such negotiations and sign any treaty to be founded thereon, and to become responsible to Her Majesty for the faithful performance by their respective bands of such obligations as shall be assumed by them, the said Indians have thereupon named for that purpose, that is to say :—representing the Indians who make the treaty at Carlton, the several Chiefs and Councillors who have subscribed hereto, and representing the Indians who make the treaty at Fort Pitt, the several Chiefs and Councillors who have subscribed hereto ;

And thereupon, in open council, the different bands having presented their Chiefs to the said Commissioners as the Chiefs and head men, for the purposes aforesaid, of the respective bands of Indians inhabiting the district hereinafter described ;

And whereas the said Commissioners then and there received and acknowledged the persons so represented, as Chiefs and head men, for the purposes
aforesaid, of the respective bands of Indians inhabiting the said district
hereinafter described ;

And whereas the said Commissioners have proceeded to negotiate a treaty
with the said Indians, and the same has been finally agreed upon and concluded as follows, that is to say :

The Plain and Wood Cree Tribes of Indians, and all other the Indians
inhabiting the district hereinafter described and defined, do hereby cede,
release, surrender and yield up to the Government of the Dominion of
Canada for Her Majesty the Queen and her successors forever, all their
rights, titles and privileges whatsoever, to the lands included within the
following limits, that is to say :

Commencing at the mouth of the river emptying into the north-west
angle of Cumberland Lake, thence westerly up the said river to the source'
thence on a straight line in a westerly direction to the head of Green Lake,
thence northerly to the elbow in the Beaver River, thence down the said
river northerly to a point twenty miles from the said elbow ; thence in a
westerly direction, keeping on a line generally parallel with the said Beaver
River (above the elbow), and about twenty miles distance therefrom, to the
source of the said river ; thence northerly to the north-easterly point of the
south shore of Red Deer Lake, continuing westerly along the said shore to
the western limit thereof, and thence due west to the Athabaska River,
thence up the said river, against the stream, to the Jasper House, in the'
Rocky Mountains ; thence on a course south-eastwardly, following the easterly range of the Mountains, to the source of the main branch of the Red
Deer River ; thence down the said river, with the stream, to the junction
therewith of the outlet of the river, being the outlet of the Buffalo Lake ;
thence due east twenty miles ; thence on a straight line south-eastwardly to
the mouth of the said Red Deer River on the South Branch of the Saskatchewan River ; thence eastwardly and northwardly, following on the
boundaries of the tracts conceded by the several Treaties numbered Four
and Five, to the place of beginning ;

And also all their rights, titles and privileges whatsoever, to all other
lands, wherever situated, in the North-West Territories, or in any other
Province or portion of Her Majesty's Dominions, situated and being within
the Dominion of Canada ;

The tract comprised within the lines above described, embracing an area
of one hundred and twenty-one thousand square miles, be the same more
or less ;

To have and to hold the same to Her Majesty the Queen and her successors forever ;

And Her Majesty the Queen hereby agrees and undertakes to lay aside
reserves for farming lands, due respect being had to lands at present cultivated by the said Indians, and other reserves for the benefit of the said

Indians, to be administered and dealt with for them by Her Majesty's Government of the Dominion of Canada, provided all such reserves shall not exceed in all one square mile for each family of five, or in that proportion for larger or smaller families, in manner following, that is to say :—

That the Chief Superintendent of Indian Affairs shall depute and send a suitable person to determine and set apart the reserves for each band, after consulting with the Indians thereof as to the locality which may be found to be most suitable for them ;

Provided, however, that Her Majesty reserves the right to deal with any settlers within the bounds of any lands reserved for any band as she shall deem fit, and also that the aforesaid reserves of land or any interest therein may be sold or otherwise disposed of by Her Majesty's Government for the use and benefit of the said Indians entitled thereto, with their consent first had and obtained ; and with a view to show the satisfaction of Her Majesty with the behavior and good conduct of her Indians, she hereby, through her Commissioners, makes them a present of twelve dollars for each man, woman and child belonging to the bands here represented, in extinguishment of all claims heretofore preferred ;

And further, Her Majesty agrees to maintain schools for instruction in such reserves hereby made, as to her Government of the Dominion of Canada may seem advisable, whenever the Indians of the reserve shall desire it ;

Her Majesty further agrees with her said Indians that within the boundary of Indian reserves, until otherwise determined by her Government of the Dominion of Canada, no intoxicating liquor shall be allowed to be introduced or sold, and all laws now in force or hereafter to be enacted to preserve her Indian subjects inhabiting the reserves or living elsewhere within her North-West Territories from the evil influence of the use of intoxicating liquors, shall be strictly enforced ;

Her Majesty further agrees with her said Indians that they, the said Indians, shall have right to pursue their avocations of hunting and fishing throughout the tract surrendered as hereinbefore described, subject to such regulations as may from time to time be made by her Government of her Dominion of Canada, and saving and excepting such tracts as may from time to time be required or taken up for settlement, mining, lumbering or other purposes by her said Government of the Dominion of Canada, or by any of the subjects thereof, duly authorized therefor, by the said Government ;

It is further agreed between Her Majesty and her said Indians, that such sections of the reserves above indicated as may at any time be required for public works or buildings of what nature soever, may be appropriated for that purpose by Her Majesty's Government of the Dominion of Canada, due compensation being made for the value of any improvements thereon ;

And further, that Her Majesty's Commissioners shall, as soon as possible after the execution of this treaty, cause to be taken, an accurate census of all the Indians inhabiting the tract above described, distributing them in families, and shall in every year ensuing the date hereof, at some period in each year, to be duly notified to the Indians, and at a place or places to be appointed for that purpose, within the territories ceded, pay to each Indian person the sum of five dollars per head yearly ;

It is further agreed between Her Majesty and the said Indians that the sum of fifteen hundred dollars per annum, shall be yearly and every year expended by Her Majesty in the purchase of ammunition and twine for nets for the use of the said Indians, in manner following, that is to say :—In the reasonable discretion as regards the distribution thereof, among the Indians inhabiting the several reserves, or otherwise included herein, of Her Majesty's Indian Agent having the supervision of this treaty ;

It is further agreed between Her Majesty and the said Indians that the following articles shall be supplied to any band of the said Indians who are now cultivating the soil, or who shall hereafter commence to cultivate the land, that is to say :—Four hoes for every family actually cultivating, also two spades per family as aforesaid ; one plough for every three families as aforesaid, one harrow for every three families as aforesaid ; two scythes, and one whetstone and two hayforks and two reaping-hooks for every family as aforesaid ; and also two axes, and also one cross-cut saw, and also one hand-saw, one pit-saw, the necessary files, one grindstone and one auger for each band ; and also for each Chief, for the use of his band, one chest of ordinary carpenter's tools ; also for each band, enough of wheat, barley, potatoes and oats to plant the land actually broken up for cultivation by such band ; also for each band, four oxen, one bull and six cows, also one boar and two sows, and one handmill when any band shall raise sufficient grain therefor ; all the aforesaid articles to be given *once for all* for the encouragement of the practice of agriculture among the Indians ;

It is further agreed between Her Majesty and the said Indians, that each Chief, duly recognized as such, shall receive an annual salary of twenty-five dollars per annum ; and each subordinate officer, not exceeding four for each band, shall receive fifteen dollars per annum ; and each such Chief and subordinate officer as aforesaid, shall also receive, once every three years, a suitable suit of clothing, and each Chief shall receive, in recognition of the closing of the treaty, a suitable flag and medal, and also, as soon as convenient, one horse, harness and waggon ;

That in the event hereafter of the Indians comprised within this treaty being overtaken by any pestilence, or by a general famine, the Queen, on being satisfied and certified thereof by her Indian Agent or Agents, will grant to the Indians assistance of such character and to such extent as her Chief Superintendent of Indian Affairs shall deem necessary and sufficient to relieve the Indians from the calamity that shall have befallen them ;

That during the next three years, after two or more of the reserves hereby agreed to be set apart to the Indians, shall have been agreed upon and surveyed, there shall be granted to the Indians included under the Chiefs adhering to the treaty at Carlton, each spring, the sum of one thousand dollars to be expended for them by Her Majesty's Indian Agents, in the purchase of provisions for the use of such of the band as are actually settled on the reserves and are engaged in cultivating the soil, to assist them in such cultivation ;

That a medicine chest shall be kept at the house of each Indian Agent for the use and benefit of the Indians, at the discretion of such Agent ;

That with regard to the Indians included under the Chiefs adhering to the treaty at Fort Pitt, and to those under Chiefs within the treaty limits who may hereafter give their adhesion hereto (exclusively, however, of the Indians of the Carlton Region) there shall, during three years, after two or more reserves shall have been agreed upon and surveyed, be distributed each spring among the bands cultivating the soil on such reserves, by Her Majesty's Chief Indian Agent for this treaty in his discretion, a sum not exceeding one thousand dollars, in the purchase of provisions for the use of such members of the band as are actually settled on the reserves and engaged in the cultivation of the soil, to assist and encourage them in such cultivation ;

That, in lieu of waggons, if they desire it, and declare their option to that effect, there shall be given to each of the Chiefs adhering hereto, at Fort Pitt or elsewhere hereafter (exclusively of those in the Carlton District) in recognition of this treaty, so soon as the same can be conveniently transported, two carts, with iron bushings and tires ;

And the undersigned Chiefs, on their behalf, and on behalf of all other Indians inhabiting the tract within ceded, do hereby solemnly promise and engage to strictly observe this treaty, and also to conduct and behave themselves as good and loyal subjects of Her Majesty the Queen ;

They promise and engage that they will in all respects obey and abide by the law, and they will maintain peace and good order between each other, and also between themselves and other tribes of Indians, and between themselves and others of Her Majesty's subjects, whether Indians or whites, now inhabiting or hereafter to inhabit any part of the said ceded tracts, and that they will not molest the person or property of any inhabitant of such ceded tracts, or the property of Her Majesty the Queen, or interfere with or trouble any person passing or travelling through the said tracts or any part thereof ; and that they will aid and assist the officers of Her Majesty in bringing to justice and punishment any Indian offending against the stipulations of this treaty, or infringing the laws in force in the country so ceded.

In witness whereof, Her Majesty's said Commissioners and the said Indian Chiefs have hereunto subscribed and set their hands, at or near Fort Carlton, on the day and year aforesaid, and near Fort Pitt on the day above aforesaid.

(Signed)   ALEXANDER MORRIS,
Lieut.-Governor, N.-W. T.

JAMES McKAY,
W. J. CHRISTIE,
 Indian Commissioners.

MIST-OW-AS-IS,	His x mark.	
AH-TUK-UK-KOOP,	" x "	
Head Chiefs of the Carlton Indians.		

PEE-YAHN-KAH-NIHK-OO-SIT,	" x "	
AH-YAH-TUS-KUM-IK-IM-UM,	" x "	
KEE-TOO-WA-HAN,	" x "	
CHA-KAS-TA-PAY-SIN,	" x "	
JOHN SMITH,	" x "	
JAMES SMITH,	" x "	
CHIP-EE-WAY-AN,	" x "	
Chiefs.		

MASSAN,	" x "
PIERRE CADIEN,	" x "
OO-YAH-TIK-WAH-PAHN,	" x "
MAHS-KEE-TE-TIM-UN,	" x "
Councillors of Mist-ow-as-is.	

SAH-SAH-KOO-MOOS,	" x "
BENJAMIN,	" x "
MEE-NOW-AH-CHAHK-WAY,	" x "
KEE-SIK-OW-ASIS,	" x "
Councillors of Ah-tuk-uk-koop.	

PEE-TOOK-AH-HAN-UP-EE-GIN-EW,	" x "
PEE-AY-CHEW,	" x "
TAH-WAH-PISK-EE-KAHP-POW,	" x "
AHS-KOOS,	" x "
Councillors of Pee-yahn-kah-nihk-oo-sit.	

PET-E-QUA-CAY,	" x "
JEAN BAPTISTE,	" x "
ISIDORE WOLFE,	" x "
KEE-KOO-HOOS,	" x "
Councillors of Kee-too-wa-han.	

OO-SAHN-ASKU-NUKIP,	" x "
YAW-YAW-LOO-WAY,	" x "
SOO-SOU-AIM-EE-LUAHN,	" x "
NUS-YOH-YAK-EE-NAH-KOOS,	" x "
Councillors of Ah-yah-tus-kum-ik-im-um.	

WILLIAM BADGER,
BENJAMIN JOYFUL,   " x "
JOHN BADGER,   .
JAMES BEAR,
 Councillors of John Smith.

KAH-TIP-IS-KOOR-AHT,	His x mark.
KAH-KEW-EE-KWAHW-AHS-UM,	" x "
NAH-PACH,	" x "
MUS-IN-AH-NE-HIM-AHN,	" x "
Councillors of Cha-kas-ta-pay-sin.	

BERNARD CONSTANT,	
HENRY SMYTH,	" x "
MAH-TUA-AHS-TIM-OO-WE-GIN,	" x "
JACOB MCLEAN,	" x "
Councillors of James Smith.	

NAH-POO-CHEE-CHEES,	" x "
NAH-WIS,	" x "
KAH-PAH-PAH-MAH-CHAHK-NAY,	" x "
KEE-YEW-AH-KAH-PIM-WAHT,	" x "
Councillors of Chip-ee-way-an.	

NAH-WEE-KAH-NICK-KAH-OO-TAH-MAH-HOTE (or Neeh-cha-aw-asis),	" x "
Chief.	

Signed by the Chiefs within named in the presence of the following witnesses, the same having been first read and explained by Peter Erasmus,
Peter Ballendine and the Rev. John McKay :

(Signed) A. G. JACKES, M.D.

JAMES WALKER,

J. H. McILLREE,
    N.-W. M. P.

PIERRE LEVAILLER. His x mark.

ISIDORE DUMOND.   " x "

JEAN DUMOND.   " x "

PETER HOURIE.

FRANÇOIS GINGRAS.

J. B. MITCHELL,
    Staff Constable, N.-W. M. P.

J. H. PRICE,
    Hospital Steward, N.-W. M. P.

XAVIER LETANGER. His x mark.

WILLIAM SINCLAIR.

A. R. KENNEDY.

R. J. PRITCHARD.

L. CLARKE.

W. McKAY.

W. D. JARVIS,
    Inspector, N.-W. M. P.

Signed by the Chiefs and head men of the Willow Indians near Fort Carlton, this 28th day of August, A.D. 1876, the same having been first read and explained by the Honorable James McKay, and Peter Erasmus, in the presence of the undersigned witnesses :

SEE-SEE-QUAM-ISH,	His x mark.
NEE-TOO-KEE-WEE-KAH-MAN,	" x "
Councillors.	
KAH-MEE-YIS-TOO-WAY-SIT,	" x "
KAH-PAY-YAK-WAHSK-OO-MUM,	" x "
SEE-SEE-KWAHN-IS,	" x "
Joint Chiefs of Willow Indians.	
KAH-NAH-KAH-SKOW-WAHT.	" x "
KAH-AH-TEE-KOO-NEW.	" x "
KAH-NAH-MAH-CHEW.	" x "
MOON-OO-YAHS.	" x "
PO-MIN-AH-KOW.	" x "
OO-TUK-KOO-PAH-KAH-MAY-TOU-MAY-YET.	" x "

(Signed)   A. G. JACKES, M.D.
JOSEPH GENTON.
JOHN A. KERR.
PIERRE LEVAILLER.   His x mark.
W. D. JARVIS,
  N.-W. M. P.

Signed by Her Majesty's Commissioners, and by the Chiefs and head men hereafter subscribing hereto, the same having been first read and explained to the Indians by the Honorable James McKay and Peter Erasmus, near Fort Pitt, this 9th day of September, A.D. 1876, in the presence of the undersigned witnesses :

(Signed)   ALEXANDER MORRIS,
  Lieut.-Governor, N.-W. T.

JAMES McKAY,
W. J. CHRISTIE,
  Indian Commissioners.

WEE-KAS-KOO-KEE-PAY-YIN,	His x mark.
PEE-YAS-EE-WAH-KAH-WE-CHAH-KOOT,	" x "
JAMES SEENUM,	" x "
OO-NAH-LAT-MEE-NAH-HOOS,	" x "
SEE-KAHS-KOOTCH,	" x "
TUS-TUSK-EE-SKWAIS,	" x "
PEE-WAY-SIS,	" x "
KEE-YE-WIN,	" x "
Cree Chiefs.	

KIN-OO-SAY-OO,   His x mark.
  Chipewayan Chief.

SEE-WAS-KWAN,   " x "

WAH-WAY-SEE-HOO-WE-YIN,   " x "
  Councillors to Wee-kas-koo-kee-pay-yin.

TIP-EE-SKOW-AH-CHAK,   " x "

PAY-PAY-SEE-SEE-MOO,   " x "
  Councillors to Pee-yas-ee-woh-kah-
  we-chah-koot.

OO-NOW-UK-EE-PAH-CHAS,   " x "

MY-OO-WAY-SEES,   " x "
  Councillors to See-kahs-kootch.

OOS-PWAH-KHUN-IS,   " x "

NEE-YE-PEE-TAY-AS-EE-KAY-SE,   " x "
  Councillors to Tus-tusk-ee-skwais.

MAH-CHAH-MEE-NIS,   " x "

ISAAC CARDINAL,   " x "
  Councillors to Pee-way-sis.

ANTOINE XAVIER,   " x "
  Councillor to Kin-oo-say-oo.

WILLIAM BULL,   " x "
  Councillor to James Seenum.

WAH-KEY-SEE-KOOT,   " x "
  Councillor to See-kahs-kootch.

CHARLES CARDINAL,   " x "

PIERRE WAHBISKAW,   " x "
  Councillors to Kee-ye-win.

KI-YAS-EE-KUN,   " x "

KAH-KEE-OO-PAH-TOW,   " x "
  Councillors to Wee-kas-koo-kee-pay-yin.

CAKE-CAKE,   " x "
  Councillor to Oo-nah-lat-mee-nah-hoos.

KAM-OO-NIN,   " x "
  Councillor to James Seenum.

AH-SIS,   " x "
  Councillor to See-kahs-kootch.

Witnesses :

(Signed) A. G. JACKES, M.D.

      JAMES MCLEOD,
          Com., N.-W. M. P.

      JAMES WALKER,
          Inspector, N.-W. M. P.

    E. DALRYMPLE CLARKE,
         Adjutant, N.-W. M. P.

VITAL J. BISH,
Of St. Albert, O. M. J.

CONSTANTINE SCOLLEN,
Priest, O. M. J.

JOHN MCDOUGALL,
Methodist Missionary.

JOHN MCKAY.

W. E. JONES.

PETER C. PAMBRUN.

A. K. KENNEDY.

PETER ERASMUS.

THOMAS MCKAY.

JAMES SIMPSON.

ELIZA HARDISTY.

MARY MCKAY.

ADHESIONS TO TREATY NUMBER SIX.

We, the undersigned Chiefs and head men of the Cree and other bands of Indians, having had communication of the treaty—a copy of which is printed in the Report of the Minister of the Interior, for the year ending 30th June, 1876, concluded at Forts Carlton and Pitt between the Indians inhabiting the country described in said treaty and Her Majesty the Queen of Great Britain and Ireland, by the Commissioners the Honorable Alexander Morris, Lieutenant-Governor of Manitoba and the North-West Territories ; the Honorable W. J. Christie, and the Honorable James McKay ; but not having been present when the negotiations were being conducted at the above-mentioned places, do hereby, for ourselves and the bands which we represent, agree to all the terms, conditions, covenants, and engagements of whatever kind enumerated in the said treaty, and accept the same as if we had been present, and had consented and agreed to the same when the treaty was first signed and executed.

Witness our hands, at Fort Pitt, this ninth day of August, in the year of Our Lord one thousand eight hundred and seventy-seven.

(Signed)   M. G. DICKIESON,
Commisisoner.

PAY-MO-TAY-AH-SOO. His x mark.
KAH-SEE-MUT-A-POO.   " x "
NAH-PAY-SIS.   " x "
KE-HI-WINS,
Head man.

Signed by the Chiefs and head men (having been first read and explained by Peter Erasmus) in the presence of

(Signed) PETER ERASMUS.
 RODERICK CAMPBELL.

Signed at Edmonton, this 21st day of August, in the year above-written, by the Chiefs and head men hereto, the whole having been first read and explained by Peter Erasmus, in the presence of the following witnesses.

(Signed) ALEXIS KEES-KEE-CHEE-CHI, His x mark.
 Chief.

OO-MUO-IN-AH-SOO-WAW-SIN-EE, " x "
 Head man.

CATSCHIS-TAH-WAY-SKUM, " x "
 Chief.

KOO-SAH-WAN-AS-KAY, " x "
 Head man.

PAHS-PAHS-CHASE. " x "

TAH-KOOTCH. " x "

Witnesses :

(Signed) RIC HARDISTY.
 H. LEDUC.
 PETER ERASMUS.
 W. D. JARVIS,
 Inspector, N.-W. M. P.

————

We, members of the Cree tribe of Indians, having had explained to us the terms of the treaty, made and concluded near Carlton, on the 23rd day of August and on the 28th day of said month respectively, and near Fort Pitt on the 9th day of September, 1876, between Her Majesty the Queen, by the Commissioners duly appointed to negotiate the said treaty, and the Plain and Wood Cree and other tribes of Indians inhabiting the country within the limits defined in said treaty; but not having been present at the council at which the articles of the said treaty were agreed upon, do now hereby, for ourselves and the band which we represent, in consideration of the provisions of the said treaty being extended to us and the band which we represent, transfer, surrender, and relinquish to Her Majesty the Queen, her heirs and successors, to and for the use of the Government of the Dominion of Canada, all our right, title and interest whatsoever which we and the said band which we represent have held or enjoyed of, in and to the territory described and fully set out in the said treaty, also all our right, title and interest whatsoever to all other lands wherever situated, whether within the limits of any other treaty heretofore made, or hereafter to be made with Indians, or elsewhere in Her Majesty's territories, to have and

24

to hold the same, unto and for the use of Her Majesty the Queen, her heirs and successors forever ;

And we hereby agree to accept the several benefits, payments, and reserves promised to the Indians under the Chiefs adhering to the said treaty at Fort Pitt ; and solemnly engage to abide by, carry out and fulfil, all the stipulations, obligations and conditions therein contained, on the part of the Chiefs and Indians therein named, to be observed and performed, and in all things to conform to the articles of the said treaty, as if we ourselves and the band which we represent had been originally contracting parties thereto, and been present at the councils held near Fort Pitt and had there attached our signatures to the said treaty.

In witness whereof Her Majesty's Lieutenant-Governor and Indian Superintendent for the North-West Territories, and the Chiefs and Councillors of the band hereby giving their adhesion to the said treaty, have hereunto subscribed and set their hands at the Blackfoot Crossing of the Bow River, this twenty-fifth day of September, in the year of Our Lord one thousand eight hundred and seventy-seven.

(Signed)   DAVID LAIRD,
*Lieut.-Governor and Indian
Superintendent, N.-W. T.*

KIS-KAY-IM   His x mark.
(or, Bob Tail),
Chief.

MEM-IN-OROU-TAW   " x "
(or, Sometimes Glad),

TCHO-WEK   " x "
(or, Passing Sound),
Councillors.

Signed by the parties hereto in the presence of the undersigned witnesses, the same having been first explained to the Indians by Rev. J. Mac-Dougall.

(Signed)   JAMES F. McLEOD,
Com., N.-W. M. P.

CONSTANTINE SCOLLEN.

A. S. IRVINE,
Assistant Commissioner.

J. McDOUGALL,
Missionary.

———

The undersigned Chiefs and head men of the Cree Nation having had communication of the treaty concluded between Her Majesty the Queen by her Commissioners and certain Chiefs of the Cree Nation, at Fort Pitt on the 9th day of September 1876, agree to surrender our title to all our lands in the North-West Territories and to abide by all the promises set forth in the said treaty, on condition that all the payments, reserves of land, and promises named therein are secured to us by Her Majesty.

And the undersigned Superintendent of Indian Affairs for the North-West Territories on behalf of Her Majesty agrees that all the payments, reserves and promises named in the said treaty to be made to each Cree Chief and his band shall be faithfully made and carried out to the Chiefs who have subscribed to this memorandum and to their people.

In witness whereof the undersigned Indian Superintendent, and the undersigned Chiefs and head men have hereto set our hands this nineteenth day of August, one thousand eight hundred and seventy-eight.

(Signed)   DAVID LAIRD.

PUS-KEE-YAH-KAY-WE-YIN.   His x mark.

MAH-KAYO.   " x "

PAY-PAHM-US-KUM-ICK-NIUM. " x "

ISIDORE.   " x "

Signed the day and year above written after having been read and interpreted to the Chiefs and head men by Peter Erasmus, in the presence of

(Signed)   JOHN FRENCH,
         Sub-Inspector N.-W. M. P.
   PETER ERASMUS.

———

We, the undersigned Chiefs and head men of the Wood Cree tribe of Indians, having had communication of the treaty made and concluded near Carlton, on the twenty-third and twenty-eighth days of August respectively, and near Fort Pitt on the ninth day of September, one thousand eight hundred and seventy-six, between Her Majesty the Queen, by her Commissioners and the Plain and Wood Cree and other tribes of Indians inhabitants of the country named therein, hereby for ourselves and the bands which we represent, in consideration of the provisions of the said treaty being extended to our bands, cede, transfer, surrender and relinquish to Her Majesty the Queen, her heirs and successors to and for the use of her Government of the Dominion of Canada, all our right, title and privileges whatsoever to all lands in the North-West Territories or elsewhere in Her Majesty's Dominions, to have and to hold the same unto and to the use of Her said Majesty the Queen, her heirs and successors forever.

And we hereby agree to accept the several provisions, payments and reserves of the said treaty as therein stated, and solemnly promise and engage to abide by and carry out all the stipulations and obligations therein contained, on the part of said Chiefs and Indians therein named to be observed and performed, and in all things to conform to the articles of the said treaty, as if we ourselves and our band had originally been contracting parties thereto.

And Her Majesty the Queen by her representative, the Honorable David Laird, Indian Superintendent of the North-West Territories, agrees that all the payments and provisions named in the said treaty to be made to each Chief and his band shall be faithfully made and fulfilled to the aforesaid Chiefs and their bands.

In witness whereof we, the said Indian Superintendent of the North-West Territories, and the said Chief and head men of the Stony tribe of Indians have hereto set our hands, at Battleford, this twenty-ninth day of August, one thousand eight hundred and seventy-eight.

(Signed)   DAVID LAIRD,
Indian Superintendent.

SW-KE-MAW   His x mark.
(or, Misketo).

ETA-WE-PE-TON   " x "
(or, Uses both Arms).

NESS-AU-ASIS   " x "
(or, Two Child).

KA-WA-SU-SKO-HO-PAT-ISK " x "
(or, Lightning).

Signed by the parties hereto in the presence of the undersigned witnesses, the same having been first explained to the Indians by Peter Ballendine.

(Signed) JAMES WALKER,
Inspector N.-W. M. P.
P. BALLENDINE.
HAYTER REED.

We the undersigned Chief and head men of the Plain Stony tribe of Indians, having had communication of the treaty made and concluded near Carlton on the twenty-third and twenty-eighth days of August respectively, and near Fort Pitt on the ninth of September, one thousand eight hundred and seventy-six, between Her Majesty the Queen by her Commissioners, and the Plain and Wood Crees and other tribes of Indians, inhabitants of the country named therein, hereby for ourselves and the band which we represent, in consideration of the provisions of the said treaty being extended to our band, cede, transfer, surrender and relinquish to Her Majesty the Queen, her heirs and successors, to and for the use of the Government of the Dominion of Canada, all our right, title and privileges whatsoever to all lands in the North-West Territories, or elsewhere in Her Majesty's Dominions, to have and to hold the same unto and to the use of Her said Majesty the Queen, her heirs and successors forever.

And we hereby agree to accept the several provisions, payments and reserves of the said treaty as therein stated, and solemnly promise and agree to abide by and carry out all the stipulations and obligations therein contained, on the part of said Chiefs and Indians therein named to be observed and performed, and in all things to conform to the articles of the said treaty, as if we ourselves and our band had originally been contracting parties thereto.

And Her Majesty the Queen by her Representative the Honorable David Laird, Indian Superintendent of the North-West Territories, agrees that all the payments and provisions named in the said treaty to be made to each Chief and his band, shall be faithfully made and fulfilled to the aforesaid Chiefs and their bands.

In witness whereof, we, the said Indian Superintendent of the North-West Territories, and the said Chiefs and head men of the Wood Cree tribe of Indians, have hereto set our hands at Carlton this third day of September, one thousand eight hundred and seventy-eight.

(Signed)   DAVID LAIRD,
                 Indian Superintendent.

KO-PAT-A-WA-KE-NUM,   His x mark.
           Chief.
BANJIEL MARISTZE,   "   x   "
JAMES (Chief's son),   "   x   "
           Councillors.
SA-SE-WA-HUM.   "   x   "
KENE-MO-LAY.   "   x   "
MAS-E-WAS-CHASE.   "   x   "

Signed by the Chiefs and Councillors within named in presence of the following witnesses, the same having first been explained by Peter Ballendine :

(Signed)   L. CLARKE.
          A. E. FORGET.
          P. BALLENDINE.

———

We, the undersigned Indian Chief and head men, having had communication of the treaty made and concluded at Forts Carlton and Pitt, in the summer of 1876, but not having been present at the conferences at which said treaty was negotiated, hereby agree to accept the terms and conditions of the said treaty, and to abide thereby in the same manner as if we had been present at the time the said treaty was first signed.

As witness our hands this eighteenth day of September, one thousand eight hundred and seventy-eight.

(Signed)   MICHAEL CALISTROIS.   His x mark.
          LOUIS PAY-PAHN-AH-WAYO. "   x   "
          AC-OO-SEE.   "   x   "

Signed by the Chief and head men, after having been read and explained by Peter Erasmus.

FORT WALSH, CYPRESS HILLS, *4th July, 1879.*

SIR,—I have the honor to enclose an agreement made with two Cree head men, who expressed to me a desire to join the treaty made at Fort Carlton and Fort Pitt, on the 9th September, 1876. Little Pine is a Cree Chief who has for some time expressed his willingness to take the treaty. Lucky Man is a head man lately made by the Indians who have been followers of Big Bear, but who have now left him.

Big Bear himself was present when both Little Pine and Lucky Man signed, and, I think, would have taken the treaty himself, had he not felt ashamed at so many of his lodges leaving him. He is now almost alone, only three or four followers having remained with him. He states that he will take the treaty at Sounding Lake at the time of the payments.

Both Little Pine and Lucky Man have requested that they may be paid at Fort Walsh, as it is impossible for them to reach the more northern agencies, and I have agreed to it. It will therefore be necessary that enough money be forwarded to pay these Indians here. Little Pine states he will have thirty-four lodges, and Lucky Man twenty-five. Taking the average of a lodge at eight, which I understand is a fair estimate, it will make four hundred and seventy-two extra Indians to be paid.

I have, &c., .

(Signed)   EDGAR DEWDNEY,
Indian Commissioner.

L. VANKOUGHNET, Esq.,
    Deputy Supt. General of Indian Affairs, Ottawa.

———

Whereas Little Pine, or Min-a-he-quo-sis, a Cree Chief on behalf of his band and certain other Cree Indians comprising twenty lodges, inhabitants of the country covered by the treaty commonly known as Treaty Number Six made between Her Majesty the Queen by her Commissioners, the Honorable Alexander Morris, the Honorable James McKay and the Honorable William Joseph Christie, of the one part, and the Plain and Wood Cree tribes of Indians of the other part, at Carlton, on the twenty-third and twenty-eighth days of August, and near Fort Pitt on the ninth day of September in the year of our Lord one thousand eight hundred and seventy-six, who have not yet given in their adhesion to the said treaty, have presented themselves to Edgar Dewdney Esq., Indian Commissioner for the North-West Territories, and expressed a desire to join in the said treaty. And whereas, the said Commissioner has recognized the said Little Pine as the head man of his band, and the said band of twenty lodges have selected and appointed Pap-a-way the Lucky Man, one of their number, as the head man of their band, and have presented him as such to the said Commissioner, who has recognized and accepted him as such head man.

Now this instrument witnesseth that the said Little Pine and Pap-a-way, or the Lucky Man, for themselves and on behalf of the bands which they represent, do transfer, surrender and relinquish to her Majesty the Queen, her heirs and successors to and for the use of her Government of the Dominion of Canada, all their right, title and interest whatsoever, which they have held or enjoyed, of, in and to the territory described and fully set out in the said treaty; also all their right, title and interest whatsoever to all other lands wherever situated, whether within their limits of any other treaty heretofore made or hereafter to be made with Indians or elsewhere in Her Majesty's territories, to have and to hold the same unto and for the use of Her Majesty the Queen, her heirs and successors forever. And do hereby agree to accept the several benefits, payments and reserves promised to the Indians adhering to the said treaty at Carlton and Fort Pitt on the dates above mentioned; and further, do solemnly engage to abide by, carry out and fulfil all the stipulations, obligations and conditions contained on the part of the Indians therein named, to be observed and performed, and in all things to conform to the articles of the said treaty, as if the said Little Pine and Pap-a-way or the Lucky Man and the bands whom they represent had been originally contracting parties thereto, and had been present at the treaty at Carlton and Fort Pitt, and had there attached their signatures to the said treaty.

In witness whereof Edgar Dewdney, Indian Commissioner for the North-West Territories, and the said Little Pine and Pap-a-way or the Lucky Man, head men of the said bands, hereby giving their adhesion to the said treaty, have hereunto subscribed and set their hands at Fort Walsh, in the said North-West Territories this second day of July in the year of our Lord one thousand eight hundred and seventy-nine.

(Signed)   EDGAR DEWDNEY,
     Indian Commissioner.

LITTLE PINE.   His x mark.
THE LUCKY MAN.   "   x   "

Signed by the parties hereto, in the presence of the undersigned witnesses, the same having been explained to the Indians by the said Edgar Dewdney, Esq., Indian Commissioner, through the interpreters Edward McKay and P. Leveiller.

(Signed)   JAMES F. McLEOD,
     Com. N.-W. M. P.

   A. G. IRVINE,
     Assistant Com. N.-W. M. P.

   FRANK NORMAN,
     Staff Constable N.-W. M. P.

THE TREATY WITH THE BLACKFEET, NUMBER SEVEN.

ARTICLES OF A TREATY made and concluded this twenty-second day of September, in the year of our Lord one thousand eight hundred and seventy-seven, between Her Most Gracious Majesty the Queen of Great Britain and Ireland, by her Commissioners, the Honorable David Laird, Lieutenant-Governor and Indian Superintendent of the North-West Territories, and James Farquharson McLeod, C.M.G., Commissioner of the North-West Mounted Police, of the one part, and the Blackfeet, Blood, Piegan, Sarcee, Stony, and other Indians, inhabitants of the territory north of the United States boundary line, east of the central range of the Rocky Mountains, and south and west of Treaties Numbers Six and Four, by their head Chiefs and minor Chiefs or Councillors, chosen as hereinafter mentioned, of the other part:

Whereas the Indians inhabiting the said territory, have pursuant to an appointment made by the said Commissioners, been convened at a meeting at the "Blackfoot crossing" of the Bow River, to deliberate upon certain matters of interest to Her Most Gracious Majesty, of the one part, and the said Indians of the other ;

And whereas the said Indians have been informed by Her Majesty's Commissioners that it is the desire of Her Majesty to open up for settlement, and such other purposes as to Her Majesty may seem meet, a tract of country, bounded and described as hereinafter mentioned, and to obtain the consent thereto of her Indian subjects inhabiting the said tract, and to make a treaty, and arrange with them, so that there may be peace and good will between them and Her Majesty, and between them and Her Majesty's other subjects ; and that her Indian people may know and feel assured of what allowance they are to count upon and receive from Her Majesty's bounty and benevolence ;

And whereas the Indians of the said tract, duly convened in council, and being requested by her Majesty's Commissioners to present their head Chiefs and minor Chiefs, or Councillors, who shall be authorized, on their behalf, to conduct such negotiations and sign any treaty to be founded thereon, and to become responsible to Her Majesty for the faithful performance by their respective bands of such obligations as should be assumed by them, the said Blackfeet, Blood, Piegan and Sarcee Indians have therefore acknowledged for that purpose, the several head and minor Chiefs, and the said Stony Indians, the Chiefs and Councillors who have subscribed hereto, that thereupon in open council the said Commissioners received and acknowledged the head and minor Chiefs and the Chiefs and Councillors presented for the purpose aforesaid ;

And whereas the said Commissioners have proceeded to negotiate a treaty with the said Indians ; and the same has been finally agreed upon and concluded as follows, that is to say : the Blackfeet, Blood, Piegan, Sarcee

Stony and other Indians inhabiting the district hereinafter more fully described and defined, do hereby cede, release, surrender, and yield up to the Government of Canada for Her Majesty the Queen and her successors forever, all their rights, titles and privileges whatsoever to the lands included within the following limits, that is to say:

Commencing at a point on the international boundary due south of the western extremity of the Cypress Hills; thence west along the said boundary to the central range of the Rocky Mountains, or to the boundary of the Province of British Columbia; thence north-westerly along the said boundary to a point due west of the source of the main branch of the Red Deer River; thence south-westerly and southerly following on the boundaries of the tracts ceded by the Treaties Numbered Six and Four to the place of commencement; and also all their rights, titles and privileges whatsoever, to all other lands wherever situated in the North-West Territories, or in any other portion of the Dominion of Canada:

To have and to hold the same to Her Majesty the Queen and her successors forever:

And Her Majesty the Queen hereby agrees with her said Indians, that they shall have right to pursue their vocations of hunting throughout the tract surrendered as heretofore described, subject to such regulations as may, from time to time, be made by the Government of the country, acting under the authority of Her Majesty; and saving and excepting such tracts as may be required or taken up from time to time for settlement, mining, trading or other purposes by her Government of Canada, or by any of her Majesty's subjects duly authorized therefor by the said Government.

It is also agreed between Her Majesty and her said Indians that reserves shall be assigned them of sufficient area to allow one square mile for each family of five persons, or in that proportion for larger and smaller families, and that said reserves shall be located as follows, that is to say:

First—The reserves of the Blackfeet, Blood and Sarcee bands of Indians, shall consist of a belt of land on the north side of the Bow and South Saskatchewan Rivers, of an average width of four miles along said rivers, down stream, commencing at a point on the Bow River twenty miles north-westerly of the "Blackfoot crossing" thereof, and extending to the Red Deer River at its junction with the South Saskatchewan; also for the term of ten years, and no longer, from the date of the concluding of this treaty, when it shall cease to be a portion of said Indian reserves, as fully to all intents and purposes as if it had not at any time been included therein, and without any compensation to individual Indians for improvements, of a similar belt of land on the south side of the Bow and Saskatchewan Rivers of an average width of one mile along said rivers, down stream; commencing at the aforesaid point on the Bow River, and extending to a point one mile west of the coal seam on said river, about five miles below the said "Blackfoot crossing;" beginning again one mile east of the said coal seam and extending to the mouth of Maple Creek at its junction with the South

Saskatchewan; and beginning again at the junction of the Bow River with the latter river, and extending on both sides of the South Satkatchewan in an average width on each side thereof of one mile, along said river against the stream, to the junction of the Little Bow River with the latter river, reserving to Her Majesty, as may now or hereafter be required by her for the use of her Indian and other subjects, from all the reserves hereinbefore described, the right to navigate the above mentioned rivers, to land and receive fuel and cargoes on the shores and banks thereof, to build bridges and establish ferries thereon, to use the fords thereof and all the trails leading thereto, and to open such other roads through the said reserves as may appear to Her Majesty's Government of Canada, necessary for the ordinary travel of her Indian and other subjects, due compensation being paid to individual Indians for improvements, when the same may be in any manner encroached upon by such roads.

Secondly—That the reserve of the Piegan band of Indians shall be on the Old Man's River, near the foot of the Porcupine Hills, at a place called "Crow's Creek."

And thirdly—The reserve of the [Stony band of Indians shall be in the vicinity of Morleyville. ·

In view of the satisfaction of Her Majesty with the recent general good conduct of her said Indians, and in extinguishment of all their past claims, she hereby, through her Commissioners, agrees to make them a present payment of twelve dollars each in cash to each man, woman, and child of the families here represented.

Her Majesty also agrees that next year, and annually afterwards forever, she will cause to be paid to the said Indians, in cash, at suitable places and dates, of which the said Indians shall be duly notified, to each Chief, twenty-five dollars, each minor Chief or Councillor (not exceeding fifteen minor Chiefs to the Blackfeet and Blood Indians, and four to the Piegan and Sarcee bands, and five Councillors to the Stony Indian Bands) fifteen dollars, and to every other Indian of whatever age, five dollars; the same, unless there be some exceptional reason, to be paid to the heads of families for those belonging thereto.

Further, Her Majesty agrees that the sum of two thousand dollars shall hereafter every year be expended in the purchase of ammunition for distribution among the said Indians; provided that if at any future time ammunition became comparatively unnecessary for said Indians, her Government, with the consent of said Indians, or any of the bands thereof, may expend the proportion due to such band otherwise for their benefit.

Further, Her Majesty agrees that each head Chief and minor Chief, and each Chief and Councillor duly recognized as such, shall, once in every three years, during the term of their office, receive a suitable suit of clothing, and each head Chief and Stony Chief, in recognition of the closing of the treaty, a suitable medal and flag, and next year, or as soon as convenient, each head Chief, and minor Chief, and Stony Chief shall receive a Winchester rifle.

Further, Her Majesty agrees to pay the salary of such teachers to instruct the children of said Indians as to her Government of Canada may seem advisable, when said Indians are settled on their reserves and shall desire teachers.

Further, Her Majesty agrees to supply each head and minor Chief, and each Stony Chief, for the use of their bands, ten axes, five handsaws, five augers, one grindstone, and the necessary files and whetstones.

And further, Her Majesty agrees that the said Indians shall be supplied as soon as convenient, after any band shall make due application therefor, with the following cattle for raising stock, that is to say : for every family of five persons, and under, two cows ; for every family of more than five persons, and less than ten persons, three cows; for every family of over ten persons, four cows ; and every head and minor Chief, and every Stony Chief, for the use of their bands, one bull ; but if any band desire to cultivate the soil as well as raise stock, each family of such band shall receive one cow less than the above mentioned number, and in lieu thereof, when settled on their reserves and prepared to break up the soil, two hoes, one spade, one scythe, and two hay forks, and for every three families, one plough and one harrow, and for each band, enough potatoes, barley, oats, and wheat (if such seeds be suited for the locality of their reserves) to plant the land actually broken up. All the aforesaid articles to be given, once for all, for the encouragement of the practice of agriculture among the Indians.

And the undersigned Blackfeet, Blood, Piegan and Sarcee head Chiefs and minor Chiefs, and Stony Chiefs and Councillors, on their own behalf and on behalf of all other Indians inhabiting the tract within ceded do hereby solemnly promise and engage to strictly observe this treaty, and also to conduct and behave themselves as good and loyal subjects of Her Majesty the Queen. They promise and engage that they will, in all respects, obey and abide by the law, that they will maintain peace and good order between each other and between themselves and other tribes of Indians, and between themselves and others of Her Majesty's subjects, whether Indians, Half breeds or whites, now inhabiting, or hereafter to inhabit, any part of the said ceded tract ; and that they will not molest the person or property of any inhabitant of such ceded tract, or the property of Her Majesty the Queen, or interfere with or trouble any person, passing or travelling through the said tract or any part thereof, and that they will assist the officers of Her Majesty in bringing to justice and punishment any Indian offending against the stipulations of this treaty, or infringing the laws in force in the country so ceded.

In witness whereof Her Majesty's said Commissioners, and the said Indian head and minor Chiefs, and Stony Chiefs and Councillors, have hereunto subscribed and set their hands, at the ''Blackfoot crossing'' of the Bow River, the day and year herein first above writtten.

(Signed)   DAVID LAIRD,

Gov. of N.-W. T., and Special Indian Commissioner.

JAMES F. McLEOD,
*Lieut.-Colonel, Com. N.-W.M.P., and
Special Indian Commissioner.*

CHAPO-MEXICO (or Crowfoot), *Head Chief of the South Blackfeet.*	His x mark.	
MATOSE-APIW (or Old Sun), *Head Chief of the North Blackfeet.*	" x "	
STAMISCOTOCAR (or Bull Head), *Head Chief of the Sarcees.*	" x "	
MEKASTO (or Red Crow), *Head Chief of the South Bloods.*	" x "	
NATOSE-ONISTORS (or Medicine Calf).	" x "	
POKAPIW-OTOIAN (or Bad Head).	" x "	
SOTENAH (or Rainy Chief), *Head Chief of the North Bloods.*	" x "	
TAKOYE-STAMIX (or Fiend Bull).	" x "	
AKKA-KITCIPIMIW-OTAS (or Many Spotted Horses).	" x "	
ATTTISTAH-MACAN (or Running Rabit).	" x "	
PITAH-PEKIS (or Eagle Rib).	" x "	
SAKOYE-AOTAN (or Heavy Shield), *Head Chief of the Middle Blackfeet.*	" x "	
ZOATZE-TAPITAPIW (or Setting on an Eagle Tail). *Head Chief of the North Piegans.*	" x "	
AKKA-MAKKOYE (or Many Swans).	" x "	
APENAKO-SAPOP, (or Morning Plume).	" x "	
* MAS-GWA-AH-SID (or Bear's Paw).	" x "	
* CHE-NE-KA (or John).	" x "	
* KI-CHI-PWOT (or Jacob).	" x "	
STAMIX-OSOK (or Bull Bacfat).	" x "	
EMITAH-APISKINNE (or White Striped Dog).	" x "	
MATAPI-KOMOTZIW (or the Captive or Stolen Person).	" x "	
APAWAWAKOSOW (or White Antelope).	" x "	
MAKOYE-KIN (or Wolf Collar).	" x "	
AYE-STIPIS-SIMAT (or Heavily Whipped).	" x "	
KISSOUM (or Day Light).	" x "	
PITAH-OTOCAN (or Eagle Head).	" x "	
APAW-STAMIX (or Weasel Bull).	" x "	
ONISTAH-POKAH (or White Calf).	" x "	
NETAH-KITEI-PI-MEW (or Only Spot).	" x "	

---

* Stony Chiefs.

Akak-otos (or Many Horses).	His x mark.
Stokimatis (or The Drum).	" x "
Pitah-annes (or Eagle Robe).	" x "
Pitah-otsikin (or Eagle Shoe).	" x "
Stamix-ota-ka-piw (or Bull Turn Round).	" x "
Maste-Pitah (or Crow Eagle).	" x "
† James Dixon.	" x "
† Abraham Kechepwot.	" x "
† Patrick Kechepwot.	" x "
† George Moy-any-men.	" x "
† George Crawlor.	" x "
Ekas-kine (or Low Horn).	" x "
Kayo-okosis (or Bear Shield).	" x "
Ponokah-stamix (or Bull Elk).	" x "
Omaksi Sapop (or Big Plume).	" x "
Onistah (or Calf Robe).	" x "
Pitah-siksinum (or White Eagle).	" x "
Apaw-onistaw (or Weasel Calf).	" x "
Attista-haes (or Rabbit Carrier).	" x "
Pitah (or Eagle).	" x "
Pitah-onistah (or Eagle White Calf).	" x "
Kaye-tapo (or Going to Bear).	" x "

Signed by the Chiefs and Councillors within named in presence of the following witnesses, the same having been first explained by James Bird, Interpreter.

(Signed) A. G. Irvine, *Ass't Com., N.-W. M. P.*

J. McDougall, *Missionary.*

Jean L' Heureux.

W. Winder.

T. N. F. Crozier, *Inspectors.*

E. Dalrymple Clark, *Lieut. and Adjutant. N.-W. M. P.*

A. Shurtliff,

C. E. Dening,

W. D. Antrobus, *Sub-Inspectors.*

Frank Norman, *Staff Constable.*

Mary J. MacLeod.

† Stony Councillors.

JULIA WINDER.

JULIA SHURTLIFF.

E. HARDISTY.

A. MCDOUGALL.

E. A. BARRETT.

CONSTANTINE SOOLLEN, *Priest*, witness to signatures of Stonixosak and those following.

CHARLES E. CONRAD.

THOS. J. BOGG.

—

ADHESION TO TREATY NUMBER SEVEN.

We, the members of the Blackfoot tribe of Indians, having had explained to us the terms of the treaty made and concluded at the Blackfoot crossing of the Bow River, on the twenty-second day of September, in the year of our Lord one thousand eight hundred and seventy-seven ;

Between Her Majesty the Queen, by her Commissioners duly appointed to negotiate the said treaty and the Blackfeet, Blood, Piegan, Sarcee, Stony and other Indian inhabitants of the country within the limits defined in the said treaty, but not having been present at the Councils at which the articles of the said treaty were agreed upon, do now hereby, for ourselves and the bands which we represent, in consideration of the provisions of the said treaty being extended to us and the bands which we represent, transfer, surrender and relinquish to Her Majesty the Queen, her heirs and successors, to and for the use of her Government of the Dominion of Canada, all our right, title, and interest whatsoever, which we and the said bands which we represent have held or enjoyed, of in and to the territory described and fully set out in the said treaty ; also, all our right, title, and interest whatsoever to all other lands wherever situated, whether within the limits of any other treaty heretofore made or hereafter to be made with Indians, or elsewhere in Her Majesty's territories, to have and to hold the same unto and for the use of Her Majesty the Queen, her heirs and successors forever ;

And we hereby agree to accept the several benefits, payments, and reserves promised to the Indians under the Chiefs adhering to the said treaty at the Blackfoot crossing of the Bow River, and we solemnly engage to abide by, carry out and fulfil all the stipulations, obligations and conditions therein contained on the part of the Chiefs and Indians therein named, to be observed and performed and in all things to conform to the articles of the said treaty, as if we ourselves and the bands which we represent had been originally contracting parties thereto and had been present at the Councils held at the Blackfoot crossing of the Bow River, and had there attached our signatures to the said treaty.

In witness whereof James Farquharson McLeod, C.M.G., one of Her

Majesty's Commissioners appointed to negotiate the said treaty, and the Chief of the band, hereby giving their adhesion to the said treaty, have hereunto subscribed and set their hands at Fort McLeod, this fourth day of December, in the year of our Lord one thousand eight hundred and seventy-seven.

(Signed)   JAMES F. McLEOD,
Lieut.-Col., Special Indian Commissioner.

MEANXKISTOMACH   His x mark.
(or Three Bulls).

Signed by the parties hereto in the presence of the undersigned witnesses, the same having been explained to the Indians by the said James Farquharson McLeod, one of the Commissioners appointed to negotiate the said treaty, through the interpreter, Jerry Potts, in the presence of

(Signed)   **A. G. IRVINE,**
Assistant Commissioner.

      E. DALRMYMLE CLARK,
Lieutenant and Adjutant N.-W. M. P.

      CHARLES E. CONRAD.

      W. WINDER,
Inspector.